Richard Wright in a Post-Racial Imaginary

Richard Wright in a Post-Racial Imaginary

Edited by
Alice Mikal Craven and William E. Dow

Associate Editor: Yoko Nakamura

With a Foreword by Amritjit Singh

B L O O M S B U R Y
NEW YORK · LONDON · NEW DELHI · SYDNEY

Bloomsbury Academic

An imprint of Bloomsbury Publishing Inc

1385 Broadway	50 Bedford Square
New York	London
NY 10018	WC1B 3DP
USA	UK

www.bloomsbury.com

Bloomsbury is a registered trade mark of Bloomsbury Publishing Plc

First published 2014

Library of Congress Cataloging-in-Publication Data
Richard Wright in a post-racial imaginary / edited by Alice Mikal Craven and William E. Dow ; associate editor, Yoko Nakamura ; with a foreword by Amritjit Singh.
pages cm
Includes bibliographical references and index.
ISBN 978-1-62356-231-1 (hardback : alk. paper) 1. Wright, Richard, 1908–1960 — Criticism and interpretation. 2. Wright, Richard, 1908–1960 — Political and social views. 3. Race in literature. 4. Blacks in literature. 5. African Americans in literature. 6. Alienation (Social psychology) in literature. I. Craven, Alice Mikal, editor of compilation. II. Dow, William (William E.) editor of compilation. III. Nakamura, Yoko, editor of compilation.
PS3545.R815Z8163 2014
813'.52—dc23
2014006808

ISBN: HB: 978-1-6235-6231-1
ePub: 978-1-6235-6232-8
ePDF: 978-1-6235-6625-8

Typeset by RefineCatch Ltd, Bungay, Suffolk
Printed and bound in the United States of America

To Olivier and Zoe Serafinowicz
Alice Mikal Craven

To Anne-Marie and my family
William E. Dow

To Tadao and Hatsuko Nakamura
Yoko Nakamura

Contents

Foreword

Richard Wright is undoubtedly a writer for the ages and he must have known that when he was writing thousands of haiku, fast and furious, at the end of his relatively short and checkered career in the United States and France. It is evident from our expanding engagements with his biography, writings, and travels that Wright continues to challenge us to think beyond our ever-shifting constructions of categories around race and region, nation and transnation, local vs. global, or in Wright's own words, "Tradition vs. Progress; Personality vs. Collectivity; the East (the colonial peoples) vs. the West (exploiters of the world)." The conference that Alice Mikal Craven and William E. Dow organized at the American University of Paris in 2008 was one of many engagements marking Wright's birth centennial. The conference demonstrated and celebrated Wright's powerful presence in the new century.

Richard Wright in a Post-Racial Imaginary, the second of the two volumes to emerge from the Paris Conference, offers an array of responses and readings that point to the diversity of contexts in which Wright speaks to us. Essays in the opening section examine Wright's intellectual trajectories in relation to Modernism, the Chicago School of Sociology, *Négritude* and such. But these essays by James Smethurst, Cynthia Tolentino, and Anthony Dawahare, in conjunction with other pieces spread throughout the volume, also show how Wright remains central to the tradition of African American literary expression that is closely tied to the lived realities of black life in the United States and in the African diaspora. In twentieth-century classics such as *Uncle Tom's Children*, *Black Boy*, *Native Son*, and *The Long Dream*, Wright exposed the limited spaces within which African Americans, especially those in the South, were expected to perform the ordinary human dance of life—to find love and nurture from individuals and communities, as well as to grow and provide for a family against the horrendous patterns of exclusion, rejection, and hateful violence. Wright highlights the absence of citizenship rights for black Americans often by not mentioning them at all, sharing instead with us his searing portrayals of the "essential bleakness of black life in America," in which "Negroes had never been allowed to catch the full spirit of Western civilization," not permitted to foster and struggle for "clean, positive tenderness, love, honor, loyalty, and the capacity to remember" (*Black Boy*, Chapter 2). And long before "post-racial" became a buzzword with the 2008 election of Barack Obama as US President, many commentators had argued that Wright's writings and perspectives had become mostly items of historical value, after the legal restoration of rights that was inaugurated, but not completed, through the Civil Rights Act of 1964, as well as by the Voting Rights Act and the Immigration and Nationality Act, both passed in 1965.

The work included in this volume is part of the exciting new scholarship on Wright that would scuttle any thought of relegating Wright's writings to a museum.

Re-reading a well-known story or novel by Wright in a classroom with young students or in your armchair at home is always full of surprises. And we have been fascinated by the voice that shapes Wright's many posthumously published works including *Rite of Passage* and *A Father's Law*. In many of his later writings, Wright comes through as one of Maxim Gorky's "unusual individuals ... [who] are not quite achieved, who are not very wise, a little mad, 'possessed.'" He was self-consciously one of those "lonely outsiders who exist precariously on the clifflike margins of many cultures," men (and women) to whom he had dedicated *White Man, Listen* in 1957. And we are barely prepared for the shocks of recognition that we will likely experience when the remaining unpublished works come out (I hope soon)—works such as *Black Hope* (see Barbara Foley's essay in this volume); *Island of Hallucination*; and Wright's letters not only to his editors and to other writers, but also to all kinds of figures around the globe.

In Wright's integral and empathetic imagination, as it captures the impact of colonialism in places such as the Gold Coast and Indonesia, in the continental realities of Africa and Asia that he evokes so powerfully in *Black Power* and *Color Curtain*, the figure of his father "standing alone upon the red clay of a Mississippi plantation," that we witness in the last two paragraphs of *Black Boy*, Chapter 1, merges with that of a farmer in the Ghanaian hinterlands, or with a street peddler in Jakarta. To me, Wright's career as an artist and man of letters displays an amazing level of unity and design, marked by his intense interest in the emerging patterns of modernity against the background of the many disenfranchising forces at work and the socioeconomic and psychic consequences they caused for millions around the world. This figure in the carpet shaped all his work, and his writings in the 1950s are very much of a piece with early works such as *Uncle Tom's Children*, *Native Son*, *Black Boy*, and his WPA-supported documentary history, *Twelve Million Black Voices* (1941). The perspectives he fashioned in the 1950s in his self-chosen new role as a global intellectual resonated well with his earlier perspectives. As early as the late 1940s, Wright began to meditate on the relationship between US racism and the global realities of colonialism and capitalism, viewing the African American as more than "America's metaphor." In 1946, he described the problem of 15 million black Americans as "symbolic" of the situation faced by over 1.5 billion people of color throughout the world.

It is against this awareness of Wright's reach into the rest of the twenty-first century that I welcome this new collection of essays. I have witnessed since 2008 the growth of both Alice and William into becoming the (W)right scholars to bring together these essays (including their own well-researched pieces). They help us appreciate Wright's layers and complexities as a man and artist; a global traveler; and a conflicted intellectual. Most of the essays are engagingly comparative (Michel Feith, Charles Scruggs, Shoshana Milgram Knapp, amongst others), compelling us to consider new connections and contexts for Wright's individual texts. Bruce Dick and Steven Tracy invite us into unexplored territories—sharpening our sense of Wright's relationship to drama and music, Blues in particular. Sandy Alexandre helps us to receive Wright's haiku with new ears, even as Marc Mvé Bekale and Sudhi Rajiv energize us for reading

Wright in relation to Senegalese writer Cheikh Hamidou Kane's novel *L'aventure ambiguë* (*Ambiguous Adventure*) and Sharankumar Limbale's life narrative, *The Outcaste*.

I hope other readers will enjoy and learn as much from this volume's many gifts as I have.

Amritjit Singh, Ohio University

Acknowledgments

We would like to thank the American University of Paris for its generous support during the editing of *Richard Wright in a Post-Racial Imaginary*. We would especially like to thank Amritjit Singh for his very generous support throughout our work on this project.

An earlier version of Marc Mvé Bekale's "The Negro Intellectual and the Tragic Sense of Hybridity: A Study in Postcolonial Existentialism" was published as "Cultural Hybridity and Existential Crisis in Richard Wright's *The Outsider* and Cheikh Hamidou Kane's *L'aventure ambiguë*" in *Transatlantica* 1/2009 (http://transatlantica.revues. org/4255). An earlier version of Alice Mikal Craven's "Richard Wright's 'Island' of Silence in *The Long Dream*" appeared in *Obsidian: Literature in the African Diaspora* 11.2 (2010): 95–106. An earlier version of Barbara Foley's " 'A Dramatic Picture . . . of Woman from Feudalism to Fascism': Richard Wright's *Black Hope*" was published in *Obsidian: Literature in the African Diaspora* 11.2 (2010): 43–54. Cynthia Tolentino's "Sociological Interests, Racial Reform: Richard Wright's Intellectual of Color" is reprinted from *America's Experts: Race and the Fictions of Sociology* (Minneapolis: University of Minnesota Press, 2009): 1–30. The lyrics of Richard Wright's "King Joe (Joe Louis Blues)," used in Steven C. Tracy's "A Wright to Sing the Blues: King Joe's Punch," is from "The Life and Work of Richard Wright" copyright © December 1971 by *New Letters*, edited by David Ray, first published in *New Letters*, volume 38, number 2, 1971. It is printed here with the permission of *New Letters* and the Curators of the University of Missouri-Kansas City.

Alice Mikal Craven and William E. Dow

Introduction

Alice Mikal Craven and William E. Dow

Richard Wright in a Post-Racial Imaginary builds upon the idea that Richard Wright is not only a *possible* literary and political prophet of his time, but that he is perhaps one of the most *plausible* prophets of America's potential to transform from a deeply racist nation to a nation where the terms *white* and *black* no longer dominate national discourses about race. The changes that took place in America during Wright's lifetime involved civil strife, political upheaval, and gender revolution. It would be counterproductive for a critical volume featuring his works to pretend that an African American man in the United States was incapable of understanding such turmoil *less* well than any of the other authors who hold prominent positions in the literary canon of twentieth-century American literature today. Nonetheless, Wright's legacy has been notoriously inhospitable to classification and definition precisely because he was a black man living in a racist society. Contemporary reassessment such as is evidenced in this volume insists upon Wright's complex and comprehensive awareness of US history in that he constantly positioned himself against any kind of essentialist approach to race, class, and American culture despite prevailing tendencies to peg him as exclusively a spokesman for his race.[1]

In what many are now calling the beginning of a post-racial America, Wright's legacy is in need of updating in terms of its value for international scholarship and his writing about race and beyond race.[2] Rethinking Wright's place as a global intellectual, as a professional writer, and as an international humanist should be taken as a priority for American studies today. Such a rethinking, as this volume argues, asserts the status of Wright as a major world-class author and explores his continuing impact on American culture as well as his anticipatory grasp of new theoretical trends concerning race and gender discourses.

Editorial choices for essays included in this volume are indeed guided by a questioning of the claim that America is currently host to a post-racialized sociopolitical environment—a concept that has garnered increasingly urgent scrutiny in the age of an Obama presidency.[3] *Richard Wright in a Post-Racial Imaginary* essentially asks if American *readers* have yet to appreciate the fruits of labor of those authors whose writings have rendered this post-racialized world *imaginable*, including, most importantly, Wright.[4] As Ramon Saldivar argues, "the relationship between race and social justice, race and identity, and indeed race and history requires a new 'imaginary' for thinking about the nature of a just society and the role of race in its construction" (574). Saldivar posits that the "post" of post-racial is indicative of a conceptual rather than a chronological shift, a position adhered to in our volume. Essays included here implicitly grant that such a new "imaginary" has its roots in the works of Wright amongst others who were writing long before the concept of post-racialization was entertained in critical circles.

Racism has by no means disappeared from America's social landscape, but this does not preclude the idea that racist trends have diminished. Indeed, race remains a central concern but it can no longer be defined exclusively in terms of a black and white binary— and this binary's attendant discourses. Given the rapidly shifting racial demographics of the United States and the world, a new "racial imaginary" is needed to explain the significance of race as a key element in American and global culture. Thus, our use of the prefix "post" in post-racial, rather than marking a final superseding of racial significance and categories, signifies an aspiration that one day the world will get beyond race as a potentially dangerous trope and that such a move will be facilitated by a thorough re-examination of Wright's works. "The political will to liberate humankind from race thinking," as Paul Gilroy argues, "must be complemented by precise historical reasons why these attempts are worth making" (12). Wright anticipated such a position by producing work that portrayed and presumed black difference as a distinct and necessary element, even as he wished to overcome the environments that created that difference.

The prefix "post" in post-racialization further entails an epistemological shift to the question of what race means for the twenty-first century. As Wright presciently understood, race as a trope provides a timely test for the democratic nature of today's cosmopolitan imaginings. Wright's racial thinking ultimately emerges as a self-conscious renunciation of "race" when this term is used in ways that divide and harmfully define human beings. As this collection emphasizes, Wright provides both a framework for a forward-looking racial imaginary and maps out possibilities for richer and larger conjectures about race, narrative theory, and narrative form in a future projection of a post-racial America.

Wright's literary and cultural hybridity is inseparable from this terminative vision. His fiction and nonfiction demand to be taken beyond borders and boundaries, to be interpreted in relation to what it means to write the African American literary text into a world literary history. Wright's strategies create discourses between distinct literary genres—between modernist, naturalist, and high cultures on the one hand, and popular, pulp, and low cultures on the other. That he writes about feeling at home (racially, culturally, and socially) *neither* in his native land (America) *nor* in his land of exile (France) is a successful form of hybridity that is only now beginning to be fully appreciated by Wright critics. Wright's literature, travel writing, and literary journalism responded both to a social world defined by the system of Jim Crow segregation *and* to a world that was increasingly diasporic, transatlantic, and global. As several essays in this volume attest, Wright accentuates "a crisis of hybridity" between America and Europe, France and Africa, Western and non-Western ways of conceiving knowledge.

Wright plugged into a cinematic bird's-eye view of his own country, its limitations, and its potential for development in relation to the rest of the world. That an African

American man raised in the South could go through a process of escaping the limitations of his environment (thereby becoming capable of identifying his heroes); fixing his preferred genres; and taking journeys into the territories in which a poor black man from the South would not be expected to travel (i.e., the European, Asian and African continents) was phenomenal. Wright accomplished all of this precisely because he was acutely mindful that race was a superimposed category, rather than a biological reality. He was aware that race consciousness had always been linked to the idea of nationality and that discourses based on a black-white binary in the United States were only ever concerned with *white Americans* and *African Americans*. His thinking here anticipated Kirin Wachter-Grene's assertion that in order to think post-racialization, American discourse about blackness "needs to invite a larger cultural conversation of different articulations of blackness in America, one in which immigrant blacks are considered and given voice" (1). Wachter-Grene implicitly calls for a separation of race and nationality in discourses about social identity in America.

Wachter-Grene further claims that taking this direction would facilitate America's need to fulfill its "social legitimacy" in its disruption of "bichromatic racialization" (2). As a celebrated author, Wright spoke differently about race and identity formation during his period of exile from the United States, and these writings need to be folded back into contemporary discourses on a post-racial imaginary in America. Wright's experiences outside the United States and his writings about them give the contemporary reader an idea of the paths he chose in carving out a space for a global humanist vision.

Wright drew from a wide array of disciplines, movements, and genres in insisting on such a vision, including sociology, proletarian literature, existentialism, popular culture, and Marxism. His recourse to these disciplines is the focus of Part 1, "Wright as Global Intellectual and Racial Reformer." The essays in this section place Wright in the context of modernism and its aftermath.[5] In this context, Wright subverted the "Negro problem" as a central problematic and contributed to, one could even suggest created, the professionalization of the black author—a creation that was successfully harmonized with the professionalization and racial "uplift" of black subjects during his lifetime and beyond.

James Smethurst's "After Modernism: Richard Wright Interprets the Black Belt" explores Wright's use of complex sources throughout crucial stages in his career in relation to the hybridic challenges he had introduced in his earlier fiction, especially in *Lawd Today!* and *Native Son*. "The result," according to Smethurst, "was a fascinating mixture of alienation, fragmentation, despair, confinement, a sense of inevitable social fate and revolutionary possibility ... [which] employed cultural forms and ways of feeling that widely circulated in US society and that were publicly accessible."

Cynthia Tolentino's "Sociological Interests, Racial Reform: Richard Wright's Intellectual of Color" likewise insists upon the need for examining Wright's literary ties to his racialized culture. Departing from entrenched views of Wright as a "proletarian writer," she interrogates "Wright's preoccupation with the professionalization of black subjects" at a moment when "the United States postwar international ascendancy was increasingly being tied to the resolution of what was known as ... the 'Negro problem.'"

Tolentino argues that Wright, "as a figure of the intellectual of color," emerges as a paradigm of "being at once the subject and the object of global processes of racial uplift." In the main, Wright's foundation for inventing a new imaginary, in which individualized questions of race feature prominently, is reliant upon the unique relationships he drew between race and modernism, race and sociology, and indeed race and the professional black writer.

Anthony Dawahare's "Richard Wright's *Native Son* and the Dialectics of Black Experience" continues this investigation by exploring how Wright "both depicts a uniquely *black* experience and surpasses it through characterization and a narrative technique that reveals black experience as a moment in an historical dialectic of social relations governed by political and economic power." Dawahare reads *Native Son* as a hybridic work that while mediating through "non-racial class forces," "both affirms and negates the very notion of black experience and presents a challenge for those . . . who want to affirm black experience as self-contained and others who want to liquidate it in some universal category." Such a revisionist reading of the canonical *Native Son* allows for a reassessment of Wright's anticipation of a post-race paradigm.

In Marc Mvé Bekale's "The Negro Intellectual and the Tragic Sense of Hybridity: A Study in Postcolonial Existentialism," Wright's notions of hybridity, as articulated in *The Outsider*, are woven into a closer relation to the literary works of Cheikh Hamidou Kane and the theoretical tracts of Homi K. Bhabha. Bekale's essay approaches the question of hybridity as a factor in "cultural mongrelization" and the need for an individual's "constant adjustments to the complex forces of the post-modern world." In keeping with the idea that Wright is a plausible prophet of a post-racial imaginary, Bekale asserts, in reference to *The Outsider*: "Having written bitter novels indicting American racism, Wright was now trying to create a literary space through which he could translate and articulate his post-racial idealism."

The volume's second part, "The Pursuit of Sovereignty in Wright's Political and Artistic Odyssey," focuses on re-contextualizing Wright from a global perspective that must be complemented by examining the literary, political, and socioeconomic paratexts of Wright's work in the 1940s and 1950s. Whereas Wright may have been anticipating the black professional writer, the editorial and marketing apparatus surrounding the publication of his works lagged far behind his literary vision. Laurence Cossu-Beaumont establishes new connections between Wright's aesthetics, his (extra-)literary influences and his growing disenchantment with the limitations of social realism for depicting black experience. The editorial history of Wright's best sellers, *Black Boy* and *Native Son*, is replete with practices of censorship and influence studies which would have been considered justified only as applied to the study and categorization of a black man's writing in Wright's time period. Cossu-Beaumont argues that the constraints in understanding Wright's full contribution to the American modernist literary tradition are largely rooted in the uncontested application of such practices.

By the same token, Wright was continually relegated to a minor role when it came to innovations in influential philosophical and sociopolitical movements of the twentieth century. Shoshana Milgram Knapp revalorizes Wright as a strong voice in mapping out an existential tradition within the context of world literature by re-examining *The Outsider*'s relation to the ideas and aesthetics of Hugo, Dostoevsky, Max Eastman, and Ayn Rand. Dismissing the critical constraints that have traditionally prevented his novel from being valued as highly as the canonical existentialist writers, due to his racial, social, and economic origins, Knapp effectively argues for a post-racial critical assessment of Wright's contribution to a race-blind scholarly debate. As a literary and philosophical movement, existentialism does not prioritize discussion of racial issues, and as a result, any author whose commentary is evaluated on the basis of the color of their skin would not initially be considered a primary contributor to the existentialist discourse (Todorov 177).

In a post-racial imaginary, obstacles to treating Wright as a key player to the existentialist debate are eradicated. Wright recognized early on "the untenability of a literary color line" (Warren 120). Like Ellison and Du Bois, Wright insisted on "a manifold literary inheritance … as both a demonstration of the irrationality of segregation and a refutation of charges that black cultural expression was inferior to works produced by whites" (Warren 120). Knapp pushes the reader to refocus the existential literary tradition by placing Wright's previously underestimated literary work, *The Outsider*, in its rightful place with respect to that tradition. Knapp's ultimate claim is that re-contextualizing *The Outsider* in this way also allows for a deeper reading of the questions of death and suicide in the novel.

Barbara Foley, in "A Dramatic Picture … of Woman from Feudalism to Fascism: Richard Wright's *Black Hope*," engages with the arguments of Cossu-Beaumont and Knapp by claiming that the editing and publication practices of Wright's time were largely responsible for keeping crucial aspects of his thought process from the public view. Therefore, those practices were directly responsible for a systemic misinterpretation of his positions on social, economic, and most importantly, gender issues. As she suggests, his failure to bring his "overwritten and redundant" manuscript of *Black Hope* to public light contributed to reinforcing his legacy as an author "oblivious to gender issues." She argues that this assessment could be rectified if his focus on "the condition of women as an issue in its own right as well as in its broader social and political connections with racism, capitalism and fascism" had been taken more seriously and *Black Hope* had been published. That "the novel was to take the alienation of its female protagonist as a means of getting at fundamental problems in modern life" signals not only the radical political value of Wright's literature but could provide our allegedly "postidentitarian" era today a basis for reassessing Wright's views on gender. Like most of Wright's fiction, *Black Hope* offers an opportunity to conceptualize race as extending beyond *whiteness* or *blackness* and to retheorize the social order that constitutes race.

Part Three focuses on the Gothic and neo-baroque strains in Wright's fiction. These peculiar strains provide insight into Wright's choices of the generic frames he should use in his exploration of African American self-fashioning and self-representation. In " 'Forged in Injustice': The Gothic Motif in the Fiction of Ernest Hemingway and Richard Wright," Charles Scruggs examines Wright's "complex simplicity" in relation to the trademark straightforward prose of Hemingway. Scruggs highlights the influence of Hemingway's "horrific-past" Gothicism on Wright's writing and signals this influence as an indicator of Wright's modernity.

William E. Dow's "Pulp Gothicism in Richard Wright's *The Outsider*" shows how *The Outsider*'s "generic hybridity" reveals new epistemological possibilities that focus on "representative relations of the Gothic to the 'interior life' of black Americans and to the social relations engendered by American capitalism." Congruently, *The Outsider* engages the effects of being denied access to social spaces of power and its privileges, and of being part of a community historically represented as deviant and dangerous. Michel Feith's "Working the Underground Seam: Richard Wright's 'The Man Who Lived Underground' in the Light of Percival Everett's *Zulus*" establishes more comparative connections in Wright's and Percival Everett's "underground," interpreted as both typography and symbol, and their respective portrayals—in Everett's *Zulus* and in Wright's "The Man Who Lived Underground"—of dystopian, neo-baroque societies. Feith explores a full range of dystopic lines of force and creates a base for new appreciation of Wright's influence on the literary tradition of taking the underground, with all of its attendant Gothic and neo-baroque tendencies, as its central theme.

Wright's experimentation with literary and artistic forms—freeing him to explore his own increasingly hybridic directions—is yet another proof that his later years afforded him a space for moving beyond the genealogical meanings of *black* and *white* and their connotative threat to individual identity. In Part Four, "Richard Wright's Sweet Airs: Experiments with Performance Genres," Bruce Allen Dick's "Forgotten Chapter: Richard Wright, Playwrights, and the Modern Theater" focuses on such theatrical productions as Wright's five-act satire, *Daddy Goodness*, and argues for a reappraisal of Wright's work in relation to his "dramatic" writing and the tradition of American and African American theater. Wright's interest in modern drama and his writing for the theater from the late 1930s until his death are rarely analysed in Wright criticism given their marginal relation to his over-determined role as a writer of protest fiction. Dick examines Wright's theatrical writing in conjunction with his constant experimentation and his nascent positioning as a global intellectual who also happened to write in performative artistic modes.

This first overview of Wright's lifelong interest in drama adds yet another dimension to understanding Wright as a thinker able to transcend imposed limits. For Wright, "the paradox and pain of having 'suffered containedly,'" as Kenneth Warren asserts, "is that he ... has come to possess a depth of experience and complexity of vision clearly superior to the dominant society he is supposed to value and emulate" (25). In taking up the forgotten or underplayed ways in which Wright wrote beyond the spaces allotted to him by mainstream publishers, this essay evaluates the influence that deeply rooted components of African American culture had on Wright's works and life while also insisting that Wright's singular experimentation with such components led him on to undiscovered creative spaces.

In like fashion, Steven C. Tracy's "A Wright to Sing the Blues: King Joe's Punch" presents the ways in which Wright's literature has been influenced by the blues tradition and details Wright's own experimentation with blues lyrics through his collaboration on a commercial recording of "King Joe." Joining Wright in this exercise were Paul Robeson, Count Basie, and John Hammond. Tracy's close analysis of the structure, language, and imagery involved attests to Wright's blending of Leftist politics and populist mythmaking that display his desire to speak to a community that might appreciate his political and aesthetic intentions.

Wright's final spaces and the lingering role that his heartfelt reflections would play for him are the focus of the last part of the volume, "Transnational Shifts: Silence and Sentiment." At the end of his life, Wright found himself far from the origins of the intimate feelings that shaped his youth as well as his early fiction. His transnationalism is reconfigured by essays in this section as a stopping place in a journey that is decidedly to be characterized as continuous rather than discontinuous, and as richly hopeful rather than aesthetically bankrupt.

To this end, Alice Mikal Craven's "Richard Wright's 'Island' of Silence in *The Long Dream*" argues that Wright's *aesthetic* development was "part of a generic trend towards constructing a transnational literary voice through deeper explorations and through literary perspectives on immigrant voices and silences." The narrative issues of Wright's transnational identities, "engage[ing] freely in an experimentation with stylistic considerations and generic forms," can be seen most clearly when compared to the works of Bernard Dadié's *Un nègre à Paris* and William Gardner Smith's *Stone Face*. Craven's claim is that the true impact of Wright's unpublished "Island of Hallucination" is more thoroughly appreciated when read in relation to *The Long Dream* (the last novel published during his lifetime) as well as being understood as an unsuccessful sequel, not in terms of Wright's thinking but, rather, in terms of its publication history. Recognition of the continuity in representations of sentiment in the early and late works can give the reader greater insight into Wright's methods for creating his humanist vision and his deep concern for social change.

Indeed, Wright's enlistments of literature in the interest of social change cross with those of the Dalit writer Sharankumar Limbale in Sudhi Rajiv's contribution to the volume. Rajiv argues that Wright's social vision can come into a sharper focus when viewed through the critical tropes of Salman Rushdie's "Imaginary Homelands" and Amritjit Singh's "Imagined Communities." These tropes designate the potential for a diasporic writer to create an imaginary homeland, a country of the mind that would envision a world of freedom and social justice. For Rajiv, *Black Power* and *The Color Curtain* demonstrate how "Wright had carved out for himself the role of global intellectual and created a means whereby he could provide inspiration to other oppressed cultures." Limbale's "interminable quest" for a "post-caste" Indian society parallels Wright's desire not just to go beyond but to eliminate racial identification as a vector of national (un)belonging. "Both Wright, the participant-observer, and Limbale, the writer-activist," Rajiv argues, "work for a reconceptualization of the pre-existing notions of identity and difference to include people situated outside the cultural and imaginary frontiers of race, caste, gender, and nation." The ultimate importance of both writers, Rajiv suggests, is their focus on the transformation, not the affirmation, of racial identities.

In "Culmination in Miniature: Late Style and the Essence of Richard Wright's Haiku," Sandy Alexandre repositions the collection of haiku that Wright composed on his deathbed as a final call for America's reflection on its own limited understanding of its human capital. Wright's haiku questions the limiting nature of African American literature as a category and "challenges and explodes the notion of compulsory allegiance to that particular, delimited culture." Alexandre interrogates how Wright mediates his intra-national experience in the American North and South with his international experience through haiku, in order to "speak for a wider community." The fervent appeal for a universal humanism, which Sandy Alexandre locates in his haiku, needs to be read carefully in order to reveal the poignancy and value of Wright's lesson to the contemporary reader. By re-situating the reading of Richard Wright's texts into the context of a post-racial imaginary, the editors of this volume hope to give contemporary audiences an opportunity to reflect on America's last 50 years of moral growth and its potential impact for a more productive discourse about race and racism in America and in an increasingly globalized culture.

Notes

1 As is made clear in the debate between Henry Louis Gates, Jr. and Tzvetan Todorov concerning writing and race, to write about race and racism is always delicate in that, as pointed out by Gates, "race, in these [certain] usages, pretends to be an objective term of classification, when in fact it is a dangerous trope" (5–6). The same scrutiny should be applied when defining the hidden ideologies possibly inherent to a term such as "post-racial." More importantly, as Todorov suggests in his responses to Gates, we risk limiting inquiry if we insist that "the content of a thought depends on the color of the thinker's skin" (177); Todorov equally posits that it is counterproductive to analyse black literature making use only of concepts formulated by black authors (177). The complexity of exploring Wright's writing from outside the construct of his role as a writer with black skin in a context as ill-delineated as the post-racial imaginary thus essentially requires jettisoning much of what constituted Wright's legacy in earlier critical discourses while simultaneously salvaging all of the very valuable commentary surrounding his most commented upon works, *Black Boy* and *Native Son*.

2 For a rigorous analysis of the difficulties involved in the superficial use of the term "post-racialization" in the mainstream media about America during the Obama presidency, see "Beyond the Binary: Obama's Hybridity and Post-Racialization" wherein Kirin Wachter-Grene argues that the term itself might also be a dangerous trope in that it "has served to reify public racial obsession" (1).

3 See, for example, Jarrett; Tesler and Sears; and Burnham.

4 A satisfying definition of the term "post-racial" is inherently difficult. The idea of a post-racial society is that in which race has lost its significance. For problems of definition, see Brooks (665–7).

5 For various relations between Wright's transnationalism and modernism, see Craven and Dow.

Works cited

Brooks, Roy L. "Making the Case for Atonement in 'Post-Racial America.'" *Journal of Gender, Race and Justice* 14 (2011): 665–78. Print.

Burnham, Linda. "Obama's Candidacy: The Advent of Post-Racial America and the End of Black Politics?" *Black Scholar* 38.4 (2008): 43–6. Print.

Craven, Alice Mikal and William E. Dow, eds. *Richard Wright: New Readings in the 21st Century.* New York: Palgrave Macmillan, 2011. Print.

Gates, Henry Louis Jr. "Editor's Introduction: Writing 'Race' and the Difference It Makes." *"Race," Writing, and Difference.* Spec. issue of *Critical Inquiry* 12.1 (1985): 1–20. Print.

Gilroy, Paul. *Against Race: Imagining Political Culture Beyond the Color Line.* Cambridge: Harvard UP, 2000. Print.

Jarrett, Gene Andrew. "The Political Audacity of Barack Obama's Literature." *Representing the Race: A New Political History of African American Literature.* New York: New York UP, 2011. 161–96. Print.

Saldívar, Ramón. "Historical Fantasy, Speculative Realism, and Postrace Aesthetics in Contemporary American Fiction." *The Twenty-First-Century American Novel.* Spec. issue of *American Literary History* 23.3 (2011): 574–99. Print.

Tesler, Michael and David O. Sears. *Obama's Race: The 2008 Election and the Dream of a Post-Racial America.* Chicago: U of Chicago P, 2010. Print. Chicago Studies in American Politics.

Todorov, Tzvetan. " 'Race,' Writing, and Culture." Trans. Loulou Mack. *Critical Inquiry* 13.1 (1986): 171–81. Print.

Wachter-Grene, Kirin. "Beyond the Binary: Obama's Hybridity and Post-Racialization." *Revue de recherche en civilization américaine* 3 (2012). http://rrca.revues.org/index448.html

Warren, Kenneth W. *What Was African American Literature?* Cambridge: Harvard UP, 2011. Print.

Part One

Wright as Global Intellectual and Racial Reformer

1

After Modernism: Richard Wright Interprets the Black Belt

James Smethurst

University of Massachusetts, Amherst

When one attempts to come to grips with the work of Richard Wright through *Native Son*, it is crucial to remember that he was a Communist throughout this portion of his career. Of course, Wright's engagement with the Communist Party of the United States of America (CPUSA) through the 1930s and into the early 1940s is well known and well documented—though, even now, following Wright's own account in the portion of *Black Boy* originally published posthumously as *American Hunger*, the emphasis is often on Wright's conflicts with national and local Chicago and New York CPUSA leaders and policies. No doubt such conflicts were real even if they did not always follow the chronology set out by Wright in his narrative. However, while nearly all the significant black poets, playwrights, and fiction writers of the 1930s and early 1940s (with the notable exception of Zora Neale Hurston) had some close connection with the Communist Left, Wright was one of the very few to publicly advertise his membership in the CPUSA (and regularly attend CPUSA branch or club meetings) during that era.

In part, Wright's public association with the CPUSA and its cultural sphere was practical, providing him with venues for literary apprenticeship, intellectual development, publication, audience, publicity, networks of distribution, contacts in "mainstream" publishing, and so on. The ideological positions of the CPUSA and the Comintern on the "National Question" and the subsidiary "Negro Question" and the Communist commitment to "Negro Liberation," particularly in the 1930s, also attracted Wright. However, it was not necessary for Wright to join the CPUSA and publicly declare his membership in order to gain the practical benefits or ideological inspiration of association with the CPUSA. Again, relatively few black artists and intellectuals made such a declaration during the 1930s and 1940s. To this day, we are not entirely sure if such artists as Langston Hughes, Sterling Brown, Paul Robeson, Countee Cullen, Robert Hayden, and Gwendolyn Bennett ever formally joined the CPUSA despite their association with the Communist Left—and in some cases, such as that of Brown, there is evidence they did not despite their Left sympathies. Others who did join, such as Margaret Walker and Frank Marshall Davis, kept their membership (though not their affiliation with the Left generally) quiet so that it is only in the relatively recent past that confirmation of their membership was discovered.

Wright, despite his recorded reluctance to spend the bulk of his writing skills and time on the writing of leaflets and pamphlets, was someone who had a commitment to practical, organizational politics. Otherwise, why formally join and why attend branch meetings, even meetings of branches of the "Artists Section," which were largely devoted to nuts-and-bolts political activity? He was, then, an artist whose work, to paraphrase Marx's famous dictum, was designed to help people understand the world, specifically the world of African Americans during the Great Depression, with the purpose of changing it.

The problem for Wright, then, was how to render the emotional, psychological, spiritual, material, and cultural reality of African Americans whose history in North America was peculiar from the rise of the peculiar institution of slavery to the triumph of Jim Crow segregation to the racialization of urban space, particularly the creation of the black ghetto (which was a comparatively recent phenomenon as Wright began his literary career). On what resources does one draw to make the journey from the Black Belt of the South to the Black Belt of the South Side vivid in a way that allows people to see avenues of group solidarity (as opposed to individual sympathy) while recognizing the special conditions of African American life in the United States? How do such pressing issues for the Left as the rise of fascism resonate or reconcile with the concerns, cultures, and psychologies of Black Belts North and South, urban and rural?

If one takes the suspicion or even rejection of universalisms of various sorts to be a hallmark of postmodernism, then Wright was certainly no postmodernist in the early portion of his career. He had a fascination with various sorts of universalist, one might say totalizing, ways of understanding, representing, and ultimately transforming reality. However, Wright also recognized the limitations of these approaches, including Marxism, for representing reality convincingly to people in the United States in ways that would potentially motivate large numbers of Americans to change the world. As a result, in creating what Lawrence P. Jackson calls his "Chicago realism," Wright drew on a wide range of resources from an equally wide spectrum of disciplines, movements, genres, and media, including sociology, modernist poetry and fiction, naturalist fiction and drama, Gothic literature, proletarian literature (particularly the work of his fellow Chicagoan James Farrell), romantic literature edging into protoexistentialism (and later a more direct engagement with existentialism), popular culture (especially the horror film with its link to the Gothic tradition), and, of course, Marxism (particularly the variant associated with the Comintern and the CPUSA).

Modernity (like modernism) is, of course, an extraordinarily elastic term. After all, Stephen Greenblatt has recently traced what he calls a "swerve" toward modernity to Poggio Bracciolini's discovery of a manuscript of Lucretius's *De rerum natura* in 1417. However, if we understand US modernity to turn on the rise of the United States as the world's premiere industrial power and an increasingly important international political force in the late nineteenth and early twentieth centuries, then the advent of the legal and extralegal system of Jim Crow segregation followed by the racialization of urban space in a more and more urbanized society are fundamental constitutive elements of this modernity. As such scholars as Michael North, Geoffrey Jacques, David Chinitz, Aldon Nielsen, and Ann Douglas have shown, the rise of Jim Crow and the racialized geography of the US city did much to shape literary modernism in the United States with its complicated parasitical but often adversarial relationship to modernity in the first three decades of the twentieth century.

In that sense, Wright, particularly in his early novels *Lawd Today!* (finished in the mid-1930s, but not published until 1963) and *Native Son* (published in 1940), can be seen as writing after modernism, if not postmodern in the usual usage of what can also be a very elastic term. While an endpoint for modernism is much debated, by the 1930s, Wright had access to and a good sense of the spectrum of modernism, including English language modernists of various stripes and nationalities as well as Central and Eastern European modernists and protomodernists, many of whose works (like those of Franz Kafka and Nikolai Gogol) were only beginning to become widely accessible (or, in the case of Gogol, accessible again) in English during the 1930s.

The modernist protagonist that Wright inherits is a person who has fallen out of society, has no roots, and is a sort of luftmensch. He or she is alienated from his or her work; has no god, no traditional values; and is a city dweller (if often born in the country) lost in the impersonal and bewildering landscape of rationalized grids of buildings (as in Baudelaire's Paris), bureaucracies, and authorities that are at one time impossibly distant and frighteningly (and inexplicably) present. Family ties, when present, instead of being a source of strength, are often chains or a deforming pressure (as was the case for Kafka's Gregor Samsa). Very often such protagonists are intense consumers of popular culture in various forms and media, a culture that serves as school, comfort, and the medium of dreams and an emotional life (as with Fitzgerald's Jay Gatsby who expresses his love for Daisy Buchanan through the display of shirts). Like Stephen Dedalus in James Joyce's *Ulysses*, these figures generally are shown to have a history, but it is one they are desperately trying to forget and/or leave far behind, generally with only limited success as the repressed history returns in various forms.

Wright's early protagonists, such as Jake Jackson in *Lawd Today!* and Bigger Thomas in *Native Son*, are often cast from this modernist mold. This connection is emphasized by the title of the final section of *Lawd Today!*, "Rats Alley," taken from T. S. Eliot's *The Wasteland*, which also provides an epigraph for the section. In *Native Son*, Bigger's desires, fears, hungers, dreams, fantasy life, and plans of action are a compound of mass culture, of B-films, newsreels, pulp magazines, and dime novels, of *The Gay Woman*, *Trader Horn*, and true crime magazines. Bigger, though born in the South, has not the least emotional or intellectual investment in the culture, the spiritual life, or the social values of his mother, who is a true product of the rural South despite her migration to and residence in the South Side of Chicago. He is leader of a gang and has a girlfriend, Bessie Mears, who is similarly, if more passively, estranged from her Southern roots. But despite what might appear to be a considerable social network, he is alienated from Bessie, whom he eventually rapes and murders, and the members of his gang. While Bigger's isolation and his saturation by mass culture products in most respects serve the purposes of social control by the ruling class, they also incite an insatiable hunger and an uncontrollable fear that result in the death of Mary Dalton, a child of the ruling elite (and the owners of the Thomas family's kitchenette apartment) on the individual level and threaten social disorder on a larger scale, much like that of the ending of Nathanael West's *Day of the Locust*—or the neo-modernist *Invisible Man* by Ralph Ellison, for that matter. And, as Brannon Costello points out, Jackson is much the same sort of multiply alienated black urbanist modernist subject adrift in a sea of mass culture with its fears, dreams, and hungers—though Costello draws too hard a line between the "typical" proletarian literature protagonist and Jackson, using Mike Gold as the familiar whipping boy of Communist orthodoxy.¹ In fact, Wright's work is much indebted to the writings of such proletarian writers as Farrell, Nelson Algren, William Attaway, John Fante, Jack Conroy, and, indeed, Gold himself in *Jews without Money*, which often feature "ethnic" protagonists lost in the city, cut off, or at least increasingly remote from older cultural roots and from an older generation whose "Old Country" or "Down Home" sensibilities and values have no real hold on them. One might add here that much of Wright's attraction to such nineteenth-century Russian writers as Gogol and Dostoevsky is in no small part due to their treatments of the existential crises of peasant, middling estate functionaries, and small landowners (or their children) who migrate to the metropolis of Petersburg, the modern Russian city built on the unstable land of marshes on the Gulf of Finland by Peter the Great. Perhaps it might be more accurate to say that Wright and many of these "proletarian" writers, including Gold, do not so much object to modernism as such, but to what they perceive as those reactionary elements of modernism and neomodernism in, say, the work of T. S. Eliot or Vanderbilt's Agrarians, which seem to promote some sort of atavistic dream of a return to an earlier organic society, whether the Old South or the Holy Roman Empire, often espousing a virulent racism, anti-Semitism, and sympathy with fascism in one form or another. Having said that, though, Wright's protagonists, like Eliot's Prufrock or the speaker(s) of *The Wasteland* or Jean Toomer's Kabnis in *Cane* for that matter, hunger for some sort of rootedness, some sort of larger meaning or context however deformed that hunger might be by the limited and limiting lexicon of mass culture. That might even lead the black subject to imagine what might seem to us a counterintuitive vision of a black Hitler, as Bigger does in *Native Son*:

> He liked to hear of how Japan was conquering China; of how Hitler was running the Jews to the ground; of how Mussolini was invading Spain. He was not concerned whether these acts were right or wrong; they simply appealed to him as possible avenues of escape. He felt that some day there would be a black man who would whip the black people into a tight band and together they would act and end fear and shame. He never thought of this in precise mental images; he felt it; he would feel it for a while and then forget. But hope was always waiting somewhere deep down in him.
>
> (*Early Works* 551)

Such mass culture dreams, even or perhaps especially those of Hitler and Mussolini caught on newsreels, can, Lacan-style, never really satisfy, but lead to another act generated by hunger, desire, and fear, culminating in individual self-destruction or mass violence. Of course, African Americans are not the only ones imprisoned by such dreams. The screaming mob that calls for Bigger's death in the third section of *Native Son* is caught in a mass culture dream of black male monstrousness circulated since Reconstruction as seen most clearly in the headlines and fragments of newspaper articles interpolated into the text of the novel. It is worth noting that the novel implies that the racist mob is made up of white people who themselves might be alienated from their cultural roots by a move to the industrial city and further dispossessed by the economic crisis. As with the violent crowd at the end of West's *Day of the Locust*, the mob's rage is a result of fear and disappointed or disappointing mass culture dreams— though Wright suggests how race and racism have long inflected such rage in the United States in a way that West does not. This is a contradictory moment in which, in negative fashion, a possible (though currently absent) class solidarity of the working-class white and black Americans is revealed along with the potential basis for a mass fascist movement in the United States—touching on the question of the nature and social base of fascism, a question that consumed the Left throughout the 1930s, especially after the triumph of the Nazis and the destruction of the largest Communist Party outside of the Soviet Union in 1933.

Of course, what is sometimes called "high" modernism had a variety of limitations as a literary model for a Communist like Wright. The racism, anti-Semitism, and fascist sympathies of a number of the "high" modernists have been noted above. In a way, the sense of alienation, of cultural and subjective fragmentation of a number of the "high" modernists, a sense that Wright found very useful in representing the experience and subjectivity of African Americans in the urban ghetto, was often grounded in some cranky vision, whether the plantation romance of the Agrarians, the Holy Roman organic society of Eliot, or the Social Credit of Pound, that did not say much about the social forces that shaped the ghetto and moved people in the United States in any way that brought satisfaction to Wright. In this regard, perhaps Joyce's vision of the day in the lives of the subject Irish people, an internal colony of the British Empire, in *Ulysses* was most akin to Wright's sensibility as seen, for example, in a day in the life of Jackson in *Lawd Today!* or in the moment in the Martello Tower when the Englishman Haines begins speaking Irish to an Irish cleaning woman anticipating and perhaps influencing the episode where Mary Dalton sings a spiritual (to the wrong tune) to Bigger in *Native Son*.

In the sort of modernism and protomodernism that most interested Wright, particularly that of Central and Eastern Europe, there was a sort of Gothic suggestion that, as in the *X-Files*, the truth was out there, that there was some sort of Kafkaesque system or authority underlying events, it just was not ever quite apprehensible to the protagonist, the modern subject.[2] This is not to say that history, or perhaps more accurately the idea of history or tradition, is absent, but it is a history that in Marx's famous Gothic formulation "weighs like a nightmare on the brains of the living" (11). Bigger has some considerable sense of his family's history in the Jim Crow South where racial violence killed his father, but like Joyce's Stephen Dedalus in *Ulysses* and his efforts to get out from under the Fenians, Parnellites, and so on, of his family's past under British rule, history for Bigger is a nightmare from which he is trying to awake—though in both the case of Bigger and of Dedalus, these efforts do not meet with much success, at least initially. Dedalus does get out from under the weight of his Irish family history by attaching himself to a new, transhistorical father figure, the wandering Jew Leopold Bloom.

This is not a satisfactory result for Wright, who looks to replace the old Gothic notion of history as a cyclical haunting with a more scientific (and Marxist) vision of history as a dialectical spiral that reveals the fundamental forces shaping society, how a system works and how it maintains itself—hence Wright's engagement with naturalism. Wright is not so much interested in the biological or Darwinian aspects of naturalism as in those moments of naturalist fiction and drama that emphasize the ways in which social systems drive the individual. Many commentators have, from the book's early reviewers, linked *Native Son* to Theodore Dreiser's *An American Tragedy* and Fyodor Dostoevsky's *Crime and Punishment*, with its story of social desire, crime, detection, and punishment.[3] However, in many respects it is the earlier naturalist novels describing the movement of rural folk to the city and the resulting social and cultural dislocations, such as Dreiser's *Sister Carrie*, Paul Laurence Dunbar's *The Sport of the Gods*, and portions of Emile Zola's *Germinal*, which are more germane to the early fiction of Wright. Wright, like his sometime protégé Ralph Ellison, was not very generous to his black literary predecessors—though where Ellison was critical about a failure to be sufficiently modern, Wright was more likely to dismiss earlier black writers for a lack of militancy.

Still, Dunbar's novel, published only a couple of years after *Sister Carrie* and among the early US naturalist novels, is an important predecessor text in its description of a black family, the Hamiltons, forced from the South only to be spiritually, economically, morally, and socially alienated and destroyed by life in the emerging black ghetto of the urban North. The black characters of Dunbar, like those of Wright, but unlike the white characters, by and large, of Dreiser, Frank Norris, and other authors associated with early US naturalism, are very publicly circumscribed in their movements, their possibilities by Jim Crow in both its northern and southern, urban and small town modes. Dunbar's black characters may dream of free will and individual choice, but they are also often aware of limitations that will undermine or betray those dreams. Carrie Meeber in *Sister Carrie* may resemble Kitty Hamilton in *Sport of the Gods* in some important respects, but the reader knows that where Meeber is morally and perhaps emotionally damaged as she floats to the top, Hamilton is not only similarly destroyed but is on a fast slide down. After all, Meeber has become a genuine star of the popular stage (and makes a commensurate amount of money) while Hamilton at her height is a modestly well-paid performer in what is basically a black burlesque show. Similarly, Bigger may entertain fantasies of marrying white heiresses, flying airplanes, giving military commands, and becoming a black Hitler for a minute or two, but he does not believe in these fantasies. Rather, he imagines exercising agency or even power through a trickster strategy in which he hides his intentions and actions beneath a mask of white expectations:

> The whole thing came to him in the form of a powerful and simple feeling; there was in everyone a great hunger to believe that made him blind, and if he could see

while others were blind, then he would get what he wanted and never be caught at it. Now, who on earth would think that he, a black timid Negro boy, would murder and burn a rich white girl and would sit and wait for his breakfast like this? Elation filled him.

(*Early Works* 543)

In short, this sort of naturalism focusing on system and the material, not spirit or ideal, in determining consciousness and psychology is a corrective, from Wright's perspective, to modernist shortcomings in revealing and making vivid the structural processes at work in producing the black subject of the urban North.

And naturalism also has an affinity with the Gothic in that it, too, has a certain cyclical logic that is not always clear to its characters, but often is to its readers. One might say that system generates the same characters over and over. As Wright implicitly points out in "How 'Bigger' Was Born" when he lists the different "Biggers" he has known, Bigger may be executed by the state of Illinois, but there will be more Biggers (including, perhaps, Bigger's younger brother, Buddy), more Mr. Daltons, more Mary Daltons, and so on. Similarly, when Big Boy flees the South after his friends are lynched in "Big Boy Leaves Home" in Wright's 1938 collection of stories *Uncle Tom's Children*, the lynchings and the flight North are part of a recurring pattern that will produce more Bobos, Lesters, and Bucks (the lynch victims), and more Big Boys. The horror and the sense of confinement of the Gothic are merged with the despair and feeling of inevitability of naturalism in order to capture the feel of the lived experience of the ghetto—especially the South Side Bronzeville of Chicago, extraordinarily packed and hemmed in by racist restrictions and violence even by the standards of US cities in the 1930s and 1940s.

As many critics have noted, Wright also drew on the Chicago School of Urban Sociology to give empirical weight to the urban alienation and fragmentation of modernism with the claustrophobia and sense of being cursed or doomed of the black Gothic and naturalism.[4] Robert Park, Louis Wirth, William Thomas, Florian Znaniecki, Horace Cayton, and the other members of the Chicago School were famously concerned with the impact of migration from abroad, particularly Eastern and Southern Europe, and from the South to Chicago and other urban centers on both the migrant generation and on the following generation that grew up in the city. This study of the second generation (or the first to grow up in the urban United States) was of particular interest to Wright. One of the drawbacks of naturalism for Wright's purposes is that when the subject of the migration to the city is taken up, as in *Sister Carrie* or *Sport of the Gods*, little distinction is made between the older and younger generations. Mrs. Hamilton in Dunbar's novel is corrupted and degraded much as her children Joe and Kitty, who come to New York as young adults. What is often missing is the distinction between generations, between those from the old country or down home and those who are truly products of the new urban environment, helping to produce a discourse of "juvenile delinquency" and of young people as a distinct (anti)social group that would migrate into social work, law enforcement, and ultimately notions of youth culture and counterculture in the 1950s and 1960s. For Wright, the gap between Mrs. Thomas, still basically a rural black Southern woman in the city, and her children shaped by the urban ghetto even if they, like Bigger, were born in South, is huge. Mrs. Thomas's religion, for example, has no hold on her son Bigger. And his world, his rage, his desires and hungers are largely inexplicable to her—at least in the form they take on the South Side. The older Jackson in *Lawd Today!* has more residual ties to the black church rooted in the rural South but in the end finds it not much more satisfying than does Bigger. The Chicago School's study of these generational differences helped anchor Wright's sense of the generations of black migrants and their children and grandchildren who had even less mobility within Chicago than, say, the Polish, Italian, and South Slav immigrants and their children.

The attraction of the Chicago School's work for Wright was, as Carla Cappetti and others (including the Chicago sociologists themselves) have pointed out, the narrative nature of the research in which the storyteller of the case histories could be a "participant observer," that is to say an insider of some sort rather than a detached outsider (Cappetti 198–210; Bone and Courage 114–38). Louis Wirth and his notion of "urbanism" that destroyed or attenuated cultural and social ties of family and community, particularly those of "minority" migrants to the city, was originally Wright's main entry point into the Chicago School. However, Park's formulation of the "marginal man," a migrant to the city from the country and, generally, from another nation, who becomes a personality type of perpetual transition, neither really fully a part of her or his old society nor of her or his new one, also dovetailed with the modernist protagonist, a Josef K. (a particular favorite of Wright's), a Gatsby, a Kabnis, a Joe Christmas, again providing an empirical underpinning for representing the black marginal man, whether Jackson or Bigger, as a social type and modern subject. In short, the Chicago School allowed Wright to anchor his rendering of the emotional, one might say existential, experience of the black ghetto in a documentary mode that was congenial in many respects with the literary resources on which he drew. It also helped him adapt the Communist notion of a "Black Belt nation" in the South to the northern ghetto, suggesting that a new national sensibility and psychology was being born, an *urban* black sensibility that had to be taken into account in any discussion of social progress in the United States—though he does not go as far as he will when he writes the introduction to the classic 1946 study of the African American South Side, *Black Metropolis* by Horace Cayton and St. Clair Drake, a study that has a far more positive vision of Bronzeville than does *Lawd Today!* or *Native Son*.

Again, circling back to Wright as a black Communist writer, this use of a variety of literary and sociological resources to make palpable and document convincingly the felt reality of the ghetto and racial/national (as it would be understood by the Communist Left) oppression was not enough. To paraphrase another famous remark of Marx in the 1845 *Theses on Feuerbach*, the point was to change the ghetto and the system that produced it, not merely study it or even accurately represent it in various ways. As a result, Wright also draws deeply on Marxism, particularly that associated with the CPUSA and the Comintern in the late 1920s and early 1930s when Stalin's idea of an impending "Third Period" was a central feature of Communist ideology and in the later 1930s when the concept of the Popular Front against fascism was dominant.

The term "Third Period" refers to Stalin's prediction of a catastrophic worldwide capitalist crisis following an earlier crisis during and immediately after the Bolshevik Revolution and the First World War (the "First Period") and a relatively short span of economic stability (the "Second Period"—basically the 1920s). The onset of the Great Depression made Stalin seem prescient. One central tenet of "Third Period" ideology is that the international working class would look for radical solutions to the crisis. The danger, argued Stalin and the Comintern, was they might be misled back into capitalism by various sorts of liberal and non-Communist Left groups, especially the various Social Democratic groups. As a result, the world Communist movement in the late 1920s emphasized the establishment of countercultural "workers'" institutions, such as theaters, bookstores, visual arts groups, writers' groups (notably the John Reed Clubs through which Wright found entree into the literary Left), journals, and so on, that were formally, thematically, and institutionally distinct from "bourgeois" culture, whether conservative, liberal, or even Social Democratic. In particular, the cultural circles and institutions of the Communist movement encouraged the development and promotion of "worker-writers," many African Americans and the children of the so-called new immigrants from Southern and Eastern Europe and many (like Wright) from the Midwest and other regions outside the usual literary centers of the urban Northeast, encouraging working-class insiders to tell their stories in their own voices and in their own styles, drawing on what might be thought of as a proletarian avant-garde and, especially in the case of African Americans, residual (to use Raymond Williams's term) folk cultures outside of bourgeois "high" culture and commercial mass culture.

Also associated with the Comintern and "Third Period" ideology was the so-called "Black Belt Thesis" formally adopted by the Comintern in 1928. This position proposed that African Americans constituted a "nation" in the South (with a significantly shared history, culture, psychology, and so on) with the right to self-determination up to and including the right to form an independent republic in the southern "Black Belt" where African Americans formed a considerable majority. The thesis also postulated black people in the urban North as a "national minority" that should be fully integrated, socially, culturally, and economically. One crucial aspect of the "Black Belt Thesis" is that it put the "National Question" and "Negro Liberation" at the center of the work of the CPUSA, including, in the cultural arena, the development and promotion of black artists, including Wright. For ideological as well as practical reasons, this "Third Period" advancement of the black "nation" and critique of mass culture had an enormous impact on Wright. Almost everywhere in *Lawd Today!* and *Native Son*, one can see how mass culture in the shape of feature films, newsreels, advertisements, popular music, pulp magazines, tabloid newspapers, and so on, sedates, seduces, intimidates, tortures, depresses, and constrains Jackson and Bigger (and Bigger's gang, his girlfriend Bessie, and all Americans, for that matter). As Bigger's Communist lawyer Boris Max says in court:

Your Honor, consider the mere physical aspect of our civilization. How alluring, how dazzling it is! How it excites the senses! How constantly and overwhelmingly the advertisements, radios, newspapers and movies play upon us! But in thinking of them remember that to many they are tokens of mockery. These bright colors may fill our hearts with elation, but to many they are daily taunts. Imagine a man walking amid such a scene, a part of it, yet knowing it is *not* for him!

(*Early Works* 815)

Also, that African Americans share a common history, culture, experience, psychology, and so on, distinct (though not absolutely disjunct) from other Americans, leaves a big mark on Wright.

The Popular Front was a response to the Nazi rise to power in Germany in 1933 and a subsequent takeover (or threatened takeover) of governments throughout European fascist or semi-fascist movements. As a result, the Communist International (Comintern) became obsessed with determining the cause and social basis of fascism (a concern that Wright took up in *Native Son* and, to a lesser extent, in *Lawd Today!*) and new methods to successfully fight it after the failure of a huge Left (including the largest Communist Party outside of the USSR) to stop Hitler in Germany. The Comintern decided that the threat of fascism was the clear and present danger to social progress and required an alliance of all democratic forces, including formerly reviled Social Democrats and liberals, from a variety of social classes ("the people"). Since the Comintern concluded that one important element of Nazi success was their superiority over the Communists, by and large, in manipulating national traditions and symbols in a manner that seemed intellectually and emotionally comprehensible to the popular majority, the Popular Front emphasized the particular democratic traditions (and iconography associated with those traditions) and popular cultures of individual countries.

Again, Wright deeply critiqued what he thought of as the hegemonic function of mass culture in gaining the consent or at least the acquiescence of African Americans in their own oppression. At the same time, again, Wright revises the "Black Belt Thesis" to suggest how a subjugated nation might exist in an urban setting without a distinct folk culture or language outside of mass culture in the "Black Metropolis" of "Bronzeville." Even Max proclaims in court that "taken collectively" African Americans "are not simply twelve million people," but "constitute a separate nation" (*Early Works* 818), blurring the distinction between a "nation" and a "national minority" made in the original formulation of the "Black Belt Thesis."

Wright also draws, Popular Front-style, on the tropes, the structure, and the structures of feeling, so to speak, of popular culture, notably 1930s film, not only to interrogate the imprisoning aspects of popular culture but also to communicate a sense of the lived horror and terror of the ghetto and a sense of sympathy and even empathy with the black subject despite his (and that subject is almost always a "he" in Wright's fiction) manifest lack of sympathetic qualities. After all, when the reader sees Jackson in *Lawd Today!*, he is unconscious on the floor after being knocked out by his wife as he assaulted her in a drunken, murderous rage. Bigger is a somewhat cowardly, small-time thug who rapes and kills his girlfriend by smashing her head and throwing her down an airshaft to make sure she is dead (though it turns out that she dies quite slowly). They are both, especially Bigger, quite monstrous in their ways. Wright invokes the 1930s Hollywood horror genre, particularly *Frankenstein* and *King Kong*, to suggest that monsters are not born but created by society.[5] One of the peculiar aspects of the horror genre, besides a surprising lack of action compared to today's horror films in many cases, is the degree to which the monster is also a victim whose monstrousness is thrust upon him/her/it, whether through a negative social nurture, as in the case of *Frankenstein*, or even capitalist exploitation, as when King Kong, in an invocation of the middle passage, is dragged from Skull Island in chains to be displayed for profit in New York. Bigger, too, as Max explains at the murder trial, is a sort of monster (a man made into a brute, to recall Frederick Douglass), created by the historical experience of slavery, Jim Crow, northern and southern racism, and "high" and popular culture:

> 'But the corpse returns and raids our homes! We find our daughters murdered and burnt! And we say "Kill! Kill!"'
>
> 'But, Your Honor, I say: "Stop! Let us look at what we are doing!" for the corpse is not dead! It still lives! It has made a home in the wild forest of our great cities, amid the rank and choking vegetation of slums! It has forgotten our language! In order to live it has sharpened its claws! It has developed a capacity for hate and fury that we cannot understand! Its movements are unpredictable! By night it creeps from its lairs and steals toward the settlements of civilization!'
>
> (*Early Works* 813)

Still, while such an invocation of the structure and tropes of the horror film might draw on the genre's explicit or implicit naturalist positing of the monster as the product of larger social forces as well as the genre's modernist promoting of at least a minimal sympathy or perhaps empathy (much like the reader's feeling that the transformation of Kafka's Gregor Samsa into a giant bug might say something about her or his own condition as a modern subject) again only studies and represents what is and how it came to be, but does not suggest the possibility of change, of what might be. In fact, like the Gothic in literature, the horror film suggests that the situation never really changes, that the monster never really dies, which is why Dracula, Frankenstein's monster, the Wolf Man, King Kong (or his son), and so on, return in so many movies after apparent death.

There is, then, a political need for historical materialist interpretation, for going beyond the horror genre and popular culture generally—and modernist, naturalist, and Gothic literature. In particular, *Native Son*, not generally thought of as an upbeat novel, proposes the possibility of changing the world through collective understanding *and* action. In part, what will allow those who grew up in the urban "Black Belt" of the South Side (and other urban centers) to act is not simply to grasp the history and folk culture of their parents and grandparents, but also (as Wright says of the folk culture in the 1937 "Blueprint for Negro Writing") to "*possess* and *understand*" popular culture, which is to say, to possess and understand the culture and psychology of Bronzeville, of the "Black Metropolis." While Bigger will not live long enough to develop such an understanding, he comes to believe that such an understanding is feasible, something that he never really believed before.

The possibility of change is also presented through an ability to develop class solidarity. For Wright in his early work, class solidarity is not simply the result of the withering away of national (in the Communist sense) differences. It is significant that Bigger's last words to Max are "Tell . . . Tell Mister . . . Tell Jan hello" (*Early Works* 850). Mary Dalton's boyfriend Jan Erlone was initially nearly as naïve about black life in the city and as patronizing of Bigger as Dalton. Yet through his contact with Bigger during the inquest and trial, Erlone, whose name suggests a non-WASP, "new immigrant" background, is able to get a much better sense of the black nation within a nation and make a meaningful contact with Bigger, who is impressed by Erlone's ability to grow and see Bigger as a human subject who can understand and who can act, not as a monster or even as a more sympathetic cipher.

So is this a kind of premature Left postmodernism? It may not be since Wright certainly believed in the reality of a totalizing, if complex, system of capitalist domination in which racial hierarchy was, and had really always been, a central pillar. And, again, he had, and would continue to have, a fascination with systems for studying, understanding, and conducting one's self in such a world even after he left the CPUSA and its variant of Marxism in the 1940s. However, he also recognized the shortcomings of even the most useful attractive (to him) literary genres, popular culture forms, intellectual disciplines, and ideological stances (even Marxism) for understanding and representing the Black Belt, South and North, its place in the world, and ways to change the ghetto and the world. As a result, he employed an extraordinarily complicated, one might say hybrid, approach to literary representation in his early fiction. In that sense, we can say that if Wright was not a postmodernist, he was certainly a black Communist writing after modernism.

Notes

1   To be fair, while Costello does make this familiar move, he also cites Barbara Foley's objection to this sort of division between the proletarian and the modernist in *Radical Representations*.

 For another discussion of *Native Son*'s debt to modernism, particularly the work of Eliot and Joyce, see Werner 183–211.
2   For a lengthier examination of *Native Son* and Gothic literature, see Smethurst, "Invented by Horror."
3   For a particularly insightful investigation of Wright's novel with respect to *An American Tragedy*, see Foley, "The Politics of Poetics."
4   For a study considering the relation of ethnography and sociology in Chicago to the work of Chicago writers, including Wright, see Cappetti.
5   For a discussion of *Native Son* and the horror films of the 1930s, see Smethurst, " 'You Reckon Folks Really Act Like That?' "

Works cited

Bone, Robert and Richard A. Courage. *The Muse in Bronzeville: African American Creative Expression in Chicago, 1932–1950*. New Brunswick: Rutgers UP, 2011. Print.

Cappetti, Carla. *Writing Chicago: Modernism, Ethnography, and the Novel.* New York: Columbia UP, 1993. Print.

Costello, Brannon. "Richard Wright's *Lawd Today!* and the Political Uses of Modernism." *African American Review* 37.1 (2003): 39–52. Print.

Foley, Barbara. "The Politics of Poetics: Ideology and Narrative Form in *An American Tragedy* and *Native Son.*" *Richard Wright: Critical Perspectives Past and Present.* Ed. Henry Louis Gates, Jr., and K. A. Appiah. New York: Amistad, 1993. 188–99. Print.

—— *Radical Representations: Politics and Form in U.S. Proletarian Fiction, 1929–1941.* Durham: Duke UP, 1993. Print.

Jackson, Lawrence P. *The Indignant Generation: A Narrative of African American Writers and Critics, 1934–1960.* Princeton: Princeton UP, 2011. Print.

Marx, Karl. *The Eighteenth Brumaire of Louis Bonaparte.* New York: International, 1963. Print.

Park, Robert E. "Human Migration and the Marginal Man." *American Journal of Sociology* 33.6 (1928): 881–93. Print.

Smethurst, James. "Invented by Horror: The Gothic and African American Literary Ideology in *Native Son.*" *African American Review* 35.1 (2001): 29–40. Print.

—— " 'You Reckon Folks Really Act Like That?': Horror Films and the Work of Popular Culture in Richard Wright's *Native Son.*" *Scandalous Fictions: The Twentieth-Century Novel in the Public Sphere.* Ed. Jago Morrison and Susan Watkins. London: Palgrave Macmillan, 2006. 83–98. Print.

Werner, Craig Hansen. *Playing the Changes: From Afro-Modernism to the Jazz Impulse.* Urbana: U of Illinois P, 1994. Print.

Wirth, Louis. "Urbanism as a Way of Life." *American Journal of Sociology* 44.1 (1938): 1–24. Print.

Wright, Richard. "Blueprint for Negro Writing." *New Challenge* Fall 1937: 53–64. Print.

—— *Early Works.* New York: Library of America, 1991. Print.

2

Sociological Interests, Racial Reform: Richard Wright's Intellectual of Color

Cynthia Tolentino
University of Oregon

I had no hope whatever of being a professional man. Not only had I been so conditioned that I did not desire it, but the fulfillment of such an ambition was beyond my capabilities. Well-to-do Negroes lived in a world that was almost as alien to me as the world inhabited by whites. What, then, was there?

Richard Wright, *Black Boy*

Many a black boy in America has seized upon the rungs of the Red ladder to climb out of his Black Belt.

Richard Wright, "White Man Listen!"

In his 1923 appraisal of black literature, "Negro Race Consciousness as Reflected in Race Literature," Robert E. Park keenly registers the way in which black literature had become an object of fascination and study (285). Citing examples of research on contemporary Negro poetry by Professor Kerlin of Virginia Military University, Negro folk songs by sociologist Howard Odum, comparative studies of Negro spirituals and Scottish ballads by Colonel Thomas Wentworth Higginson, and what he deems a "very good collection" of Negro poetry in the US Department of Justice investigation reports that followed the 1919 race riots in US cities including Chicago, Washington DC, Knoxville, and Omaha, he offers an intriguing description of US state-sponsored interest in black literature by government and military personnel working in intelligence operations and academic contexts.

Describing his interest in African American poetry as that of a "student of human nature," Park positions himself within a group of state-sponsored professional experts reading black literature with "profound appreciation," rather than amateur enthusiasm (284). Indeed, for the US State no less than Park, these accounts of black literature could advance notions of scientific objectivity while also organizing a hierarchical relationship that defined white sociologists as cultivated experts and authorities in relation to black subjects. In arguing that African American writers were contributing to the model established by writers of "all the disinherited races of Europe," Park frames black literary production, including black radical writings, as stemming from an established "American" process of assimilation that centered on an immigrant's journey to the New World and the gradual sloughing off of ethnic customs and habits. Following this logic, he envisions the African American writer as a sociologically generated figure that is defined in relation to white European immigrants. The State-sponsored studies of African American literary production might thus be seen as constituting an important site by which the Chicago School of sociology positioned itself intellectually and institutionally as an arbiter of African American literary value and an agent of US national progress and racial reform.

On an institutional level, then, such studies opened up modes of self-authorization and access to integrated workplaces to African Americans as informants and researchers. Sociology especially was a privileged discourse on race that generated liberal narratives that envisioned racial reform as central to the possibility of imagining national progress and the expansion of US political power in the postwar period. I refer to these nationalized negotiations of racial reform within an understanding or reading of the existing system of capitalism as "liberal narratives of race," for a number of reasons.[1] Not only did liberal narratives—as an apparatus of sociology—define race as the source and figure of conflict, consensus, destiny, and difference, but they also enabled writers of color—as interpellated subjects—to develop strategies of self-authorization that both supported and critiqued the process of economic racial uplift for black subjects. Such economic regeneration was central to the concept of racial reform, in fact. Literature was its material or evidence.

Sociology's production of people of color as both the subjects and objects of race generates models of black professionalization, defined as racialized notions of vocation, which also structure and define the criterion for literary value. Park goes on to argue, for example, that black literature is naturally sociological, claiming that it is "more true if possible of the Negro than of any other people, that the Negro poetry is a transcript of Negro life" (285). According to Park, African American writing offers a valuable record first, of the Negro's self-understanding, and second, of the Negro's development of a new race consciousness, or attempt to redefine himself and his relationship to the past. In defining aesthetic expression as the Negro's native tendency, Park proposes, "Expression is perhaps his *métier*, his vocation" (285). In so doing, he figures documentary writing as an inherently African American profession and the Negro as a natural producer of sociological texts. In praising poet Paul Laurence Dunbar for studying the Negro "objectively, without apology and without prejudice," Park also claims that Dunbar has moved the tradition of black literature forward. Using sociological criteria to define literary value, he contends that Dunbar's aesthetic of scientific disinterestedness provided him with privileged access to the Negro's understanding of the "Negro problem," which he interprets as the struggle to be both a Negro and an American citizen.

Two decades later, Richard Wright would offer a different and critically important gloss on the relationship between canonical sociology, African American writing, and economic mobility. In his famous essay "I Tried to be a Communist," Wright claims, "I was a Communist because I was a Negro. Indeed, the Communist Party had been the only road out of the Black Belt for me."[2] Numerous commentators have interpreted Wright's statement as representative of his battle with Party orthodoxy and as a reference to the appeal that communism held for black Americans in imagining alternatives to Jim Crow society.[3] But his remarks are, I believe, less interested in explaining or justifying his Red past than emphasizing the uneven institutional and intellectual impact of sociology and communism on the emerging mobility signified by the professional writer of color. My purpose is neither to emphasize Wright's definitive break with communism nor to argue for "Left continuity" in his writings. As Wright suggests, taking up the subject position of "Communist" enabled him to reflect upon, without completely rejecting, the sociologically generated, pathologized figure of the impoverished "Negro." Similarly, the Communist Party, as an institution that viewed literary production as a professionalization process for black subjects, gave him an alternative way of interpreting liberal sociology's nationalist emphasis on economic and cultural assimilation and racial tolerance ("Be like us and we like you maybe"), and in so doing, created the conditions for him to figuratively depart from the "Black Belt," the sociologically produced space assigned to blacks under the US system of racial segregation.[4]

I am interested in how Wright's specific focus on the relationship between communism and sociology allows us to see his engagement of the promise of the professionalization of black subjects as a critical discourse at the moment in which US postwar world ascendancy was increasingly being tied to the resolution of the "Negro problem." The destiny of blacks came to represent the future of America during the late thirties, propelling the question of black assimilation into mainstream white America into the center of debates over national reform that were also concerned with articulating and legitimating the expanding global power of the United States. Even as Wright depicts communism as generating the conditions that enabled him to re-evaluate sociologically produced black subjectivities, he puts particular emphasis on communism's and sociology's joint conceptualization of African Americans as both social problems in need of revolutionary intervention and liberal "uplift" and as potential professionalized subjects who could, as native informants and documentary producers, facilitate that intervention. How, I ask, did this contradictory production of black subjects complicate the process of professionalization?

Professionalization, as envisioned by both US communism and Chicago School sociology, democratized knowledge production by giving intellectual and institutional value to marginalized works and experiences, and, in doing so, broadening definitions of cultural producers. For Wright, the professional becomes both a synecdoche and agent for discourses of uplift that incorporated black subjects into professions from which they were formerly excluded but that also exposed the limits and contradictions of uplift. The professional of color, he suggests, emerges through the tension of being at once the subject and object of processes of racial uplift. Rather than emphasizing the professionalized subject's purity, Wright seems more interested in its "impurity," or ability to understand and articulate its own positioning within processes of objectification. The professional writer of color, as Wright sees it, is not defined in opposition to market forces or by being in control of one's own labor. Rather, he seeks to carve out a figure that registers an awareness of both models and their investments in black subjects, rather than to prove the professionalized figures imagined by communism and sociology as "counterfeit." Wright's engagement of ideologies of professionalism is not only a testament to its power at this particular historical juncture, but represents more sharply an attempt to understand its implications for people of color, as the subjects and objects of their expanding forms.

To this day, revisionist literary historians credit "I Tried to be a Communist" with having inaugurated a new genre of black cultural history in which black Americans struggle to negotiate an artistic and political voice in relation to the white US Left.[5] Similarly, the publication of Wright's novel *Native Son* in 1939–40 is frequently cited as marking the definitive withdrawal of black writers from the Old Left as well as the Nazi-Soviet non-aggression pact and the decade following the Depression. Although "I Tried to be a Communist" is conventionally read as an allegory of Wright's fraught relationship and break with the US Communist Party (CPUSA), it actually offers a detailed account of the narrator's gradual realization of the synchronicity between communism's and sociology's construction of black subjects. Through the essays "How 'Bigger' Was Born" and "Blueprint for Negro Writing," I consider his complex engagement with communism and sociology of race through his figuration of engaged readers and knowledge producers that selectively took up and contested historic and representational conventions in an emergent liberal discourse of race of which they were a part.

The first part of this chapter proposes that Wright's critical essays and novel *Native Son* narrate a less understood historical juncture: the emergence of his figure of the professional writer of color in relation to competing models for the professionalization of black subjects. Situating Wright's figure of the writer of color in the same discursive universe as the professionalized subjects envisioned by communism and sociology helps us to see his interest in engaging an embattled discourse of professionalization in the context of overlapping questions about US national progress and the institutionalization of race experts.[6] At the same time, this interpretive move offers us a more nuanced view of the tense and contradictory relationship that Wright and other African American writers had with sociological modes of representation and the discipline of sociology.[7]

The second part of the chapter examines Wright's struggle to formulate a critique of the modernist notion of Universalism, but also to avoid the pitfalls of racial particularity. According to Paul Gilroy, Wright inaugurated a "new kind of black author" and also represented the ideal figure through which to explore what George Kent had famously labeled "blackness and the adventure of western culture." I adapt this interpretation in order to argue that Wright's production of a new type of black writer was linked to his ability to "see" blackness as an object of study and interest in a larger narrative of Western Civilization.[8] Whereas Gilroy suggests that this "newness" comes from Wright's open political affiliations and the creative possibilities that they produced, I show how Wright located the black radical writer as emerging from the tension with processes of literary professionalization envisioned by canonical sociology and communism. Pursuant to this logic, I read *Native Son* as suggesting that black writers need not be concerned with portraying black specificity because this difference, in the form of racialization, already structures Bigger's relationship to the material and economic relations that position him vis-à-vis both black bourgeois culture and the nation-state. By focusing on the way in which the state and dominant culture would perceive a black man in a wealthy white woman's bedroom, Wright emphasizes that racial difference is already scripted. My reading of Wright's text suggests that he engages with the contradictions of particularisms of Universalism's Other in order to point out how they were complementary and self-reinforcing discourses. Particularism actually reinforced the need for Universalism's emphasis on uniformity, social order, and civil society.

In "I Tried to be a Communist," the Communist Editor concludes that the African American narrator's poems are "crude, but good for us," accepting them for publication and promoting his work to other left-wing literary publications. Wright evokes the synchronicity between Communist conceptions of black writing as primitive, yet socially useful, and Park's view of Negro slave songs as "crude and elemental" windows into the Negro's early race consciousness. Like liberal sociologists such as Park, white American and particularly Jewish American writers linked with the CPUSA read black literature as a direct reflection of the Negro's consciousness, but also saw it as fostering Communist interracialism and cooperation between black and white comrades and, in so doing, solving the problems of blacks. Communist Party writers such as Mike Gold interpreted Negro spirituals as protest songs, rather than religious texts, arguing that they prefigured Communist deliverance of the Negro from class exploitation.[9] Both sociologists and Communists saw rural African Americans as New World peasants that could, respectively, assimilate to mainstream US culture in a limited way or take their place in the class struggle as the most exploited part of the proletariat. So imagined, their readings of African American writing as folk expression essentialized black culture and made it difficult for African American writers to be viewed as "legitimate" intellectuals and artists and evaluated on the same criteria.

Wright could also be seen as promoting sociological modes of study in order to develop an alternative to the limitations that he identified with communism's literary criteria and vision. For example, in "I Tried to be a Communist," he ironically describes the pleasure that he takes in his work at a South Side Boy's Club, which includes transcribing the figures of speech used by the adolescent African American boys that he encountered and taking notes on their lives. In relating his decision to write short stories, rather than biographical sketches, he certainly remarks on the inadequacy of communism's literary approach, noting that it could never "know these boys, their twisted dreams, their all too clear destinies." Though Wright registers his own ability to gain access to his subjects, he expresses doubts over his own capacity to convey such "tragedy." Wright thus defines the labor of writing as building upon notes and inventing in a way that reveals aspects unseen and undervalued by communism's literary approach.

But does Wright, in response, directly endorse Chicago School sociology in his efforts to publicly assert a "black reality"? In his introductory essay for St. Clair Drake's and Horace Cayton's 1945 sociological study *Black Metropolis*, for example, Wright seems to defend the authenticity of his published books by pointing to sociological data and encouraging fiction readers to consult sociological studies:

If, in reading my novel, *Native Son*, you doubted the reality of Bigger Thomas, then examine the delinquency rates cited in this book; if, in reading my autobiography, *Black Boy*, you doubted the picture of family life shown there, then study the figures on family disorganization given here. (xx)

Here, even as Wright sought to critique sociology's hold on African American writing, he also drew on its objective status and institutional presence in order to legitimate his own creative work. The instability of his relationship with sociology reveals the authority of sociology in representing and authenticating black lives, but also provides the conditions for Wright's analysis of communism's and sociology's visions of black professionalization and production of black subjects.

But even as Wright appropriates sociological modes of analysis to develop his literary technique, he also struggles to distinguish his literary production from communism and sociology. Rather than explaining Wright's rejection and support for Chicago School sociology as isolated, aberrant episodes or signs of unevenness, I argue that such expressions are symptomatic of the complex melding of literary authority and sociological practices of knowledge production. I read Wright's novel *Native Son* (1939) as an account of the emergence of the radical African American writer as an incipient and fraught professional knowledge producer. As I suggest, this figure is distinguished by sociologically informed knowledge-producing techniques.[10] Before turning back to Wright's texts, let me consider the intellectual and institutional intersections that shape the conditions of emergence for this figure.

The "Black Belt"

For Wright, Communism represented a necessary stage in the reform of racial inequality and the emergence of black consciousness. His description of the Party as the passageway through which he was able to leave the "Black Belt," the space assigned to blacks under racial segregation, can be read as a metaphor for the process that enabled him to envision himself in terms other than the prescribed paths of professionalization for black subjects within the racial discourse of the 1930s. Wright specifically depicts the "Communist Party" as the institutional site that enabled him to break with the vision of progress associated with the "Black Belt," the term used to refer to contiguous and predominantly African American counties in the US South and, later, to the urban ghetto of Chicago's South Side that figured centrally in sociological studies of race.

But the "Black Belt" is not a geographical area or political district, but rather an *assemblage* of racial imaginings that emerged on the global stage in the early part of the twentieth century. Loosely and then, over time, inextricably linked with black pathology, social reform, and US progress, the Black Belt might be seen as embodying the intellectual and institutional intersection between conceptions of nature and racial destiny. Conflating blackness with nature tropes and imagery advances essentialist conceptions of blacks as exploitable primitives that require surveillance and management. The racial image of the Black Belt, with its historic associations of doomed populations, extreme poverty, overcrowded housing, economic decline, social backwardness and disorganization, particularly in relation to African Americans, stood as a reminder of the US legacy of slavery and a pre-industrial plantation economy. The impulses to engage the Black Belt at home and abroad enabled the United States and the Communist Party to define itself, respectively, as democratic and revolutionary, and to defend its political vision and global influence.

According to Booker T. Washington, the term was first used to refer to a region in the southern United States that had particularly rich soil and that consequently became the area where slaves drew the largest profits and came to outnumber the white inhabitants (52). The idea of the "Black Belt" took on new significance with the rapid growth of northern cities in the late nineteenth century that brought almost 50,000 African Americans from the South to the South Side of Chicago, followed by another 70,000 during what was popularly known as the Great Migration of the next two decades. Emerging out of the encounter between the mass migration of African Americans and institutionalized racial segregation, the Black Belt came to denote the ethnically homogenous and predominantly African American communities on Chicago's South Side. It was during this time that the term entered into mainstream discourse in US culture, signaled by the publication of growing up narratives and academic studies of the Black Belt that attempted to respond to widespread concern over overcrowded cities and urban poverty.[11]

Noting that he is frequently asked to define the term "Black Belt," Washington figures the "Black Belt" as an intellectual construction ("So far as I can learn") in order to emphasize his "objective" perspective as the basis for his explanatory authority and to thus separate it from essentialist constructions of black intellect and knowledge production. Significantly, explanations of the Black Belt also became a way for black intellectuals to assert their acquired expertise and authority over and against dominant figurations of the Negro as naturally expressive. Such expressions of explanatory authority did not constitute a solution, enlightenment, or freedom, but were rather challenged and limited, as I will show through Wright's texts.

With the democratic, antifascist mission in Europe calling attention to the contradictions of racism "at home," narratives of US national progress had become increasingly tied to the resolution of the "Negro problem." Significantly, the destiny of blacks came to represent the future of America during the late 1930s, and the question of black assimilation into mainstream white America moved to the center of debates over national reform, propelled by attempts to explain and legitimate the expanding role of the United States as a global power.[12] Representing the Black Belt proved to be pivotal to such narratives of US progress in the mid-twentieth century. Was the Black Belt to be a relic of plantation agriculture and black slavery, or an emblem of liberal reform?

The "Black Belt" was not only a subject of concern to white liberals and sociologists, but specifically opened up ways for Marxists to challenge traditional liberals and more radical separatist movements, including Garveyism. As many American cultural and intellectual historians have observed, the political Left during the 1930s was hardly a unified political field, but was undergoing a series of political shifts, as the Communist Party attempted to address forms of oppression that were not class-based.[13] The "Black Belt" nation, as a metaphor for black oppression, became the centerpiece of Communist policy in the 1930s and greatly enhanced Communism's allure to black Americans. Before 1928, the Communist Party in the United States had not recognized the particularity of blacks or other racial minorities within the general class struggle. In 1928, the Sixth World Congress of the Comintern passed a resolution that supported the redefinition of the "Negro Question" proposed by Claude McKay and other New Negro writers. Their new formulation held that African Americans in the US South constituted a "nation within a nation" and thus possessed the right to self-determination as part of a larger global and anti-imperialist struggle. Following this logic, blacks in the North were viewed as an "oppressed national minority" whose emancipation could be secured through solidarity with white workers in the class struggle. By situating race within a nationalist framework, this Marxist theory of racism was intended to resolve racial divisions within the Party and also to challenge Garveyism and other so-called "bourgeois" separatist movements. The resolution asserted that there was an autonomous tradition of black radicalism, but also gave support to the notion that black history and culture were hopeful sites of black self-determination, rather than symbols of black pathology. The Black Belt nation thesis offered a vision of racial redemption through an emphasis on the distinctiveness of black culture and black oppression. In doing so, it also outlined a trajectory for the authorization of black subjects.

Through representations of the Black Belt, Communists shaped the contours of African American writing and also defined processes of professionalization for black subjects. On an institutional level, the CPUSA leadership solicited narratives about the Black Belt and opened up publication, public lecturing, and professional opportunities for African American writers. They supported national literary organizations such as the John Reed Clubs that enabled African American writers to develop intellectual and professional networks. At the same time, Communist writers conceptualized the Black Belt as part of a project of black literary reform, encouraging African American literary "reconnections" with life and culture in the Black Belt, or southern cotton-producing regions of the United States (Maxwell 70). Communist Party writers such as Mike Gold saw African American writing that focused on working-class and rural subjects as a logical supplement to proletarian writing, one that could enhance its critique of the Greenwich Village literary movement by fostering Communist interracialism, as a condition of possibility for bringing about Proletarian revolution and the downfall of capitalist power. Commenting on the Black Belt's capacity to authorize and authenticate African American writers and their work, William Maxwell suggestively notes, "Black intellectuals such as Richard Wright thus had good reason to read the party as both a relative haven of integration and a reracializing institution offering privileged reconnection with the racy vernacular earth of the Black Belt" (7). Through its focus on the Black Belt, CPUSA opened up a professionalization process for black writers that specifically encouraged them to give expression to pathological conceptions of the US South, which was also the territory of liberal reformers and Chicago School sociologists, including Washington and Park.[14]

By 1940, the "road out of the Black Belt" had become a central focus for white liberals and social scientists in the United States, as well as for African American and Communist writers, including Wright. If Communists figured the Black Belt as a nation that could create the conditions needed to deliver black subjects from nationalist pathologies to the global class struggle, liberal sociology depicted the "road out of the Black Belt" as a progressive program of racial uplift and moral reform that could help to close the gap between American ideals and social practices.

In my readings of his critical essays and the novel *Native Son*, I examine Wright's pairing of communism's conception of the Black Belt as the racial redemption of black Americans and the liberal emphasis on the "road out of the Black Belt." Whereas the demand for sociological and proletarian narratives about the Black Belt transformed the "Black Belt" into a site of self-authorization for black intellectuals and writers, Wright takes up the "road out of the Black Belt" as a powerful fiction that allows him to examine the processes that it outlines for the professionalization of black subjects. As an object of interest and study, the Black Belt also brought Wright into contact with black middle-class intellectuals such as Horace Cayton and St. Clair Drake. By analysing intellectual constructions of the "Black Belt," Wright considers the respective roles and developmental teleologies that they imagine for black culture and political consciousness. Depicting the "Black Belt" as a sociologically produced figure enables Wright to critique communist narratives of racial redemption and liberal narratives of racial reform, and to script an alternative process of professionalization for black subjects.

For Wright, taking up the Black Belt as a metaphor for black oppression provided a way to situate communism and sociology in the same discursive universe, and to thus call attention to their intellectual and institutional impact on black literature. Their joint interest in and demand for narratives of the Black Belt encouraged him to revalue his past life in the South while also giving significance to his interpretation of the Black Belt of Chicago. Most importantly, Wright connected the textualizations of black folk materials in communist narratives of racial redemption and sociological narratives of racial reform and called attention to the ways in which they outlined processes for the professionalization of black subjects. He then sought to use the intersection of these narratives—their readings of black literature and production of black professional subjects—as the basis for articulating an indigenous and independent black radicalism.

Recovering black pathology

Wright's essay "How 'Bigger' Was Born" depicts the genesis of Bigger Thomas, the protagonist of *Native Son*, and also serves as an account of his writing process, in which he identifies the factors, including moving from the South to Chicago and coming into contact with the labor movement, that led him to see Bigger as a "meaningful and prophetic symbol."[15] I read "How 'Bigger' Was Born" as a text that offers a detailed description of the emergence of an independent black radicalism through the recognition of racial pathology, an evaluation of how black Americans and white Americans are interpellated by antiracist narratives, and a reconfiguration of liberal and communist concepts of interracialism.

To illuminate the specific conditions for the recognition of black pathology that could bring about black radicalism, Wright posits the development of knowledge of racist conventions as forming the basis for the refiguration of standard narratives. Through detailed descriptions of Bigger Numbers 1–5, black male figures with whom he identifies, admires, and fears, Wright painstakingly explains how each represents a different form of racial protest against the restrictions of Jim Crow laws. His sociological construction of black subjectivity depicts individual responses to racism, the social effects of individual actions, and the legal consequences for each Bigger. While the lives of Bigger Numbers 1–4 end in violence, prison, or insanity, it is Bigger Number 5 who presents a more hopeful and effective form of protest. Unlike Bigger Number 1, who uses brute force to bully other blacks, or Bigger Number 2, who can only express himself in terms of his hatred of whites, Bigger Number 5 is able to generate a sense of pride in and solidarity with other blacks. If Bigger Number 3 is a black man who uses force against other black workers for individual gain, and Bigger Number 4 represents an ineffectual intellectual who is paralyzed by his belief that "white folks won't let us do nothing," then Bigger Number 5 takes a different direction by using his knowledge to expose the hypocrisy, racism, and social sanctions that enforce segregation laws and exclude blacks from culture and education. Unlike Bigger Number 3, who only uses force, and Bigger Number 4, who resembles the defeated intellectual, Bigger Number 5 uses both force and intellect to challenge racial segregation. When asked by the conductor to move from a street car designated for "white only," he refuses, claiming that he is unable to read the sign that separates the streetcar into white and black sections.

As Wright suggests, Bigger Number 5 is exceptional—an exemplary text for the beginnings of the articulation of an indigenous and independent black radicalism—for his skillful appropriation of black pathology; in this case, Bigger takes up the withholding of literacy from blacks and transforms it into a form of protest. Although Wright emphasizes the potential that Bigger Number 5 represents for an antiracist politics that can also generate black collective consciousness and solidarity, he also reminds us that this Bigger probably met the same end—lynching or another violent death—as the others. In doing so, he suggests that individual recognition is not equivalent to institutional and structural change.

What Wright's account of Bigger Numbers 1–4 makes clear are the processes by which blacks have been interpellated by narratives of race that subsequently provide the languages and terms through which they envision their lives. In order to consider the possibilities for self-determination and racial autonomy, Wright probes the way in which black subjection needed to be reinforced through the restriction of social mobility and opportunity, through segregated housing and public facilities, employment, and ideologies that advanced the racial superiority of whites. In his view, the shared intent of these strategies was to enlist the participation of blacks in their own subjection:

But, because the blacks were so close to the very civilization which sought to keep them out, because they could not but react in some way to its incentives and prizes, and because the very tissue of their consciousness received its tone and timbre from the strivings of that dominant civilization, oppression spawned among them a myriad variety of reactions, reaching from outright blind rebellion to a sweet, other-worldly submissiveness. (858)

By suggesting that the interpellation of blacks by conceptions of advancement and achievement ("incentives and prizes") is inevitable, Wright also notes that black self-conceptions are forged in relation to dominant "strivings," or narratives of self-making, development, and progress. The multiple ways in which narratives of mobility and egalitarianism address blacks reveal the discursive formation that Frantz Fanon identifies as counter-hegemony. For Fanon, the process through which marginalized subjects are invited to identify with dominant discourse is encoded by a set of heterogeneous social practices that enable the articulation of dissent and resistance.[16] So imagined, the hailing process opens up the possibility of putting askew totalizing concepts of domination and subjugation, and instead illuminating dynamics such as unevenness, incompleteness, and failure. By taking into account the complex ways in which blacks have been interpellated by and also reproduce dominant cultural narratives of race and national progress, Wright reveals the tenuousness of conceptions of race and antiracist narratives.

In contrast to figurations of communist interracialism as a condition for class revolution and the sociological concept of assimilation as the solution to the "Negro problem," Wright portrays exchanges between African Americans and white writers as formative to the development of independent modes for conceptualizing and representing the "locked-in life of the Black Belt areas" (862). Commenting on how novels by white writers enabled him to develop strategies for evaluating the "effects of American civilization upon the personalities of people," his exchanges with white writers also provided him with the critical tools and language needed to depict black life in fiction. Remarking that African Americans did not have a background in such "sharp and critical testing of experience, no novels that went with a deep and fearless will down to the dark roots of life," Wright references the presumed documentary nature of African American writing in order to argue that such conceptions have prevented African Americans from being regarded as legitimate artists and developing their skills and techniques as writers (862–3).

When Wright describes a pamphlet that features Gorky and Lenin in exile in London, looking upon landmarks such as Big Ben and Westminster Abbey, he recounts how Lenin points out each site to Gorky through the language of cultural proximity and comparison: "Here is *their* Big Ben. There is *their* Westminster Abbey. There is *their* library" (863). This scene—and the essay more generally—illustrates a critical theme for Wright: how knowledge emerges through comparisons to one's own context. But what is most compelling about Wright's description is that it calls attention to his own memory of himself reading the story about Lenin and Gorky ("There is in me a memory of me reading an interesting pamphlet" 863). As Wright implies, it is his remembered experience of reading that is significant, not only the story. In contrast to sociological and communist renderings of African American writers as conveyors of authentic and unmediated racial experience, Wright depicts his interior life through his remembered encounter with a textual account of knowledge production. In his appraisal, he assigns the same value to vernacular accounts ("Sometimes I'd hear a Negro say . . .") and written materials, and thus gives value to informal and unofficial knowledge practices, incorporating them as part of the historical record.

Arguing against the desirability of "pure particularism," Ernesto Laclau writes, "If the particular asserts itself as mere particularity, in a purely differential relation with other particularities, it is sanctioning the status quo in the relation of power between the groups" (99). As he explains, stressing only the differential aspect can generate the notion of separate developments—as seen in the system of apartheid—and promote an approach that leaves intact and unexamined the power relations on which this differential aspect is based. "How 'Bigger' Was Born" registers the constant struggle to avoid the pitfalls of particularity as sketched by Laclau. In the text, reading does not represent achievement or escape, but rather a starting point that leads to the recognition of patterns that, in turn, enables him to develop an understanding of the specificity of a particular situation and conditions, while also positioning them within larger contexts and pointing to their implications. What matters for Wright is not a mimetic political identification, but rather familiarity as a form of perspective. The inspiration that Wright finds, for example, in a passage about feudal Russia demonstrates his interest in using the "actions and feelings of men ten thousand miles from home" to better understand the "moods and impulses" of those in Chicago and the US South (863). As he theorizes, focusing on the comparison enables him to feel that he has gained worldly knowledge that allows him to interpret Bigger in relation to broader contexts than his individual experience. Yet he also suggests that criticism alone does not create change. At the moment that massive urbanization is transforming the Black Belt of the South into the Black Ghetto, he also points out how it can also reinforce unequal structures of power.

As I have suggested, Wright expresses the need for a specific kind of professional writer, one whose authority emerges through the ability to draw relationships between histories and cultures. But he specifically portrays himself as a knowledge producer in competition with sociologists studying the Negro problem (Wright, "Introduction" xx). Depicting himself as a writer sanctioned by self-knowledge and acquired knowledge, he envisions himself working in parallel with their scientific studies: "So, with this much knowledge of myself and the world gained and known, why should I not try to work out on paper the problem of what will happen to Bigger? Why should I not, like a scientist in a laboratory, use my imagination and invent test-tube situations, place Bigger in them, and following the guidance of my own hopes and fears, what I had learned and remembered, work out in fictional form an emotional statement and resolution of this problem?" (867). By juxtaposing his literary exploration of Bigger in *Native Son* with scientific studies of the "Negro problem," Wright asserts his authority to offer an account of racism and its solution. Closely mirroring sociological challenges to biological and essentialist views of race, his interpretive authority draws from both scholarly knowledge and his "lived experience" as a black man in the United States. What separates *Native Son* most markedly from the sociological studies of race in the 1930s is the way in which Wright posits blacks as the central protagonists of American social reform. While liberal narratives of race have traditionally figured black Americans as the subjects and beneficiaries of racial reforms carried out by white Americans, Wright's focus on the different forms of black agency constituted within the restrictions of Jim Crow society represents an important historical intervention in the ascription of social and developmental roles in liberal discourse. Instead of viewing the moral reform of white Americans as the primary weapon in the fight against racial bigotry, Wright turns attention to the development of political consciousness and agency in black Americans.

The relation of Bigger Thomas to other nations and races represents a turning point in the narrative of Wright's political formation. As he explains, "The extension of my sense of the personality of Bigger was the pivot of my life; it altered the *complexion of my existence*" (860). The extension of Bigger, as a metaphor for black oppression, to other contexts transformed the way that Wright saw himself as a racialized Other. The new perspective generated through his extension of black subjectivity enables him to see himself in terms other than those assigned to blacks by dominant culture, which defines them negatively through the rhetoric of segregation and in opposition to "white" notions of freedom, modernity, and productivity. The transformation that Wright attributes to his negotiation of black specificity with other forms of subjectivity represents a de-centering of debates over the assimilation of blacks into white American culture.

Wright tells us that his protagonist emerged from a recognition of similarities between racism in the United States and the rhetoric of fascism in Europe: "I was startled to detect, either from the side of the Fascists or from the side of the oppressed, reactions, moods, phrases, attitudes that reminded me strongly of Bigger, that helped to bring out more clearly the shadowy outlines of the negative that lay in the back of my mind" (864). In a comparison of fascism in Germany to racism in the United States, he points to the Nazi preoccupation with the "construction of a society in which there would exist among all people (*German* people, of course!) *one* solidarity of ideals, *one* continuous circulation of fundamental beliefs, notions, and assumptions" (864). Wright focuses here on the contradictions within a key element of classical liberalism, the notion of a civil society, or an alternative to a hierarchical social order, which both German fascism and American racism hold in common. At another moment, he compares the Nazi reliance upon rituals and symbols to the quest for black leaders in Marcus Garvey's "Back to Africa" movement. Although he rejects Garvey's separatist political agenda, he acknowledges the desire for a place in which blacks could be political leaders and participate in the nation as full citizens that inspired Garvey's vision of remaking a "home" for black Americans in Africa. Wright calls attention to the cultural alienation that has produced a sense of estrangement in Bigger, remarking that "the civilization that had given birth to Bigger contained no spiritual sustenance, had created no culture which could hold and claim his allegiance and faith" (865).

By rewriting the traditional narrative in which America's uniqueness is defined through its opposition to Nazi fascism and Russian totalitarianism, Wright reveals the degree to which articulations of US national power drew strength from the separation of racism from international politics. The parallels that he sees in "the emotional tensions of Bigger in America and Bigger in Nazi Germany and Bigger in old Russia" challenge the dominant narrative of American exceptionalism (865). By appropriating the terms of opposition through which America's cultural and political coherence is achieved, Wright then uses them to question the exceptionalism of American democratic culture—through its presumed, absolute difference—from Nazi Germany. Wright's belief that Bigger, "an American product, a native son of this land, carried with him the potentialities of either Communism or Fascism" places Bigger within an international context, implying that Bigger's political allegiance has not yet been articulated (866).

Between "communist" and "sociologist"

As Wright suggests, reading leads to acts of comparison and revaluation, in contrast to the humanist enlightenment that would lead him to identify more closely with projects for racial reform and racial redemption. To explain the conditions for the emergence of a black radical writer, Wright turns to the constellation of racial knowledge produced about black subjects. Where, he asks, does the figure of the African American writer intersect with the intellectual practices by which knowledge about African Americans is produced? In the 1937 literary manifesto, "Blueprint for Negro Writing," he suggests that the goal for African American writers is to generate a "relationship between the Negro woman hoeing cotton in the South and the men who loll in swivel chairs on Wall Street and take the fruits of her toil" (51). Though Wright appears, at first glance, to be urging writers to focus on US capitalism's exploitation of black workers in the South, I argue that he is more interested in recovering the figures of the black rural proletarian and liberal capitalist as key protagonists in both communism's and sociology's fictions of the Black Belt. These figures were part of larger discourses that worked to interpellate supporters of a Black Belt nation as well as the citizens of a nation that was largely believed to have adopted a course of racial reform. By emphasizing the connection between a romanticized black peasantry and the US captains of industry that were also the liberal philanthropists funding sociological studies of the Negro problem, Wright shows how such framings of blackness enabled sociology to proclaim itself as an agent of racial reform and Americanization over and against communism, which was also asserting itself as an alternative to liberal projects that pursued the moral reform of white Americans as a means of securing the racial uplift of African Americans.[17] As Maxwell observes, many African American activists and writers were drawn to the Party precisely because they saw it as a way to counteract a problematic white philanthropy and the negative reactions it stirred up (8). By examining how both sociologists and communists read black literature as sociological in order to figure black Americans as the chosen objects of Communist deliverance and racial reform, Wright suggests that this intersection called into being the need for an independent black radical writer.

In "Blueprint for Negro Writing," Wright offers a detailed account of black literature through an analysis of the overlap between processes of objectification, racialization, and professionalization. The essay is divided into ten sections, and begins by analysing two definitions of the social role of Negro writing and then goes on to construct nationalism, perspective and theme as "problems" that are racial and literary, concluding with sections on professional autonomy and an argument for the necessity for writing to take place as collective work. Sociology and communism produced a discourse around African American writing that emphasized authenticity and transparency, while also establishing a particular role for writers as transcribers of the Negro's consciousness. In contrast, Wright depicts a black radical writer as a historical formation that emerges from the intersection between the processes for the professionalization of black subjects imagined by communism and sociology. By analysing the convergence of sociological and communist productions of black subjects, Wright reconstructs the role of the black writer to show how fiction opens up a space for the articulation of an independent and indigenous black radicalism.[18] In order to gain perspective beyond "cold facts" produced in sociological interpretations, Wright argues that African American writers need to reflect upon the "harsh lot of their race" in relation to representations of the aspirations and struggles of other marginalized groups ("Blueprint for Negro Writing" 51). On the one hand, Wright suggests that relating black Americans to other political contexts and struggles can lead to a broader understanding of the "interdependence of people in modern society" and that connecting the lives of black urban individuals to the working classes will offer perspective on the majority of the world's population. But he is also, I believe, calling upon writers to reflect upon the ways in which they have been constructed as objects through black pathology.

Wright addresses his conceptions of African American literary heritage by pointing to the impact of readings of black literature as social documentary by sociologists and communist writers. To redefine the figure of the African American writer, he identifies Marxism as offering the unique possibility of restoring the African American writer's "lost heritage," or his role as a "creator of the world in which he lives, and as a creator of himself" (49). By identifying creative agency as the African American writer's heritage, Wright counters sociological conceptions of black literary formation as the recovery of black folklore and Southern cultural roots. Instead, he posits a genealogy for black literature in which folklore is an important source of literary inspiration among others: "Eliot, Stein, Joyce, Proust, Hemingway, and Anderson; Gorky, Barbusse, Nexo, and Jack London no less than the folklore of the Negro himself should form the heritage of the Negro writer" (50). Following Wright's formulation, the process of becoming a writer is synonymous with the development of an understanding of how processes of objectification, racialization, and professionalization are mutually constitutive; this understanding then forms the basis for literary strategies of self-authorization.

I see Wright as using the convergence of communism and sociology—particularly their sociological readings of black literature and joint investment in the professionalization of black subjects—as a basis for articulating an independent and indigenous black radicalism. To do so, he has to negotiate the conflation of black literature with documentary and conceptions of the Negro writer as naturally expressive, rather than a self-determined creative subject. Perhaps Wright's analysis of perspective offers the best illustration of the conditions for the emergence of the figure of the black radical writer. As he explains, perspective is a vantage point in "intellectual space where a writer stands to view the struggles, hopes, and sufferings of his people" (50). Perspective cannot be "discovered" in the Negro's consciousness, he contends, but rather emerges as a combination of a "pre-conscious assumption" and a "difficult achievement." By constructing "perspective" as a particular "problem" in black literary culture, he identifies it as a key element in the process of professionalization that also enables him to outline a process for the formation of a black radical writer.

Strange white people

Wright advances a view of race and racism that reproduces and contests the universalizing tendencies of both liberal and Communist orthodoxy while also staking out a position of racial specificity. Instead of positing the recognition of black specificity and self-determination as the ultimate goal of politics, or what Ernesto Laclau has termed "pure particularism," Wright points to the development of class consciousness through black disidentification with the processes of professionalization imagined by liberal integration and communist interracialism.[19] As he explains, the recognition of alliances of class and race amongst blacks and also between blacks and whites will enable the formation of black consciousness and culture, or a brand of cultural nationalism that does not require the social isolation of blacks from other political groups and contexts.

The novel tells the story of Bigger Thomas, a young African American man whose first day as a chauffeur for Mr. and Mrs. Henry Dalton, a wealthy white family with vast real estate holdings in Chicago, culminates in the accidental murder of their twenty-three-year-old daughter Mary, a University of Chicago student. Organized into three parts, *Native Son* begins with "Fear," an account of Bigger's domestic life and disastrous debut as the Daltons's chauffeur. The second part, "Flight," begins after Bigger accidentally kills Mary and becomes a fugitive, later attempting to extort ransom money and blaming Jan Erlone, Mary's boyfriend and Communist Party member, for the murder. The third part, "Fate," tells the story of Bigger's trial, ending with his execution. I consider how the novel brings into focus Bigger's encounters with members of the Dalton household in order to show how liberalism envisions a professionalizing process for black subjects at the same time that it advances black pathology in order to regulate the inclusionary process for black subjects.

If Bigger's job with the Daltons places him on the path to self-making and upward mobility, then this process of professionalization is violently derailed by his murder of Mary, his employer's daughter, and to a different extent his African American girlfriend Bessie Mears. More than once, the novel showcases Bigger's attempts to interpret the racial logic of liberalism. In one scene, Bigger persuades himself to go to the interview at the Dalton household by taking into account his mother's analysis of the dynamics that defined black Americans as the fetishized objects of elite white Americans:

And rich white people were not so hard on Negroes; it was the poor whites who hated Negroes. They hated Negroes because they didn't have their share of the money. His mother had always told him that rich white people liked Negroes better than they did poor whites. (36)

By repeating his mother's assessment, Bigger also underscores her focus on white benevolence and its impact on black people. To revise this emphasis, he later connects assertions of white heterogeneity, or the recognition of cultural and ethnic differences amongst white people, to a liberal discourse of race, which outlines a process in which the recognition of white heterogeneity will lead to black integration and, in doing so, facilitate the continuation of racial uplift and US national progress. Bigger's recognition of white heterogeneity, for example, does not change the ways in which his racial construction continues to haunt him and shape his actions. Indeed, the account of the events that lead up to Mary's death suggests that the crime is largely motivated by Bigger's confusion and fear over how he will be perceived as a black man. When he helps the intoxicated Mary to her room, he wonders "what a white man would think seeing him here with her like this?" (*Native Son* 81). The contradictory impulses that Mary's presence evokes for Bigger articulate the threat that white women carried for the professionalization of black men:

He watched her with a mingled feeling of helplessness, admiration, and hate. If her father saw him with her now, his job would be over. But she was beautiful, slender, with an air that made him feel that she did not hate him with the hate of other white people. But, for all that, she was white and he hated her. (81)

This passage suggests how a white woman is predominantly figured as an irreducible marker of race and a potential threat to the economic and physical survival of black men. But it also offers more than a description of the degree to which the symbolic presence of white women defined social boundaries for black men. When Bigger distinguishes Mary's regard for black people from the overtly racist views of "other white people," his recognition of white hetereogeneity also narrates his attempt to critically evaluate the production of racial knowledge. Even as he recognizes Mary as "different," he concludes that it does not justify another type of reaction from him. What matters, he tells us, is her racial classification as white.

While Wright exposes the falsity of America's egalitarian rhetoric by pointing out the exclusion of black Americans from narratives of national progress, he also explores the terms that constitute nationalist affiliation and subjectivity. In the novel, Bigger persuades his friend Gus to play "White," a game in which they imitate the actions and manners of powerful white men. Taking on the roles of an Army general, financial tycoon J. P. Morgan, and the President of the United States, they act out scenes of authority borrowed from movies and other media associated with white men (21–2). Through their performances, Bigger and Gus figure whiteness as heightened masculine authority and economic empowerment through which they are able to participate in public decision-making, direct the allocation of financial resources, and discipline others.

Their performances of whiteness temporarily claim authority and agency in a way that reveals the fabricated nature of American subjectivity. By appropriating the words, gestures, and forms of entitlement that constitute white male authority, Bigger and Gus challenge the naturalized appearance of the white male subject. As Richard Dyer reminds us, power "works in a particularly seductive way with whiteness, because of the way it seems rooted, in common-sense thought, in things other than ethnic difference" (White 46). What Bigger and Gus expose in their game is the way in which black subjectivity is traditionally defined in a negative relation to white power and agency, thus throwing into question the possibility of black autonomy and agency within such a binary definition of racial difference.

I see Wright as most forcefully questioning framings of blackness in liberal narratives of racial reform in scenes that feature Bigger and Peggy O'Flagherty, the Irish cook and housekeeper. Liberalism, he suggests, frames blackness as an obstacle to a process assimilation that was seen as central to Americanization. The liberal narrative of progress intersects with a process of professionalization at the point where the black subject is called upon to self-identify as the pathological object that will then be reformed and uplifted by white Americans in a national process of racial reform. Scenes between Bigger and Peggy dramatize the logic of racial reform, as a counterpoint to communism's view of interracialism as a key component in the class struggle.

By relating Bigger to Peggy, Wright explores the processes of professionalization for black subjects and white immigrants inscribed within a liberal narrative of racial reform. More than once, Peggy compares Bigger to the "last colored man who worked for us" in a way that encourages him to see himself as the object of racial uplift and that also allows her to lay claim to the same racial category as her wealthy employers, even though she holds a subordinate position as their servant (56). So imagined, liberal narratives of race position blacks as the privileged objects of white racial reform while also opening up new forms of identification to non-elite whites.

Peggy attempts to instruct Bigger on the benefits of racial reform by impressing upon him that Mr. Dalton has "done a lot for your people." But Bigger's puzzled response of "My people?" demonstrates that he does not identify with Peggy's view of him as part of a racialized group that is also the object of racial uplift. Peggy's characterization of the Dalton household as "one big family" also leads Bigger to distrust her. Unable to imagine becoming part of this idealized white family formation, Bigger suspects Peggy as having courted his cooperation in order to shift some of her work onto him. To reject the concept of ethnic assimilation that Peggy represents, he recovers a history of racialized class antagonism between black and white working classes and, in doing so, articulates a racial critique of reform. For Bigger, it isn't just blackness, but other socially constructed differences that matter in creating disparities of power and economic opportunity. By inferring that the results of differential access are differential opportunities and outcomes, he also suggests that access, as the possible possibility within a range of options, and opportunity, as possibility in a wider and more general sense, are not the same.

Through Peggy, Wright suggests that the notion of shared ethnic oppression generates and helps to legitimate a racialized hierarchy in which the Irish are assigned a managerial role in the professionalization process imagined for black subjects. By identifying the similarities between the histories of black Americans and Irish Americans, David Roediger emphasizes their shared histories of oppression and displacement from a homeland.[20] Yet it is precisely Roediger's superficial assumption of a "common history" as colonial subjects and exploited workers that the novel complicates through the interactions of Bigger and Peggy. Theses scenes enable Wright to link the histories of African Americans and Irish Americans through the purportedly universal concept of ethnic assimilation. Yet rather than connecting these histories through a logic of commonality that can elide differences, the novel points to the possibility of a cross-racial alliance by portraying the link between African Americans and Irish Americans as relational, or structured by differential access to employment and life chances. Peggy's insistence on an ethnic equivalence with Bigger actually helps to install and legitimate a racialized hierarchy in which Irish Americans are positioned as a managerial class of privileged experts that is key to the process of the professionalization of black subjects and, more generally, to the liberal project of racial reform.

By foregrounding the investment of non-elite whites such as Peggy in a cross-racial alliance, the novel shows how non-elite and elite whites are recruited in different, yet critically linked ways by the logic of liberal racial reform. I read Peggy's positioning of Bigger as the privileged object in a larger narrative of racial uplift as a concise description of the interpellations of non-elite whites as agents of racial reform that play critical pedagogical roles by pointing to individual examples of successful racial reform and, in doing so, normalizing ethnic assimilation as the standard process for subject formation and Americanization. To further instruct Bigger on the benefits of liberal racial reform, Peggy holds up the example of Green, the former chauffeur who attended night school and obtained a US government job. Though she expresses admiration for Green in a way that invites Bigger to follow in his path, Bigger fixates on the ten years of service to the Daltons that it took for Green to "pull himself up by his bootstraps," thus rejecting the developmental trajectory of self-making and middle-class mobility that he represents. By questioning the liberal myth of self-making in which a black man obtains an education through the patronage of white liberals and uses the opportunity to gain middle-class respectability, Bigger brings into focus the intersection between liberal narratives of racial reform, the professionalization process for the incorporation of African Americans into mainstream society, and the elevation of non-elite whites through the expansion of forms of identification with a white racial category.[21]

Peggy's self-identification as a member of the extended Dalton family and mimicking of their commitment to helping African Americans illustrates the process by which the dominant classes secure their positions through the reproduction of their thought, practices, and social vision. Like her employer's "deep interest" in African Americans, Peggy also professes to "know something about colored people" (58). But she distinguishes her privileged knowledge from the benevolent regard of her employers, noting that her family "felt about England like the colored folks feel about this country" (58). Peggy parallels the British colonization of the Irish to the subjugation of black Americans and, in doing so, connects African Americans and Irish immigrants as oppressed ethnic groups. I interpret Bigger's encounter with Peggy as staking out points of identification and disidentification between African Americans and white European immigrants in order to assert the irreducible difference between race and ethnicity, but also to question its logic of commonality. Rather than pursuing an alliance between Peggy and Bigger, the novel instead represents their relationship in terms of a racialized hierarchy in which white European immigrants are on top.

Sociology speaking through

As I suggested in my earlier discussion of African American writing and literary value, sociology positioned itself intellectually and institutionally as an agent of US liberalism. As the official national discourse on race, sociological narratives of race helped to bridge academic knowledge production of race and important cultural and institutional apparatuses of liberalism, including philanthrophy and Christianity. In *Native Son*, Bigger's encounters with members of the Dalton household dramatize the ways in which elite and non-elite whites are interpellated by sociologically generated liberal narratives of race, in which they are the protagonists and Bigger is the pathologized object and beneficiary of their project of uplift and racial reform. By thematizing the conflicted feelings that arise through Bigger's encounters with the Daltons and Jan Erlone, Mary's boyfriend and Communist Party member, Wright suggests that Bigger begins to develop a form of racial consciousness through his recognition of himself as a pathologized object that will, in turn, enable the emergence of black agency and an independent black radicalism.

The Dalton's "deep interest in colored people" suggests how a program of racial reform was increasingly interpreted as a moral duty for white Americans. From their first meeting, the Daltons view Bigger through the critical lens of sociology, particularly in their debate over whether it would be "wise procedure to inject [Bigger] into his new environment at once" and whether it would be too "abrupt," based on the analysis found in Bigger's relief organization case record, to "invoke an immediate feeling of confidence" (48; 1940 and later editions). Bigger's inability to understand the Dalton's conversation about him is symbolically figured both as a form of blindness and as a physical obstruction to his development of self-knowledge:

> The long strange words they used made no sense to him; it was another language. He felt from the tone of their words that they were having a difference of opinion about him, but he could not determine what it was about. It made him feel uneasy, tense, as though there were influences and presences about him which he could feel but not see. He felt strangely blind. (48)

Bigger's awareness of the way in which he is inscribed by scientific language calls attention to his estrangement from a position in which he would be able to participate or produce a counter-discourse on race. When Bigger encounters the language of social science, as voiced by the Daltons, he feels its power and re-racializing effect on him, but is not able to name its source. By directly linking the Daltons' ability to understand and deploy these scientific terms and models to the power and privilege that they possess over Bigger's future, the scene depicts the intertwined relationship of culture and domination. The Daltons' ability to make Bigger see himself as an "Other" of dominant discourse is symptomatic of the power that white liberals possess through their appropriation and deployment of narratives that revolve around a pathological model of black culture, as linked to the notion of national progress. While Mr. and Mrs. Dalton assume roles as Bigger's social guardians, they also take responsibility for the process that is directed at his transformation into a productive citizen.

I read Mary Dalton's expression of desire to "see" and "know" how blacks live as a complement to Mr. and Mrs. Daltons's sociological conception of Bigger as their moral duty as well as Jan's view that organizing African Americans is a key to the class revolution. Significantly, Mary uses the language and tropes of social science closely associated with her school, the University of Chicago, the institutional base for the Chicago School sociologists and a key site for knowledge production of race during the early twentieth century. In foregrounding her desire to learn the "ways of black folks," Mary asserts what she sees as their common, if unequal, humanity in a way that also frames their differences as cultural ones. Her lament to Bigger that blacks and whites "know so little about each other" implies that racism can be resolved if white people become better educated about black culture.[22] This scene locates Mary as part of the University of Chicago social science discourse and underscores how ineffectual her intepretation of race is, when seen from Bigger's perspective.

In this sense, Bigger's murder of Mary also represents an attempt to kill off that discourse. Wright literally showcases the University's suppression of intellectuals of color in a scene in which Bigger sees six white men take something from a "brown skinned Negro" and throw him into a cell. Eventually, the man is taken away in a straitjacket, leaving a white man to explain the incident to Bigger: "He went off his nut from studying too much at the university. He was writing a book on how colored people live and he says somebody stole all the facts he'd found. He says he's got to the bottom of why colored folks are treated bad and he's going to tell the President and have things changed, see? He's nuts! He swears that his university professor locked him up" (765). Here, the University is depicted as a knowledge-producing institution that participates in the suppression of sociological accounts generated by African American researchers. The end of the novel gives further emphasis to the linkages between University of Chicago social scientists, the production of racialized sexual pathologies, and the policing of black subjects. By reading the newspaper reportage of his trial, Bigger considers the testimony of two academics: a "psychiatric attaché of the police department" who deems Bigger more "cagy" than he appears and concludes that he may be hiding other crimes, and a psychology professor who comments that white women have an "unusual fascination" with black men and that black men cannot control themselves around white women (787). Even though Bigger has already begun to articulate an independent perspective, this scene implies that he continues to be haunted by black racial pathologies.

When Mary and Jan talk with Bigger and ask him to dine with them in a South Side restaurant, their actions reinforce their racial privilege. Upon meeting Bigger, Jan tells him not to use the hierarchical address "sir" and characterizes their relationship as purportedly horizontal: "I'll call you Bigger and you'll call me Jan. That's the way it'll be between us" (507). Jan's assertion of a shared humanity with Bigger does not lead him to feel liberated or equal, but instead results in his feeling even "blacker" than before:

> He was very conscious of his black skin and there was in him a prodding conviction that Jan and men like him had made it so that he would be conscious of that black skin. Did not white people despise a black skin? Then why was Jan doing this? Why was Mary standing there so eagerly, with shining eyes? What could they get out of this? Maybe they did not despise him? But they made him feel his black skin by just standing there looking at him, one holding his hand and the other smiling. (508)

In relating the unsettling effect that Jan and Mary have on him, Bigger also indicates that it has provided him with the critical distance that allows him to analyse his own objectification. Connecting their benevolent treatment to his sense of racial Otherness leads him to rethink the racial knowledge that he already possesses ("Did not white people despise a black skin?"), and to conclude that their regard for him is different, but still dehumanizing. Though Bigger does not generate a counter-narrative, he connects his recognition of black pathology to his ability to locate himself at the intersection of intellectual and institutional knowledge of race: "He felt he had no physical existence at all right then; he was something he hated, the badge of shame which he knew was attached to a black skin. It was a shadowy region, a No Man's Land, the ground that separated the white world from the black that he stood upon" (508). Bigger thus frames recognition of black pathology as creating the possibility for achieving a fuller perspective:

> He felt naked, transparent: he felt that this white man, having helped to put him down, having helped to deform him, held him up now to look at him and be amused. At that moment he felt toward Mary and Jan a dumb, cold, and inarticulate hate. (68)

By suggesting that Jan's assertion of equality actively pursues a racial hierarchy, rather than neutralizing racial difference, these scenes also sketch the emergence of Bigger's independent vantage point and perspective, described here as his sense of "inarticulate hate."

Jan's belief that a revolution cannot take place without the support of black Americans reflects a specific Party vision of communist interracialism as an enabling condition for class revolution. According to Jan, black Americans will "give the Party something it needs" (517). Recalling Robert Park's remarks that black Americans are "naturally expressive," the "something" that Jan attributes to African Americans is described by Mary as "emotion" or "spirit" and can be found in black vernacular culture, such as songs and spirituals. Both positions envision a social role for black Americans, but fall short of a politics that involve restructuring power relations, opening leadership, and defining a visionary and intellectual role. Amidst the backdrop of Jan and Mary singing a Negro spiritual together, Wright offers a close-up of Bigger's "derisive" reaction: "Hell that ain't the tune."

Jan and Mary's pursuit of interracialism by eating in a restaurant in an African American neighborhood, imitating black speech, and expressing general admiration for black culture, make Bigger increasingly uncomfortable. By illustrating the way in which Bigger's ability to feel like himself depends upon white people acting "white," or, in this case, authoritative and dominant in relation to blacks, Wright suggests that black people see themselves as "black" negatively, through the terms of racial domination and segregation. As we will see, the possibilities for the development of black autonomy and self-determination within the limited space of Jim Crow is repeatedly raised through a negotiation of liberal narratives of race and class consciousness.

"Not the only object of hate": On pathologization and racial particularity

In the novel, Bigger's recognition of pathologized images serves as a springboard for his gradual reframing of black pathology. Hearing the legal and dominant cultural interpretation of Bessie's dead body helps to articulate for Bigger the way in which racial domination is secured not only through physical means, but rather through the assertion of particular forms of subjectivity that shape the boundaries of his present and future. Remembering Bessie enables Bigger to recover something he did not experience individually and, in so doing, links his development of racial consciousness to the assertion of his explanatory authority:

> He knew that Bessie, too, though dead, though killed by him, would resent her dead body being used in this way. Anger quickened in him: an old feeling that Bessie had often described to him when she had come from long hours of hot toil in the white folks' kitchens, a feeling of being forever commanded by others so much that thinking and feeling for one's self was impossible. (755)

By making a seamless transition from a description of Bessie's life to his own feelings of rage kindled by a racist culture, Bigger constructs their relationship as a racial alliance that authorizes him to speak for her and also displaces the misogyny that led to her murder. What this scene implies is that Bigger is able to develop race consciousness and to assume the persona of an analyst through his physical and symbolic domination of women.

In reflecting on his alliance with Jan, Bigger claims to have gained a new type of perspective, one that emerges through the developments of explanatory authority through collective racial identification. To explain his decision to serve as Bigger's advocate, Jan claims that his experiences of imprisonment and the loss of Mary, as a white woman and loved one, have led him to identify with "black men who've been killed" and "black men who had to grieve" and, consequently, to view the murder case as part of a system of black racial oppression (714). According to Bigger, the knowledge that Jan does not blame him for Mary's death generates familiar feelings of guilt, but "in a different sense" (714). He goes on to figuratively depict this change as the feeling that a "white man had flung aside the curtain and walked into the room of his life" (714). Bigger locates his new perspective as emerging from the shift in Jan's interpretative framework for the murder from an isolated crime to an example within a racialized and historicized system.

When Reverend Hammond, the black preacher, urges him to adopt a universalist discourse of "eternal life" as an alternative to the pathologized images of himself in the newspapers, Bigger reacts by throwing away his cross (709). Rather than taking comfort in the Reverend's black vernacular speech and the familiarity of the images that he evokes, Bigger rejects the Reverend's raceless, Universalist vision as a viable analytical framework, resolving "never again to trust anybody or anything. Not even Jan. Or Max. They were all right, maybe; but whatever he thought or did from now on would have to come from him and him alone" (315). Bigger's remark distances himself from the Universalist discourse that the Reverend represents, but also from the Black Belt nation thesis and Marxist economic discourse associated, respectively, with Jan and his lawyer, Max. Though he regards Jan and Max as potentially "all right," he also asserts the need to be independently responsible for generating his own course of action. Bigger's independent perspective, his ability to imagine an alternative form of happiness, might thus be seen as emerging through his interpretation of the synchronicity between white liberalism and Christianity, particularly the ways that their interpellations of black subjects through discourses of domesticity work to maintain hegemonic discourses. Significantly, his new perspective takes its definition from Bigger's recognition of the ways in which black people are encouraged to participate in hegemonic processes. When his lawyer Max asks him whether he could feel "at home" in church, as a place where nobody hated him, Bigger replies: "I wanted to be happy in this world, not out of it. I didn't want that kind of happiness. The white folks like for us to be religious, then they can do what they want to with us" (778). By highlighting Bigger's attempt to navigate the investments of liberalism and communism in the development of black subjects, such expressions of how he is both a subject and object in these discourses might be seen as narrating the beginnings of an independent black radicalism.

The novel's final scene offers an extended demonstration of Bigger's failure to develop into a coherent, self-actualizing subject and emphasizes instead the significance of his attempts to view himself in relational terms. According to Cedric Robinson, *Native Son* offers an extended demonstration of Wright's critical stance toward Marxism. Suggesting that even Max never understands Bigger and is actually frightened by Bigger's vision of himself, Robinson implies that the purposes of Marxism employed in US Communism were more political than analytical, directed toward enabling people to achieve power, rather than produce theory or praxis. Extending Robinson's argument, I read this scene as illustrating Bigger's development of analytical skills through his negotiating of the demands of racial liberalism and communism. In registering the legal function of the questions that his lawyer Max asks him, he relates that they provide him with a sense of value, or "recognition of his life, of his feelings, of his person that he had never encountered before" (782). Emboldened by this new self-understanding, Bigger tries to view himself in relation to others, a feat that he claims he had always been afraid to undertake, given the entrenched perspectives wrought from experience.

Coda

In *Native Son* and his literary model for African American writing, Wright manages to define a position from which he could understand liberal discourse on race as a problem that involved the professionalization of black subjects. In *Native Son*, Bigger Thomas witnesses an African American sociologist shouting that his university professor stole his research on the "Negro problem," as he resists police efforts to isolate him in the jail. After ignoring Bigger's attempts to find out what has been stolen, the black sociologist is led away in a straitjacket, leaving the white prison guard to explain:

> He was writing a book on how colored people live and he says somebody stole all the facts he'd found. He says he's got to the bottom of why colored folks are treated bad and he's going to tell the President and have things changed, see? He's nuts! He swears that his university professor locked him up. (765)

Tempting as it is to read this scene as marking the exclusions of African Americans from the academy or depicting the gap between black intellectuals and working classes, the scene seems more interested in pointing to the rising significance of the "Negro problem" as a national issue as it disenfranchises African Americans and displaces African American knowledge production.

Notes

1 My work on liberal narratives of race draws from Thomas Hill Schaub's study of liberalism and Cold War American fiction of the 1950s. As Schaub writes, "The word 'liberalism' refers not to a monolithic or univocal event, set of people, or doctrine, but to a moiré of usage, invoking an indeterminate array of connotations, each of which brings into play other terms and meanings" (5).
2 Wright's essay "I Tried to be a Communist" is seen as having inaugurated a new genre of black cultural history that centers on African American creative struggles with a white US literary and political Left.
3 I use the word "communist" with lowercase "c" to refer to individuals, movements, and ideas that saw themselves as communist generally. "Communist" with capital "C" will be used to denote individuals, events, and ideas directly connected to the Third International, founded in 1919 by Soviet Bolsheviks.
4 "It was not the economics of Communism, nor the great power of trade unions, nor the excitement of underground politics that claimed me; my attention was caught by

the similarity of the experiences of workers in other lands, by the possibility of uniting scattered but kindred people into a whole. It seemed to me that here at last, in the realm of revolutionary expression, Negro experience could find a home, a functioning value and role" (Wright, "I Tried to Be a Communist").

5 See, for example, Bill V. Mullen's characterization of the essay as ushering a new era in which "black Americans struggle to find their artistic and political voice in relationship to the brutalizing tendencies of the white Left" (qtd. in Singh, "Retracing the Black-Red Thread" 831–2).

6 My reading of *Native Son* as a novel about the professionalization of black subjects departs from the narratives through which it is usually discussed. In speaking of the novel's proletarian themes, Walter B. Rideout contends that the "imaginative expansion of the book, the quality which survives both melodrama and didacticism, comes from the relating of the truncated lives of Negroes in the United States to those of all the other 'have nots,' the humiliated and despised, who are goaded on by the American dream and whose tragedy it is to be blocked from the dream's fulfillment" (261). Whereas Rideout emphasizes the novel's interest in depicting the possibility of a united proletariat, I argue that the novel is more interested in thematizing the processes of professionalization imagined for black subjects. Rather than contrasting these professionalization processes as categorically different, the novel depicts them as jointly invested in the articulation of a professional black subject. Cedric J. Robinson also emphasizes the book's proletarian themes, but productively connects them to a transnational framework: "Bigger Thomas's character was specific to the historical experience of Blacks in the US, but his nature was proletarian, that is world-historical" (297). My chapter takes a different approach to *Native Son* by proposing that Wright positions Bigger Thomas at the crossroads of competing discourses regarding the professionalization of black subjects.

7 I take up William J. Maxwell's location of theoretical crossings in the works of Zora Neale Hurston and Richard Wright in order to analyse its implications for the professionalization of black subjects. As he writes, "For Hurston, rural-disposed Boasian anthropology; for Wright, urban-disposed Chicago School sociology crossed with the Communist party theorizations of the Negro Question" (159). Given the chapter's focus on the professionalization of black subjects, my chapter is less concerned with Wright the person and more concerned with how he envisioned the radical writer of color as emerging from the intersection between sociology of race and Communism.

8 Paul Gilroy, "Without the Consolation of Tears: Richard Wright, France, and the Ambivalence of Community." *The Black Atlantic*. London and New York: Verso, 1993. 146–86. 147.

9 As Robin D. G. Kelley cogently notes, "Most Communist theoreticians assumed (even during the Third Period) that 'genuine' black folk culture was at least implicitly, if not explicitly, revolutionary" (116). Following this logic, antireligious Communists such as Mike Gold could positively regard African American spiritual expressions as making reference to the religious past only in order to refer to their Communist present (qtd. in Kelley 116–17). Similarly, other Communists such as Harold Preece found Communist protest in Negro spirituals and described them as "living prophesies of deliverance" (qtd. in Kelley 117).

10 Writing against entrenched assumptions that depict Wright's and Ellison's rejection of the Party as simply "their movement away from leftwing radicalism into liberalism and literary celebrity, as some critics have suggested," Nikhil Pal Singh points out that the

wartime views of both Wright and Ellison cannot only be regarded as "anticommunist," but also sought to generate an independent black radicalism (*Black Is a Country* 122).

11 See, for example, Charles S. Johnson's *Growing up in the Black Belt* and E. Franklin Frazier's *Negro Youth at the Crossway*, both of which were published around 1940.

12 Oscar V. Campomanes and Amy Kaplan have argued persuasively that historical accounts that trace US global power and political expansion only to World War II have largely contributed to the erasure of the US' colonization of the Philippines during the Spanish-American War.

13 As Paula Rabinowitz reminds us, there were "abrupt shifts in line among leftists as the Communist Party in the United States (CPUSA) instituted its own version of Stalinism" (17). For other accounts of the political Left in the United States, see Pells. See also Wald.

14 Maxwell comments on Wright's use of the term "peasant" in his autobiography, where he describes the "tragic toll that the urban environment exacted of the black peasant" (Wright, *Black Boy* 271; Maxwell 160). We also need to remember that Park traveled through the South as Washington's emissary. See Robert Bone, "Richard Wright," *The Negro Novel in America* (New Haven: Yale UP, 1958) 455, which is cited in Maxwell 160.

15 "How 'Bigger' Was Born" was originally a talk that Wright gave at Columbia University on March 12, 1940, and at the Schomberg Library in Harlem a few weeks later. A shorter version was later published in the *Saturday Review of Literature* issue of June 1, 1940, and also in an even more condensed essay in *Negro Digest* in the fall of 1940. In August 1940, Harper and Brothers published the first complete text as a separate pamphlet of 39 pages and, in 1942, added the essay as the introduction to later printings of Wright's novel *Native Son*. This account and textual references for "How 'Bigger' Was Born" are drawn from *Richard Wright: Early Works*.

16 See Fanon's discussion of counter-hegemony and the role of culture in his theory of formation of national consciousness, particularly his theorization of national culture as "contested culture" (206–48).

17 As Singh notes, Wright found US communist views of blacks stereotypical and sentimental and hence believed that they "failed to recognize the remarkable transformations of black life under conditions of mass migration, urbanization, and print culture" (*Black Is a Country* 120).

18 In his study of nationalism, Benedict Anderson links print culture to the formation of collective national consciousness. As he explains, print capitalism, or the mass distribution of texts, effectively changed the way in which people imagined their relationships to one another and envisioned their place within a nation. While Anderson sees literary production as a condition of national consciousness, he locates the origins of the process through which consciousness is formed in the economic system that produces these texts, rather than in fiction. By blurring the distinction between fiction and sociology, Wright suggests a different view: that the formation of collective consciousness, and hence new types of agency and subjectivity, takes place through fiction, not as a result of it. For a critique of Anderson, see Armstrong and Tennenhouse.

19 Arguing against the desirability of "pure particularism," Ernesto Laclau writes, "if the particular asserts itself as mere particularity, in a purely differential relation with other particularities, it is sanctioning the status quo in the relation of power between the groups. This is exactly the notion 'separate developments' as formulated in apartheid: only the differential aspect is stressed, while the relations of power on which the latter are based are systematically ignored" (99).

20 In his study of the constitution of the white working class in the nineteenth century, David R. Roediger remarks that comparisons between African Americans and the Irish stemmed from a number of environmental and historical—rather than biological—factors, including job competition and neighborhood rivalries. As he observes, "Shared oppression need not generate solidarity but neither must it necessarily breed contempt of one group for the other" (134). Although Roediger points to moments in which there were "strong signs that the Irish might not fully embrace white supremacy," he follows this observation with a catalogue of the ways in which the Irish working class appropriated and defended the entitlements and rights associated with whiteness, most often through violence directed at blacks. With the rise in immigration during the 1840s and 1850s, the Irish increasingly began to assert themselves as "white" rather than Irish, thereby distancing themselves from blacks and other immigrant groups, such as Jews, Eastern Europeans, and Italians (134).

21 Aside from Green, other black characters are positioned in varying degrees of identification and difference from Bigger Thomas, marking out various paths available to him as a black man in the 1930s. For example, Bigger's mother, with her tired resignation to Jim Crow laws, longing for middle-class domesticity, and pleas for Christian mercy, represents the suffering black subject begging for recognition of black humanity that Wright rejects in his essay on African American writing.

22 In her chapter, "Fashioning Obligation: Indebted Servitude and the Fetters of Slavery," Saidiya V. Hartman argues that the transition from chattel slavery to Reconstruction generated a new genre of literature directed toward instructing freed blacks on the "ways of white folks" in order to improve interactions between blacks and whites (149). In *Native Son*, we see a different dynamic in which white Americans are being encouraged to learn about black culture as part of a process of national reform and the repudiation of racial bigotry. In both cases, however, racial knowledge is posited as a crucial factor in narratives of social progress and the nation's democratic well-being.

Works cited

Anderson, Benedict. *Imagined Communities: Reflections on the Origin and Spread of Nationalism*. Ithaca: Cornell UP, 2006. Print.

Armstrong, Nancy and Leonard Tennenhouse. "A Novel Nation; or, How to Rethink Modern England as an Emergent Culture." *Modern Language Quarterly* 54.3 (1993): 327–44. Print.

Campomanes, Oscar V. "The New Empire's Forgetful and Forgotten Citizens: Unrepresentability and Unassimilability in Filipino American Postcolonialities." *Critical Mass: A Journal of Asian American Cultural Criticism* 2.2 (1995): 145–200. Print.

Drake, St. Clair and Horace R. Cayton. *Black Metropolis: A Study of Negro Life in a Northern City*. Chicago: U of Chicago P, 1993. Print.

Dyer, Richard. *White: Essays on Race and Culture*. London: Routledge, 1997. Print.

Fanon, Frantz. *The Wretched of the Earth*. Trans. Constance Farrington. New York: Penguin, 1967. Print.

Frazier, E. Franklin. *Negro Youth at the Crossroads: Their Personality Development in the Middle States*. Washington, DC: American Council of Education, 1940. Print.

Gilroy, Paul. *The Black Atlantic: Modernity and Double Consciousness.* London: Verso, 1993. Print.

Hartman, Saidiya V. *Scenes of Subjection: Terror, Slavery, and Self-Making in Nineteenth-Century America.* New York: Oxford UP, 1997. Print.

Johnson, Charles S. *Growing Up in the Black Belt: Negro Youth in the Rural South.* Washington, DC: American Council on Education, 1941. Print.

Kaplan, Amy. "'Left Alone with America': The Absence of Empire in the Study of American Culture." *Cultures of United States Imperialism.* Ed. Amy Kaplan and Donald E. Pease. Durham: Duke UP, 1993. 3–21. Print.

Kelley, Robin D. G. *Race Rebels: Culture, Politics, and the Black Working Class.* New York: The Free Press, 1996. Print.

Laclau, Ernesto. "Universalism, Particularism, and the Question of Identity." *The Identity in Question.* Ed. John Rajchman. New York: Routledge, 1993. 93–108. Print.

Maxwell, William J. *New Negro, Old Left: African-American Writing and Communism between the Wars.* New York: Columbia UP, 1999. Print.

Park, Robert Ezra. *Race and Culture: The Collected Papers of Robert Ezra Park.* New York: Arno Press, 1974. Print.

Pells, Richard H. *The Liberal Mind in a Conservative Age: American Intellectuals in the 1940s and 1950s.* Middletown: Wesleyan UP, 1985. Print.

Rabinowitz, Paula. *Labor and Desire: Women's Revolutionary Fiction in Depression America.* Chapel Hill: U of North Carolina P, 1991. Print.

Rideout, Walter B. *The Radical Novel in the United States, 1900–1954.* Cambridge: Harvard UP, 1957. Print.

Robinson, Cedric J. *Black Marxism: The Making of the Black Radical Tradition.* Chapel Hill: U of North Carolina P, 2000. Print.

Roediger, David R. *The Wages of Whiteness: Race and the Making of the American Working Class.* Rev. edn. New York: Verso, 1991. Print.

Schaub, Thomas Hill. *American Fiction in the Cold War.* Madison: U of Wisconsin P, 1991. Print.

Singh, Nikhil Pal. *Black Is a Country: Race and the Unfinished Struggle for Democracy.* Cambridge: Harvard UP, 2004. Print.

—— "Retracing the Black-Red Thread." *American Literary History* 15.4 (2003): 830–40. Print.

Wald, Alan M. *The New York Intellectuals: The Rise and Decline of the Anti-Stalinist Left from the 1930s to the 1980s.* Chapel Hill: U of North Carolina P, 1987. Print.

Washington, Booker T. *Up from Slavery.* New York: Norton, 1996. Print.

Wright, Richard. *Black Boy. Richard Wright: Later Works.* New York: Literary Classics of the United States, 1991. 1–366. Print.

—— Introduction. *Black Metropolis: A Study of Negro Life in a Northern City.* By St. Clair Drake and Horace R. Cayton. Chicago: U of Chicago P, 1993. xvii–xxxiv. Print.

—— "Blueprint for Negro Writing." 1937. *African American Literary Theory: A Reader.* Ed. Winston Napier. New York: New York UP, 2000. Print.

—— "How 'Bigger' Was Born." *Richard Wright: Early Works.* Ed. Arnold Rampersad. New York: Library of America, 1991. 851–82. Print.

—— "I Tried to Be a Communist." *Atlantic Monthly* Aug. 1944: 61–74; Sept. 1944: 48–56. Print.

3

The Negro Intellectual and the Tragic Sense of Hybridity: A Study in Postcolonial Existentialism

Marc Mvé Bekale
University of Reims

In a letter to Michel Fabre in 1964, Léopold Sédar Senghor wrote about Richard Wright: "His whole life and work tend to be the proof that he was a torn man, very much like me, all things considered. A man torn between the past and the future of his race, between the values of Négritude and those of European civilization" (qtd. in Fabre, "Richard Wright" 46). That Senghor identified himself with Wright is particularly revealing in the sense that Senghor's trajectory epitomizes the intellectual journey of the postcolonial subject. In many ways, Wright's literary works of the 1950s fit into the philosophical, cultural, and political agenda of the Négritude writers, most of whom were trying to redefine the Western conception of Reason and Being through the assertion of Negro cultural values. Discussing the substance of *The Outsider* with Paul Reynolds, his literary agent, Wright stated:

> The break from the U.S. was more than a geographical change. It was a break with my former attitudes as a Negro and a communist—an attempt to think over and redefine my attitudes and my thinking. I was trying to grapple with the big problem—*the problem and meaning of Western civilization as a whole and the relation of Negroes and other minority groups to it.*
>
> (qtd. in Fabre, *Unfinished Quest* 366; emphasis added)

It seems that the "big problem" Wright set out to explore in *The Outsider* forms the nexus of the African literature of _the 1950s and 1960s. For the emerging African elite, those years were marked by cultural and existential insecurity as African countries, transitioning from European colonies to modern states, had to broker new cultural values. *The Outsider* is filled with echoes of this historical mutation, which had forced the Third World people "to leave their tribal, ancestral anchorages of living by being sucked into the orbit of industrial enterprises" (Wright 451).

Elsewhere, I have argued that the term "anchorage," a central metaphor in Wright's fiction, is invested with ontological and psychological meaning since it underlies the Negro's quest for his historically negated humanity (Mvé Bekale 42–58). The notion of "anchorage" is then an instantiation of Frantz Fanon's concept of "disalienation." An avid reader of Wright's literature, Fanon saw in the tragic destiny of Bigger Thomas in *Native Son* an eloquent expression of "the existential deviation" white oppression has imposed on the Negro as well as a struggle against the "inessentiality of servitude" to which the Negro race has been confined since its encounter with European civilization (178). Wright initiated the dialectics of "disalienation" with the publication of "Big Boy Leaves Home," a story about a Negro boy's traumatic confrontation with racism in the South. The racial fears instilled in Big Boy find a psychotic outlet in *Native Son*, whereas *The Outsider* attempts to transcend those irrational fears by raising philosophical questions about human freedom. The evolution of Wright's heroes, from Big Boy to Cross Damon, reflects strikingly the moral and psychological dilemma of contemporary African intellectuals, most of whom go through a painful process of "Westernization" in order to realize themselves.

Building on the theoretical perspective of postcolonial hybridity, I will examine the spiritual and moral odyssey of black intellectual characters in Wright's *The Outsider* and Cheikh Hamidou Kane's *L'aventure ambiguë*. I will discuss two different categories of hybridity:[1] the creative or transcendental form of hybridity theorized by Homi K. Bhabha as the "Third Space of enunciation" of identity (38), and the pathological hybridity that rather paralyzes the self and is best exemplified in African literature by Samba Diallo, the protagonist of *L'aventure ambiguë*. I will, however, slightly depart from Bhabha's line of thinking to consider the Negro's hybridization in connection with the problem of alienation and existential angst.

The notion of hybridity is historically loaded. Initially associated with miscegenation and impurity, it was introduced in the postcolonial discourse to challenge the essentialist models of culture and identity. In *The Location of Culture*, Bhabha has made it a major concept allowing him to reject the validity of any idea based on cultural authenticity. For Bhabha, the social reality of hybridity translates into a liminal space or "Third Space" wherein complex forms of identities are formulated:

> It is only when we understand that all cultural statements and systems are constructed in this contradictory and ambivalent space of enunciation that we begin to understand why hierarchical claims to the inherent originality or 'purity' of cultures are untenable, even before we resort to empirical historical instances that demonstrate their hybridity. (37)

Bhabha's argument resonates with Stuart Hall's view that identity, far from being a fixed essence, is experienced in terms of "dispersal and fragmentation," historical and cultural positioning:

> Cultural identities come from somewhere, have histories. But, like everything which is historical, they undergo constant transformation. Far from being eternally fixed in some essentialised past, they are subject to the continuous 'play' of history, culture and power. Far from being grounded in mere 'recovery' of the past, which is waiting to be found, and which when found, will secure our sense of ourselves

into eternity, identities are names we give to the different ways we are positioned by, and position ourselves within, the narratives of the past.

(qtd. in Ashcroft 4)

The Outsider and *L'aventure ambiguë* offer interesting perspectives on the question of identity as a constant negotiation and re-enunciation of self. These novels stage two black intellectual characters who find themselves trapped by the ideological and moral forces of their social environment. As we follow Cross Damon and Samba Diallo in their adventures, we realize that these forces are related to the dialectics of displacement, which leads to the dislocation of their individuality. For *The Outsider*, it should be underlined that 13 years after the publication of *Native Son*, Wright made it clear that he wanted to move beyond racial issues to confront the world with a new vision of man. While Bigger Thomas was the product of American racial politics, Cross Damon is portrayed as a symbol of the modern fragmented individual who thinks that man is "nothing in particular" (Wright 174). Such a vision was caused by Wright's disillusionment with the foundational values of Western societies, the evolution of which has resulted in "a kind of war against mankind" (Wright 457). *The Outsider* then represents a new dimension in the development of Wright's literature. Having written bitter novels indicting American racism, Wright was now trying to create a literary space through which he could articulate his post-racial existentialism.

In much the same way, the quest for new values informs *L'aventure ambiguë*. Kane's novel, now a classic African text, raises fundamental questions about the nature of African independence, both culturally and politically. The story unfolds in colonial times, and we first meet Samba Diallo as a young man caught between two ideological systems. He must navigate the Islamic spirituality of his native Diallobé country and liberal Western ideas. When Samba Diallo migrates to Paris to pursue his studies in philosophy, he ends up voicing scepticism about his identity. In various ways, Samba Diallo's experience at school and university calls to mind Cross Damon's enrollment in a college philosophy class, a choice he made not for practical use of knowledge but for an abstract understanding of the meaning of life. As displaced individuals, both characters are struggling to make sense of the materialistic ethics of Western society. This may account for their interest in philosophy, although their constant involvement with metaphysical issues deepens their existential plight, leaving them with the tragic sense of nothingness. Indeed, the insight they acquire from their spiritual search does not open any doors to them other than those of solitude and dereliction. Samba Diallo's exposure to Western values prompts him to question the traditions that used to cement his being. In Paris, he explains to his friends,

I am not a distinct country of the Diallobé facing a distinct Occident, and appreciating with a cool head what I must take from it and what I must leave with it by way of counterbalance. I have become the two. There is not a clear mind deciding between the two factors of a choice. There is a strange nature in distress over not being two.

(Kane 164; translation mine)

This passage not only echoes W. E. B. Du Bois's contention about the agony of "double consciousness" (the young African admits that "I have become the two") but also highlights Samba Diallo's inability to handle the ordeal generated by the process of cultural mongrelization. His "distress over not being two" then underlies the psychological and moral tension faced by some postcolonial intellectuals who, suspicious of modern values and no longer able to find footing in traditional society, had to live with a Janus-faced identity.[2]

L'aventure ambiguë came out at the time when Senghor was reassessing his ideas about the African-Negro personality. Turning from a narrow view of Négritude as "antiracist racism," he became a strong advocate of "cultural hybridity" ("métissage culturel"), which, he writes, was, along with art, "one of the essential features of *Homo sapiens*" (Biondi 121). While Senghor emphasizes the richness of the mongrelized self, Kane attempts to bring into the open its dark side. Samba Diallo's inability to cope with his "two-ness" then signals the failure of Senghor's politics of "métissage," for the cultural landscape described in *L'aventure ambiguë* shows a sharp contrast with the intersectional space "of giving and receiving" that was supposed to pave the way for "la Civilisation de l'Universel."[3] Rather than fostering any viable individuality, "le métissage" results in what Jean-Paul Sartre has called "engleuement" caused by the blurring and destabilization of cultural boundaries. In that regard, Samba Diallo's adventure recalls Obi Okonkwo's fate, the antihero (not to be confused with Ogbuefi Okonkwo of *Things Fall Apart*) of Chinua Achebe's *No Longer at Ease*. Like Samba Diallo, Obi Okonkwo is a man of words and books, a product of "mission-house upbringing and European education" (Achebe 71). The two men are emblematic of the African elite who, evolving between opposite worlds, had to create an "interstitial space" through which they could assert their postcolonial individuality. But such a space proves perilous and unstable, as Samba Diallo realizes: "I have chosen an itinerary liable to get me lost" (Kane 125). Samba Diallo goes on to meditate on the fate awaiting the postcolonial intellectual:

> It may be that we shall be captured at the end of our itinerary, vanquished by our adventure itself. It suddenly occurs to us that, all along the road, we have not ceased to metamorphose ourselves, and we see ourselves other than what we were. Sometimes the metamorphosis is not even finished. We have turned ourselves into hybrids, and there we are left. Then we hide ourselves filled with shame.
>
> (Kane 124–5)

The condition of African students is stressed again when Samba Diallo compares their fate with that of a courier: "at the moment of leaving our home, we do not know whether we shall ever come back" (Kane 124).

Cross Damon's journey in *The Outsider* is similarly dominated by the haunting sense of existential precariousness. After miraculously surviving a subway accident in Chicago, Cross Damon chooses a marginal life before turning himself into a nihilistic criminal. Here, marginality fits into Bhabha's definition of "liminal space" or "Third Space," one in which the modern self was to be reinvented. Indeed, Cross Damon is given the chance to start from scratch. Once in Harlem, he visits a cemetery to select a name from a tomb. After forging an identity card, he could live incognito and act like a "little God," showing ruthless determination to "blot out" anyone trying to infringe upon his newfound freedom. On a train heading to New York, Cross Damon comes upon Elly Houston, the New York General Attorney, who also embodies marginality because of his hunchback deformity. The men engage in a long philosophical conversation about the position of the Negro in American society. When Cross Damon later commits a double manslaughter, Elly Houston is asked to investigate the crime. It does not take him long to realize that the potential killer (Cross Damon) is a nihilist who lives in an isolated moral and metaphysical space. Cross Damon has become something of an enlightened pagan in whose head and heart ancient myths are dying. "And what's there to guide him? Nothing at all but his own desires, which would be his only values" (Wright 403–4).

We have seen that Samba Diallo too evolves in a world where African myths are falling apart, accentuating his sense of loss and dereliction. However, while Samba Diallo finds himself bogged down in pathological hybridity, Cross Damon asserts freedom as an absolute staple of his existence. Alienation (both moral and psychological) gives Cross Damon a new lease on life. He enters a new temporality (pre-Christian time) after erasing his past and choosing his destiny for the first time. A transcendental gesture, the exile into a marginal "Third Space" literally turns him into a virtual being. He is a man deprived of any ethical and ideological references because in his "mind and consciousness all the hopes and inhibitions of the last two thousand years have died."

Samba Diallo's tragic experience stems from cultural and spiritual displacement, whereas Cross Damon's retreat from the world, a personal choice, underlies an attempt at re-historicizing himself. After "blotting out" his past and "old consciousness," Cross Damon "was without a name, a past, a future; no promises or pledges bound him to those about him" (Wright 177). In *Native Son*, re-historicization, coming after the completion of existential metamorphosis, was set in motion by Bigger Thomas's accidental murder of Mary Dalton. Cross Damon moves this idea further as murder—now an "act of creative destruction"—turns out to be a manner of ontological rebellion. It is driven by the Nietzschean ideal of "transvaluation," an ideal meant to pave the way for the emergence of a Zarathustrian type of man and for the advent of a new "historical or temporal regime."[4]

The Outsider and *L'aventure ambiguë* are clearly philosophical novels. One finds strong Conradian undertones in the depiction of Cross Damon's and Samba Diallo's adventure. Their stories can be construed as a reverse enactment of Kurtz's voyage in *Heart of Darkness*. Joseph Conrad describes the way alienation or marginality provides man with a deep insight into human existence. Both Cross Damon and Samba Diallo are lost souls because they are endowed with a disillusioned vision of the world, what Sartre, commenting on Albert Camus's *L'Etranger*, has referred to as "l'illumination désolée" ("desolate illumination") or "la lucidité sans espoir" ("hopeless lucidity") (124). At the end of their spiritual odyssey, Cross Damon and Samba Diallo acquire a deep understanding of man. But rather than setting them free, this "understanding" leads to moral exile and changes them into both existential and social outcasts. Asked why he chose to live as an outsider, Cross Damon is unable to provide any rational answer.

Instead, "His mind reeled at the question. There was so much and yet it was so little..."
(Wright 562). And the only words he managed to utter during his agony echoes
Marlow's elliptical evocation of Kurtz's vision of horror. Answering one last question
from Elly Houston, who is determined to make sense of his absurd life, Cross Damon,
with a bleak stare reminiscent of Kurtz's look, confesses: "It ... It was ... horrible ..."
(Wright 563). Similarly, the end of *L'aventure ambiguë* is permeated by the sense of
existential despair. In Paris, Samba Diallo feels like "a broken balafong, like a musical
instrument that has gone dead" (Kane 163). Before he is killed by a character named
"The Fool," Samba Diallo, like Cross Damon, finds himself enmeshed in metaphysical
brooding: "Master, what is left for me? Darkness is closing on me. I no longer burn at
the heart of beings and things" (Kane 174). Although the metaphor of "darkness"
bespeaks the failure of cultural mongrelization, it also partakes of a deconstructive
politics of Western philosophical ideas, most of which are rooted in the concept Martin
Jay has called "ocularcentrism" (qtd. in Ashcroft 125). Since the Ancient Greeks, Thomas
Seifrid contends, "ocularcentrism" has remained a key paradigm in epistemology and
ontology, a dominant trope of knowledge and Being:

> That one of the defining eras of modernity is called the Enlightenment merely
> underscores ocularcentrism's persistence since the Greeks, as do a multiplicity of
> cultural forms belonging to the twentieth century, from our now thoroughly visual
> everyday vocabulary (including casually deployed words and phrases like *evidence,
> insight, shed light on, obvious, appears,* and *brilliant*) to the rampant videoism of
> popular culture. (438)

It should be recalled that Greek ontology emphasized "sight" or "vision" over all other
senses. Aristotle opens his *Metaphysics* by claiming the pre-eminence of sight, which
alone among other senses "enables us to acquire knowledge and bring to light many
differences between things" (Aristote 2). Another famous example on this issue relates
to the allegory of the cave explored by Plato in book 7 of the *Republic*. At the heart of
this myth lies the question of light and vision: the encounter with higher essences or
truths depends on whether the inhabitants of the cave, living in darkness, can see real
things in the light of day or as mere shadows. For Plato, and for Western society, vision,
knowledge, and reason were inextricably tied to each other as they were considered the
locus of truth.

How can Plato's allegory apply to the spiritual journey of the black intellectual? For
centuries, the Negro was ideologically and racially confined to a "sub-human" status. In
Cahier d'un retour au pays natal, Aimé Césaire writes ironically about it:

> Those who have invented neither powder nor compass
> those who could harness neither steam nor electricity
> those who exploited neither seas nor the sky. (44)

In the Hegelian perspective, History means the transition from "darkness" to higher
civilization, the fulfilment of "absolute knowledge." But the dynamics at work in *The*

Outsider and *L'aventure ambiguë* suggest a radical subversion of that dialectics. Although endowed with acute vision of life, the "Westernized" Negro is unable to undertake the platonic ascension towards transcendent essences. A similar outcome points to the failure of Western "ocularcentrism" and the values it embodies. This view is expressed by Cross Damon when he contends that "to see was not to control, self-understanding was far short of self-mastery" (Wright 153). And for the African-Negro, the centrality of "Sight" or rationality in understanding the world proves irreconcilable with African ontology, premised upon the unity and the existence of spirits in all living things. The loss of this sense of unity as well as the clash between Western and non-Western ways of conceiving knowledge accentuates the crisis of hybridity in *The Outsider* and *L'aventure ambiguë*.

Notes

1   On the different categories of hybridity, Ella Shohat suggests that we "discriminate between the diverse modalities of hybridity, for example, forced assimilation, internalized self-rejection, political cooptation, social conformism, cultural mimicry, and creative transcendence" (110). For Ray Oldenburg, "third spaces" in American society are intermediary spaces. They refer to a "generic designation for a great variety of public places that host the regular, voluntary, informal, and happily anticipated gatherings of individuals beyond the realms of home and work" (16).
2   See Sougou.
3   The phrases "encounter of giving and receiving" ("le rendez-vous du donner et du recevoir") and "la Civilisation de l'Universel" were coined by Pierre Teilhard de Chardin and Aimé Césaire.
4   See Hartog.

Works cited

Achebe, Chinua. *No Longer at Ease*. London: Heinemann, 1960. Print.

Aristotle. *Métaphysique*. Tome 1, Livre A–Z. Paris: Librairie Philosophique J. Vrin, 1991. Print.

Ashcroft, Bill. *Post-Colonial Transformation*. London: Routledge, 2001. Print.

Bhabha, Homi K. *The Location of Culture*. London: Routledge, 1994. Print.

Biondi, Jean-Pierre. *Senghor ou La tentation de l'universel*. Paris: Editions Denoël, 1993. Print.

Césaire, Aimé. *Cahier d'un retour au pays natal*. 1947. Paris: Présence Africaine, 1983. Print.

Fabre, Michel. "Richard Wright et l'Afrique." *Notre Librairie* 77 (1984). Print.

—— *The Unfinished Quest of Richard Wright*. Trans. Isabel Barzun. 2nd edn. Urbana: U of Illinois P, 1993. Print.

Fanon, Frantz. *Peau noire, masques blancs*. Paris: Editions du Seuil, 1952. Print.

Hartog, François. *Régime d'historicité: Présentisme et expérience du temps*. Paris: Editions du Seuil, 2003. Print.

Kane, Cheikh Hamidou. *L'aventure ambiguë*. Paris: Julliard, 1961. Print.

Mvé Bekale, Marc. *Traite négrière et expérience du temps dans le roman afro-américain.* Paris: L'Harmattan, 2006. Print. Etudes Africaines-Américaines et Diasporiques.

Oldenburg, Ray. *The Great Good Place: Cafés, Coffee Shops, Community Centers, Beauty Parlors, General Stores, Bars, Hangouts, and How They Get You Through the Day.* New York: Paragon, 1986. Print.

Sartre, Jean-Paul. *Critiques littéraires (Situations, I).* Paris: Gallimard, 1947. Print. Idées.

Seifrid, Thomas. "Gazing on Life's Page: Perspectival Vision in Tolstoy." *PMLA* 113.3 (1998): 436–48. Print.

Senghor, Léopold Sédar. *Liberté 1: Négritude et humanisme.* Paris: Editions du Seuil, 1964. Print.

Shohat, Ella. "Notes on the 'Post-Colonial.'" *Social Text* 31/32 (1992): 99–113. Print.

Sougou, Omar. "Resisting Hybridity: Colonial and Postcolonial Youth in *Ambiguous Adventure* by Cheikh Hamidou Kane and *L'Appel des arènes* by Aminata Sow Fall." *Matatu: Journal for African Culture and Society* 25–6 (2002): 213–27. Print.

Wright, Richard. *The Outsider.* New York: Harper, 1953. Print.

4

Richard Wright's *Native Son* and the Dialectics of Black Experience

Anthony Dawahare
California State University, Northridge

But anyone destitute of a theory about the meaning, structure and direction of modern society is a lost victim in a world he cannot understand or control.
Richard Wright, "Blueprint for Negro Writing"

A consciousness committed to experience is ignorant, has to be ignorant, of the essences and determinations of its being.
Frantz Fanon, *Black Skin, White Masks*

Many critics have written about or commented upon Richard Wright's Marxist politics from the 1930s. While this scholarship has been of great value to our understanding of Wright's work, the analyses and assessments of his interactions with the Communist Party of the United States (CPUSA) and his adoption of Marxism usually ignore the ways in which the dialectical materialist methodology informs his writing from the 1930s—despite the fact that dialectical materialism is synonymous with Marxism and the philosophy of the Communist movement of which he was a part.[1] Perhaps his somewhat embattled relationship and eventual break with the CPUSA has become too much of a distraction for critics, a distraction retrospectively created and/or reinforced by Wright's highly publicized biographies and his disavowal of Communism in "I Tried To Be a Communist," for one can certainly be a dialectical materialist and critical of the CPUSA. To be sure, one can be a critic of the CPUSA precisely from a dialectical materialist perspective, as many were at the time and in the decades that followed the "Red Decade." To say Wright's disagreements and eventual break with the CPUSA was a rejection of Marxism would be as fallacious as saying that Martin Luther's break with the Catholic Church was a rejection of Christianity.

The purpose of this essay is to explore in some depth the ways in which Wright's dialectical materialism informs his major fictional work from the 1930s, *Native Son*. While an explication of the dialectics of *Native Son* can proceed in a number of directions, my goal here is to focus on Wright's dialectical representation of *black experience*, a concept that by the 1930s had already become somewhat of a fetish object. It is precisely his dialectical representation of black experience that cuts to the heart of a kind of racial positivism produced by the outpouring of literary works during the Harlem Renaissance. This validation of black experience by Harlem Renaissance spokesmen like W. E. B Du Bois, Alain Locke, and James Weldon Johnson or writers such as Jesse Fauset, Langston Hughes, and Countee Cullen is well known. Its commodification for a white, middle-class America has also been documented.[2] Black experience has also been the basis of political programs and cultural movements. Today, the concept of "the black experience" is omnipresent, from the Schomburg Studies on the Black Experience at the Schomburg Center to countless studies and documentaries.

The reasons for the recording and validation of black experience are fairly clear, given the historical effacement of the African and African American social histories within US culture. Yet the backlash to the effacement of black experience produced new problems for writers and intellectuals concerned ultimately with black liberation. As George Schuyler pointed out in the 1920s, the championing of racial difference and a distinctly racial literature replays the myths of racial difference that white racists used to enslave African Americans in the first place (54). Perhaps this is one reason why Locke, Du Bois, Hughes, and others insisted that blacks are not altogether different: they are American too. Nonetheless, the notion of racial difference tended to be the keynote in black literature after the war; it is what made it unique and (well) different from other literature written at the time. It affirmed what white Americans already knew through their ideological training: that black Americans are a separate race, even if "American," and, if the movement was successful, they could be said to be "equal" as well.

Wright engages this problem by producing a novel that both depicts a uniquely *black* experience and surpasses it through characterization and a narrative technique that reveals black experience as a moment in an historical dialectic of social relations governed by political and economic power. That is, the novel's development involves Bigger's own emergence from a racial positivism that coincides with a narrative that moves from thick description of narrative details to a dialectical-theoretical presentation of black experience. In both cases, the novel shows black experience as mediated by nonracial class forces and relations. Consequently, *Native Son* both affirms and negates the very notion of black experience and presents a challenge for those then and now who want to affirm black experience as somehow self-contained and others who want to liquidate it in some universal category, whether in Americanism or in a reductive Marxist class analysis. Wright's novel, in other words, speaks both to nationalists and Marxists and provides a powerful representation of the pitfalls of especially a positivistic approach to racism wherein political and economic slavery are dependent on a psychological slavery to the "facts" of one's (black) experience.

As a way to appreciate the dialectical form and content of *Native Son*, it is instructive to recall G. W. F. Hegel's dialectical analysis of experience that influenced Marxism and thus the dialectical perspective of Depression-era black Communists. Hegel points out that one of the most trenchant positions in modern philosophy and life in general is empiricism. Empiricism, of course, is a rather common-sense view of how we know what is true and real since, in general, there are a multitude of "experiences in life by which we know things immediately" (*Lectures* 64). An empirical perspective assumes that immediate experience equals immediate knowledge about things. I know what I know because I have seen, felt, heard, or tasted it. He terms this mode of knowing as "sense-certainty" (*Phenomenology* 58) since it relies on the senses for knowledge about what is real and true. Sense-certainty constitutes a form of consciousness, although one that naively believes what it experiences is the whole "truth." This is not to say that experience is simply deceptive; dialectical philosophy understands experience as essential to knowledge about the world. The issue is only that knowledge based on one's immediate experience is necessarily partial. What I am calling racial positivism is a variant of empiricism, a variant that also ignores and/or mistrusts knowledge not gained and/or confirmed by immediate experience.

Book One of *Native Son* (Fear) focuses on the power and limitations of immediate experience and the formation of Bigger's racial positivism. Wright shows how immediate experience is a force that shapes consciousness and self-consciousness: the immediate experience of racism convinces one that one is in fact different, other, a "race" unto itself, and worse, inferior, less than human, not entitled to a good education, job, or living conditions. The initial moment of this experience has been memorably depicted by many black writers, including W. E. B. Du Bois in *The Souls of Black Folk* when he writes about the moment that the racial "veil" descended upon him separating him from his classmates (38), and Countee Cullen in "Incident" concerning an eight-year-old boy whose smiling acknowledgment of another boy is returned with a tongue that pokes out and calls him a "Nigger" (15). Fanon also tells of a similar encounter with whites who through their gaze, pointing, and objectifying interpellation—"Look, a Negro" (and worse)—"sealed [him] into that crushing objecthood" of racism (109). Wright begins the novel long after Bigger's veil-experience and the "sealing" of his racial consciousness, yet we clearly see its lasting effects in the dialogue between Bigger and Gus. Both Bigger and Gus are resigned to their "fate" as black men living in a racist society in the 1930s: they will never be US presidents, rich, generals, or aviators; hence, they can only "play" at these things. Bigger's reaction to his experience of racist limits is further defined by a sense of dread: he expects "something awful's going to happen" to him (23). In each case, both young black men are shaped by their experiences of inequality and do not expect to be treated any differently. They know that they are and will remain "on the outside of the world peeping in through a knot-hole in the fence" (20). What differentiates Bigger from Gus is that he is more clearly what Abdul JanMohamed terms "the death-bound subject," "the subject who is formed, from infancy on, by the immanent and ubiquitous threat of death" (2). That is, the sense of catastrophe (of killing or dying) is the most he expects, even though he cannot get used to inequality (*Native Son* 20). They are graduates of what Wright terms elsewhere a "Jim Crow" education ("Ethics" 1).

For Wright, the collective reaction to racism—the sense that one is on the outside looking in—has created "a Negro way of life in America," replete with black churches, presses, school systems, professions, a sporting world, a business world, and a social world ("Blueprint" 100) and, as we read in *Native Son*, a ghettoized black community in major American urban centers. Wright depicts the oppressiveness of a "Negro way of life" in the opening pages of *Native Son*. Hence, from the old, creaking bed, to the alarm clock that awakes his entire family confined to one room, to his mother's exploitation as a domestic servant who washes white people's clothes, and so on *ad infinitum*, his experience is shaped by a racist political economy. As Bill V. Mullen notes, the kitchenette Bigger lives in within the confines of Chicago's South Side is akin to the prison cell he will later occupy (10). His spatial confinement defines the dimensions of his black experience, and he knows from experience that life for a black man is like being in jail (*Native Son* 20).

The formation of a black society within the United States—or of a "nation within a nation," as the Communists theorized it[3]—is an essentially defensive position born out of necessity. It is, as Max tells the courtroom, a natural enough response to injustices that have lasted for over two hundred years for millions of people: "Men adjust themselves to their land; they create their own laws of being; their notions of right and wrong. A common way earning a living gives them a common attitude toward life" (*Native Son* 454–5). The overall ideological effect is, as in the case of Gus and Bigger, one of reification, since black Americans "accepted these negative conditions with the inevitability of a tree which must live or perish in whatever soil it finds itself in" ("Blueprint" 100).

Wright makes the issue of Bigger's *consciousness* of his experience central, since he wants to show how Bigger's sense of self and futility is tied to his difficulty in thinking beyond his immediate experience. His consciousness of his experience is unable to scale the walls of that experience. He has not yet learned the ways in which the immediate is always mediated and, therefore, he feels hopelessly trapped (like the rat). Thus, when he asks himself "what he can do" about changing his experience, "his mind hit a blank wall and he stopped thinking" (12). Moreover, as we earlier learn, he cannot allow the meaning of his experience to "enter fully into his consciousness," namely his family's "shame and misery," since this would unleash a desire to destroy himself or others (9). This circumstantial and willful restriction of the consciousness of his experience contributes to his sense of imprisonment and is an expression of his racial positivism. His thinking is tied to his senses and avoids the kind of theoretical abstraction necessary to understanding the relationship between immediate experience and mediating social systems. And when he feels most confined by his experience, as in the scene where he first meets Jan, he is "[s]o intensely taken up ... with his own immediate sensations" as to render thinking or critical reflection on his experience nearly impossible (80).

Bigger's inability as yet to understand his experience in terms of its mediation is central to the catastrophe of his meeting with Jan and Mary—the turning point of his life. His mind is unable to comprehend the actions of a well-intentioned but naively racist white Communist and his rich and naively racist sympathetic girlfriend. He can, of course, relate a particular experience to a general notion, but even here the movement of his thought is trapped by his understanding of the ways in which truth experientially *appears* and its appearance is ideologically conditioned. He cannot get around the fact that Jan and Mary are optically white, and while in the Dalton car sitting between Jan and Mary, he felt "he was sitting between two vast white looming walls" (77), an apt metaphor for his sense of racial confinement. He will later confirm this metaphor for how white people appear to him when he refers to them as a "white looming mountain of hate" (418).

This issue of the phenomenology of whiteness is crucial to understanding the racial positivism of the novel and its dialectical critique. The whiteness of Jan and Mary is the way in which the social system of class inequality manifests itself in this particular case. They bear within them history (the legacy of slave relations) and the then present social relations of capitalist inequality. "Essence must appear," as Hegel says (*Science* 418), and there is a necessary relationship between the content/essence and appearance/form of this dialectic. Their coloring—or the significance of their color—is historically produced by class systems. To Bigger, they (as all white people in the novel) are simply embodiments of power over him. They are a menace, a terror, a composite of all he fears, and he knows this because of the way he, his family, and other black Americans are and have been treated by whites. Bigger's experience and experiences told by other black Americans have convinced him that Jan and Mary cannot be other than a menace precisely because they are white. One could say that, ideologically, the relationship between form and content is inverted (as in a "cameral obscura" [Marx and Engels 32]): their whiteness (form) determines their power (content). Bigger, in other words, is enthralled with the historically overdetermined appearance and assumes that it can be nothing other than it is, a menace, etc. In fact, it is probably more accurate to say that he can see nothing other than the appearance since he ontologizes or reifies it as a thing or a natural force (a wall, a mountain).

Yet Jan and Mary, as appearance, as existents, bear within them the contradictions of the system as well, and the fact that, while shaped, they are not determined by the history of a racist political economy. They have chosen to take the side of the proletariat and the oppressed in the class struggle and therefore contradict their whiteness. Bigger's positivist perspective struggles with this contradiction. In their first meeting, he continually asks a form of the question, who are these people? What do they want from him? He tries "desperately to understand" (76), yet he cannot reconcile some of their behaviors with their color. The most powerful and disarming contradiction for Bigger is that Mary and Jan treat "him" (as he says about Mary in the following passage) "as if he were human, as if he lived in the same world as she. And he had never felt that before in a white person. But why?" (74). Here we see the slippage emerge for him between form and content, something that contradicts *all* of his previous experience and understanding.

One cannot fault Bigger for being trapped in the immediacy of his experience; Wright sympathetically shows that not only does he lack other and more experiences to expand his understanding (83), and that he as yet lacks political theory, but also his treatment by Jan and Mary is contradictory: they also treat him as subordinate to them and therefore their appearance is not wholly contradictory since they are still structurally in the position of the master and ideologically tied to inegalitarian social relations. Thus, when Bigger first meets Jan, we read that Jan wants Bigger to treat him as an equal. Bigger's response is a mix of confusion, self-loathing, and hatred. Bigger thinks to himself:

> [W]hy was Jan doing this? Why was Mary standing there so eagerly, with shining eyes? What could they get out of this? Maybe they did not despise him? But they made him feel his black skin by just standing there looking at him, one holding out his hand and the other smiling. He felt he had not a physical existence at all right then; he was something he hated, the badge of shame which he knew was attached to a black skin ... At that moment he felt toward Mary and Jan a dumb, cold, and inarticulate hate. (76)

Wright's thick description of Bigger's immediate experience, the way he felt and thought, is as profound as its revelation of the mediation of Bigger's experience. Wright shows that Bigger's immediate feelings about himself and whites are mediated by a social relation of power that precedes them all: he is placed in the role of one who must obey those who have power over his life, and, ironically, even their contradictory demand that he be treated equal. The social contradictions are too much for Bigger to resolve intellectually, and when confronted with the sharpness of a contradiction (as in the above scene), his "solution" is expressed in a desire to "blot [it] out" through a devastating act of violence against one or both terms of the contradiction, namely against himself or Mary, Jan, Bessie, and so on (80, 159, 197).

The slippage between form and content is actually part of a dialectical process of historical development that Wright depicts. The older assumption—so often articulated in Harlem Renaissance writing—that whiteness equals wealth and power began to come undone due to the contradictions made visible during the Great Depression. The old form itself began to break apart under pressure from the internal class contradictions of America as masses of white workers were thrown out of work, congregated in bread and soup lines, and participated in mass and sometimes multiracial labor and social actions. While Mary is a character easily ridiculed or despised for her ignorance and class position, she is nonetheless reflective of larger social transformations and specifically the way in which the children of the bourgeoisie allied themselves with the proletariat as inequality and other social problems became more acute. This alliance did not mean, of course, that they could slough off their prior ideological conditioning and consequential behaviors. Yet history—the economic crisis, the rise of an international racist (fascist) movement, the growth of Communism in and out of the United States—bears them all along to a moment they have not yet had time fully to come to terms with.

Oddly, Bigger's murder of Mary and later of Bessie is crucial to his overcoming of racial positivism. His eventual actions of "blotting out" painful contradictions allow him to transcend momentarily and partially his sense of imprisonment. Thus, Bigger has new eyes (118) after the murder of Mary; he claims to penetrate below the surface of things and in some ways he does. He now perceives the difference between his home and that of the Daltons; his mother's and Vera's weariness; Buddy's aimlessness, and everyone's "blindness" to accept their fates as black in the United States. His murder creates a distance between himself and the world, allowing for a space of observation and understanding (hence Buddy's and Vera's discomfort with his stares) (120–2). His negating acts set loose his thinking from some of its previous ruts and, as Hegel argues, "thinking is in fact essentially the negation of something given" (*Encyclopaedia* 36). Dialectically, the murder is a negation of a negation, that is to say, a negation of those who are symbolically and/or potentially the cause of his own negation/death.[4] This, of course, is a form of cognitive freedom rather than that of a social or political freedom, a freedom mainly to view his experience differently and to make some choices within the narrowing circuit of the South Side. Bigger "felt" free (131). The murders are, of course, as ineffectual as any individual solution to collective or social problems, as Max tells the court about the uselessness of giving Bigger the death sentence (462). Yet, to Bigger, the murders are (as he thinks after killing Mary) "a supreme and meaningful act" (131), an act he can call his own and that cannot be taken away. He becomes aware of himself for the first time in his life as a subject (and not simply as an object) of history, even though the bloody "history" he has created is far from the world-making actions Georg Lukács envisioned for the proletariat, when the proletariat will "become the identical subject-object of history whose praxis will change reality" (197).

It is not until Bigger's "fate" as a black man in America is fulfilled (i.e., not until his imprisonment and [social] death becomes manifest) that he more fully overcomes the immediacy of his experience with the help of dialectical theory. Boris Max—whose name evokes both Marx and the Soviet Union—schools Bigger in a dialectical theory so that Bigger begins to understand how white and black people are caught up in a social drama of class.[5] A two-directional movement of thinking develops for Bigger that allows him to transcend and understand his experience: he learns to place the individual fact under the general notion, which is a form of abstraction necessary to dialectical thinking (and critical thinking in general), and just as importantly, he learns to differentiate the individual from the general.[6] These two movements of his thought occur at different times, and the latter movement is more important than the former to his newly acquired understanding of his experience. The first movement, from the particular to the general, is evident when, immediately after his first candid talk with Max, he comes to see that he was not alone in his feelings or experiences:

> He wondered if it were possible that after all everybody in the world felt alike? Did those who hated him have the same thing Max had seen in him, the thing that made Max ask him those questions? . . . For the first time in his life he had gained a pinnacle of feeling upon which he could stand and see vague relations that he had never dreamed of. (418)

He begins to see, in other words, that irrespective of color, he was not alone and that his own feelings had a social value he had not imagined. Max validated his problems and perceptions of life as important and shared. We later read that his recognition that the personal is also social, that perhaps "he was in relation to all the others that lived," made his death acceptable to him (420). His individual death would not invalidate his life since its importance was "bigger" than his finite self. He comes to see that his individual "I" is also social, shared by countless others. Hegel's comment on the immanent supersession of sense-certainty applies to Bigger's own supersession, with the proviso that Bigger supersedes by experience and theory: "Sense-certainty thus comes to know by experience that its essence is neither in the [immediate] object not in the 'I', and that its immediacy is neither an immediacy of the one nor of the other" (*Phenomenology* 62).

More importantly, his imprisonment and talks with Max and Jan allow him to recognize that society is composed of individuals who are irreducible to class or race. He overcomes the consciousness he had previously gained from the immediacy of his experience that whites are necessarily to be hated and feared. Multiple passages are indicative of this transformation in Bigger but arguably none more so than those on the "looming mountain of white hate" (333). After Jan visits Bigger in his cell and takes responsibility for his "blindness" (331), Bigger has a revelation that transforms all white people from being a natural force or an abstraction to being a collection of individuals who have wills:

> Suddenly, this white man had come up to him, flung aside the curtain and walked into the room of his life. Jan had spoken a declaration of friendship that would make other white men hate him: a particle of white rock had detached itself from that looming mountain of white hate and had rolled down the slope, stopping at his feet. The word had become flesh. For the first time in his life a white man became a human being to him ... He saw Jan as though someone had performed an operation upon his eyes, or as though someone had snatched a deforming mask from Jan's face. (333–4)

This passage, the epiphanic moment of the novel, alludes to several other texts as a way to register the significance of Bigger's revelation. First, it evokes Du Bois's *The Souls of Black Folk* but in reverse: whereas Du Bois uses the metaphor of the veil to register the moment when he realized the existence of the color line as a child (38), Wright uses the rending of the curtain as an entering into a non-racialized relationship with a white man. His use of the curtain also evokes Matthew 27:51 (from the New International Standard Version of the New Testament): "Suddenly the curtain in the temple was torn in two from top to bottom; and the earth shook and the rocks were split." Other translations, including King James, translate curtain as "veil." The passage refers to the moment of Christ's death, which rends the curtain of the Jewish temples that separated humanity from God, the Holy Place from the Most Holy Place, thereby giving believers direct access to God without the need of priests or sacrifices. For Bigger, the rending of the curtain is a revelation of the truth about Jan, a man who previously appeared to him *as though* a god one could not approach.[7] Rather than having a divine illumination, Bigger has what Walter Benjamin terms a "profane illumination, a materialist, anthropological inspiration" (209). This in turn makes sense of why "The word became flesh," a direct quote from John 1:14 that discusses the way in which God, as the Word, became flesh in Jesus, and, significantly, John equates the Word/God with love. That is, Jan's "declaration of friendship" is itself revolutionary and separates him (a white "particle" in *Native Son* or part of the "split" rock in the NT) from "that looming mountain of white hate" and unites him in "brotherly love" with Jan. Additionally, his overcoming of racist abstraction is akin to eye surgery, which therefore suggests that Bigger's previous assumption that he could see and all are blind was itself a misperception or a partial truth. Lastly, Bigger comes to see that the historically overdetermined appearance of Jan is a "deforming mask," an appearance now contradicted by Jan's "content" or "essence" as a hurt man seeking forgiveness and understanding for having been caught up in the phenomenology of racism as well (*Native Son* 331–2).

Bigger's movements from the particular to general and general to particular meet in a dialectical synthesis that is the basis of his new hope. For if people are not hopelessly alienated from each other or hopelessly formed into races (mountains), then they can choose to align themselves together to make changes that are in their collective interests. As Bigger later thinks to himself:

> If that white looming mountain of hate were not a mountain at all, but people, people like himself, and like Jan—then he was faced with a high hope the like of which he had never thought could be, and a despair the full depths of which he knew he could not stand to feel. (418)

His hope then takes shape in a fantasy of belonging to a multiracial collectivity whose shared desires for a good life "melted away [like the sun] the many differences, the colors, the clothes" (420). Bigger's hope comes from a new understanding of change, of history as made by human beings. To refer back to an epigraph for this essay, Bigger has come to understand that "anyone destitute of a theory about the meaning, structure and direction of modern society is a lost victim in a world he cannot understand or control" ("Blueprint" 103). It is also significant, if we follow the Biblical allusions further, that the "resurrection" of Jan's humanity for Bigger entails the splitting of the rock/mountain, which releases the dead saints who are reunited with God (Matthew 27:52) so that that which was many becomes one and "what was common and good [was drawn] upward toward the sun" (*Native Son* 418).

In spite of the scriptural allusions and the general form of Bigger's own political fantasies of collectivity, it is important to underscore that Wright's critique of racial positivism shows how the immediate and mediating social relations are, at bottom, those of class or, as the "Red" Langston Hughes said, "the rich over the poor, no matter what their color" (102). That is, *Native Son* works to show that Bigger's experience of being black and his transcendence of racial positivism cannot be fully understood outside of the class relations that produce them. Max again provides the consciousness that established the links between Bigger's immediate experience of inequality and the systemic (capitalist) determinations of that experience. He links, in other words, the profits of landlords (the Daltons) to the immiseration of the black working class (renters, the Thomases) (457) and the economic interests of finance capital ("the Loop bankers") and capitalists ("the Manufacturers' Association") to the political state (the district attorney, the governor, and the mayor) (449) that is prosecuting him so harshly and terrorizing the South Side. More broadly, Max reveals "the laws and processes" governing the exploitation and oppression of black Americans (451). As James Smethurst correctly notes, Bigger emerges from a mystified ("Gothic") consciousness to one that "begins to understand the motivations for his actions and the social laws which have shaped his actions, or at least he sees that such an understanding may be possible" (37).[8]

It is no wonder, then, that in "How 'Bigger' Was Born," Wright explains that his "discovery" that Bigger was also white "was the pivot of [Wright's] life" (515), and that these newly acquired X-ray specs (to use his metaphor) allowed him to see that "the Southern scheme of oppression was but an appendage of a far vaster and in many respects more ruthless and impersonal commodity-profit machine" (515). His X-ray vision allowed him to see below surfaces or appearances into the motivating causes of those appearances. Additionally, Wright's dialectical perspective allowed him to see that Bigger's experience of alienation was part of the mass alienation of the working class from its labor and the world its has produced ("How 'Bigger'" 518). He even goes so far as to say "that certain modern experiences were creating types of personalities whose existence ignored racial and national lines of demarcation ... [and] ... carried with them a more universal drama-element than anything I'd ever encountered before" (520–21). Put differently, Wright's conception of experience transcends that of racial experience, and black experience is in fact part of a vaster drama, namely that of an international contradiction and struggle between labor and capital, between the oppressed and the oppressors.

Consequently, Wright shows that if Bigger's experiences are also those of the "white" working class, then it makes little sense to insist that his experience is so unique that he should join (say) a black nationalist party and fight for the creation of a black nation, which, of course, Wright did not advocate.[9] To be sure, to make the concept of black experience the basis of one's politics was to reproduce ideologically and institutionally the prison house of racism and nationalism that obscured the significant ways that all experiences are mediated by capitalism—from the way people work to their relationships to each other, relationships so alienated by racism that they are led to believe that their diverse experiences are unrelatable or incomprehensible to each other. Thus, while Bigger is a "vague" nationalist due to his hatred of white people ("How 'Bigger'" 527), he cannot easily identify with black people either. He is, as Wright and countless commentators on the novel note, in a "No Man's Land" between the white and black world (66). His momentary fantasy of a black nationalist leader (130) is undercut by his desire to break out of the prison of race and live beyond the color line.

The conclusion of *Native Son* may seem to contradict the foregoing analysis. Max and Bigger seem no longer to see eye to eye. Yet, in spite of claims that Bigger's assertion of his rationale for the murders are affirmations of his racial particularity and/or difference in contrast to Max's totalizing Marxist framework of understanding,[10] nowhere in the concluding paragraphs do we find Wright racializing Bigger's newfound consciousness, understanding, and peace before death. He simply affirms that the killing, which we earlier identified with a negation of the negation, must have been "good" if he felt strong enough to do it. He also identifies the *motivation* for the killing as essential to his identity (501), and the motivations are precisely those of freedom from the narrow walls of the prison house of his experience of racism and its class determinations, of being "crowd[ed] ... too close" (496).

From this perspective, Bigger's new understanding is existentialist, since he comes to learn and to accept that his existence (his actions) defines his essence (his identity), and, in this regard, his understanding is as nonracial as Jean-Paul Sartre's own conception of humanity (*Existentialism* 22). He learns that he is free to act even in the small realm of freedom the prison affords, "for man is characterized above all by his going beyond a situation, and by what he succeeds in making what he has been made—even if he never recognizes himself in his objectification" (Sartre, *Search* 91). Bigger does in fact recognize himself—his needs and desires to be free—in his objectification. It is no wonder that Sartre (a dialectical thinker in his own right) and Wright became good friends and shared similar beliefs on philosophy, politics, and art.[11]

From another angle, his nonracialized motivations and sense of freedom are affirmed in his decision to ask Max to tell Jan, not "Mister" (or Master) Jan, good-bye (*Native Son* 502): an act that transcends the physical walls of his prison and contributes to the crumbling of the "racial" mountain. Hence, it is itself an individual act become political, a "positive" outcome of the prior negations that he does not renounce and, instead, claims as his own essential to his being. And, in this sense, he attests to the dialectical notion that negation does indeed lie at the heart of (his) being and is a power to be feared by all who want to maintain the status quo. For as Marx notes in his postface to *Capital,*

> dialectic is a scandal and an abomination to the bourgeoisie and its doctrinaire spokesmen, because it includes in its positive understanding of what exists a simultaneous recognition of its negation, its inevitable destruction; because it regards every historically developed form as being in a fluid state, in motion, and therefore grasps its transient aspect as well; and because it does not let itself be impressed by anything, being in its very essence critical and revolutionary. (103)

Max is not in disagreement with what Bigger says so much as that he says it days before he will be put to death (495, 497). Bigger's hard-won understanding of his relation to others is almost too tragic for Max to bear, for, as Max tells him, "Men die alone, Bigger" (496), which is why he stumbles away as though "blind" (501). Tragically, the moment that Bigger is no longer "sealed into that crushing objecthood" of racism (Fanon 109) is the moment in which death shall "seal" him eternally.

Theoretically, then, *Native Son* illustrates the dialectical view that the recourse to immediate experience as the basis of one's truth and literary or political practice is always incomplete. A perspective based on immediate experience is necessarily one-sided since it cannot comprehend the ways in which experience is mediated by what is not immediately present. As this essay has been suggesting, and as Hegel states, "It turns out that immediacy and mediation are unseparated and indeed inseparable" (*Lectures*

64). Even our understanding of experience is mediated, whether we are conscious of it or not, in the sense that our understanding is never simply based on the immediate experience, since, objectively, it is part of processes and relationships that extend beyond the moment. Lukács, one of the more dialectical thinkers of the twentieth century, explains that the concept of mediation is like a "lever" that elucidates the concrete mediations that bind together the disparate experiences and parts of a social totality:

> [T]o leave [the particulars and immediacy of] empirical reality behind can only mean that the objects of the empirical world are to be understood as aspects of a totality, i.e., as aspects of a total social situation caught up in the process of historical change. Thus the category of mediation is a lever with which to overcome the mere immediacy of the empirical world. (162)

Hegel referred to the concept of mediation as a ladder by which we climb out of the limits of our understanding (*Phenomenology* 14; *Lectures* 47). Wright's ladder is the narration of *Native Son*, whose moments are like steps that ascend to the higher standpoint of dialectical philosophy and that lead to the dramatic-theoretical plateau Max affords in his defense of Bigger. The novel like "[e]very first-rate novel, poem, or play lifts the level of consciousness higher" ("Blueprint" 106).

One of the consequences of an understanding of the dialectical mediation of experience is that it seems to drop out the "racial" ground of black identity, culture, and politics, especially if one properly understands that the ground of black experience is not some metaphysical or eternal racial essence but, rather, historical processes defined by change. Once blackness is seen as a lived "moment" and not an essence, or once it is seen as a social relation in a political economy antagonistic to the well-being of working people (irrespective of color), it becomes difficult to reify it, to embrace it as a fixed identity, or as the origin and end of one's political practice. This is not to suggest that for Wright black experience is not real, valid, and more complex than any representations can make out. To be sure, Wright says that Bigger "was more important than what any person, white or black, would say or try to make of him, more important than any political analysis designed to explain or deny him" ("How 'Bigger'" 526). In "Blueprint," Wright also insists on the importance of representing a uniquely unified black culture, since its folklore, spirituals, blues, works songs, and vernacular are "the channels through which the racial wisdom flowed" from generation to generation, from mother to daughter, and father to son (99). One should not read, in other words, *Native Son* as ignoring the texture and density of experiences specific to black Americans—and yet, at the same time, Wright's work suggests that we would be mistaken to overlook the ways in which "racial" experience is mediated by what Lukács describes as "aspects of a total social situation caught up in the process of historical change" (162), namely, the global system of capitalism and its inherent contradictions. We must, as Wright says, "view society as something becoming rather than as something fixed and admired" ("Blueprint" 98–9). Or, more precisely, black writers "must accept the nationalist implications of their lives, not in order to encourage them, but in order to change and transcend them" (101). Wright's dialectical presentation of Bigger's own *becoming* other than he is at each moment, of moving from racial positivism and his "vague" black nationalism to a dialectical and internationalist perspective of his black experience exemplifies Wright's own political development in the 1930s that he understood as part of a larger historical dialectic.

This dialectical view of black experience is, of course, similar to the view of Sartre in "Black Orpheus," his preface to a collection of writings by negritude poets that did not endear him to Fanon. Sartre viewed negritude as a "moment" in the dialectic of history: white supremacy is a thesis, negritude is a negation of white supremacy, and social equality is the negation of the negation (or negritude). As he wrote, "[n]egritude is dedicated to its own destruction, it is a passage and not objective, means and not the ultimate goal," since it posits, in Marxist terms, universal brotherhood as its goal, "the human society without racism" (60), which is akin to Bigger's own vision of the "vast crowd of men" who are united by "the common and the good." Fanon, stunned, feeling amputated by Sartre's remarks, asserts negritude nonetheless as real, as existential—he affirms the "moment" of his blackness against the fate of all things that are caught in the circle of being and nothingness; his blackness, he says, echoing Langston Hughes, is "truly a soul as deep as the deepest of rivers" (140). Yet Fanon reveals a profound point about his defense of negritude, or, we can add, about any racial positivism: "A consciousness committed to experience is ignorant, has to be ignorant, of the essences and determinations [or mediations] of its being" (134). To be sure, to be "committed to [black] experience," one must ignore the mediations of that experience that have nothing to do with being black. The resistance to the concept of mediation is a hallmark of racial positivism, of the affirmation of black experience as the ground of one's literary or political practices, past and prospective.

In the spirit of a true dialectical narrative, then, Wright's novel challenges us to hold both the immediacy and the mediation of black experience in mind, and not to deny one for the other, but to see them as a unity of opposites. Its brilliance and continuing relevance is its refusal to reduce black experience to a "monochromatic formalism" (Hegel, *Phenomenology* 9) wherein the experience of racial difference is either reified as an absolute of racial identity or liquidated in an absolute of class identity. Put differently, the novel challenges us to grasp both the horrors of the experience of racism and the global inequalities of a class system so that we may, like Bigger, come to imagine a world no longer defined by race or class but, rather, by a community of shared interests defined by "what was common and good."

Notes

1   The major exception is Abdul R. JanMohamed's perceptive study of "the dialectics of death" in Wright's fiction. Notable studies of Wright's politics include Reilly, Kinnamon, Irr, and Hakutani.
2   See Huggins and Lewis.
3   See Solomon on the Communist's Black Nation Thesis.

4   For another view of "the dialectic of death," see JanMohamed. Using the tripartite structure of the dialectic, JanMohamed claims that Bigger's development involves transcending his "social-death" (a thesis) by accepting the possibility of "actual-death" (an antithesis), resulting in his understanding of his death as a "symbolic-death" (a synthesis) (85).

5   JanMohamed's otherwise illuminating reading of "the dialectics of death" in *Native Son* diminishes the importance of Ma[r]x to "Bigger's victory over death [since it] is severely compromised because he has not won it by struggling directly against the master; rather, he has won it by killing two women who are, in their own, different ways, in weaker positions than Bigger" (136–7). He assumes that "a thoroughly horrified Max withdraws his approval" when Bigger morally affirms his killing (137), an idea I interpret somewhat differently below.

6   See Allred's chapter on Wright. He writes here of Wright's influence by the Chicago School of Urban Sociology whose method "blended the abstraction of quantitative methods ... with the particularity and humanizing force of documentary materials" (155). See also Miller on the influence of Burke's *Permanence and Change* and the latter's use of the concept of a dialectic.

7   Perhaps the text also alludes to that more popular rending of the curtain in *The Wizard of Oz*, although it is unclear if Wright could have seen the movie prior to submitting proofs of his manuscript.

8   Paul N. Siegel's claim that Max was not a member of the CPUSA (95) is beside the point with regard to his influence on Bigger: one need not be a "card-carrying member" of the CPUSA to think dialectically. And, besides, why would the ILD hire a lawyer who did not understand the complex political and economic determinations of a case involving an African American?

9   See my chapter on Wright in *Nationalism, Marxism, and African American Literature between the Wars: A New Pandora's Box*.

10 See Gibson 39; Irr 209; Scruggs 168; Skerret 118; and Margolies 51–2 for readings that emphasize Bigger's difference from Max in the concluding scene.

11 For a useful discussion of the Wright–Sartre relationship, see Fabre.

Works cited

Allred, Jeff. *American Modernism and Depression Documentary*. Oxford: Oxford UP, 2010. Print.

Benjamin, Walter. "Surrealism: The Last Snapshot of the European Intelligentsia." Trans. Rodney Livingston et al. *Walter Benjamin. Selected Writings*. Ed. Michael W. Jennings et al. Vol. 2. Cambridge: Belknap Press of Harvard UP, 1999. 207–21. Print.

Cullen, Countee. "Incident." *Color*. New York: Harper & Brothers, 1925. 15. Print.

Dawahare, Anthony. *Nationalism, Marxism, and African American Literature between the Wars: A New Pandora's Box*. Jackson: UP of Mississippi, 2003. Print.

Du Bois, W. E. B. *The Souls of Black Folk*. New York: Bedford, 1997. Print.

Fabre, Michel. "Richard Wright and the French Existentialists." *MELUS* 5.2 (1978): 39–51. Print.

Fanon, Frantz. *Black Skin, White Masks*. Trans. Charles Lam Markmann. New York: Grove, 1967. Print.

Hakutani, Yoshinobu. "*Native Son, Pudd'nhead Wilson*, and Racial Discourse." Kinnamon 183–95.

Hegel, G. W. F. *The Encyclopaedia Logic: Part I of the Encyclopaedia of Philosophical Sciences with the Zusätze.* Trans. T. F. Geraets, W. A. Suchting, and H. S. Harris. Indianapolis: Hackett, 1991. Print.

—— *Lectures on Logic.* Trans. Clark Butler. Bloomington: Indiana UP, 2008. Print.

—— *The Phenomenology of Spirit.* Trans. A. V. Miller. Oxford: Oxford UP, 1977. Print.

—— *Science of Logic.* Cambridge: Cambridge UP, 2010. Print.

Holy Bible Containing the Old and New Testaments. Cambridge: Cambridge UP, 2007. Print. King James Version.

Holy Bible Containing the Old and New Testaments. Cambridge: UP, 2008. Print. New International Version.

Huggins, Nathan Irvin. *Harlem Renaissance.* Oxford: Oxford UP, 2007. Print.

Hughes, Langston. "Too Much of Race." *Good Morning Revolution: Uncollected Writings of Langston Hughes.* Ed. Faith Berry. New York: Carol Publishing, 1992. 101–4. Print.

Irr, Caren. "The Politics of Spatial Phobias in *Native Son.*" Kinnamon 196–212.

JanMohamed, Abdul R. *The Death-Bound-Subject: Richard Wright's Archeology of Death.* Durham: Duke UP, 2005. Print.

Kinnamon, Keneth, ed. *Critical Essays on Richard Wright's Native Son.* New York: Twayne, 1997. Print.

Lewis, David Levering. *When Harlem Was in Vogue.* New York: Penguin, 1997. Print.

Lukács, Georg. "Reification and the Consciousness of the Proletariat." *History and Class Consciousness: Studies in Marxist Dialectics.* Trans. Rodney Livingstone. Cambridge: MIT Press, 1968. 83–222. Print.

Margolies, Edward. "*Native Son* and Three Kinds of Revolution." *Bigger Thomas.* Ed. Harold Bloom. New York: Chelsea House, 1990. 43–53. Print.

Marx, Karl. *Capital: A Critique of Political Economy.* Intro. Ernest Mandel. Trans. Ben Fowkes. Vol. 1. New York: Vintage, 1977. Print.

Marx, Karl and Frederick Engels. *The German Ideology: Critique of Modern German Philosophy According to Its Representatives Feuerbach, B. Bauer and Stirner, and of German Socialism According to Its Various Prophets. Collected Works.* Vol. 5. New York: International Publishers, 1976. 19–539. Print.

Miller, Eugene E. *Voice of a Native Son: The Poetics of Richard Wright.* Jackson: UP of Mississippi, 1990. Print.

Mullen, Bill V. "Space and Capital in Richard Wright's *Native Son* and *Twelve Million Black Voices.*" *Reconstruction* 8.1 (2008). Web.

Reilly, John M. "Giving Bigger a Voice: The Politics of Narrative in *Native Son.*" *New Essays on Native Son.* Ed. Keneth Kinnamon. Cambridge: Cambridge UP, 1990. 35–62. Print.

Sartre, Jean-Paul. *Black Orpheus.* Trans. S. W. Allen. Paris: Gallimard, n.d. Print.

—— *Existentialism Is a Humanism.* Trans. Carol Macomber. Intro. Annie Cohen-Solal. New Haven: Yale UP, 2007. Print.

—— *Search for a Method.* Trans. Hazel E. Barnes. New York: Knopf, 1963. Print.

Schuyler, George S. "The Negro-Art Hokum." *Within the Circle: An Anthology of African American Literary Criticism from the Harlem Renaissance to the Present.* Ed. Angelyn Mitchell. Durham: Duke UP, 1994. 51–4. Print.

Scruggs, Charles. "The City without Maps in Richard Wright's *Native Son.*" Kinnamon 147–79.

Siegel, Paul N. "The Conclusion of Richard Wright's *Native Son.*" Kinnamon 94–103.

Skerret, Joseph T., Jr. "Composing Bigger: Wright and the Making of *Native Son.*" Kinnamon 104–18.

Smethurst, James. "Invented by Horror: The Gothic and African American Literary Ideology in *Native Son.*" *African American Review* 35.1 (2001): 29–40. Print.

Solomon, Mark. *The Cry Was Unity: Communists and African Americans, 1917–1936.* Jackson: UP of Mississippi, 1998. Print.

Wright, Richard. "Blueprint for Negro Writing." *Within the Circle: An Anthology of African American Literary Criticism from the Harlem Renaissance to the Present.* Ed. Angelyn Mitchell. Durham: Duke UP, 1994. 97–106. Print.

—— "The Ethics of Living Jim Crow." *Uncle Tom's Children.* 1940. New York: HarperPerennial, 1993. Print.

—— "How 'Bigger' Was Born." *Native Son.* New York: HarperPerennial, 1993. 505–40. Print.

—— "I Tried to Be a Communist." *The God That Failed.* Ed. Richard H. Crossman. New York: Harper & Brothers, 1949. 115–62. Print.

—— *Native Son.* New York: HarperPerennial, 1993. Print.

Part Two

The Pursuit of Sovereignty in Wright's Political and Artistic Odyssey

5

Richard Wright and his Editors: A Work under the Influence? From the *Signifyin(g)* Rebel to the Exiled Intellectual

Laurence Cossu-Beaumont

Université Sorbonne Nouvelle – Paris 3

This chapter engages in a reflection on several commonly held views regarding Richard Wright's career and work and offers a new critical approach and methodology. Wright was and still is such a well-known novelist that his reputation has sometimes overshadowed not just the texts but also the specific context of such unlikely success. In 1939, he was the first African American writer selected by the Book-of-the-Month Club. The popular mail-order book sales club was founded in 1926 and circulated an estimated 363,000 book copies in 1939. More recently, in 1991, Wright became a Library of America author, only the second African American after W. E. B. Du Bois in 1987.[1] The nonprofit publisher was—and still is—dedicated to preserving America's canon texts in authoritative editions.[2] The 1991 volume gave editor Arnold Rampersad the opportunity to restore Wright's original texts and exposed the significant cuts demanded by the publishers and distributors. In that respect, new approaches (book history, influence studies) and the focus on new sources (the correspondence) may contribute to a perhaps alternative reading of Wright's famous texts in the light of editorial stakes. We hope to inscribe Wright's now classical and timeless works back into the relevant economic and racial politics of their days through an analysis of the publishers' attempts at censorship and marketing targets.

First of all, homage needs to be paid to Michel Fabre, who was undoubtedly the most important Wright scholar in the sense that he initiated the scholarship on Wright with his astute insight and unprecedented documentation in the seminal *The Unfinished Quest of Richard Wright*. It was indeed Fabre who first and most successfully suggested that Wright's exile in Paris offered him a continuation of a *lifetime quest* instead of the contemporary view that leaving his native land had cut Wright off from his creative roots. Furthermore, the outstanding archives at the Beinecke Rare Book and Manuscript Library at Yale University, the Wright Papers in the James Weldon Johnson Collection, donated by Wright's widow, Ellen Wright, were really made accessible to future researchers by the unparalleled dedication of Fabre, who sorted the thousands of documents there.

There is at the Beinecke a mine of unexplored and still little-used documentation, especially the extensive correspondence with Wright's fellow *literati* or with his publishers and editors. The letters have never been published and have been little exploited. When it comes to the later period of Wright's career, after his 1947 expatriation to Paris, the cross-reading resulting from a book history approach and the interest for correspondence shows the way African American authors remained connected with the motherland. Although personally free in Paris, they were still submitted to the diktats, prudery, and prejudice of American society through the book market. Their economic survival in exile depended on selling books to American readers and convincing American publishers to publish and adequately promote their books. In this respect, the extensive editorial correspondence (between Wright and his publisher and agent) kept at the Beinecke pleads for a new reading of some commonly held judgments on Wright's exile works for instance, now seen as hasty "reductive literary criticism" (Davis 2). Too often considered as impoverished by distance and by the supposed loss of contact with his African American roots, Wright's 1950s fiction is read as a signal of a creative impediment brought about by the distracting influence of existentialism and cosmopolitanism:

> The underlying assumption here is that Wright's strength as a writer depended wholly upon the intense nearness of American experience and that the experience of expatriation deprived him, then, of his legitimate materials and signaled his end as an artist. That assumption is wrong, and the tale itself is not an uncommon instance of American provincialism posing as critical truth.
>
> (Davis 2)

The exile "tale" has been denounced as early as 1973 by Charles T. Davis and others, including Fabre. The Beinecke letters, however, offer a new background for the understanding of Wright's last published novel, *The Long Dream*, two years before his death. I suggest here that the boundaries of editorial pressure may have superseded the boundaries of the artist's inspiration, especially at a time of doubt and waning success. This chapter delves into the correspondence to suggest that editorial pressure, not lack of inspiration or remoteness from his roots, dictated Wright's choices and writing in the 1950s. Evidence can be found in the Beinecke letters of the responsibility of agent Paul Reynolds and editor Edward Aswell in pushing Wright away from his original writing projects in the 1950s while securing texts they felt were Wright's landmark and a guaranty of success, thus producing *The Long Dream* and not the more ambitious and innovative works Wright had been planning.

The chapter first unearths the letters exchanged between Wright; Dorothy Canfield Fisher, a member of the Book-of-the-Month Club committee; Aswell, Wright's publisher at Harper; and Reynolds, Wright's literary agent. The 1939 and 1944 correspondence dealing with the preparation of the final volumes of respectively *Native Son* and *Black Boy* to be selected and distributed by the Book-of-the-Month Club reveals that, in the very making of his career and definition of his work, the young author had been, if not controlled, at least channeled by editorial forces. In the characterization of Bigger and Mary, the central figures of his 1940 best seller *Native Son*, or in the delineation of their relationship, the writer's creative freedom met the requests of a powerful editor and the limits of early 1940s American society concerning interracial relationships. Similarly, although for political reasons, editorial interference loomed in the final stages of *Black Boy*'s publishing process in 1944. The first developments of the chapter will thus be devoted to the making of a best seller colliding with censorship, the demands of the editorial world, and the aspirations of a budding writer.

Fisher emerged as a central figure among Wright's editorial correspondents. As a member of the committee of the Book-of-the-Month Club, she pushed for the selection of both *Native Son* and *Black Boy* and thus contributed to their outstanding sales and large circulation. Wright's biographer, Hazel Rowley, has uncovered Fisher's influence, the "white shadow," over Wright's best sellers: "the Richard Wright we know is a censored, mediated, packaged Richard Wright" (625). Other scholars have identified Fisher as the "white mental censor" that kept Bigger "in his place" (Sumner 142). The influential Fisher did demand and obtain significant cuts and modifications. Much less known, however, is Wright's witty resistance to this disguised censorship, which he strikingly devised along the lines of African American *signifyin(g)*. This resistance is at play in the correspondence between Wright and Fisher in 1944 and will be the main resource for our study.

Although much has been written on Wright being forced (or not) to make such cuts or to rewrite, especially in the wake of the 1991 publication of the unexpurgated versions of *Native Son* and *Black Boy* in the Library of America edition, Wright's resistance has not been documented, for the Beinecke letters have not been exploited. Scholars have extensively commented on the differences between the "censored" text and Wright's original draft, but the epistolary battle made of refusal and compromise remains unknown. Scholars have debated the authority of an "original" text: Rampersad called his careful restoration a "major salvage operation." Julia Wright concurred, while others expressed their disagreement with the fraud, which they considered disrespectful of Wright's choice: "How do we know the form in which Wright intended the books to be read?" they wonder (Olney 524).[3]

We will not engage in such a debate here but rather offer a counterpoint with the vantage point allowed by the correspondence. The correspondence is like the backstage space where white censors, the author's self-censorship, and the limits of it are interplaying their respective strength, authority, and resisting strategies. This engages historical, political, and economic if not business considerations, rather than literary ones: beyond the admittedly bold choice of the Book-of-the-Month Club, there remained the stake of marketing a book that was fit for the white middle-class readers of the Club, in other words that was fit for mainstream America. Rampersad acknowledged that "I don't think of the Book-of-the-Month Club as the villains ... You have to safeguard your product. The members of the club's selection committee ... were keenly aware of an audience not as enlightened as they were" (qtd. in Blau). In the end, the equation between a brutal murder story with a backdrop of segregation and a popular best seller remains a puzzle.

While Wright's witty and strategic rebellion against censorship is documented in the first two sections of the article dealing with the making or framing of Wright's early best sellers, the third section will turn to the "exile tale" and a less flamboyant career end. In both instances, only the unpublished letters kept at the Beinecke can fully reveal the complex process that gave birth to the celebrated *Native Son* and *Black Boy* or to the underrated *The Long Dream*. It has been our choice, in this chapter, to offer a continuing thread by focusing on autobiography and fiction and by drawing a parallel between the editorial making of an African American best-selling author with *Native Son* and *Black Boy* and the returning editorial control of a doubting exile for *The Long Dream*. The two key stages of Wright's career—beginning and end—are both to be understood through the editorial power, either imposed on, internalized by, or resisted by the fiction writer. Beyond the editorial debates, one can grasp the backdrop of the racial question, informing every editorial demand, as well as the firm resistance of the author, while all parties seem to carefully avoid direct references to their real political motives. In the end, both the celebrated launch of Wright's career and its more criticized close will be read in the light of editorial framing. The study of correspondence thus brings a new light in the perspective of rethinking Wright and his times, and the American society's complex relation to race and communism.

The launching of a career

In 1939, Wright was about to become a confirmed author with the publication of his first novel, *Native Son*; his publishing debut with the collection *Uncle Tom's Children* in 1938 had been promising. On August 22, 1939, Edward Aswell, Wright's publisher at Harper, informed him that *Native Son* was under consideration by the Book-of-the-Month Club. The final decision was to be reached in their September board meeting: "If this happens, the chances are very good that the book will have a general sale considerably greater than might otherwise be expected, and, in addition, a Book Club choice would mean a nice sum of money for you" (Richard Wright Papers [hereafter RWP], box 98, folder 1379). Aswell urged Wright to accept the Club's conditions:

> And incidentally the Book Club wants to know whether, if they do choose *Native Son*, you would be willing to make some changes in that scene early in the book where Bigger and his friends are sitting in the movie picture theater. I think you will recognize the scene I mean and will understand why the Book Club finds it objectionable. They are not a particularly squeamish crowd, but that scene, after all, is a bit on the raw side. I daresay you could revise it in a way to suggest what happens rather than to tell it explicitly. Please let me hear about this as soon as possible so that I can convey your answer to the Book Club.
>
> (August 22, 1939, RWP, box 98, folder 1379)

This was to considerably delay the publishing of *Native Son*. The book had been ready for printing when news of the Book-of-the-Month Club's interest reached the publisher in August 1939: on August 8, Aswell had written, "the jacket is already made" (RWP). Yet it was only in January 1940 that the board decided on a March selection. *Native Son* came out on March 1, 1940. In that span, *Native Son* was made readable for the book club members and fit for popular and commercial success. Wright's literary agent, Reynolds, insisted on the golden opportunity: "Mr Aswell was going down to see Mr Sherman and he would write you about some changes which he said would be very, very minor . . . with war and misery everywhere it is kind of nice to be able to think of you and realize that you must be feeling on top of the world" (October 11, 1939, RWP, box 103, folder 1531). Success was at hand. Indeed, on April 4, 1940, Aswell wrote to Wright rejoicing about reviews and sales beyond expectation (RWP, box 98, folder 1379). The Beinecke archive contains weekly letters thereafter updating Wright on the astounding sales: "the book sold 2,000 copies last Friday alone" (April 8 letter); by May 1, 50,000 copies (May 2 letter). Both Rowley and Rampersad quote the exceptional figure of 215,000 copies sold within three weeks, the fastest sale for a Harper book in 20 years. There was much to gain: as far as revenues are concerned, the letters indicate that Wright received $17,869.50 in author's rights for the year 1940 (RWP, box 98, folder 1379, leaf 132). But what was the price paid?

Critics have been harsh, especially since the restored texts became available in 1991: references to "cleansing" and "emasculation" abound. Some are particularly cynical about the prevailing commercial interest:

> But let's look on the bright side: this is a story that makes money, and *Native Son* sold close to 215,000 copies in three weeks. If the racial ideology is right, the profits will follow; so for profit's sake, Bigger, don't look at that white lady! And you, reader, don't ask for the text in which Bigger feels the itch to look at her.
>
> (Sumner 142)

The allusions are to the cuts pertaining to a possible—even if imagined—sexual relationship between the young African American (anti)hero, Bigger Thomas, and his white victim, Mary Dalton. Indeed, the brutal narrative of Bigger's fall was to be remodeled to fit the Club's subscribers. What followed was, in the words of Julia Wright, "the emasculation of Bigger" (qtd. in Butler 171), for the most significant cuts dealt with the few openly sexual scenes.

> It is important to us that Bigger Thomas, who was "castrated" because deprived of his sexual life in the edited 1940 text, is made whole again—and made human—by the reinstatement of the masturbation scene at the beginning of *Native Son* and of references to his guilt-ridden desire for rich, white Mary prior to the panic which leads him to smother her accidentally.
>
> (Julia Wright qtd. in Butler)

The first scene that Wright agreed to cut on the Club's demand is indeed an explicit masturbation scene (actually a contest between Bigger and his friends). Sentences like

"I am polishing my nightstick" were deemed too "raw," as Aswell indicated in his August 1939 letter to Wright (RWP).

Interestingly enough, the masturbation scene originally takes place after Bigger and his friends discovered Mary in a newsreel showing a group of rich young men and women on a Miami beach. Her little-dressed figure clearly rouses the sexual interest of the boys and this is the crude comment, that "white women'll go to bed with anybody ... they even have their chauffeurs" (Wright 474). Later in the narrative, Bigger will become the Daltons' chauffeur. The scene thus makes it possible for Mary and her soon-to-be driver Bigger to be sexually connected. The possibility of a (fantasized) sexual relationship between Bigger and Mary is suggested again when Bigger witnesses the love-making of Mary and Jan, her fiancé, in the back of the car he is now driving for the Daltons. The glimpse of Mary's thigh and the fascination of Bigger glancing back through the mirror are cut from the 1940 version. Finally, the third and last passage cut from the original manuscript is the expression of Bigger's desire while he takes the drunk Mary to bed and holds her unconscious body.

In other words, although the late-1930s readers were deemed ready to accept a violent and desperate murder story and the tragic destiny of a young black man, they were spared the suggestion of a possible sexual ambiguity between Bigger Thomas and his white victim Mary—even if only imagined by Bigger.[4] The representation of a young white woman whose sexuality was freely exposed was the boundary of 1940s American society and for the targeted mainstream readership. Sexual prudery is not the sole explanation here as Bigger and his black girlfriend Bessie engage in sexual intercourse later in the narrative. The looming taboo of miscegenation is a more plausible reason for the demanded cuts. Rampersad concludes:

> Most of the major areas of textual controversy in Wright's work can be traced to the inevitable conflict that pitted an extraordinarily forceful and brilliant black writer, one who was bent on speaking the unspeakable, against white agents, editors and publishers who, often with what they construed to be Wright's best interests in mind, had very determining ideas of what whites were willing to accept from such a source.

Although the boldness and irreverence were tuned down, *Native Son* turned out to be both a commercial success and an emotional and political shock for the mainstream readership to which the Book-of-the-Month Club selection made it widely accessible. As Irving Howe famously cornered, "the day *Native Son* appeared, American culture was changed for ever."

Signifyin(g) and the making of a political best seller

Five years later, the publishing of *Black Boy* offered a very similar scenario. In January 1944, Wright's autobiography, then entitled *American Hunger*, was ready to come out: "Our spring publishing schedule has now been worked out, and I am glad to inform you that the date set for the publication of *American Hunger* is June 14" (Aswell to Wright, January 25, 1944, RWP, box 99, folder 1381). Yet at the last minute, news was heard of a new Book-of-the-Month Club selection, and throughout the summer and fall of 1944, adjustments had to be discussed and agreed on for what ended up being a spring 1945 publication. Success was just as outstanding as that for *Native Son*: "Dear Dick, Hold your hat again! In the week just ended we had reorders from *Black Boy* amounting to 4438 copies. This brings the total to 134,000" (Aswell to Wright, 6 July 1945, RWP, box 99, folder 1382). Only this time, the unpublished correspondence at the Beinecke sheds light on Wright's resistance to new demands voiced by Fisher on behalf of the Club.

Indeed, by 1944, Wright had become a celebrated best-selling author. Offered this new Book-of-the-Month Club selection for his upcoming autobiography, Wright did yield to the main request of the Club—that the projected publication be cut in half to focus on the Mississippi childhood only.[5] Cutting the second part, and thus the disillusions of Wright's experiences in Chicago, produced a text focusing the criticism on the racist distant South only. The new ending portrayed a hopeful "Dick" on board a train northbound to the conquest of his long fought for freedom. In other words, though admittedly flawed in the South, American society could offer hope and fulfillment to anyone, the concluding chapter seemed to promise. Likewise, from *American Hunger*, its first title and the portrayal of an American deceived by the promises of his country, the book became the plea of a "black boy" whose only burden is the racial situation. Clearly, the editorial interference ensured that exposing Southern segregation triggered no suggestion of an *American* failure, although Wright originally tried to maintain that aspect before giving in. On August 15, 1944, Reynolds reported a conversation he had with Fisher about the title and stated that *she* did not like *American Hunger* and liked *Black Boy* better: "She said she felt strongly that the Book-of-the-Month Club should not try to dictate or enforce the title but she said she would speak to the judges. I told her you and Harper wanted that title and she said, 'Well, I'll say that to the judges and I'm sure it will be the title" ' (Reynolds to Wright, August 15, 1944, RWP, box 103, folder 1535). *American Hunger* was not the title ultimately chosen in spite of Wright's preference. The word "American" had actually been the bone of contention of previous exchanges.

In 1944, the Club wanted more than just the initial split of Wright's life story. The United States was at the time leading the allies in the Second World War, and Fisher's exacerbated patriotism met Wright's integrity and wish to maintain a critical view, not just of the racist society he grew up in but of the shortcomings of the American value system at large. Bill Mullen describes the domestic racial context of the Second World War as explosive: "Archibald MacLeish, director of the Office of Facts and Figures for the Roosevelt administration, convened a conference of black newspaper editors to ask that they tone down calls for racial reform in respect for national wartime unity" (7). Even *Native Son* was read in a new light after the conflict broke out. This 1941 newspaper clipping from *PM*, an editorial magazine, is kept in the Wright Papers at the Beinecke:

Bigger Thomas is the tragic protagonist of a great novel, *Native Son*, written by a Negro, Richard Wright, and published by Harper's. Bigger's life was a disaster, because he was a Negro oppressed—as all his people are oppressed—by the blind misunderstanding and hostility of whites. He had many thwarted longings. One of them was to be an airplane pilot. We print one moving passage from *Native Son* here, because it has a special meaning to a country arming against Fascism. We are making Bigger Thomases every day. We make them by barring Negroes from the Army, from the Navy and from the Air Corps. We make them by depriving Negroes of jobs in defense industries. And Bigger Thomases don't make soldiers for democracy.

                              (May 7, 1941, RWP, box 6, folder 111)

Was *Black Boy* going to further fuel such debates by providing new examples of the racial hardships endured by popular author Richard Wright? Here, in the necessary amendments that the amputation of the original manuscript entailed, Wright strove to resist more authoritative demands and openly political requests. An epistolary duel ensued.

To ensure closure after the split of the original work, Wright wrote an additive conclusion of *Black Boy* pondering on such questions as "What made me conscious of possibilities? From where in this southern darkness had I caught a sense of freedom?" (Wright 878). The answer, he explains, lies in his readings of influential authors like "Dreiser, Masters, Mencken, Anderson and Lewis" (Wright 878). The answer, he concludes, lies in "books" only (Wright 878).

In the Beinecke correspondence discussing this new ending, Fisher repeatedly tries to bring Wright to advocate his faith in the American values that supposedly gave him the strength and courage to overcome his hardships. On April 1, 1944, she literally suggests that Wright add a more patriotic tone to the ending passage:[6]

What I'm trying to put in such a tentative way as not to make it a suggestion, much less a request, is the question whether it might be possible for you, somehow, somewhere in this fine epilogue, to answer your own question "What was it that made me conscious of possibilities? From where had I caught a sense of freedom?" Perhaps you might answer it by another question such as I put myself, only I put into old-fashioned phrases, "From what other source than from the basic tradition of our country could the soul of an American have been filled with that 'hazy notion' that life could be lived with dignity?" Could it be that even from inside the prison of injustice, through the barred windows of that Bastille of racial oppression, Richard Wright had caught a glimpse of the American flag?

                              (RWP, box 97, folder 1333)

Though apparently respectful of Wright's choices, Fisher imposes an ideology she feels is lacking in the original page. In a surge of lyrical patriotism, she invites him to acknowledge that only the American tradition could have freed him from his Southern prison.

In a July 6, 1944 letter, Wright submits a text that he states he has redrafted accordingly. He underlines the changes he has conceded but also remains adamant on one point. Fiction saved him from the Southern doom, not the "American flag": "For me, it had been my reading of fiction—far removed from political consideration—that evoked in me a sense of personal freedom, or the possibility of escaping the South" (RWP, box 97, folder 1333). He intends to remain faithful to the spirit of the text and pushes away Fisher's inappropriate optimism:

> I fully understand the value of what you are driving at, but, frankly, the narrative as it now stands simply will not support a more general or hopeful conclusion. The Negro who flees the South is really a refugee; he is so pinched and straitened in his environment that his leaving is more an avoidance than an embrace.
> (Wright to Fisher, July 6, 1944, RWP, box 97, folder 1333)

Nevertheless, in her July 12 answer, Fisher formulates another attempt at bending the narrative her way. She tries praising Wright and goes on bargaining for "one word":

> I gather you cannot bring yourself to use, even once, the word *"American"* in speaking of the "tinge of warmth which came from an unseen light"—such a beautiful sensitive phrase! Some of the novel and stories you read were—it is probable—laid in *your own country of America*. Hence some of the characters in books through whom you had "glimpsed life's possibilities" were *fellow Americans of yours* ... Those characters could have been no other than products of *American tradition* ... Was it only in Russian, British or French fiction that you found anything to give you tidings from afar that there were human brothers of yours on the globe, who had ideals, who tried, however fitfully, to live up to them, who never never dreamed of denying their validity ... Did you not, in any book-character, encounter a white *fellow-citizen* of yours who tried to live up to that ideal?
> (RWP, box 97, folder 1333; emphasis added)

Wright has already expressed the absurdity of being over-enthusiastic about the supposed American values after pages of atrocities and sufferings. Confronted with such insistence and wary not to antagonize the committee, Wright responds with a rather clever strategy. Fisher wants "the word American," she says? Wright gives in. Literally. He uses the word "American" and proudly announces it in his next letter:

> As a writer, I'm always willing to react again and again to anyone's reactions, and I have reworded again the section of the ending dealing with my revelation of the American scene. I have stated the names of those American writers that influenced me and tried to give the reasons for my being able to respond to them. I did manage to use the word "American", and I want to assure you that I did not omit it previously by intention.
> (July 20, 1944, RWP, box 97, folder 1333)

This is nothing short of a *signifyin(g)*, an oral African American strategy whereby the weaker speaker defeats his opponent by taking his word literally and by faking naivety.

Wright did in all appearances respectfully surrender to Fisher's demands and offer an explicit connection with the American tradition. Yet the wording of the ultimate passage of the 1945 version of *Black Boy* points to American writers as among the harshest critics of their country, those Wright also described in his July 20 letter as "rebels of a sort":

> It had been through books—at best, no more than vicarious cultural transformations—that I had managed to keep myself alive in a negatively vital way … What enabled me to overcome my chronic distrust was that these books— written by men like Dreiser, Masters, Mencken, Anderson and Lewis—seemed defensively critical of the straitened American environment. These writers seemed to feel that America could be shaped nearer to the hearts of those who lived in it.
>
> (Wright 878–9)

Interestingly enough, this African American strategy, brought to the fore by the work of Henry Louis Gates, Jr., is usually not associated with Wright's aesthetics. Nevertheless, in this unequal fight between an African American writer and the representative of a white editorial institution, the recourse to a specifically black strategy, to an oral trick, to a street practice is what offers Wright access to the homes of thousands of white readers subscribing to the Book-of-the-Month Club. This is a rather unknown way in which Wright fulfilled the lifetime quest he first articulated in *Black Boy*: "Could words be weapons?" (Wright 237). Wright's famous formula is mostly read as evidencing his radical engagement, his pledge to denounce (the racial situation) through his prose. Yet "words as weapons" adequately describes what *signifyin(g)* has always meant for African Americans in their oppressing environment: it was their only possibility to "fight back with words," before the decade of civil rights fights and collective political action. This should serve as a compelling invitation to consider that Wright's committed writing is not necessarily exclusive of African American tropes. In this episode, white censorship may actually have shattered, and not erected, barriers between Wright and his African American inheritance.

The way the book was promoted and marketed, though, reinforces the notion that publishers were trying to to sell the book as an account of America's limitless possibilities and opportunities for all. The 1945 dust jacket of *Black Boy* is thus described by Howard Rambsy:

> The words on the cover appear over what are apparently clouds, and a small opening in the clouds shows what are presumably stars. The image of clouds and stars alludes to the closing of the autobiography where Wright states that "I headed North, full of a hazy notion" that "if men were lucky in their living on earth they might win some redeeming meaning for their having struggled and suffered here beneath the stars." (228)

Such optimism seems fit with the political control of the editorial world in times of war. Interestingly, Rambsy also points out, the *Black Boy* jacket will feature the figure of what is to be interpreted as a rebel in the 1960s editions, the jacket offering the reader guidance in keeping with the spirit of the times.

For the safekeepers of social and racial order, however, *Black Boy*, in spite of the cuts and rewriting, was not deemed patriotic, optimistic enough, or even accurate at all. *Black Boy* managed the interesting feat of being on the year's best-sellers list (for nonfiction) released by *Publishers Weekly* and being the object of a congressional debate. Mississippi Senator Bilbo denounced the narrative and tried to have the book banned:

> There is another book which should be taken off the book racks of the Nation, it should be removed from the book stores; its sales should be stopped. It is the recent book of the month which has had such a great sale. Senators can understand why it has had such a sale if they will read it. It is entitled "Black Boy", by Richard Wright. Richard Wright is a Mississippian. He was born in Natchez, Miss. He went from Natchez to Jackson, from Jackson to Memphis, from Memphis to Chicago, and from Chicago to Brooklyn, N.Y., where he is married to a white wife and is living happily, he says. He wrote the book *Black Boy* ostensibly as the story of his life. Actually it is a damnable lie from beginning to end. It is practically all fiction. There is just enough truth to it to enable him to build his fabulous lies about his experiences in the South and his description of the people of the South and the culture, education, and life of the southern people. The purpose of this book is to plant the seeds of hate in every Negro in America against the white men of the South or against the white race anywhere, for that matter. That is the purpose. Its purpose is to plant the seeds of devilment and trouble-breeding in the days to come in the mind and heart of every American Negro. Read the book if you do not believe what I am telling you. It is the dirtiest, filthiest, lousiest, most obscene piece of writing that I ever seen in print. I would hate to have a son or a daughter of mine permitted to read it; it is so filthy and dirty. But it comes from a Negro and you cannot expect any better from a person of his type.
>
> (*Congressional Record*, 91, pt. 5, June 27, 1945, RWP, box 14, folder 244)

Although Bilbo failed to have the book banned nationally (Mississippi did ban it), the "danger" he describes in the spreading of such discourse and examples is clearly made more immediate by the wide circulation of the book and the exceptional sales.

Exile and editorial pressure

At the crossroads of book history and Wright scholarship, the Beinecke archive offers another opportunity to reconsider a commonly held judgment, namely that Wright's exile meant the unfortunate end of his masterpieces. The European fiction writing tends to be regarded as minor, and this has not been often interrogated by scholars, unless to provide the too obvious contention that the loss of his US-rooted inspiration was the answer. There is ground, however, for a new appreciation of the reasons of such underrated fiction works in exile in the Beinecke archive. First of all, Wright's first "European" novel, *The Outsider*, dubbed too artificially existentialist, was originally conceived in the United States, before the exile of 1947.[7] Further contradiction of the usual reading of the exile work lies in the 1955 correspondence between Wright and his agent, Reynolds, and between Wright and his lifetime editor, Aswell. The exchanges deal with the possibility of repeating the success of *Black Boy*, hence our choice to focus on these letters in particular and offer a mirroring analysis of our first sections, from early career to later one. As John A. Williams suggested, editorial pressure may also have intervened before the writing of the books and not in the immediate pre-publishing stages:

> I don't believe Wright (like his compatriot, Himes) was ever out of touch with what was happening here. The critics are wrong. Wright is still being rediscovered because new aspects and new subtleties of American racism, thus new negatives, are being revealed on levels he might have imagined but never got to write about.

Aswell was Wright's editor at Harper from the start of his career, that is to say from the publication of *Uncle Tom's Children* by Harper in 1938. He guided Wright through the successes of *Black Boy* and *Native Son*, and the mutual trust that oozes from the long and numerous letters is undoubtedly a positive influence on Wright's work, in particular as far as Aswell's advice on the various manuscript rewritings is concerned. However, Aswell did refuse texts like "The Man Who Lived Underground" in 1944; the novella was published in the collection *Cross Section* edited by Edwin Seaver in 1945 and was later included in *Eight Men*. Even in times of success, Aswell did not believe in the modernist non-biographical kind of narrative Wright experimented with in "The Man Who Lived Undergound" and later in *The Outsider*. Nevertheless, when Aswell left Harper for McGraw-Hill in 1947, Wright considered leaving with Aswell, but his agent recommended he stay with the more prestigious Harper. He quickly found himself isolated for by 1947 he was in Europe and had no trustworthy correspondent at Harper. After Aswell's departure, the collaboration between Wright and John Fischer, his new contact, was marred with incomprehension and the relative failure of *The Outsider*.[8] Though Wright published *Black Power* with Harper the following year, when it came to tackling fiction again he turned to Aswell, in need of support more than in need of a publisher—indeed, Harper would publish one more book by Wright, *Pagan Spain*. By 1955, the two men planned to resume collaboration with sincere enthusiasm.

> The thought of working with you again fills me with the most pleasurable anticipations. I look back upon the early work you and I did together as one of the most rewarding experiences of my life and one of the things of which I am most proud.
>   (Aswell to Wright, August 11, 1955, RWP, box 101, folder 1459)

Wright's answer ten days later testifies to the need for the writer to find a trustworthy and reliable partner to guide him through his next works after a period of doubt and failures:

To tell you the truth I've really had no editor since you left Harpers. There were editors there, of course, and they are all good men in general. But they were really *not* editors. I guess, without my knowing it, I'd been spoiled while I was at Harpers and you were my editor. I got into the habit of taking editors for granted and I never knew the difference until you left.

(August 21, 1955, RWP, box 85, folder 983; emphasis in original)

Immediately, in a forty-page letter written from August to October 1955,[9] Wright develops proposals for future works. More importantly, perhaps, in this document, he gives his own understanding of his exile, which he does not associate in any manner with a loss of inspiration. In 1955, eight years after leaving the United States, the satisfaction is unmitigated:

Freed of racial preoccupations, I opened my eyes and looked upon the world sort of innocently for the first time. *Slowly, the kind of things that I really wanted to write made themselves manifest in me* ... Now, freed of this (which most people assume was the only thing that a black writer could write out of, that is racial fear and feelings), I've let what would have normally come to the fore on me become my main preoccupation. That preoccupation is: the individual and his society ... That problem poses for me many paradoxes: society and man form one organic whole, yet both, by the very nature of their relationship, are in sharp conflict ... This preoccupation of mine cuts across racial, class, sexual, religious, and political questions.

(RWP, box 85, folder 983; emphasis added)

Wright thus appears as rather enthusiastic on the positive effects of his exile and entirely inspired by the latter; he offers Aswell no less than forty pages of prospective works designed beyond the racial question and around what could be understood as modern alienation. In fact, that theme had already been tackled in the short story "The Man Who Lived Underground" and in an unpublished essay "Memories of my Grand Mother," both from the mid-1940s and much anterior to the exile. It remains that for Reynolds, his agent, and Aswell, his soon-to-be new editor, the European exile solely explained Wright's new ambitions and had been detrimental to his writing. Reynolds had voiced his pessimism two years before: "I have been worried for a long time as to what Wright should do ... *The Outsider* showed evidence of a man out of touch" (Reynolds to Fischer, April 30, 1953, Selected Records of Harper & Brothers, box 34, folder 3).

Accordingly, Aswell pushed Wright away from those unmapped projects while pulling him back to the familiar African American tragic fate. In January 1956, he refused Wright's proposals: "What it comes down to, as I see it, is my belief, even my conviction, that these novels which you outlined for me at such length are *not really the right thing for you to tackle*" (Aswell to Wright, January 24, 1956, RWP, box 101, folder 1459; emphasis added). Wright, in doubt, and attentive to a trustworthy advisor, relinquished, and offered another project in tune with what was expected from him. Aswell expresses his relief in this February 9 letter:

I am relieved to learn that you have given up the projects you outlined to me in such great detail, and it seems to me that the new one about the young man from Mississippi who fouled things up so badly in France offers a very promising subject for you. This is something that you can write about with intuitive knowledge and something with which you can make effective use of your own experience— even though your experience, happily, is not at all the same as that of this young man.

                                                      (RWP, box 101, folder 1459)

In other words, Wright should go back to his original inspiration, draw from his own experience—from Mississippi to Paris. Aswell basically demands that Wright produce the same ingredients that made his success. *The Long Dream* is launched. Whether it is the role of the editor to maintain an author in his familiar themes or to accompany him in new ventures is the question that stems from this exchange. Aswell congratulates Wright on his agreement to "return to the essence of [his] own living which [he had] drawn upon so richly in the past" (August 7, 1956, RWP, box 96, folder 1301), but upon its publication in 1958, the critics will precisely criticize *The Long Dream* for merely repeating, and less successfully, the "recipe" of *Black Boy*. Interestingly enough, *The Long Dream* is dedicated to Reynolds and Aswell: whether the novel is the fruit of Wright's desire or of his advisors' editorial strategy is worth asking in the light of what precedes.

More generally, the example offered here might invite scholars to reconsider different book proposals and unpublished texts available in the Beinecke papers, or even published texts that have been given little attention. *Rite of Passage*, a short novel from the 1940s, blocked by editorial decisions, offers an interesting representation of a woman's voice and comes to tune down the usual outcry against Wright's lack of positive female figures in his works. "Man of All Work," a short story included in *Eight Men* but written in 1957—at the same time the deemed unoriginal *The Long Dream* was being produced—displays a rarely quoted example of a successful black man whose empowerment, courage, and sense of responsibility contrast with the apparent determinism looming on the characters in *Uncle Tom's Children* or on Bigger Thomas. In that respect, "*Eight Men* challenges the brute machismo and uncomplicated misogyny so often imputed to [Wright]" (Gilroy xiv) and, it should be added, confirms the writer's delight for witty *signifyin(g)* bits. Indeed "Man of All Work" is a funny rewriting of the Shakespearian tradition of transgender disguise, with an amusing mockery of the famous white tale "Little Red Riding Hood." Black empowerment and black successful resistance through a traditional African American strategy, here understood as applying to both the author and some of his heroes: these are only a couple of examples of how many of Wright's known and less-known texts fiction could be brought forward to shed a new light on the diversity and complexity of his life-time project, which suffers from being summed up by the shadows of his two best sellers and by the reputation of his exile texts.

Editorial history thus brings to the fore new connections: some of the short stories of *Eight Men* written at the same time as *The Long Dream* were unaffected by editorial pressure because they were not designed to become Wright's next best seller. This chapter seeks to offer new perspectives not just to the literary critics of Wright's best-selling or less-known texts but for scholars in political, economic, and cultural fields as well. The questions of editorial pressure informed by the political demands of the time or the issues of marketing racial narratives in segregated America (and turning them into best sellers) open new vistas for our understanding of American history through popular culture.

Notes

1   More volumes from the Library of America have since been dedicated to African American texts: Frederick Douglass, Zora Neale Hurston, James Baldwin, Slave Narratives, Charles W. Chesnutt, and James Weldon Johnson.

2   On the foundation and significance of the Library of America, modeled on the French Pléiade edition of classics, see Kenneth M. Price's interview of Daniel Aaron. Aaron was co-founder and director of the Library of America.

3   More dissent on the Library of America edition stemmed from James W. Tuttleton and James Campbell.

4   To be accurate, one should mention one other notable cut, in Bigger's lawyer's speech at his trial in the final pages; the latter does not, however, illustrate the race/sex politics at play in the cuts considered in this chapter.

5   The original project and manuscript Wright handed to Harper in December 1943 was entitled *American Hunger* and was composed of two parts: the Mississippi childhood and the Chicago coming of age.

6   Most of the correspondence between Wright and Fisher on the selection of *Black Boy* by the Club is fully available at the Beinecke; Wright kept a carbon copy of the letters he sent and kept Fisher's letters as well (RWP, box 97, folder 1333).

7   On November 16, 1944, Harper and Wright signed a contract for a new novel, "title and subject to be determined later." It was canceled in 1949 as Wright had failed to meet the original deadline of January 1, 1947 (Fischer to Reynolds, May 18, 1949, RWP, box 99, folder 1382). But after *Native Son*, Wright had planned to address the issue of black alienation. The unpublished novel, *Black Hope*, the short story "The Man Who Lived Underground," all written before Wright's first trip to Paris in 1946, can be seen as early explorations of the main theme of *The Outsider*.

8   The Richard Wright–John Fischer correspondence is located at the Firestone Library of Princeton University in the Harper fund ("Selected Papers of Harper and Brothers").

9   This document, not exactly a letter, is classified as "Proposal" in the Beinecke archive (box 85, folder 983) and entitled "Celebration of Life" from Wright's own title. It comprises "When the World Was Red," the draft for a novel on an Atzec king where Wright introduces the encounter of this traditional culture with the Spanish one as a first experience of modernity. Also drafted is "A Strange Daughter/Girl," a fiction about the murder of a young pregnant white woman by her black lover around the theme of reversed miscegenation.

Works cited

Blau, Eleanor. "The Works of Richard Wright." *New York Times* 28 Aug. 1991. Print.

Campbell, James. "The Wright Version?" *Times Literary Supplement* 13 Dec. 1991: 14. Print.

Cossu-Beaumont, Laurence. "Orality in Richard Wright's Short Stories: Playing and Surviving." *Orality*. Spec. issue of *Journal of the Short Story in English* 47 (2006). Print.

Cossu-Beaumont, Laurence and Claire Parfait. "Book History and African American Studies." *Transatlantica* (2009). Web. http://www.transatlantica.org/

Davis, Charles T. Introduction. *Richard Wright: Impressions and Perspectives*. Ed. David Ray and Robert M. Farnsworth. Ann Arbor: U of Michigan P, 1973. 1–6. Print.

Fabre, Michel. *The Unfinished Quest of Richard Wright*. Trans. Isabel Barzun. New York: William Morrow, 1973. Print.

Gates, Henry Louis, Jr. *The Signifying Monkey: A Theory of African-American Literary Criticism*. New York: Oxford UP, 1988. Print.

Gilroy, Paul. Introduction. *Eight Men*. By Richard Wright. 1961. New York: HarperPerennial, 1996. Print.

Harper & Brothers. Selected Records. Manuscripts Division, Department of Rare Books and Special Collections, Princeton University Library. Print.

Howe, Irving. "Native Son and Black Boys." *Dissent* Autumn 1963: 353–68. Print.

Mullen, Bill. "Popular Fronts: Negro Story Magazine and the African American Literary Response to World War II." *African American Review* 30.1 (1996): 5–15. Print.

Olney, James. "Richard Wright in the Library of America." *Partisan Review* 61.3 (1994): 518–28. Print.

Price, Kenneth M. "An Interview with Daniel Aaron on the Library of America." *South Central Review* 5.4 (1988): 60–71. Print.

Rambsy, Howard. "Re-presenting Black Boy: The Evolving Packaging History of Richard Wright's Autobiography." *Southern Quarterly* 46.2 (2009): 71–85. Print.

Rampersad, Arnold. "Too Honest for His Own Time." *New York Times Book Review* 29 Dec. 1993: 3. Print.

Rowley, Hazel. "The Shadow of the White Woman: Richard Wright and the Book-of-the-Month Club." *Partisan Review* 66.4 (1999): 625–34. Print.

Sumner, Charles. "For Profit's Sake! Don't Look at That White Lady!" *Southern Quarterly* 46.2 (2009): 134–42. Print.

Tuttleton, James W. "The Problematic Texts of Richard Wright." *Hudson Review* 45.2 (1992): 261–71. Repr. in *The Critical Response to Richard Wright*. Ed. Robert Butler. Westport: Greenwood, 1995. 167–72. Print.

Williams, John A. "Richard Wright: The Legacy of a Native Son." *Washington Post* 22 Sept. 1991. Print.

Wright, Julia and Ellen Wright. "Letter to *Time Literary Supplement*." *Time Literary Supplement* 31 Jan. 1992. Repr. in *The Critical Response to Richard Wright*. Ed. Robert Butler. Westport: Greenwood, 1995. 171–2. Print.

Wright, Richard. *Black Boy*. 1945. Ed. Arnold Rampersad. New York: Library of America, 1991. Print.

—— Papers. James Weldon Johnson Collection, Yale Collection of American Literature. Beinecke Rare Book and Manuscript Library, Yale University, New Haven.

6

Recontextualizing Richard Wright's *The Outsider*: Hugo, Dostoevsky, Max Eastman, and Ayn Rand

Shoshana Milgram Knapp
Virginia Tech

Picture a group of novelists "seated together in a room, a circular room, a sort of British Museum reading-room—all writing their novels simultaneously." This was the advice of E. M. Forster, himself a superb novelist, in his admirably sensible *Aspects of the Novel* (9). Such an image of simultaneous composition, to be sure, should not be our exclusive avenue of access to fiction. We are enriched, after all, by studying writers in the settings of their times, their places, the events of their lives, and the textures of their personal experiences. Forster's image, however, brings with it the opportunity for new juxtapositions and for the insight to be gained by regarding individual texts as part of world literature, which is "not an infinite, ungraspable canon of works but rather a mode of circulation and of reading" (Damrosch 5). The present article, accordingly, is an invitation to consider Richard Wright's *The Outsider* in the light of several other novels that were composed, as it were, in the same passion-drenched moments and around the same glorious circular literary room. To the extent that Cross Damon is a psychological and spiritual outsider from conventional morality, he has company—and his company encompasses Victor Hugo's Jean Valjean and Fyodor Dostoevsky's Rodion Raskolnikov. To the extent, moreover, that *The Outsider* has an aesthetic identity as a novel of ideas, it too has company—and that company includes Ayn Rand's *Atlas Shrugged*.

In the concluding chapters of *The Outsider*, the protagonist's secrets unravel. Ely Houston, the district attorney in New York, tells Damon that the library of books Damon left behind him in Chicago amounted to an implicit confession of his motives, his crimes, and his anguished relationships: "Your Nietzsche, your Hegel, your Jaspers, your Heidegger, your Husserl, your Kierkegaard, and your Dostoevsky were the clues" (560). Because of the timing of the composition of the novel (the first novel to be published by Wright after he left the United States for Paris), because of Wright's own political circumstances, and because of numerous specific allusions and plot features, *The Outsider* is frequently, and understandably, discussed in terms of Wright's rejection of Communism, his affinity for existentialism, and his reading of Kierkegaard and Nietzsche. But there are terms other than these terms, and one of them—i.e., Dostoevsky—appeared in Houston's inventory of Damon's library.

By viewing Damon's library as clues to his nature, Houston is not thereby implying that these books are the only possible clues, that there is no other information relevant to the man's life or his crimes. The books, however, constitute a distinct and revealing angle of approach. Houston has chosen to focus on such figures as Nietzsche and Kierkegaard as composing Damon's intellectual or spiritual community. This community—of European thinkers and writers—share with Wright's protagonist the paradoxical status of being outsiders from the standpoints of convention, religion, or society—and of being outsiders, together. They are, so to speak, members of his tribe, in a way that fellow African Americans are not.

In order to grasp the relevant essence of Damon, Houston needs to go beyond his initial understanding of him from the standpoint of race. At their first meeting on the train, Houston stated that, as a hunchback, he was qualified to empathize with the outsider status of African Americans. He believes, moreover, that blacks, all blacks, are outsiders *per se*: "They are outsiders and they are going to know that they have these problems. They are going to be self-conscious; they are going to be gifted with a double vision, for, being Negroes, they are going to be both inside and outside of our culture at the same time" (163–4). Yet Damon himself sees his race as irrelevant to his "decisive life struggle":

> His consciousness of the color of his skin had played no role in it. Militating against racial consciousness in him were the general circumstances of his upbringing which had shielded him from the more barbaric forms of white racism; also the insistent claims of his own inner life had made him too concerned with himself to cast his lot wholeheartedly with Negroes in terms of racial struggle. Practically he was with them, but emotionally he was not of them. He felt keenly their sufferings and would have battled desperately for any Negro trapped in a racial conflict, but his character had been so shaped that his decisive life struggle was a personal fight for the realization of himself. (195)

Nor does he regard his race as relevant to his abandonment of his family and his past: "There was no racial tone to his reactions; he was just a man, any man who had had an opportunity to flee and had seized upon it" (109).

In his doomed relationship with Eva Blount, she is drawn to him in part because of his race ("I'm noticing other victims now, I've become aware of colored people" [283]); she wishes, in fact, "to experience the hurt and shame of being black" (385). Yet he asks himself: "Could he allow her to love him for his color when being a Negro was the least important thing in his life?" His race is "the least important thing in his life" even though he relies on racial stereotypes in order to acquire a false birth certificate: "In his role of an ignorant, frightened Negro, each white man—except those few who were free from the race bias of their group—would leap to supply him with a background and could safely hide behind it" (217).

He makes the point that he never joined the race to which he belongs (234), and this statement is important: from the perspective of his library of books—a library that includes no books by members of his ethnic group—one's actual identity is the identity one chooses to join. Damon would ask us to "read" the story of his life as anything but an alternative version of Wright's *Native Son*. His own library of books, after all, did not include any works of black literature. If, therefore, we read him as the protagonist of the sort of book he would have chosen to have on his library shelf, we accede to Damon's position that his ethnic identity does not define him. We adopt the perspective Houston reaches at last, though not at once: the understanding that Damon considers himself an outsider because of choice rather than chance, because of reasons that cannot be reduced to race.

The present article, therefore, seeks to recontextualize this novel by viewing one of its key elements in relation to two texts Wright knew: *Les Misérables* by Victor Hugo and *Crime and Punishment* by Fyodor Dostoevsky. Wright's admiration for Dostoevsky is well-documented, and his familiarity with Hugo is also part of his background.[1] The three books combine knuckle-biting suspense with heart-breaking loss and breath-taking intellectual passion. In all three, moral drama meets melodrama. We begin, as does *The Outsider*, with the idea of the aborted fresh start.

In *Les Misérables*, Valjean—an ex-convict whom prison has transformed into Prisoner 24601—claims a new identity as Monsieur Madeleine, the beneficent factory owner and mayor of Montreuil-sur-Mer. When another man is mistakenly accused of a minor crime he has committed, he reclaims his prison identity for the limited purpose of clearing the man wrongly accused then flees and reinvents himself again as Fauchelevent, brother of the gardener in a Paris convent, and, outside the convent, as Leblanc and again Fauchelevent. Years go by. Although Javert, who has been pursuing him relentlessly, lets him go free, Valjean is nonetheless unwilling to accept the gift of a blameless, threat-free life. With no explanation, he removes himself from contact with the one person he loves, because he refuses to let his past taint her future. In the end, the hidden truth is revealed, and death is not far behind. Although he never re-entered prison, the prison never left him—yet Hugo presents him as worthy of a better fate.

In *Crime and Punishment*, Raskolnikov, an impoverished, moody student whose dreams are beyond his practical grasp, plans to murder and rob a nasty pawnbroker in order to make possible a "fresh start." (He intended, he says, to use the resulting money to finance this start.) After the crime, he finds himself starting fresh in a way that he did not expect (i.e., separated emotionally from all human beings). He ultimately explains to Sonya, the prostitute who is his confidante/confessor, that he could not make a fresh start because he could not "cross over." In the novel's epilogue, after the truth has come out, he achieves his fresh start only through imagining a future in which he must abandon all of his ideas, and he must abandon the very act of thinking, and replace these with Sonya's religious faith. "Instead of dialectics, there was life"; the future is to be "his gradual regeneration, ... his acquaintance with a new, hitherto completely unknown reality" (551).

The most striking feature of the narrative of *The Outsider* is the audacity of Damon's attempt at a fresh start. Mistakenly considered dead, he deliberately abandons his family, job, and identity, an abandonment that he protects through the impulsive killing of a friend and then through flight and a succession of new names and crimes. In the end, as in *Les Misérables*, the hidden truth is revealed, and death is not far behind.

Damon's fresh start, his bold relinquishing of his past choices and burdens, presents parallels with the actions of Valjean and Raskolnikov; there are also significant differences. Like Valjean, he has no intention of recrossing the bridge behind him. He changes names, repeatedly, to evade capture and exposure. But Hugo's protagonist is inspired by a desire not merely for escape, or for an existence unhaunted by prison, but by a *positive* vision, by the knowledge that the Bishop of Digne has seen goodness in his soul and has made him promise to be loyal to his own best self: "Jean Valjean, my brother, you no longer belong to evil, but to good" (106). The symbol of his moral self-obligation is a pair of silver candlesticks, the Bishop's gift. Damon, by contrast, is focused on the burdens he is escaping and on the radical possibility of framing an existence without any burdens or responsibilities. For him, there are no candlesticks; there is no ideal self to incarnate. There is no freedom *for*, only freedom *from*. In his own internal words:

> For years he had been longing for his own way to live and act, and now that it was almost his, all he could feel was an uncomfortable sense of looseness. What puzzled him most was that he could not think of concrete things to do . . . That all men were free was the fondest and deepest conviction of his life. And his acting upon this wild plan would be but one expression of his perfect freedom. He would do with himself what he would, what he liked. (109, 111)

Like Raskolnikov, he has spent time brooding over the dolors and drudgery of his present, without taking steps to construct a more fulfilling life—until, one dark day, he decides to take a transgressive leap. And, like Raskolnikov, he commits an impulsive killing in order to protect the deliberate leap. And, like Raskolnikov, he comes to question the isolation that was the inspiration for his self-uprooting, the belief that no ties or traditions can or should inhibit him in any way. Raskolnikov asks, disingenuously, "Crime? What crime?" (518). Dostoevsky writes, moreover, that Raskolnikov's "hardened conscience did not see any especially terrible guilt in his past" (543). In a similar spirit, Damon proclaims, in his dying words, the true horror: that, in his heart, he has always believed himself to be innocent. But for him, there is no reading of the Bible, no spiritual re-enactment of the resurrection of Lazarus, no prison term in Siberia, and, in spite of his expressed wish to "make a bridge from man to man" (585), no second chance for a second chance.

The three narratives share several additional elements. In all three novels, a damaged man, himself in jeopardy, saves, or attempts to rescue, innocent victims: Valjean, for example, takes responsibility for the prostitute Fantine and her orphaned daughter Cosette, and engages in systematic acts of kindness and benevolence; Raskolnikov, in effect, adopts the Marmeladov family, including the chief breadwinner, the prostitute Sonya; Damon buys the prostitute Jenny a bus ticket to Denver and a better life, and he also meets with, and tries to intimidate, the men who have swindled Hattie Turner out of her home. But the generous actions of Damon—unlike those of Valjean and

Raskolnikov—are limited by his unwillingness to become personally involved or to follow through, much as he allows Bob Hunter, on the train, to count on him as a witness and then gives him an untraceable address.

All three works contain long passages of intellectual discourse, in such a way that ideas themselves become heroes or villains. Hugo's novel features numerous lectures on the part of the narrator (including the long background piece about the Battle of Waterloo, in which we learn that Napoleon was defeated not on account of military incompetence or inferior strength but because he annoyed God) and a long speech by Enjolras, a revolutionary leader in the 1832 uprising. Dostoevsky's novel, which is illuminated (or shadowed) by an essay we never read—Raskolnikov's published article about the extraordinary man who is justified in breaking the law if breaking the law is necessary for the development of an idea—also features conversations about the implications of this article. Although *The Outsider* features numerous passages of philosophical introspection on the part of Damon, and a revealing (perhaps too revealing) conversation with Houston on the train in Part Two, the most salient such passages occur in Part Four (when he is asked to talk for his life, and does) and in Part Five (when he is asked to talk in the face of imminent death, and he gasps out his final thoughts).

In all three novels, moreover, the protagonist faces pursuit by a man of the law who is a kind of spiritual double. In *Les Misérables*, Valjean is pursued by Javert (the name is virtually an echo), who first saw Valjean in prison and who, himself prison-born, defends the law relentlessly in order to resist the temptation to violate it. In *Crime and Punishment*, the prosecutor Porfiry Petrovich is himself implicitly tempted by Raskolnikov's idea; he has read Raskolnikov's article about what is permitted to extraordinary men. He confesses that he too imagines himself a Napoleon. He brings the crime home to Raskolnikov not through the accumulation of forensic physical evidence but through grasping Raskolnikov's philosophical/psychological motivation. It is no surprise to learn that Wright's copy of *Crime and Punishment* was dog-eared at the chapter in which the prosecutor reveals his intimate acquaintance with Raskolnikov's inner state (Fabre, *Richard Wright* 39). In *The Outsider*, Houston feels an admiration for Damon and an intellectual affinity with him as a fellow outsider; Houston is said to know "the demonic feelings of men who played god because he himself was of the demonic clan" (341). When they meet for the second time, Houston says, "At last I've tracked you down" (352). At the end, Houston tries to extract, from the dying Damon, a coherent statement—not primarily in order to resolve the remnants of the police case but in order to resolve Houston's own personal agony.

Wright's novel combines the Hugo–Dostoevsky pattern with distinctly powerful personal concerns. *The Outsider*, evidently, makes use of familiar tropes—the chase, the disguise, the debate, and the criminal who both creates and destroys himself. But Wright raises the body count, intensifies the access to the protagonist's consciousness, and deepens the ensuing despair. Similar developments are relevant to two additional elements of *The Outsider*: the multiple murders and the suicide of Eva. Through the lenses of Hugo and Dostoevsky, both of these can be illuminated.

In *The Outsider*, Damon commits two pairs of linked acts: he kills Joe Thomas *impulsively* to protect the secrecy of his having *deliberately* "killed" himself by changing his identity, and he kills Hilton, almost as *impulsively*, to protect the secrecy of his having *deliberately* killed Herndon and Gil Blount. In *Crime and Punishment*, similarly, Raskolnikov kills Lizaveta Ivanovna, impulsively, to protect the planned killing of Alyona Ivanovna, the pawnbroker. Although Valjean's actions do not include murder, he too has a pair of crimes (not counting the crime of stealing a loaf of bread, a crime he commits prior to the narrative proper): he deliberately steals silver cutlery from a bishop and then impulsively steals a coin from a child. It is the need to pay for this latter crime (i.e., by declaring himself guilty in order to clear someone wrongly accused) that forces him out of his new identity. Hugo says of the latter, impulsive crime:

> Was it the final effect, the final effort of the evil thought he had brought from prison, a remaining impulse . . .? To put it plainly, it was not he who had stolen, it was not the man, it was the beast that, from habit and instinct, had stupidly set its foot on that money, while the intellect was struggling in the midst of so many new and unknown influences . . . It was a strange phenomenon . . . but the fact is that in stealing this money from the child, he had done a thing of which he was no longer capable. (111–12)

In all three novels, the impulsive actions of the protagonists stand as potential indices of moral status. Here is the key question: is he primarily what he does by *deliberation*, or what he does in the *moment*, or *both*? Hugo answers, in the voice of the narrator, that Valjean's second crime is one of which he was not capable, but the man himself recognizes that it stands for a potential against which he must guard himself. Dostoevsky answers, in the voice of Sonya, that both actions (i.e., the planned and the spontaneous) are offenses against God and the earth, for which Raskolnikov must seek atonement and redemption. The question is: to what extent does an individual own his actions? And this becomes a significant question for Damon: he is concerned not primarily with the rightness or wrongness of what he has done, but with the extent to which he claims his own actions.

Consider a crucial passage from the concluding chapter of Part Three. First, we observe Damon's state of mind as he acts: "Suddenly a fullness of knowledge declared itself within Cross and he knew what he wanted to do. He was acting before he knew it" (302–3). But after he has left two corpses on the floor of Herndon's apartment, he insists, for the past, present, and future, that his choice was volitional: "He knew exactly what he had done; he had done it deliberately, even though he had not planned it. He had not been blank of mind when he had done it, and he was resolved that he would never claim any such thing" (304). His insistence, mandated by his personal code of accountability, is also implicitly a declaration in the context of analogous introspective acts of Valjean and Raskolnikov.

Damon's treatment of Eva (treatment that arguably contributes to her suicide) offers similarly instructive parallels to episodes in Hugo and Dostoevsky. Eva, an abstract artist, has been exploited by a loveless marriage to the Communist Gil Blount, whom Damon kills. Eva learns that Damon, to whom she has offered her love, has a secret and troubling past: he deserted and disowned his family; by withholding this information, he has deceived her. When he attempts to tell what he now believes to be the truth about why he killed Gil and Herndon, he insists that she understand, pity, and love him. She responds by taking her own life, seizing her own death. She jumps out the window sooner than remain with a man who says "If you turn from me, the world collapses" (530) because "If ever a man needed your love, I need it." He asks her to be his judge, to tell him if he is to live now; he is, in effect, demanding her complicity. She refuses him.

A reading of *Les Misérables* is relevant here, as contrast. Valjean makes strenuous efforts to shield Cosette, his adopted daughter, from his past, even though the past he is concealing entails less actual guilt than was the case for Damon. And yet Valjean removes himself from Cosette's life after her marriage to Marius Pontmercy. He refuses to live with the young couple and severely restricts his contact with them. As he explains to Marius, any alternative is impossible: "I would have brought the prison to your hearth, I would have sat down at your table with the thought that, if you knew who I was, you would drive me away" (1396). In his initial concealment of the killings he has committed, Damon is protecting Eva not only from the knowledge of his guilt, but from its burden.

A reading of *Crime and Punishment* is similarly relevant here. When Raskolnikov confesses the murders to Sonya, her first response is pity and concern: "'What, what have you done to yourself!' she said desperately, and, jumping from her knees, threw herself on his neck, embraced him, and pressed him very, very tightly in her arms" (411). Along with the offer of firm and direct emotional support and intimacy, she also provides a specific method of atonement: he is to confess publicly, to kiss the ground he has outraged, to embrace legal and spiritual punishment. But the fervor and immediacy of her offer of empathy and support are not contingent on the demands she makes, the actions she recommends. Before he takes a step toward the police and the prison, she embraces him, guilt and all.

Damon tries, in his relationship with Eva, to have it both ways (i.e., to be alternately Valjean and Raskolnikov). He affords himself the release of confession, in his delirium, yet, when fully conscious, chooses to shield Eva from his guilt; then, after Houston has exposed his desertion of his family, he chooses to tell her that he killed in order to affirm his vision of life over one he abhorred. He burdens her with his anguished self-justification, and he begs her to give him the love he craves. In doing so, however, he reckons without the fact of the facts. He disregards the record of actions that cannot be gainsaid or excused. Tragically, that very truth sends Eva—still reeling from the deception practiced on her by the Communists in what she had not realized was an arranged marriage—beyond the bounds of bearable pain. Instead of keeping his peace to protect Cosette as did Valjean, he overwhelms with his confession—twice—a woman who does not have the resources Sonya brought to the redemption of Raskolnikov.[2] The contrast with nineteenth-century fictional protagonists highlights Damon's limitations and limns the extent of his anguished descent into betrayal of the love he has discovered too late.

Further contrasts, and contexts, can be found in two of Wright's contemporaries. These two, although not part of the novel's past, represent part of its future or afterlife, part of the conversation in which *The Outsider* participates. It is well known that Max Eastman, a former Communist, wrote for *The Freeman* a thoughtful, yet puzzlingly mixed, review of *The Outsider* ("Man as a Promise"). Alternately admiring and ridiculing the novel's narrative drive, Eastman is similarly ambivalent about Wright's ideas: although he appears to approve of the attack on Communism, he disparages what he dismisses as "the Existentialist racket" (567). The review illustrates not only Eastman's wish to call attention to the novel without fully endorsing it, but also the unusual nature of the novel's approach to ideas. *The Outsider*, although saturated with ideas, is not propaganda. In the case of propaganda, the primary measure of success is the reader's agreement with the ideas propounded. *The Outsider* is (and is praised for being) compelling without necessarily being persuasive.

Eastman initially sought another reviewer for the novel. On February 27, 1953, Eastman wrote to the novelist Ayn Rand soliciting a review of *The Outsider*, stating, "I have a feeling we might have a like interest in it, since we did the other night on one other momentous question." The night in question was February 13, at a dinner they both attended in New York in honor of J. B. Matthews (Lichtman and Cohen 76). The "other momentous question" in which they were both interested probably pertained to their shared opposition to Communism and their shared enthusiasm for the anti-Communist investigations of J. B. Matthews, who was (like Eastman) an ex-Communist now turned anti-Communist.

Although Rand ultimately did not write the requested review, her final novel, *Atlas Shrugged*, has parallels with *The Outsider*. There is no evidence of a direct influence. From the standpoint of the timing of the novel's composition (as evident in the holograph first draft of *Atlas Shrugged*, where she indicated the starting date of each chapter), it is not plausible to speculate that her contact with *The Outsider* influenced the composition of *Atlas Shrugged*. By February 1953, she had already planned the entire novel, and she was well into writing the third of its three parts. But, as Eastman may have realized, Rand's fiction shares with *The Outsider* an affinity with the fiction of Hugo and Dostoevsky, both of whom, indeed, she admired (*The Romantic Manifesto* 86–7, 107, 153–61). And if we imagine Rand and Wright at work around a circular literary table, there are several possible points of imaginative contact.

One dramatic parallel pertains to the suicide of Eva. A sequence in *Atlas Shrugged* involves an innocent young woman, Cherryl Brooks, who offers her love to a man because she believes the world has wronged him. She ultimately learns that he has deceived her about his true nature, and when she confronts him, he has no answer to her repeated question: "Why didn't you tell me the truth? . . . Why did you lie? Why did you let me think what I thought?" (810). On the longest, and last, night of her life, she considers the personal meaning of his deception and its consequences for her: she sees the world as this man writ large and views this prospect as a fate worse than death. Cherryl's life, like Eva's, is incomprehensible and unbearable after a lover revealed as a liar continues to demand her love.

Houston described as follows Damon's intentions toward Eva: "You'd want to lead her, remake her, save her, and at bottom you'd be wanting, in doing this, to save yourself ... And she was ripe to respond on the same basis; she wanted to *help* you ..." (560). Damon had said to Eva: "Have mercy on me ... Pity me, but not for what has been done to me, but for what I've done to others and myself ... You be my judge; you tell me if I'm to live now ..." (534). Eva's reaction: "She was still as a block of ice. Her eyes stared unseeingly into the shadows of the room" (534). Finally, she "looked at Cross and while she was looking he saw the light go out of her eyes" (535).

In *Atlas Shrugged*, after a plea for an understanding she cannot summon up even if she so desired, Cherryl's "face looked suddenly worn, an odd, aged look that seemed haggard and lost" (804). Her husband, James Taggart, demands her sanction: "His eyes were desperate; she did not know whether he was boasting or begging for forgiveness; she did not know whether this was triumph or terror" (809). He tells her: "I've always been misunderstood and I should have been accustomed to it by now, only I thought that you were different and that I had a chance" (811). He continues: "I'm all alone ... You're all I have" (812). But she tells him she feels fear: "Not fear of what you can do to me, but of what you are" (814). When, in anger, he tells her to go to hell, she reflects upon the hell that her life has become, and seeks death: "I feel blinder than any animal right now, blinder and more helpless. An animal knows who are its friends and who are its enemies, and when to defend itself. It doesn't expect a friend to step on it or to cut its throat" (819–21).

Cherryl believes that her husband's alleged love and demand for understanding is in fact a threat, a threat she cannot escape, and that wherever she walks, the horror will follow her. "There is no place to go, she thought and stumbled on—I can't stand still, nor move much longer—I can neither work nor rest—I can neither surrender nor fight—but this ... *this* is what they want of me, *this* is where they want me ..." (833). "She went on, seeing nothing around her, feeling trapped in a maze with no exit ... No exit ... no exit ... no refuge ... no signals ... no way to tell destruction from safety, or enemy from friend ..." (835).

In *The Outsider*, we do not have access to Eva's consciousness. The tortured thoughts of Rand's Cherryl, however, suggest the unheard voice of Wright's Eva. Through reading Cherryl, we can infer the core and the cause of Eva's despair: Damon is seeking from her a validation that would violate her nature, and, in the name of love, he is attempting to burden her with his own spiritual contradictions. To understand Damon in the way he seeks to be understood would be to condone as well as comprehend, and thus to lose herself. If Eva did what he asked, she would surrender, perhaps irrevocably, her vision and moral independence.

Part Three of *Atlas Shrugged* features another striking parallel with *The Outsider*. The seventh chapter, "This Is John Galt Speaking," contains a 60-page speech. This speech makes clear not only the development of the plot (and, indeed, the narrative depends on a *plot* in the sense of a plan or conspiracy), but also the philosophical principles that underlie that plot. Rand's archival notes for the novel indicate that the hero was to give (at least) two important speeches, one to be delivered over the radio and the other to be delivered while he was in physical jeopardy, confronting a handful of men committed to torturing him. In 1946, she wrote part of the torture-chamber speech. In 1947 and 1948, she made notes for the radio speech then outlined the key points in 1949; she wrote more in 1951, outlined again in 1953, and wrote for two years (1953–5), completing the speech on October 13, 1955. She did not, however, develop a torture-chamber speech—not in her preparatory notes and not in the chapter she ultimately wrote ("The Generator," the ninth chapter of "A is A," Part Three of the novel).

She ultimately decided, in other words, not to place an important philosophical speech in the context of danger and pain. One reason may be that she viewed force as the enemy of thought, not as a stimulus to it. Indeed, as her hero says in the radio speech, "To interpose the threat of physical destruction between a man and his perception of reality, is to negate and paralyze his means of survival . . . Force and mind are opposites" (940). Damon, who condemns the Communist cult and culture of intimidation, has an inkling of this perspective. Yet, when ordered by Menti to talk for his life, he complies. He is articulate, thoughtful, dazzling.

Eastman's review praised this sequence:

> The fifteen-page speech with which Cross Damon stalls and baffles them [the Communist Party central committee] when they get him in a corner, and seem on the point of exterminating him, is a masterpiece of learned reflection. As an essay in the *Freeman* it would provoke arguments to fill the magazine for a year. And what an ingenious way to compel a lazy-minded nation to read an essay! (47)

But is the fear of imminent death an appropriate inspiration for learned reflection? Is the threat of extermination likely to motivate the threatened man to do what Damon does (i.e., to expound his view about the frightening truth revealed by science behind the discarded veils of mysticism)? In Rand's omission of the projected torture-chamber speech, we see that her hero will not talk for his life, will not think under duress. He speaks, instead, at his own time and on his own terms.

Galt's radio speech advocates reason as the basis of a moral code for living on earth. In the words of Galt:

> Whoever you are—you who are alone with my words in this moment, with nothing but your honesty to help you understand—the choice is still open to be a human being, but the price is to start from scratch, to stand naked in the face of reality and, reversing a costly historical error, to declare: "I am, therefore I'll think." (973)

And Damon, in the context of his critique of both Fascism and Communism, advocates using one's honesty to help one understand: "But there is one little thing, it seems to me, that a man owes to himself. He can look bravely at the horrible totalitarian reptile and, while doing so, discipline his dread, his fear and study it coolly, . . . and note down with calmness the pertinent facts" (492). He himself has aspired and struggled to do so. When Menti says that Damon, with his eloquence, should be on the Central Committee, Damon points out what Menti has not grasped: "No. You don't want men in your Party who can think" (493).

In an important sense, of course, every book is what it is, and *The Outsider* is not an imitation of Hugo or Dostoevsky, or a precursor of *Atlas Shrugged*. Damon had asked himself, back in Chicago, if there might not be a community of outsiders: "Were there not somewhere in this world rebels with whom he could feel at home, men who were outsiders not because they had been born black and poor, but because they had thought their way through the many veils of illusion? But where were they? How could one find them?" (35). Perhaps they can be found in that circular room in which the novelists compose their visions, in the plaintive confession of Valjean, who said, "I am not part of the family of men ... I am outside" (1395); in the agonized self-awareness of Raskolnikov, in whose soul a "dark sensation of tormenting, infinite solitude and estrangement suddenly rose to consciousness" (103); and in the principled withdrawal of Galt, who rejected as intolerable the terms of existence in a corrupt world. By reading Wright's first expatriate novel in relation to his nineteenth-century predecessors and his twentieth-century contemporaries, the present article constitutes an attempt to bring *The Outsider* back "in" to a relevant literary context.

Notes

1   The most detailed treatments of *The Outsider* and Dostoevsky are those by Michael F. Lynch, who identifies a number of suggestive parallels in narrative, characterization, and dialogue. Michel Fabre, too, has documented Wright's knowledge of Dostoevsky in *Richard Wright: Books and Writers* (39–40), *The Unfinished Quest of Richard Wright* (84, 170–1, 175), and *The World of Richard Wright* (20–1). Other critical treatments of Wright and Dostoevsky include Widmer, Reed, Fishburn (114), Nisula, Magistrale, Peterson, Bloshteyn, and Cappetti.

Regarding Wright and Hugo, see Margolies on "The Man Who Lived Underground" and the sewer sequence in Hugo's *Les Misérables* (81). Felgar also mentions this novel (157). In *The Unfinished Quest of Richard Wright*, Fabre notes the sewer setting in "The Man Who Lived Underground" (241), but, in his note (574), points out that there is no evidence of Wright's having read *Les Misérables* at that time. Gibson describes a sequence in Wright's unpublished novel as "a pastiche scene" from Hugo's *Notre-Dame de Paris*. The fact that Houston in *The Outsider* is a hunchback, like Quasimodo in *Notre-Dame de Paris* (often translated as *The Hunchback of Notre Dame*), may be more than a mere coincidence. Several contemporary reviews of *Native Son* mentioned Hugo (see, for example, Cooper and McDowell). An anonymous *Newsweek* review of *The Outsider* invoked both Hugo and Dostoevsky ("Wright's Second").

2   An additional text by Dostoevsky may be pertinent here: "A Gentle Spirit," the first-person story of a husband, alone with the lifeless body of a wife who chose suicide rather than live with her husband's lies. Dostoevsky's "A Gentle Spirit" was available in a translation by Constance Garnett (in *The Eternal Husband, and Other Stories* and in *Short Stories of Dostoevsky*), whose translations of other works by Dostoevsky Wright is known to have read and owned; it also appeared in the November 1876 number of Dostoevsky's *Diary of a Writer*, which, according to Bloshteyn, Wright is likely to have read (284). This story, part of the Dostoevsky canon that Ayn Rand read while growing up in Russia, has parallels to the Cherryl subplot in *Atlas Shrugged*, discussed in the present article.

Works cited

Bloshteyn, Maria R. "Rage and Revolt: Dostoevsky and Three African-American Writers." *Comparative Literature Studies* 38.4 (2001): 277–309. Print.

Cappetti, Carla. "Black Orpheus: Richard Wright's 'The Man Who Lived Underground.'" *MELUS* 26.4 (2001): 41–68. Print.

Cooper, Anna J. "Writer Flays 'Native Son'; Would Like Story on Victor Hugo Theme." *Washington Tribune* 17 Aug. 1940: 7. Print.

Damrosch, David. *What is World Literature?* Princeton: Princeton UP, 2003. Print.

Dostoevsky, Fyodor. *Crime and Punishment*. Trans. Richard Pevear and Larissa Volokhonsky. New York: Vintage, 1992. Print. Trans. of *Prestuplenie i Nakazanie*.

—— "A Gentle Spirit: A Fantastic Story." *The Eternal Husband, and Other Stories*. Trans. Constance Garnett. New York: Macmillan, 1917. Also in *Short Stories of Dostoevsky*. Trans. Constance Garnett. New York: Dial, 1946. Print. Trans. of "Krotkaja."

Eastman, Max. Letter to Ayn Rand. Feb. 27, 1953. Ayn Rand Papers, Ayn Rand Archives. Ayn Rand Institute, Irvine.

—— "Man as a Promise." Rev. of *The Outsider*, by Richard Wright. *The Freeman* 4 May 1953: 567–8. Repr. in *Richard Wright: Critical Perspectives Past and Present*. Ed. Henry Louis Gates, Jr., and K. A. Appiah. New York: Amistad, 1993. Print.

Fabre, Michel. *Richard Wright: Books and Writers*. Jackson: UP of Mississippi, 1990. Print.

—— *The Unfinished Quest of Richard Wright*. New York: Morrow, 1973. Print.

—— *The World of Richard Wright*. Jackson: UP of Mississippi, 1985. Print.

Felgar, Robert. *Richard Wright*. New York: Twayne, 1980. Print.

Fishburn, Katherine. *Richard Wright's Hero: The Faces of a Rebel Victim*. Metuchen: Scarecrow, 1970. Print.

Forster, E. M. *Aspects of the Novel*. 1927. New York: Harcourt, 1954. Print.

Gibson, Richard. "Richard Wright's 'Island of Hallucination' and the 'Gibson Affair.'" *Modern Fiction Studies* 51.4 (2005): 896–920. Print.

Hugo, Victor. *Les Misérables*. Trans. Lee Fahnestock and Norman MacAfee, based on C. E. Wilbour's translation. New York: Signet, 1987. Print.

Lichtman, Robert M. and Ronald D. Cohen. *Deadly Farce: Harvey Matusow and the Informer System in the McCarthy Era*. Urbana: U of Illinois P, 2004. Print.

Lynch, Michael F. *Creative Revolt: A Study of Wright, Ellison, and Dostoevsky*. New York: Peter Lang, 1990. Print.

—— "Haunted by Innocence: The Debate with Dostoevsky in Wright's 'Other Novel,' *The Outsider*." *African American Review* 30.2 (1996): 255–66. Print.

Magistrale, Tony. "From St. Petersburg to Chicago: Wright's *Crime and Punishment*." *Comparative Literature Studies* 23.1 (1986): 59–70. Print.

Margolies, Edward. *The Art of Richard Wright*. Carbondale: Southern Illinois UP, 1969. Print.

McDowell, Doris. "Black Joads." Rev. of *Native Son*, by Richard Wright. *Courier-Journal* [Louisville] 10 Mar. 1940, Sunday Magazine: 7. Print.

Nisula, Dasha Culic. "Dostoevski and Richard Wright: From St. Petersburg to Chicago." *Dostoevski and the Human Condition after a Century*. Ed. Alexej Ugrinsky, Frank S. Lambasa, and Valija K. Ozolins. New York: Greenwood, 1986. 163–70. Print.

Peterson, Dale E. "Richard Wright's Long Journey from Gorky to Dostoevsky." *African American Review* 28.3 (1994): 375–87. Print.

Rand, Ayn. *Atlas Shrugged*. 1957. New York: Signet, 1992. Print.

—— *Atlas Shrugged* First Draft. Ayn Rand Papers. Library of Congress, Washington, DC.

—— *Atlas Shrugged* Notes. Ayn Rand Papers, Ayn Rand Archives. Ayn Rand Institute, Irvine.

—— *The Romantic Manifesto: A Philosophy of Literature*. Rev. ed. New York: Signet, 1975. Print.

Reed, Kenneth T. "*Native Son*: An American *Crime and Punishment*." *Studies in Black Literature* 1.2 (1970): 33–4. Print.

Widmer, Kingsley. "The Existential Darkness: Richard Wright's *The Outsider*." *Wisconsin Studies in Contemporary Literature* 1.3 (1960): 13–21. Print.

Wright, Richard. *The Outsider*. New York: Harper Collins, 1993. Print.

"Wright's Second." Rev. of *The Outsider*, by Richard Wright. *Newsweek* 23 Mar. 1953: 113. Print.

7

"A Dramatic Picture … of Woman from Feudalism to Fascism": Richard Wright's *Black Hope*

Barbara Foley

Rutgers University, Newark

In February 1940, Richard Wright sent to his literary agent, Paul Reynolds, the 961-word manuscript of an untitled novel for which the working title was "Slave Market"; he would later title the manuscript "Black Hope." Apologizing for what he acknowledged to be the "over-written and redundant, and too vague and abstract" nature of the text, he noted that its present state was no worse than the "same crude condition" of the original typescript of *Native Son*, which was then on its way to publication. Wright summarized the plot of his new novel as "a dramatic picture … of woman from feudalism to fascism" (February 6, 1940, Richard Wright Papers [hereafter RWP], box 18, folder 292). Only briefly alluded to in the scholarship on Wright, and never reproduced even in excerpted segments, *Black Hope* is indeed an unwieldy novel. It warrants far more attention than it has received, however, and ought to find its way to publication. The novel demonstrates that Wright, who is often viewed as oblivious to gender issues, if not outrightly misogynist, was in fact deeply interested in the condition of women as an issue in its own right as well as in its broader social and political connections with racism, capitalism, and fascism. The novel further illuminates Wright's concerns—as a political thinker, a student of psychology, and a creative artist—in the intensely productive period when he was working on not only *Native Son* but also "The Man Who Lived Underground" and *Twelve Million Black Voices*. In this essay, I will describe what Wright was attempting to accomplish in *Black Hope*; examine the novel's significance in Wright's political and artistic odyssey; and suggest the text's relevance to the mid-twentieth-century Left's attempts to link Marx with Freud in a formulation of the necessary connections between women's liberation, the defeat of fascism, and the fight for egalitarian Communism.[1]

A summary of this complex novel is rendered difficult by the fact that Wright produced not only three different drafts of the first version but also a second version, apparently composed about a year later but left incomplete. The second version, which I will call *Black Hope 2*, begins in North Carolina and features the experiences of Maud Wilson, a light-skinned African American woman who is entrapped by Ed Basin, a trafficker in indentured labor who transports young—and usually illiterate—black women to the urban North, where they are coerced either into low-wage domestic work, prostitution, or some combination of the two. His practice of keeping them indebted, unable to escape his grasp, establishes a clear parallel with the economics of sharecropping. Basin first rapes Maud but then, realizing the value of her skin color, subjects her to arsenic poisoning, which, while nearly killing her, bleaches her skin. Although Maud is deeply ambivalent about her newfound whiteness, after her ordeal, she glimpses herself in a mirror and imagines new possibilities for herself—possibilities that, it is implied, will bring her into conflict with the criminal use that Basin plans to make of her (RWP, box 21, folders 323–7). The manuscript breaks off here. Drawing upon journalistic exposés of the so-called slave markets in the Bronx and Brooklyn, where middle-class housewives would drive to busy intersections seeking domestic labor on a daily or weekly basis, Wright supplemented this information by over 150 interviews of his own with Negro domestic workers. It is to be regretted that Wright did not complete this version of *Slave Market/Black Hope*, since his detailed research had prepared him to write a proletarian novel focusing on the experiences of a segment of the US population—African American women workers—rarely portrayed in the literature of the day.[2]

Because *Black Hope 2* is incomplete, the discussion will focus primarily upon the first version of the novel that Wright sent to Reynolds in early 1940. I will call this text *Black Hope 1* when it is necessary to distinguish between the two versions. Set in the late 1930s—there are a number of references to the military build-up toward impending war—the novel takes as its protagonist Maud (alternatively named Eva) Hampton, clearly an early version of Maud Wilson. Although Maud presumably was born in the South, she is introduced as a sophisticated college graduate (hailing from the University of Chicago) living in Harlem and used to northern urban life. Ailing from overwork and frustrated by her racially glass-ceilinged job as a social worker, however, she decides to lighten her skin by taking arsenic (an entirely voluntary activity in this version), thereby passing over the color line. She does this over the objections of her lover, Freddie—an intellectual, an aspiring writer, and a political radical. Maud is hired to be the housekeeper of an invalid elderly millionaire widower, Cleveland Spencer, who likes to discharge his pistol at the wall across from his bed (the Freudian symbolism is not far to seek). Not paid adequately in this feminized job category, Maud appropriates some of the wages of the still more exploited Ollie Knight, a woman who has been brought North by a Mr. Downy (an early version of the nefarious Basin) to work for a low-wage employment agency. Old Spencer becomes infatuated with Maud. She entices him into promises of marriage and is named as inheritor of his estate; on the night of their first sexual intercourse, she kills him and becomes a rich woman (RWP, box 19, folders 302–5).

But the living is not easy. Maud has to deal with Spencer's insane adult daughter, Lily (Wright's version of the madwoman in the attic), who apparently has lost her mind through witnessing her father's abuse of her mother and his subsequent mistresses. Maud also has to contend with Spencer's lawyer, Henry Beach, who, having discovered that she is a Negro and has murdered the old man, blackmails her. While Maud has no regrets about passing, she struggles with her racial conscience, which is embodied not just in Ollie and Freddie but also in Freddie's deeply Christian mother Clara, who has worked as Spencer's cook for many years and, like the rest of the Negro staff, knows of Maud's racial subterfuge. Also working at the Spencer mansion is Dot, a selfish, somewhat frivolous white woman whom Maud has recruited to take care of Lily (RWP, box 19, folders 306–9; RWP, box 10, folders 310–11).

The plot thickens as Beach gets involved in catastrophic gambling on Wall Street and gradually drains Maud's fortune. Beach's son, Henry Beach, Junior, comes on the scene as a dissolute, alienated, and violent young man who fills the void of his life with petty crime. At first delighting in shooting out streetlamps (the phallic parallel with old Spencer is explicit), Beach Junior moves on to joining a gang and committing a murder, for which he is sentenced to death. His son's impending execution traumatizes Beach Senior, who founds a fascist organization named NAUR (National American Union Rehabilitation) that attempts to co-opt the appeal of proletarian solidarity in support of a Wall Street-financed militaristic movement aimed at taking over large portions of the globe. (Embodying the organization's opportunistic propaganda, the NAUR anthem is titled "Sing a Song of Struggle.") That white women are open to the appeal of NAUR is shown in Dot's eroticized attraction to NAUR's doctrine of "American manhood." NAUR also founds a Harlem chapter whose all-male constituents are drawn by the promise of their serving as the shock troops in an invasion of South America (to which, once it is conquered, Beach secretly plans to deport his black supporters). Since the United States is, Beach asserts, a "nation of minorities," racial doctrines need to be molded to coexist with pluralism. There will be no need for genocide; sectors of the population—"the nigger . . . the kike . . . the pope-lovers . . . the crazy modern women taking jobs from honest men"—will simply be manipulated and turned against one another, leaving NAUR free to amass wealth and prepare for global conquest. Beach even attempts to recruit Freddie to his cause, praising his leadership potential and quoting Stalin to the effect that "Reds [are] the engineers of the human soul" (RWP, box 18, folders 290–1).

Maud is selfish and unprincipled, but even she is repelled by Beach's present activity and future outlook. She had killed, she ponders, because she felt "shunted out of the world" and wanted to get back in; Beach and his associates wanted to kill "not to get back into the world but in order to feel alive." The novel approaches its finale when Maud, refusing to continue bankrolling Beach's schemes, is outed by him as a Negro murderess and commits suicide. Lily, bent on revenge on the male sex, attacks and decapitates Beach, causing the collapse of NAUR. The grieving Freddie goes off to write his novel. It is Ollie who emerges as the hero of *Black Hope 1*, since she becomes an organizer for a multiracial union, Domestic Workers Union Local 567 (a fictional stand-in for Domestic Workers Local 149, which by 1940 had become an active force among New York's superexploited domestic workers). Maud, we learn, has left the remains of her fortune, as well as the Spencer mansion, to the union, so there is a glimmer of light at the end of this otherwise doleful tale (RWP, box 17, folder 289).[3]

*   *   *

Wright was entering new territory in *Black Hope 1* in several ways. Although in "Blueprint for Negro Writing" he had ruthlessly lampooned writers of the Harlem

Renaissance who featured as protagonist members of the Negro middle class, his portraiture of Maud required him to address the ways in which capitalism affects African Americans other than those on the lowest echelons of society. Maud is hardly as comfortably situated as Clare Kendry, the wealthy, thrill-seeking protagonist of Nella Larsen's *Passing*; Maud's actions are motivated largely by economic insecurity. But neither is she caught in the dire poverty that entraps Bessie or Bigger's mother in *Native Son*, or the constrained situation of a proletarian housewife that is the lot of Lil Jackson in *Lawd Today!*—much less, of course, the violent and degraded conditions endured by the women inhabiting the Jim Crow South of *Uncle Tom's Children*. Moreover, as in Larsen's novel—and other novels of the 1910s and 1920s such as James Weldon Johnson's *The Autobiography of an Ex-Colored Man* and Jessie Redmon Fauset's *Plum Bun*—Wright placed front and center the psychological consequences of racial passing. However he might wish to subvert them, then, he was engaging with the conventions accompanying the figure of the tragic mulatto.[4]

Black Hope 1 also shows Wright making his first serious foray into the genre of the novel of ideas. The long conversations between Freddie and Maud, Maud and Beach, and Freddie and Beach display Wright's influence by philosophical novelists from Feodor Dostoevsky to Thomas Mann to André Malraux (whose *Man's Fate* in fact is directly quoted in the novel) and anticipate Cross Damon's debates with his various antagonists in *The Outsider*. Beach discourses at considerable length about the fragmentation and anomie of modern life and couches the appeal of fascism in proto-existentialist terms. Maud consciously crafts her career as an assault on the citadel of white supremacist, male-dominated capitalism. The key to the intellectual energy of *Black Hope*, however, is Wright's idealized (and somewhat long-winded) alter ego, Freddie, who—albeit never directly identified as a Communist—plans to attend an upcoming gathering of the National Negro Congress and expatiates on the connections between and among the "woman question," the "Negro question," the class struggle, and the USSR as well as, more broadly, the human need to assert the value of life in the face of certain death. The obverse of Bigger Thomas and Jake Jackson in many ways, Freddie demonstrates that as early as 1940 Wright was capable of creating an intellectually sophisticated male character who is also a political leftist; he did not need to embrace existentialism and anticommunism in order to invent a character who could dub himself a "rebel" and an "outsider" and talk about the meaning of life. If James Baldwin had encountered Freddie before he wrote his famous critique of Wright in "Everybody's Protest Novel," he might not so readily have dismissed the older writer as incapable of delineating a hero as thoughtful and intelligent as himself.[5]

*   *   *

In the plot synopsis that he conveyed to Reynolds in February 1940, Wright hastened to point out that what he was sending was "*not* a novel with a feminist theme." If by "feminist" he meant a text built around a valorized woman protagonist whose resistance to sexism attracts the reader's sympathy and admiration, this was an accurate statement. Maud, who tries to beat patriarchal capitalism on its own terms, ends up being destroyed by her greed. She is, moreover, less articulate about her own oppression as a woman than is the loquacious Freddie, who sets forth the parallels between women and Negroes as victims of the capitalist drive for profit and power. But the text displays Wright's intense interest in the economic, sexual, and psychological dimensions of sexism. The "slave market" where the black migrant Ollie is sold to the highest bidder is a degraded microcosm of the situation of all the novel's women, from the upwardly mobile African American Maud to the white working-class Dot to the white ruling-class Lily.

Indeed, in a note to the manuscript, Wright meditated on various meanings conveyed by his working title that indicate the broad range of issues he saw embedded in Maud's story. The title signified not only "the status of women in society," he wrote, but also domestic labor—"the most common and hard symbol"—as well as woman as "slave of biology" in her status as "wife and mother." But the title went beyond gender, encompassing "the compulsive role of the outcast, . . . the woman (as man) [who is] a slave of the mental and physical limits of life," as well as the slave market as a "social unit, the voluntary union for living" (RWP, box 21, folder 329). While these vague formulations show that Wright had not quite figured out how to make the various meanings of "slave market" intersect in his narrative, it is evident that the novel was to take the alienation of its female protagonist as a means of getting at fundamental problems in modern life. As Wright remarked in another fragmentary note, the novel would explore, through Maud's act of murder, her "deep and consuming sense of estrangement"; this in turn would symbolize "how man gets cut off from his fellow man because of the 'breaking images' in capitalist society . . . The girl was cut off in the break up of feudal ties, and each new move is an effort to become at home" (RWP, box 21, folder 332). Wright evidently intended for Maud's situation as a woman to figure metonymically in a historical, political, and philosophical commentary on modern alienation.

Wright hardly neglects the racialized nature of Ollie's and Maud's subjection to men. Maud can be successfully blackmailed by Beach because she is passing over the color line, while Ollie, in one particularly horrific scene, is shown being forced to have sexual intercourse with a dog while Downy watches and pleasures himself. But Wright was most interested in the shared features of female experience. According to the biographer Hazel Rowley, Wright, as he worked on the novel, was strongly influenced by his first wife Dhimah Rose Meidman and her mother, two Jewish women who made him "aware that white women shared many of the same experiences as black women" (188). His goal in having Maud exchange racial identities was, Wright wrote to Reynolds, not so much to explore the racial aspects of passing as to find a way to feature "the personality and consciousness of *any* modern woman" (February 6, 1940, RWP, box 21, folder 331)—a comment that, while suggesting Wright's acceptance of the notion that whiteness equals universality, nonetheless indicates his interest in gender in a transracial register. In this context, Ollie's closing transformation into a class-conscious organizer for a multiracial union of female domestic workers takes shape not just as an individual triumph but as an affirmation of the leading role played by African American women "so situated in this system," says Freddie, "that their fight for their rights will be a fight in defense of all women" (RWP, box 18, folder 291). And, perhaps, all people: Wright ended his five-page synopsis of the novel's plot with the remark that his novel was to "reveal in a symbolic manner the potentially strategic position, socially and politically, which women occupy in the world today" (RWP, box 21, folder 329).[6]

Black Hope thus requires that we readjust the lenses through which we view and assess Wright's understanding of the relationship of gender oppression to racism and capitalism. In *Lawd Today!*, Wright treated the male supremacist attitudes of Jake and his friends as central to their entrapment within capitalist ideology: Al's delight in imagining soldiers' freedom to commit rape facilitates his own participation in the strike-breaking militarism of the National Guard, while Jake's view of his female coworkers as "cunts" displaces his rage at his own position in the plantation-style hierarchy of the post office. In *Native Son*, Bigger's economic and social emasculation figures centrally in his violent attack on Gus, his spiraling antagonism toward Mary, and his rape of Bessie. In neither of these novels, however, did Wright allow the reader entry into the thoughts of the women who are used and abused by the male characters. In *Black Hope 1*, Wright may not have featured a praiseworthy protagonist, but, perhaps more significantly, he entered the consciousness of a complex, bold, and intelligent woman who chafes against her confined condition as "a Negro and a woman and a worker" and decides to do something—however misdirected—to change it (RWP, box 17, folder 284). Maud Hampton is, arguably, the most complex woman character to appear in Wright's entire *oeuvre*.[7]

To be sure, in neither of its versions does *Black Hope* show Wright transcending reified gender dualisms of various kinds. Dot and Lily hardly escape the respective stereotypes of airhead and hysteric. Although Freddie insists that men's subordination of women is "conditioned" rather than "natural," in what appear to be valorized assertions, he insistently declares that women are closer to the natural world than men, thus affirming the dualisms he presumably rejects. The scene of Ollie's sexual degradation with the dog encourages a pornographic gaze even as it condemns Downy's vicious appropriation of the young black woman's body. Despite these and other manifestations of abiding sexism, however, in *Black Hope*, Wright was clearly attempting to explore the complexities, material and psychological, of women's oppression. In creating Ollie and Maud, Wright undertook not only to view gendered and raced identities from the standpoint of women but also to anchor this standpoint in an analysis of capitalist political economy. In his awareness of the economics of housekeeping—whether the supervisory work performed by Maud or the hard labor performed by Ollie—he would appear to have been familiar with the contemporaneous leftist discourse about women's reproductive labor that was set forth in such texts as Grace Hutchins's *Women Who Work* and Mary Inman's *In Woman's Defense*.[8] Moreover, his portrait of Maud's conviction that assuming power entails abandoning femininity, as well as of Lily's fear that all men are rapists and Dot's willingness to worship at the shrine of phallic militarism, suggest his acquaintance with such analyses of internalized sexism as were set forth in Rebecca Pitts's 1934 *New Masses* article titled "Women and Communism."

Perhaps the most interesting feature of Wright's engagement with the Left's theorization of women's emancipation consists in Freddie's various comments about the situation of women in the USSR, as well as, more broadly, the necessary connection between women's full emancipation and Communist egalitarianism. Criticizing the limitations of bourgeois feminism, with its fixation on legal equality and voting rights, Freddie proposes that in capitalist society women live under a "dictatorship": their fight for liberation is inseparable from "the global struggle for freedom." Indeed, he posits, "Like [sic] Negroes in this country live, so women live all over the world." Freddie asserts that the view of women as property in capitalist countries shores up the regime of private property both materially and ideologically. The Soviet Union, where "millions have found [the good]," has made significant strides toward women's emancipation. As of yet, however,

> nowhere does the ideology of woman prevail, coexist with that of man, interpenetrate with that of man, fuse with it ... [Only] when we change the structure of society so that the idea and life of woman is interwoven into the warp and woof of our everyday existence ... shot through with woman's modifying intuition ... will the race [not] be narrowed down to just owning things.
>
> (RWP, box 17, folders 284, 288)

In other words, women will attain full freedom only with the abolition of exchange value. Wright's abiding embrace of essentialist gender dualisms thus coincides with a commitment to transcending not just capitalism but also socialism—as an intermediary social formation—in order to achieve a classless social order free of exploitation of all kinds. In its meditation on what such an emancipated future might look like, *Black Hope* is, in some respects, the most radical novel Wright ever wrote.[9]

* * *

While Wright's preoccupation with "the woman question" makes *Black Hope* distinct in his *oeuvre*, the novel's imaginative investigation into the nature of fascism is an equally intriguing feature of the text. In *Lawd Today!, Native Son*, and "How 'Bigger' Was Born," Wright had already evinced his fascination with the possibility that a native-born US fascism could, however paradoxically, appeal to the most disenfranchised and dispossessed segment of the population: African Americans. In this concern, Wright was hardly alone. As early as 1919, the Jamaican-born Leftist W. A. Domingo had warned the Socialist Party that its failure to fight racism would result in antagonizing black workers toward their white counterparts and enlisting them in the ranks of the capitalist class as strikebreakers and thugs. As the Communist movement gained in numbers and influence in the course of the Depression decade, its commitment to fighting for class-based multiracial solidarity was interwoven with its recognition of the links between fascism and Jim Crow, as well as the threat posed to the revolutionary movement by the appeal of Japanese fascism as a challenge to global white supremacy. But most Depression-era scenarios linked the possible growth of black fascism with the anticommunist black nationalism articulated by the Garveyites—Marcus Garvey had, after all, claimed that he and the Universal Negro Improvement Association (UNIA) were the "first fascists"—as well as by various Harlem organizers as Sufi Abdul

Hamid and Randolph Wilson, the latter of whom dubbed himself the "Black Hitler." Although Ralph Ellison's Ras the Exhorter somewhat soft-pedals the anti-Semitism characteristic of these organizers, he conveys a vivid composite portrait of one such black reactionary.[10]

In *Black Hope*, however, Wright pushed the possibilities of black fascism further by postulating that a *white*-organized fascist movement, complete with anti-Semitism *and* anti-black racism, could flourish among the very people against whom it was largely, if not exclusively, targeted. The most famous white Depression-era American writer who had prophetically imagined the growth of a native American fascism—Sinclair Lewis, in his 1935 novel *It Can't Happen Here*—had stipulated that the movement would be so overtly racist (aimed in fact at black re-enslavement) that it would garner no support among its black victims. The only novelist besides Wright who would attempt to treat the phenomenon of a white-led fascist movement with a black popular base was the African American writer Carl Ruthven Offord, whose 1943 novel, *The White Face*, represented Nazi-led organizing as having at least temporary success in Harlem. Evidently, Wright and Offord discerned a fascist potential embedded in black alienation that was inconceivable to Lewis.

Yet Wright's and Offord's portrayals of a white-led black fascism were not without historical plausibility. After all, the premier fascist theorist in the United States during the 1930s, Lawrence Dennis—author of *The Coming American Fascism* and *The Dynamics of War and Revolution*—was a light-skinned black man who had passed over the color line and, in the late 1930s, hobnobbed with Benito Mussolini, Rudolph Hess, Herman Goering, and Josef Goebbels. As the historian Gerald Horne has pointed out, Dennis envisioned an American fascism that would be premised upon smashing the labor movement and conjoining big business with the state, but that would not prominently feature white supremacist doctrine (*Color of Fascism*). Nonetheless, the fact that a man who had seen his family suffer the slings and arrows of Jim Crow racism could theorize that American capitalism would be best served by a state modeled on Nazi Germany speaks volumes about black alienation from American "democracy" during the Depression years. In the closing sections of *Black Hope*, Wright dared to extrapolate what a movement led based on Dennis's goals might look like in the streets of Harlem.[11]

Like a number of other Marxists of his day—the psychologists Reuben Osborn and Wilhelm Reich, the critics Kenneth Burke and Harry Slochower—Wright was absorbed by the project of articulating psychoanalysis with historical materialism. These cultural Marxists agreed that the Left's theorization of fascism as the brutal class rule of finance capital in crisis was adequate to describe its material underpinnings. Indeed, in *Black Hope 1*, Wright makes it clear that fascism is a ruling-class-instigated movement. Not only is Beach a minion of Wall Street, but old Spencer, alert to his class interests in a time of economic crisis, turns out to have been investing for several years in steel production in the expectation—indeed, the hope—that he would profit from the burgeoning armament industry in the coming war. Wright's portrait of NAUR thus adheres to current leftist doctrine about the links between finance and industrial capital, the state, and right-wing mass movements. At the same time, Wright, along with other Marxists working in the spheres of psychology and culture, felt that the psychodynamics of fascism, while hardly autonomous, required understanding in their own right. Wright had previously explored the raced and gendered appeal of fascism to oppressed African Americans. In *Lawd Today!*, Jake's frustrated sexuality is intimately linked with his vision of black warships attacking—indeed, symbolically raping—a helpless (and very white) Statue of Liberty. In *Native Son*, Bigger's attraction to Hitler is presented as integral to his felt need for community. Where the issue of fascism figures marginally in Wright's two earlier novels, however, *Black Hope* allowed him to place the issue of fascism front and center, focusing upon its potential psychological appeal to all sectors of the population—even those whose material interest should lead them to reject it most passionately.

The core of this appeal, Wright proposes, is fascism's function as an antidote—at least an apparent antidote—to alienation. The Beaches, Junior and Senior, most fully exemplify the impulse to fill the inner void with external destruction. The son, nihilistic, overindulged, and undisciplined, organizes a gang that descends into sociopathic violence. The father organizes NAUR in large part out of a need for "something" to lift him out of the "valley of dry bones" that he feels his "life of fragments" has become (RWP, box 17, folder 289). As a servant of Wall Street, he organizes a movement that will advance the global interests of American capitalism; as a hollow man of the modern world, he seeks fullness in the mindless chanting of an apocalyptic mass movement over which he wields demagogic control. The eroticization of aggression plays no small role in compounding the thrill of authoritarian power. Beach Junior's obsessive shooting out the globes of lampposts, like the millionaire Spencer's spraying bullets on his bedroom wall, displays the link between phallic propulsion and fascist domination for both the young man and the old. Dot's attraction to NAUR's militarized masculinism displaces and sublimates her sexual longings, returning her to a state of "clapping her hands like a baby" (RWP, box 18, folder 280). While these patently Freudianized portraits are somewhat cartoonish in their exaggerated outlines, they amply illustrate Wright's preoccupation with the psychological soil where the seeds of fascism can germinate and take root.

Alienation is not the preserve solely of the novel's neurotic antagonists, however. Maud decides to cross the color line not just because she seeks a more comfortable life but also because she feels the need to be "in unison with others"; she identifies with male power because otherwise "she was an atom flying about in cold space." Freddie views himself and Maud as "outsiders" to mainstream political and cultural life. Indeed, his proposition that men need the otherness presumably embodied in women reflects his sense of separation from himself; his romantic yearning for Maud expresses a desire at once concretely fulfillable and abstractly infinite. But while fascism supplies one answer to alienated modernity, communism supplies another. Fundamentally at issue in the debate between Freddie and Beach is the type of collectivity that will satisfy the human hunger for a meaningful social identity. Beach holds that NAUR, with its deft scapegoating of "others," answers the human need for recognition and affirmation. Freddie, while acknowledging that Beach, in his "queer, warped way" was reacting against the reduction of life to "bread grubbing," declares that he is "for workers taking power and reconstructing life on earth" because only in this way will humanity find meaning in life (RWP, box 17, folder 287; RWP, box 18, folder 291).

While *Black Hope* resembles *The Outsider* in its long disquisitions over communism and fascism, being and nothingness, its political standpoint is thus the obverse of that proposed in the 1953 novel. For *The Outsider*, articulating the thesis of "two totalitarianisms," groups fascism and communism as psychological/authoritarian twins, to be jointly counterposed with the existential doctrine of individual freedom espoused by Cross Damon and his double/nemesis, Ely Houston. These two characters' joint status as "outsiders" derives from their shared antipathy to authoritarian group-think. *Black Hope*, by contrast, pits communism *against* fascism. Freddie and Maud are "outsiders" because they refuse to settle for the restricted state of existence that is required by capitalist reality: they seek rather than flee from a meaningful collective identity. In *Black Hope*, both systems of social organization speak to the loneliness and dislocation experienced by modern humanity, but one contains the potential to negate and sublate alienation, while the other promises a descent into atavism and still greater existential loneliness.[12]

The somewhat melodramatic trajectory of the plot of *Black Hope* limns Wright's conviction—at least in the early 1940s—that a native-born American fascism could not succeed in attracting more than passing support from ordinary people. The ranks of NAUR's soldiers disband once the charismatic leader is killed; the easily seduced Dot is left without a great leader to follow. The determining roles played by most of the novel's women, moreover, indicate Wright's positive estimate of women's potential leadership in defeating a native US fascism. It is Maud's refusal to go along with Beach's fascist project that puts him into a tailspin. It is the "crazy" Lily who then murders the demagogic Beach, leading one to wonder whether she is in fact so crazy after all. And it is the proletarian Ollie who ends up taking over the Spencer mansion and turning it into a site of women workers' collective resistance to exploitation. The estimable Freddie, by contrast, is relegated to the margins of the action by the novel's end. Women may be drawn into the fascist web, it seems, but they will not remain there. Indeed, the pivotal actions performed by Maud, Lily, and Ollie in the plot of *Black Hope* suggest the rationale for Wright's chosen title: if the "hope" of all oppressed people consists in the egalitarian future that Freddie imagines, and if black people are to be principal articulators and agents of that hope, then women—whose emancipation is, after all, contingent upon "the global struggle for freedom"—will figure centrally in this liberatory project.

We will recall Wright's statement to Reynolds that he wished his novel-in-progress to "reveal in a symbolic manner the potentially strategic position, socially and politically, which women occupy in the world today." Women were—at least "potentially"—the vanguard of antifascism. *Black Hope* reveals a radical appreciation of women's positioning in the struggle for a better world that must be taken into account in overall assessments of the politics and ethics of one of the most important revolutionary writers of the past century.

Notes

1 While Reynolds advised Wright to cut his original manuscript by 50 percent and to undertake extensive revisions, he encouraged the novelist, opining that *Black Hope* was "a larger and deeper book than *Native Son*" (Reynolds to Wright, April 13, 1942, qtd. in Rowley 264). Wright continued to work on *Black Hope* on and off for many years, substantially abandoning it when he started working hard on *Black Boy (American Hunger)* in 1943, but dropping it "for once and for all" only in 1948 (Rowley 354). The *locus classicus* of feminist commentary targeting Wright's negative attitudes toward women is Maria K. Mootry's "Bitches, Whores and Woman Haters: Archetypes and Typologies in the Art of Richard Wright." See also Green. Because of stringent prohibitions surrounding the Wright estate, I am constrained in my ability to quote directly from the manuscript; paraphrase and summary will have to bear much of the burden of my commentary on the text.

2 The "Slave Market" at the corner of 167th Street and Jerome Avenue in the Bronx was first exposed by Ella Baker and Marvel Cooke in "The Bronx Slave Market." By 1940, the many such sites of labor exchange had become the object of a government investigation, the report of which is among Wright's notes for his novel (RWP, box 21, folder 332). While Wright appears to have completed *Black Hope 1* before he left for Mexico in March 1940, he evidently worked on *Black Hope 2* while south of the border, since he wrote to Ralph Ellison from Mexico requesting assistance in tracking down information about the conditions of domestic workers in New York. Ellison sent back the municipal report and the name of a contact, as well as his own observations on the conjunction of domestic labor with prostitution; "Hope this is food for your imagination," he wrote (Ellison to Wright, April 14, 1940, RWP, box 97, folder 1314). See also Ellison to Wright, April 22, 1940; Wright to Ellison, March 23, 1940; and Wright to Ellison, n.d. (Ralph Ellison Papers, box I:76). A number of Wright's interviews detailed sexual harassment of black maids and cooks by white husbands/fathers; this material evidently supplied the basis of Wright's comedic short story, "Man of All Work," which treats a black man who "passes" as a black female housekeeper and is subjected to the sexual aggression of his white male employer.

3 The five-page synopsis of the plot of *Black Hope 1* that Wright sent to Reynolds corresponds with the manuscript in most of the particulars about Maud as inheritor of Spencer's estate, but it contains very little about Beach and NAUR—material that must have been added to later drafts (RWP, box 21, folder 329). An addendum to the synopsis added still more murders—including Dot's killing Lily and Maud's choking Clara to death—as well as a bizarre scene in which Freddie sees Maud's body "turning back to her old color now" after she has committed suicide (RWP, box 21, folder 331).

4 For more on racial passing and hybridity in novels of the Harlem Renaissance, see Kawash and Sherrard-Johnson.

5 In his February 6, 1940 letter to Reynolds, Wright wrote that he intended to "cut down . . . the long tirade of Freddie," as well as "insert a foreshortened flashback of Maud's early life" (RWP, box 18, folder 292). At the 1936 National Negro Congress, Wright chaired a session on "Negro Writers and Artists in the Changing Social Order"; he reported in *New Masses* that the Congress had sparked "new hope" for African Americans ("Two Million Black Voices" 15).

6 The scene in which Ollie is abused by the man with the dog is based upon one of Wright's interviews with domestic workers (RWP, box 21, folder 332).

7 For more on the links between emasculation, sexism, and black male disempowerment in Wright's fiction, see Dawahare.

8 Inman's book, which would spark a significant intra-party debate in the 1940s over whether or not housework should qualify as "productive" labor, was serially published in the Communist Party's *People's Daily World* in 1939 and, according to Kate Weigand, was "used in Communist Party schools around the country . . . as a textbook in their courses on the woman question" (36). Michel Fabre indicates that Wright owned a copy of Inman's book (78).

9 For contemporaneous leftist commentaries on the situation of women in the Soviet Union, see Winter and Halle.

10 For more on leftist warnings of right-wing black reactions to US racism, see Thompson; Hill; Horne, *Race War!*, especially "War/Race" (105–27); and Gilroy, especially "Black Fascists" (231–7).

11 I examine the connection between Lawrence Dennis, *Invisible Man*'s Rinehart, and *Juneteenth*'s Bliss/Sunraider in *Wrestling with the Left: The Making of Ralph Ellison's* Invisible Man.

12 While scholars disagree about the nature and extent of Wright's embrace of existentialism in *The Outsider*, there is general accord about his endorsement of Hannah Arendt's thesis of "two totalitarianisms" and his identification with the figure of the embattled, individualistic "outsider." See Atteberry.

Works cited

Atteberry, Jeffrey. "Entering the Politics of the Outside: Richard Wright's Critique of Marxism and Existentialism." *Modern Fiction Studies* 51.4 (2005): 873–95. Print.

Baker, Ella and Marvel Cooke. "The Bronx Slave Market." *Crisis* Nov. 1935: 330–1, 340. Print.

Baldwin, James. "Everybody's Protest Novel." *Notes of a Native Son.* 1955. *Collected Essays.* Ed. Toni Morrison. New York: Library of America, 1998. 11–18. Print.

Burke, Kenneth. "The Rhetoric of Hitler's 'Battle.'" 1939. *The Philosophy of Literary Form: Studies in Symbolic Action.* New York: Vintage, 1941. 191–220. Print.

Dawahare, Anthony. *Nationalism, Marxism, and American Literature between the Wars: A New Pandora's Box.* Jackson: UP of Mississippi, 2003. Print.

Dennis, Lawrence. *The Coming American Fascism.* New York: Harper, 1936. Print.

—— *The Dynamics of War and Revolution.* New York: Weekly Foreign Letter, 1940. Print.

Ellison, Ralph. *Invisible Man.* 1947. New York: Vintage, 1980. Print.

—— *Juneteenth: A Novel.* New York: Vintage, 1999. Print.

—— Papers. Library of Congress, Washington, DC.

Fabre, Michel. *Richard Wright: Books and Writers.* Jackson: UP of Mississippi, 1990. Print.

Fauset, Jessie Redmon. *Plum Bun: A Novel without a Moral.* 1929. Boston: Beacon, 1990. Print. Black Women Writers Series.

Foley, Barbara. *Wrestling with the Left: The Making of Ralph Ellison's* Invisible Man. Durham: Duke UP, 2010. Print.

Gilroy, Paul. *Against Race: Imagining Political Culture beyond the Color Line.* Cambridge: Belknap P of Harvard UP, 2000. Print.

Green, Tara T. "The Virgin Mary, Eve, and Mary Magdalene in Richard Wright's Novels." *CLA Journal* 46.2 (2002): 168–93. Print.

Halle, Fannina. *Women in Soviet Russia*. Trans. Margaret M. Green. London: Routledge, 1933. Print.

Hill, Robert A., comp. and ed. *The FBI's RACON: Racial Conditions in the United States during World War II*. Boston: Northeastern UP, 1995. Print.

Horne, Gerald. *The Color of Fascism: Lawrence Dennis, Racial Passing, and the Rise of Right-Wing Extremism in the United States*. New York: New York UP, 2006. Print.

—— *Race War! White Supremacy and the Japanese Attack on the British Empire*. New York: New York UP, 2004. Print.

Hutchins, Grace. *Women Who Work*. New York: International Publishers, 1934. Print.

Inman, Mary. *In Woman's Defense*. Los Angeles: Committee to Organize the Advancement of Women, 1940. Print.

Johnson, James Weldon. *The Autobiography of an Ex-Colored Man*. New York: Penguin, 1990. Print.

Kawash, Samira. *Dislocating the Color Line: Identity, Hybridity, and Singularity in African-American Narrative*. Stanford: Stanford UP, 1997. Print.

Larsen, Nella. *Passing*. New York: Modern Library, 2002. Print.

Lewis, Sinclair. *It Can't Happen Here*. New York: Collier, 1935. Print.

Malraux, André. *Man's Fate (La Condition Humaine)*. Trans. Haakon M. Chevalier. New York: Modern Library, 1934. Print.

Mootry, Maria K. "Bitches, Whores and Woman Haters: Archetypes and Typologies in the Art of Richard Wright." *Richard Wright: A Collection of Critical Essays*. Ed. Richard Macksey and Frank E. Moorer. Englewood Cliffs: Prentice-Hall, 1984. 117–27. Print.

Offord, Carl Ruthven. *The White Face*. New York: McBride, 1943. Print.

Osborn, Reuben. *Freud and Marx: A Dialectical Study*. New York: Equinox Co-Operative P, 1937. Print.

Pitts, Rebecca. "Women and Communism." *New Masses* February 19, 1934: 14–16, 20. Print.

Reich, Wilhelm. *The Mass Psychology of Fascism*. Trans. Vincent R. Carfagno. 1942. 3rd edn. New York: Farrar, 1970. Print.

Rowley, Hazel. *Richard Wright: The Life and Times*. New York: Holt, 2001. Print.

Sherrard-Johnson, Cherene. *Portraits of the New Negro Woman: Visual and Literary Culture in the Harlem Renaissance*. New Brunswick: Rutgers UP, 2007. Print.

Slochower, Harry. *No Voice Is Wholly Lost: Writers and Thinkers in War and Peace*. New York: Creative Age P, 1945. Print.

Thompson, Mark Christian. *Black Fascisms: African American Literature and Culture between the Wars*. Charlottesville: U of Virginia P, 2007. Print.

Weigand, Kate. *Red Feminism: American Communism and the Making of Women's Liberation*. Baltimore: Johns Hopkins UP, 2001. Print.

Winter, Ella. *Red Virtue: Human Relations in the New Russia*. New York: Harcourt, 1933. Print.

Wright, Richard. *Black Boy (American Hunger)*. 1944. New York: HarperPerennial, 1993. Print.

—— "Blueprint for Negro Writing." *New Challenge* 2.2 (1937): 53–65. Repr. in *African American Literary Theory: A Reader*. Ed. Winston Napier. New York: New York UP, 2000. 45–53. Print.

—— "How 'Bigger' Was Born." *Native Son*. New York: Perennial, 1993. 505–40. Print.

—— *Lawd Today!* 1963. Boston: Northeastern UP, 1993. Print.

—— "Man of All Work." *Eight Men*. 1961. New York: HarperPerennial, 2008. 109–54. Print.

—— "The Man Who Lived Underground." *Eight Men*. 1961. New York: HarperPerennial, 2008. 19–84. Print.

—— *Native Son*. 1940. New York: Perennial, 1993. Print.

—— *The Outsider*. 1953. New York: Perennial, 2003. Print.

—— Papers. James Weldon Johnson Collection, Yale Collection of American Literature. Beinecke Rare Book and Manuscript Library, Yale University, New Haven.

—— *Twelve Million Black Voices*. 1941. New York: Basic, 2008. Print.

—— "Two Million Black Voices." *New Masses* February 25, 1936: 15. Print.

—— *Uncle Tom's Children*. 1936. New York: Perennial, 2008. Print.

Part Three

Wright's Other Destinies: Gothicism and the Neo-Baroque

8

"Forged in Injustice": The Gothic Motif in the Fiction of Ernest Hemingway and Richard Wright

Charles Scruggs
University of Arizona

"We live in a time," said Richard Wright in "Blueprint for Negro Writing," "when the majority of the most basic assumptions of life can no longer be taken for granted. Tradition is no longer a guide. The world has grown huge and cold" (1388). This modernist theme of what Georg Lukács has called "transcendental homelessness" explains why Wright would be drawn to the fiction of Ernest Hemingway (41). In different ways, both American writers confronted and articulated the "nada" of existence in Hemingway's "A Clean, Well-Lighted Place" (*Complete Short Stories* 291), and both looked for a place of refuge in a "cold" world. Hemingway would find his clean, well-lighted place in the post-World War I cafés in Paris in which he wrote his stories, or on the big two-hearted river that helped restore Nick Adams to psychic health after the trauma of the war. For Wright, his clean, well-lighted place would be a room in a Memphis boarding house in which he read the books recommended by H. L. Mencken, books "stolen" from the library because literacy and subterfuge would be his only weapons in a war waged against him by the American South (*Black Boy* 246–51). It would be the writers of those books that would give the young Wright a sense of himself and a sense that he was not alone, that there were others in America who fought the good fight.

When we come to think of the "white" literary influences upon Wright, Hemingway is not an author who immediately comes to mind. We would certainly put others before him: Theodore Dreiser, Sinclair Lewis, and James T. Farrell among the realists and literary naturalists, and Dostoevsky, Gertrude Stein, John Dos Passos, and James Joyce among the modernists. But in an interview, Wright would single out Hemingway as a modernist whose presence is too obvious to be ignored: "I like the work of Hemingway, of course. Who does not?" (Kinnamon and Fabre 10).

What exactly did Wright "like" about Hemingway? One theme that connected the two writers is expressed by Hemingway's famous remark that "writers are forged in injustice as a sword is forged" (*Green Hills* 71), and, as Hemingway's metaphor of the "sword" suggests, warfare is a central concern in the fiction of both men. Growing up in Mississippi for Wright was comparable to Hemingway's experiences in World War I, but that similarity also links them to a specific American literary tradition. Malcolm Cowley said of Hemingway in 1944 that contrary to the popular belief that he wrote within the realist or naturalist tradition, Hemingway should be placed in the company of "Poe and Hawthorne and Melville," those "haunted and nocturnal writers" of American literature (317). Cowley's observation finds an echo in Wright's memorable words at the end of his essay "How 'Bigger' Was Born": "We have in the oppression of the Negro a shadow athwart our national life dense and heavy enough to satisfy even the gloomy broodings of a Hawthorne. And if Poe were alive, he would not have to invent horror, horror would invent him" (*Native Son* 540). It is the Gothic motif in Hemingway that fascinated Wright, especially its manifestation in three different but related ways: the precarious or unstable nature of the "normal" world, the sudden eruption of a horrific past into the present (with the consequence of things rapidly falling apart), and, finally, "a certain persistence of *strangeness* in the reality described" (Punter 404; Botting 11; Goddu 26; Lloyd-Smith 136). These themes appear often in Hemingway's fiction, as they do in Wright's, but Wright would add a racial dimension to Hemingway's preoccupation with the themes of dread, isolation, and loneliness.

As Wright's biographers tell us (Fabre, *Unfinished Quest* 176; Rowley 158), Wright was reading Hemingway's short stories before he wrote *Native Son*, but there is considerable intertextual evidence that Hemingway's great short-story cycle *In Our Time* helped Wright structure his own short-story collection *Uncle Tom's Children*. "Indian Camp" is the first story in *In Our Time* just as "Big Boy Leaves Home" is the introductory story of *Uncle Tom's Children*, and both involve a pastoral setting that is changed radically by an unexpected Gothic moment. For the adolescent Nick, that moment is the grotesque suicide of the Indian husband of the woman who gives birth, and for Wright's Big Boy, it is the sudden appearance of a white woman at the Edenic swimming hole that results in the shooting death of two friends and the lynching of another. Both stories involve a witness, a child or adolescent, who will be permanently scarred by what he has experienced. But the relationship between the two stories is even more explosive.

Wright had earlier used the phrase "*complex simplicity*" in "Blueprint for Negro Writing" to define the modernist mode (1385), and although he named a number of modernists, including Hemingway, who shared this quality, he undoubtedly had Hemingway's minimalist style in mind, especially his famous statement in *Death in the Afternoon* that came to be known as the "ice-berg theory." Hemingway had observed that a good writer "can omit things that he knows" and the story will be even stronger because what remains unstated and silent is ominously present. "The dignity of movement of an ice-berg," he observed, "is due to only one-eighth of it being above water" (*Death* 192). In a recent article, Cedric Gael Bryant has brilliantly called attention to the Titanic effect that a hidden iceberg has in "Big Boy Leaves Home." Bryant does not mention Hemingway, but what he says about the "vertiginous excess of meaning" unleashed by the sudden presence of a white woman at the forbidden swimming hole is precisely the kind of effect Hemingway had in mind. The seemingly innocent moment "is punishable" for the adolescent boys "in unspeakable ways—beatings, public humiliation, adjudicated fines and/or imprisonment, and greater still, 'their' crime summons the specter of family suffering, loss of property, and death" (542–3). So too Hemingway's Nick experiences emotions that he will not be able to process until much later—the relationship between love and death, the history of American genocide against Native Americans, the bond between father and son—but one thing does separate Nick from Big Boy. Nick leaves the Indian camp in the dawn for home with the exhilarating feeling (albeit delusory) that "he would never die" (*In Our Time* 19), whereas Big Boy flees home in the dawn, "his intestines . . . drawing into a tight knot" (*Uncle Tom's Children* 275).

In Hemingway's stories, unexpected violence or a radical change in circumstances can suddenly tumble the "normal" world into nightmare. In *In Our Time*, Nick Adams in "The Battler" thinks he sees a loving relationship between a nurturing black man and a battered fighter, but the focus suddenly shifts to another kind of relationship, that of predator to prey, and Nick is not sure what he has seen. As James Smethurst notes in his excellent article on *Native Son*, one key Gothic "convention" is the "terror of incomprehension" (34). What Nick does not understand is that his "incomprehension" is tied to a Gothic past that "'weighs like a nightmare on the brain of the living'" (Smethurst 31). In "The Battler," an African American named Bugs travels the country with Ad Francis, a crazed ex-boxing champion whose face looks "like putty" (*In Our Time* 55). The two become a grotesque parody of Jim and Huck, the black Bugs seemingly looking out for the demented Ad, but the Gothic element occurs when Bugs has to whack Ad over the head with a blackjack to keep him from assaulting Nick. Hidden behind Bugs's "polite" behavior may be the sinister enjoyment of brutalizing a helpless Ad, a reversal of the master and slave relationship of American history. The ambiguity of Bugs's character and Ad's brutalization, first in the ring and now in the present, will haunt Nick for the rest of his days.

That ambiguity, of course, goes into Wright's Gothic portrayal of Bigger Thomas in his famous novel *Native Son*. At the end of the novel, Max's "eyes were full of terror" as he listens to Bigger's unapologetic defense of life. Bigger tells his lawyer that "what I killed for, I *am*! . . . What I killed for must've been good! . . . I didn't know I was really alive in this world until I felt things hard enough to kill for 'em" (501). Refusing to repent and defining himself through violence, Bigger is both a monster and distinctly human—he, like Bugs, wants to be more than a servant. Moreover, both refused to be defined as a "Negro" character. They remain mercurial from beginning to end, something that shocks both Max and Nick alike. Although Bigger makes a gesture toward reconciliation at the novel's end ("Tell Jan hello"), what remains is a Gothic portrayal of the African American character that eludes easy stereotypes. Ironically, Bigger has been defined by two views of the past: the nightmare of history and the past that he will not be a slave to. At the novel's end, Bigger is a moral monster who has reinvented himself in the great American tradition—he's a true "native son."

In his article on *Native Son*, Smethurst calls attention to the alarm clock whose sudden, grating sound opens the novel. Smethurst notes that instead of the clock signifying the beginning of a day that will end, it expresses a "cyclical journey" (36) that has been, and will be, repeated by other Biggers. Wright's "Long Black Song" is another story in *Uncle Tom's Children* that echoes Smethurst's point. Set in the pastoral South, the story contains a line that could serve as an ironic epigraph to many Hemingway stories. The traveling white salesman from Chicago wants to sell Sarah a "clock," a clock built into a "graphophone." Sarah tells him that she has no need of a clock, that the rhythms of her day do not require one, but the salesman is insistent: "I don't see how in the world anybody can live without time" (*Uncle Tom's Children* 108). The salesman's conception of "time" is commensurate with his field of study at school when he returns to Chicago: "science." Puzzled by a word she's never heard, she asks him what "science" is. His answer is a model of Enlightenment naïveté: "It's about why things are as they are" (110). In both Hemingway's and Wright's fiction, not only do things never stay as they are, they never are "as they are" in the first place. In this case, Freud's "uncanny," as many critics of the Gothic have noted, is relevant to things not being "as they are" or staying put "as they are." Freud's *heimlichkeit* as "the familiar" is also tied to the root word "family" (Edwards xxv) and the boundaries implied by that word are obvious—home, father, mother—concepts that are seemly clear and distinct, but, as Jerrold Hogle and Justin D. Edwards have noted, the "return of the repressed familiar" in "external, repellant, and *un*familiar forms" threatens not only the stability of the self but the stability of place (Hogle 6, 15; Edwards xxv). In Hemingway's story "My Old Man," the adolescent narrator discovers that his father, a jockey who was involved with a gambling syndicate, is unable to escape a past that erupts into the present with a vengeance and kills him. The child must not only deal with the shattered image of his father, but the story ends with a line that could stand as a theme of "primordial dissolution" (Hogle 11) in both Hemingway's and Wright's fiction: "Seems like when they get started they don't leave a guy nothing" (*In Our Time* 129).

Leaving "a guy" with "nothing" is a ubiquitous theme in Hemingway. "A Clean, Well-Lighted Place," "In Another Country," "A Way You'll Never Be" are just a few examples of the presence in Hemingway's fiction of that Gothic motif, but it also occurs in Wright's fiction when he seems to be looking over his shoulder at Hemingway. One the clearest examples of Hemingway's influence on Wright occurs in one of his best stories in *Uncle Tom's Children*: "Down By the Riverside." In that story, Wright rewrites the famous retreat from Caporetto in *A Farewell to Arms*. In Hemingway's novel, the retreat begins orderly and ends in confusion, chaos, and terrifying absurdity. Frederic Henry's own men are killed by fellow Italians, and the self-appointed "battle police" think him a deserter or a German disguised as an Italian and are going to summarily execute him without a trial. Jumping into a river, Henry escapes, making "a separate peace" with the war (222, 243). Wright's protagonist, Mann—he has no first name—is not so lucky. Caught in a monstrous Mississippi flood (probably that of 1927), Mann finds himself in a world whose spatial dimensions are completely distorted. As he tries to get his pregnant wife to a hospital, an allusion perhaps to the ending of *A Farewell to Arms*, he takes a boat that his brother has stolen, kills its owner in self-defense, and embarks on a journey through sheets of rain, floating houses, and an unrecognizable landscape. Mann "had," Wright says, "the feeling that he was in a dream" (*Uncle Tom's Children* 89). The dream turns into nightmare as his wife dies before she can give birth, and he is discovered by soldiers to be the killer of the white man who owned the boat. He is murdered by the soldiers "down by the riverside," an ironic commentary on Henry's escape from the battle police and on the song in which war will be made "no more" (an allusion perhaps to Hemingway's title). As in Hemingway's *A Farewell to Arms*, laying down sword and shield is an illusion. Catherine and Henry escaped the war to Switzerland but not the mortality that comes with being alive. Henry walks back home "in the rain" (332). Mann dies in it.

Hemingway's fiction would find its way into *Native Son*. Wright's graphic description of Bigger severing Mary's head to fit her into the furnace becomes a grotesque illustration of her well-intentioned remark to Bigger of wanting "to *see*" how Negroes "live" (79). Her dismembered body is squeezed into a furnace the size of Bigger's family's "kitchenette." The same grim irony exists in Hemingway's story "An Alpine Idyll" in which a woodsman, living alone in the Swiss mountains in the dead of winter, puts his dead wife in a shed, props up her frozen body against a wall, and uses her mouth as a place to hang his lantern (*Complete Short Stories* 262–6).

Human isolation results in the Gothic grotesque, a situation that will be repeated in Wright's story "The Man Who Killed a Shadow." Saul, Wright's protagonist, grows up in a world in which white people are as unreal to him as he is to them. They are simply "shadows." Saul moves from job to job as in a dream, but one day he becomes a janitor in a cathedral, one that has a library. His placid life might have gone on forever except for an unexpected encounter with a white female librarian who comes on to him but also insults him and denies her sexual advances. Saul kills her simply to shut her up. He then "propped her clumsily against a wall" (*Eight Men* 165), as Hemingway's Alpine peasant propped up his wife, while he cleaned up the blood: "He had been trained to keep floors clean, just as he had been trained to fear shadows" (165). Wright takes Hemingway's Gothic theme of human isolation and places it within a racial context. The librarian's death is no more real to Wright's nameless protagonist than is a "shadow," a play upon the African American as "spook." The story asks the question: Who is the "spook" now?

As in Hemingway, Gothic dread permeates Wright's fiction. In Wright's last published novel *The Long Dream*, Fishbelly says of a white man that his "father had come to America and had found a dream," whereas Fishbelly "had been born in America and found a nightmare" (380). For Wright, a "nightmare" was a bad dream that took a material form that in Wright's case expressed the terror of American history (Sedgwick 136). That terror could be the "Southern Night" in *Black Boy*, "the terror from which I fled" (257) or the "hysterical terror" felt by Bigger in Mary's bedroom when Mary's mother opens the door. It was as though "he were falling from a great height in a dream. A white blur was standing by the door, silent, ghostlike" (*Native Son* 97).

The nightmare of the past erupting into the present at any time occurs in Hemingway's great short story "The Killers," as Nick's life is changed forever when two hired gangsters from the city walk into a small town diner. George, the manager of the diner, tries to deflect the potential violence of the two Alpha males upon Sam the cook. When asked by one of them who's in the back, George responds not by saying Sam's name or "the cook" but "the nigger" (*Complete Short Stories* 217). It is that racial epithet that links Sam with the Swede, the fugitive that the gangsters are going to kill for some unexplained crime. When Nick tries to warn him, the Swede says, as though he is a runaway slave, that he is "through with all that running around" and waits patiently for death (221). Nick's "education" is brutal, sudden, and grotesque. He learns that death comes unexpectedly in all forms, as urban thugs who dress like fops, and that people on the run give up for no discernible reason. Significantly, he learns as well that man dies alone, a Hemingway theme that finds its way into Wright's masterpiece, *The Outsider*.

In that novel, Wright deliberately alludes to Harry Morgan's dying words in Hemingway's *To Have and Have Not*: "One man alone ain't got . . . No matter how a man alone ain't got no bloody fucking chance" (225). In *The Outsider*, a dying Cross Damon tells Ely Houston that "the search can't be done alone . . . Never alone . . . alone a man is nothing" (585). Wright clearly had Harry in mind when he wrote the final scene in *The Outsider*. In death, both men struggle to find words to articulate their lives but can do so only in broken sentences. In his unpublished review of *To Have and Have Not*, Wright saw Hemingway's Harry as a member of the inarticulate working class, something that reflected both a strength and weakness in the novel. Hemingway, he said, did not want to "falsify" Harry, for "an intellectual Harry Morgan discussing the obscure causes of individual loneliness and isolation in America would simply not ring true" (Fabre, *Books and Writers* 207–8). However, making Harry inarticulate forced Hemingway to write about the rich from an outside perspective, thereby failing to fuse the novel into an organic whole. The problem that Wright saw in Harry Morgan he sought to solve in *Native Son*. By including the articulate Max into the novel's third section, Wright gives us two interpretations of the meaning of Bigger's life. Bigger struggles to find an authentic voice to define his own life, and Max attempts to put that life into a larger intellectual and political context.

In the opening of *To Have and Have Not*, Harry is working hard to be upwardly mobile. He owns his own boat, makes a living taking rich people out fishing, and refuses an offer of three thousand dollars—because it is too "risky"—to smuggle Cuban revolutionaries to the United States. Harry begins on a downward spiral, however, when one of the wealthy skips out without paying his bill. In desperation, he not only takes risks but murders, first killing Mr. Singe, a corrupt businessman, and then losing his arm and his boat to the police attempting to smuggle booze from Havana to Key West. From this point on, the odds are against him, and he dies gallantly (but futilely), killing four bank-robbing Cubans who plan to double-cross him when they reach Cuba.

This downward spiral needs to be kept in mind when we hear Harry's dying words: "No matter how a man alone ain't got no bloody fucking chance." These lines echo a famous passage in *A Farewell to Arms* when Henry says that "you did not know what it was about. You never had time to learn. They threw you in and told you the rules and the first time they caught you off base they killed you" (327). *To Have and Have Not* is less about social conditions during the Depression, despite Hemingway's satire on the rich, than it is about the thin line between "having" and "not having." Harry's "no matter how" suggests that nothing anyone does—no matter how one tries to plan his life—will save a person from being killed if one small thing goes wrong, as things have a tendency to do.

In *The Outsider*, Wright created an intellectual Harry Morgan in Cross Damon who is self-educated despite his job sorting mail in a post office in Chicago, thus making Cross an outsider who is intellectually aware of his condition but who, driven by demons, is helpless to change his fate. On the surface, Cross's life is quite different from Harry's. At the beginning of the novel, he is caught in a network of social relationships—a vengeful wife, a calculating mistress, a dead-end job—that threatens to suffocate him. Finding himself in a freak train accident, he is mistaken for another man, and in the classic American pattern, reinvents himself in a new city (New York) with a new identity. However, starting from scratch does not give him a better or different life. He lies, murders, and betrays to preserve the self he has created. Ironically, he has not escaped the past at all, first murdering an old friend in Chicago to preserve his new identity and then betraying a woman, appropriately named Eva, who might have given him what he had been searching for all along, a sense of belonging, a "home" in this world. This is what Cross tries to say, as he's dying, by using words that echo Harry's: "The search can't be done alone."

Harry's emphasis is on the word "chance," not "search." A man alone does not have a "chance" in a world of chance. In *To Have and Have Not*, Hemingway sees the human condition through the lens of Ecclesiastes in which the "vanity" of earthly things creates the existential condition of "man alone." In his next novel, *For Whom the Bell Tolls*, he attempted to solve the problem of "man alone" by juxtaposing the cruelty of the Spanish Civil War (on both sides) with the need to find a cause that builds a bridge between self and other. Wright will borrow that theme in the ending of *The Outsider*. He tells Houston that "man is a promise that he must never break" (585). That "promise" is the potential to fulfill one's humanity by, as Cross says with his last breath, making "a bridge from man to man . . . Starting from scratch every time is . . . is no good" (585).

Nonetheless, terror remains a theme in both *For Whom the Bell Tolls* and *The Outsider*. Hemingway compares the Loyalists' brutal murder of the fascists in Ronda, Spain (making them run a gauntlet before throwing them into a gorge), to a lynching Robert Jordan witnessed as a child (116–17), and Wright uses a stanza from Blake's "A Divine Image" as the epigraph to his novel in which "Cruelty has a Human heart, / And Jealousy a Human Face; / Terror the Human form Divine, /And Secrecy the Human Dress." Cruelty is only one expression of the human condition, but it is the path Cross travels when he reinvents himself after the train accident. Separated from "tradition," an inherited moral order, he becomes a "little god," murdering others not only to protect his new identity but because he can. Left to himself, he descends to "man alone" in which man expresses himself through an unrestrained love of power. The "horror" Cross feels at the end, as he tells Houston, is that he "felt . . . *innocent*" (586). That is, he believed that reinventing himself was a natural, even a human, act, but the "horror" lay in the consequence. He reinvented himself as a monster. He forgot that "love"—the bridge between man and man—is the essence of the human: *the* divine image and not *a* divine image (Blake 55). Earlier, he had told Houston, when they met on a train going to New York, that perhaps "man is nothing in particular . . . Maybe that's the terror of it. Man may be just anything at all" (172). If man is no longer made in God's image (the theme of Cross's long speech on the impact of the Industrial Revolution), then he may become "anything at all," either fulfilling the "promise" of his humanity or distorting that "form" to the image of "terror." Cross has not only betrayed everyone whose path he has crossed, but he has become his name, a demon. If "man is nothing in particular," then to "blot" out another is as natural as blotting out a fly.

The Outsider is, in part, a revisionist treatment of *To Have and Have Not*. Wright takes Hemingway's "man alone" and turns it into a philosophical reverie upon the modern condition, one in which racial identity becomes a metaphor for "the outsider." We also see this revisionist perspective in *Pagan Spain* as Wright's treatment of the Spanish bullfight ratchets up the Gothic implications of Hemingway's *Death in the Afternoon*. In that extraordinary text on bullfighting, Hemingway said that the authentic bullfighter is a "truly great killer," who must have a sense of pride in his craft and "a sense of honor and a sense of glory beyond that of the ordinary bullfighter" (232–3). What he confronts in the bull is death on wheels, and his courage in confronting death is his pride, just as killing the bull cleanly is his honor. It is precisely here that Hemingway makes a connection between the craft of storytelling and the ritual of bullfighting: "all stories, if continued far enough, end in death, and he is no true story teller who would keep that from you" (122). Just as the great bullfighter must confront the reality of death in the bullring, so too the "true" story teller must never forget the one subject that gives his story authenticity.

In *Pagan Spain*, Wright said that he intended to investigate the "emotional" side of bullfighting that Hemingway ignored (150), just as he had described in *Black Boy* (playing off Hemingway's "grace under fire") the "frenzy under pressure" of African Americans when placed within the bullring of the American South (*Black Boy* 37). For Wright, the bull in the bullfight symbolizes the dark side of human nature, "the undistracted lust to kill" (*Pagan Spain* 113). What the ritual of the bullfight accomplishes is to distract us by displacing that "lust to kill" upon the bull. Thus the bullfighter, in killing it, assures us that our lives have been cleansed of guilt and sin. But the fact that the bull must be killed again and again only reminds us of the violence that remains in human nature. To illustrate this, Wright describes the violence of a crowd who "mutilated the testicles" of the bull once the fight was over, an echo of the gratuitous cruelty of a lynching mob in the South (155). The fact that it is the "testicles" that are violated calls attention to another theme that Wright develops. The bullfight vicariously satisfies the repressed sexuality of the crowd, a point Wright makes by noting the "little orgiastic moan" of one woman in the crowd (122). The Freudian connection between sexuality and violence is already there in Hemingway, especially in a story like "Indian Camp."

Curiously, there is another Gothic theme that links Wright and Hemingway: the fragility of the male ego. In *The Sun Also Rises*, Jake Barnes learns that his moral superiority over Robert Cohn evaporates when he has to acknowledge that he has betrayed the values that he believed had restored his masculinity lost in the war. In *For Whom the Bell Tolls*, Pablo's heroic behavior during the early part of the Spanish Civil War inexplicably crumbles into cowardice and drunkenness. Perhaps the best example of Hemingway's theme of male vulnerability lies in his great short story "In Another Country." The brilliance of this story is that it works by indirection, appearing to focus on one thing only to lead us down a different path. Nick Adams is undergoing rehabilitation in Milan for an injury sustained during the war. Since his wound was accidental and not the result of valorous action, he is not one of the "hunting-hawks" (*Complete Short Stories* 208), the three soldiers at the hospital who were awarded medals because of their bravery. Nick's medals were given to him because he is an American. Although the soldiers make a distinction among themselves in terms of hawks and non-hawks, this hierarchy of masculinity is not what the story is about.

One of the hawks is a major, a former fencing champion of Italy who will never fence again because of an injury to his hand. The doctors at the hospital fatuously boast that his hand will be as good as new, but the major is a realist and a stoic who indulges in no such illusions. Ironically, his "illusion" is the Enlightenment belief that his life can be controlled through discipline and reason. Hence his insistence that if Nick is to speak Italian, he should learn "grammar" (*Complete Short Stories* 208). For the major, "grammar" is life's syntax, its underlying rational structure, but the Gothic motif in the story lies in something his "grammar" has not taken into account. He purposely waited until he was invalided out of the war before he married, but fate has blindsided him. Nick comes to the hospital one day to find the major completely distraught, unable to "resign" himself to a terrible turn of events: his young wife has caught pneumonia and died (209–10). The major can control his emotions when it comes to himself, but he had not understood how much of his emotional life he had invested in another person. Her death, not his, is the other "country" he had not foreseen.

One does not have to search far in Wright's fiction to find the theme of male identity suddenly falling apart: Big Boy, Fishbelly, Bigger, "Fred Daniels" ("The Man Who Lived Underground" [in *Eight Men*]), Jake Jackson (*Lawd Today!*), Erskine Fowler (*Savage Holiday*), and Cross Damon all experience a collapse of identity as the circumstances of their life are radically altered or disrupted. But one comic version of this Gothic motif in Wright's fiction needs to be underscored because it bears an odd resemblance to Hemingway's "In Another Country." In his short story "Man of All Work" (originally written as a radio play), Wright uses Freud's notion of the "uncanny" to satirize Carl's belief in reason, his belief that what is "familiar" (*heimlich*) in his house can also be made familiar in another's house, even that of a white family. To save his "home," he answers an advertisement for domestic help, but he must cross-dress in his wife's clothes to get the job. He was a cook in the army and is a master at taking care of his own kids (changing diapers, warming bottles of milk), so why not use his skills in a new context? Is he not a self-sufficient black male? But he does not know that once he re-creates his sexual identity, he has already stepped over into the "unfamiliar" (*unheimlich*). And when he enters a white household, he crosses a threshold into the void, for the white "family" is a grotesque parody of the "familiar" (Freud 371–7).

To his dismay, he discovers the father to be a lecherous drunk and his wife a cowardly whiner. In this nightmarish world, Carl finds himself sexually assaulted by the husband and shot by the wife (in an act of transferred aggression). Though the story ends happily (Carl is bought off by enough money to make the final payments on his home), he tells his wife that "I was a woman for almost six hours and it almost killed me. Two hours after I put that dress on I thought I was going crazy" (*Eight Men* 131).

Not only does he discover what it means to be a black woman in a white world, but his conception of himself as a "man" capable of doing "all work" is completely shattered. The Gothic mode, as Hogle has observed, obscures "boundaries," even those separating male and female (11).

Perhaps the most important connection between Hemingway and Wright can only be described as one of sensibility. Wright said in *Black Boy* that his experience growing up in Mississippi created "a somberness of spirit that I was never to lose . . . a somberness that was to make me stand apart and look upon excessive joy with suspicion." Moreover, watching his mother suffer as she lay dying gave him a sense of the "fear" and "dread" and "uncertainty" of life that was never to leave him. All his subsequent writing, he continued, would thus become an attempt to wring "a meaning out of meaningless suffering" (*Black Boy* 100). This is very close to Hemingway's own attitude toward life and art, especially as expressed in his short story "A Clean, Well-Lighted Place." This well-known story is as much about an older and younger waiter as it is about the old man who finds some solace from his own mortality by frequenting a "well-lighted" café. The young waiter cannot understand the old man's despair, his need for ritual and order and a place in which chaos is kept at bay, but the older waiter knows all too well the dread that comes from having to face the engulfing night. It is the story's last two lines that link Wright and Hemingway. The older waiter conjectures as to why he cannot fall asleep until dawn: "After all, he said to himself, it is probably only insomnia. Many must have it" (*Complete Short Stories* 291).

Works cited

Blake, William. "The Divine Image." *English Romantic Writers*. Ed. David Perkins. New York: Harcourt, 1967. Print.

Botting, Fred. *Gothic*. London: Routledge, 1996. Print. The New Critical Idiom.

Bryant, Cedric Gael. "'The Soul Has Bandaged Moments': Reading the African American Gothic in Wright's 'Big Boy Leaves Home,' Morrison's *Beloved*, and Gomez's *Gilda*." *African American Review* 39.4 (2005): 541–53. Print.

Cowley, Malcolm. *The Portable Malcolm Cowley*. Ed. Donald W. Faulkner. New York: Viking, 1990. Print.

Edwards, Justin D. *Gothic Passages: Racial Ambiguity and the American Gothic*. Iowa City: Iowa UP, 2003. Print.

Fabre, Michel. *Richard Wright: Books and Writers*. Jackson: UP of Mississippi, 1990. Print.

—— *The Unfinished Quest of Richard Wright*. Trans. Isabel Barzun. New York: Morrow, 1973. Print.

Freud, Sigmund. "The 'Uncanny.'" *Standard Edition of the Complete Psychological Works*. Trans. Alix Strachey. London: Hogarth, 1953–64. 368–407. Print.

Goddu, Teresa A. *Gothic America: Narrative, History, and Nation*. New York: Columbia UP, 1997. Print.

Hemingway, Ernest. *The Complete Short Stories of Ernest Hemingway: The Finca Vigia Edition*. New York: Scribner, 2003. Print.

—— *Death in the Afternoon*. New York: Scribner's, 1932. Print.

—— *A Farewell to Arms.* 1929. New York: Macmillan, 1986. Print.

—— *For Whom the Bell Tolls.* New York: Scribner's, 1940. Print.

—— *Green Hills of Africa.* New York: Scribner's, 1935. Print.

—— *In Our Time.* 1925. New York: ScribnerCollier, 1986. Print.

—— *The Sun Also Rises.* 1926. New York: Scribner, 2003. Print.

—— *To Have and Have Not.* New York: Scribner's, 1937. Print.

Hogle, Jerrold E. "Introduction: The Gothic in Western Culture." *The Cambridge Companion to Gothic Fiction.* Ed. Hogle. Cambridge: Cambridge UP, 2002. 1–20. Print.

Kinnamon, Keneth and Michel Fabre, eds. *Conversations with Richard Wright.* Jackson: UP of Mississippi, 1993. Print.

Lloyd-Smith, Allan. *American Gothic Fiction: An Introduction.* New York: Continuum, 2004. Print.

Lukács, Georg. *The Theory of the Novel: A Historico-Philosophical Essay on the Forms of Great Epic Literature.* Trans. Anna Bostock. Cambridge: MIT Press, 1971. Print.

Punter, David. *The Literature of Terror: A History of Gothic Fictions from 1765 to the Present Day.* London: Longman, 1980. Print.

Rowley, Hazel. *Richard Wright: The Life and Times.* New York: Holt, 2001. Print.

Sedgwick, Eve Kosofsky. *The Coherence of Gothic Conventions.* New York: Arno, 1980. Print.

Smethurst, James. "Invented by Horror: The Gothic and African American Literary Ideology in *Native Son.*" *African American Review* 35.1 (2001): 29–40. Print.

Wright, Richard. *Black Boy: A Record of Childhood and Youth (American Hunger).* 1945. New York: Harper Row, 1998. Print.

—— "Blueprint for Negro Writing." *The Norton Anthology of African American Literature.* Ed. Henry Louis Gates, Jr., and Nellie Y. McKay. New York: Norton, 1997. 1380–8. Print.

—— *Eight Men.* 1961. New York: Harcourt Brace Jovanovich, 1976. Print.

—— *Lawd Today!* 1954. Jackson: UP of Mississippi, 1994. Print.

—— *The Long Dream.* Boston: Northeastern UP, 1958. Print.

—— *Native Son.* 1940. New York: HarperCollins, 1993. Print.

—— *The Outsider.* 1953. New York: HarperCollins, 1993. Print.

—— *Pagan Spain.* 1957. New York: HarperCollins, 1995. Print.

—— *Savage Holiday.* 1954. Jackson: UP of Mississippi, 1994. Print.

—— *Uncle Tom's Children.* 1938. New York: Harper, 1965. Print.

9

Pulp Gothicism in Richard Wright's *The Outsider*

William E. Dow
The American University of Paris

> *We black men and women in America today, as we look back upon scenes of rapine, sacrifice, and death, seem to be children of a devilish aberration, descendants of an interval of nightmare in history, fledglings of a period of amnesia on the part of men who once dreamed a great dream and forgot.*
>
> Richard Wright, *Twelve Million Black Voices*

I

Continuing the Gothic-like historical nightmares and "devilish aberrations" that he conceptualizes in *Twelve Million Black Voices*, Richard Wright's *The Outsider* comments on US race relations while examining the philosophical and psychological forms of alienation with which Wright tries to avenge his "outsider" status. This essay makes a claim for the importance of what I'm calling Wright's "pulp Gothicism," a mode keyed to various popular cultural forms of the 1940s and 50s that provide a vantage point for re-examining an African American version of the Gothic and crime genres.[1] As Suzanne B. Dietzel has recently remarked, "The field of African American popular culture studies has almost exclusively focused on music, film, and popular (folk) heroes, especially with the emergence and popularity of rap, hip-hop, and black youth culture in the 1980s and 1990s" (156). Much less attention has been given to ways in which African Americans have represented themselves in popular narrative genres or in literatures meant primarily—or at least on the surface—for public entertainment. This essay builds on recent developments in cultural and American studies that view such popular cultural forms (pulp fiction, novels of crime, mystery, suspense) as rendering powerful commentaries on dominant social orders and ideologies.[2]

The Outsider is a particularly interesting case because its generic hybridity brings together two of the most popular narrative forms of the 1940s–1950s—the crime novel and the Gothic horror story—to highlight racial and ethical dimensions that can be seen as taking us to a larger sense of "human possibilities" (Ward 181) than exist, for example, in *Native Son* and *Black Boy*. This essay responds to *The Outsider*'s interpretive challenges by focusing on this hybridity: Wright's combination of pulp fiction in which lurid and sensational subjects offer compelling alternative or parallel realities with his Gothic vision that centers on evocations of fear, immoderacy, startling shifts and reversals, and a racially directed epistemology. *The Outsider*'s generic hybridity shows us new epistemological possibilities through "the specific kind of unease created by the Gothic" (Soltysik 5) and its "disruptive potential" (Goddu 8). "A major theme of the Gothic," according to Steven Bruhm, "has always been the interior life … as a contemporary Gothic subject … [which] becomes a/the field on which national, racial, and gender anxieties … get played out and symbolized over and over again" (Bruhm 162). Wright's Gothic sensibility focuses on representative relations of the Gothic to "the interior life" of black Americans and the social relations engendered by American capitalism.[3]

Cross Damon, Chicago postal worker, working-class intellectual, and the novel's protagonist, exemplifies Wright's 1950s fascination with forms of identity "that arise from hostile, negating conditions of oppression" (Relyea 191) from which he creates Cross's "modern consciousness." In a word, Wright can be seen as extending the African American Gothicism of such writers as W. E. B. Dubois, Jean Toomer, Ralph Ellison, and Nella Larsen to encompass questions of identity inseparable from such a consciousness and inseparable from popular cultural forms.[4] Because Wright uses pulp and "popular" writing in the generic mix of *The Outsider*, his Gothicism results in a sustained historical-materialist critique from both inside and outside an African-American literary and political tradition.

Wright's Gothic undertones can help locate him in a tradition that takes him far from the usual categories in which he is placed—naturalist, realist, political propagandist, modernist *manqué*. *The Outsider* is filled with allusions to what might be called the topoi or landmarks of the Gothic: premonitions, curses, the subterranean, confinement, doubles, conspiracies, and premature burial. These topoi are especially effective when serving as a filter and backdrop for Wright's questions and positions on race and racial relations. Although some critics have claimed that race is incidental to *The Outsider*,[5] I will argue that Wright retained from the Gothic horror story devices that he connected to the crime plot of 1950s popular culture to uncover the social aberrations of racism and the terrors of modernity. The abilities of Cross Damon concern foremost his skill in moving unobserved through the multiple levels of a city and illuminating the concealed vices of a modernist society. Such depictions reinforce Valerie Babb's assertion in relation to Wright's racial intentions, "As concerned as Wright was with having readers see racial truth, he was more concerned with having them see themselves in that truth" (Babb 710). Wright wished to create a world in which his readers could comprehend the consequences of the pulp and Gothic impulses that Cross illustrates but cannot control.

As *The Outsider* opens, Cross is desperately trying to deal with his failed marriage, increasing debt, and his girlfriend's threats to charge him with statutory rape. A working-class intellectual, a reader of Nietzsche and Hegel, he is trying to find a belief system that will vanquish his constant fear of social extinction: "His life was a delicate bridge spanning a gaping chasm and hostile hands were heaping heavy loads upon that bridge and it was about to crack and crash downward" (19). Cross's pervasive fear powers the racialized Gothicism of *The Outsider*. Indeed, the meanings of Cross's fear hover undecidably between the psychological and the political, between the sense of a free humanized self and the countervailing sense of being (racially) deselved. In the novel's opening chapter, he overhears a group of black men in a Chicago bar discussing how whites are the "scardest folks on earth" (34) because they're guilty—guilty of racial intimidation and oppression of all non-whites:

[A] man said soberly [,] "White folks in America, France, England, and Italy are the scardest folks that ever lived on this earth. They're scareda Reds, Chinese, Indians, Africans, *everybody*."
    "But how come you reckon they so scared?" an elderly man asked.
    "'Cause they're guilty," the tall man explained. "And guilty folks are *scared* folks!" (34)

The perceived racial fear of whites towards blacks and other people of color—and vice versa—however, appears to affect Cross less on a communal level than on a personal level. This conversation foreshadows the unrelenting back and forth forces of Cross's own guilt and fear. As *The Outsider* goes on to demonstrate, Cross cannot exorcize such forces from his personal history (he can, for example, only "instinctively choose to love himself over and against all others" because he feels threatened by "a mysterious God," 22); nor can he dissociate fear and guilt from his racial roots. His blackness is a status that places him both inside and outside Western society, a position Wright viewed as applying to himself.[6]

Reminiscent of Ellison's "invisible man," Cross's personal fear centers on his ongoing dread of *non-identity*. Although at times being crucially aware of his race and the desires it engenders in him ("he hungered for her [Gladys his future wife] ... as a woman of his own color who was longing to conquer the shame imposed upon her by her native land because of her social and racial origin" [66]), he never stops trying to shunt, question or defer his racial consciousness:

[T]he insistent claims of his own inner life had made him too concerned with himself to cast his lot wholeheartedly with Negroes in terms of racial struggle. Practically he was with him but emotionally he was not of them. He felt keenly their sufferings and would have battled desperately for any Negro trapped in a racial conflict, but his character had been so shaped that his decisive life struggle was a personal fight for the realization of himself. (195)

Cross's fear about being entrapped in one constrictive racial identity underlies other fears.

One evening he is trapped in a subway wreck from which he escapes leaving behind his coat and identification papers, which are later mistakenly matched with a dead man. Cross is besieged by the fear of being discovered alive after deciding to feign his death in this accident. His fear is compounded by his mother "attempting to reduce him again to the status of a fearfully impressionable child" (24); his later fears of being exposed as a murderer;[7] and his constant fear that his true identity be discovered. Wright transforms the core of these fears into Cross's quest for a modern racial self—a self that in constantly testing ethical limits dreads an unknown future that appears to convert any attempt at progress into decline. Wright describes this self through the form of a pulp-Gothic crime story.

After the tramway accident, Cross decides to desert his wife, mother, and children; he flees Chicago for New York and there becomes associated with the American Communist Party. He later develops a relationship with Eva, an abstract painter and the wife of a Party leader, Gil Blount. Following Cross's murder of Gil, Cross cannot appease Eva because, as he himself realizes, *he* embodies her deepest fears:

> Could he tell her of how he had abandoned his mother, Gladys, his three sons, how he had killed Joe Thomas, Gil, Hendon . . .? Could he tell her that his life was steeped in deception, that he was the essence of the world that she hated and feared? (385)

Resonant of conventional Gothic literature, a fear of disclosure subsumes Cross's past and present decisions. Most of these fears, however, involve a racial identity, an identity subsumed by fear and resistance to it, readily recognized by the novel's other characters: e.g., Eva, Jack Hilton, a leading CPUSA member, Ely Houston, the District Attorney who will later try to convict Cross, and Joe Thomas, a fellow postal worker. Eva, for example, fearing for Cross's life, tells him that she "want[s] to feel the hurt and shame of being black" (385), to look into "the black depths of his heart" (538). Self-servingly, Hilton, just after Gil is murdered, proclaims to Cross, "Watching and coping with the racially charged behavior of white Americans are a part of your learning how to live in this country. Look, every day in this land some white man is cussing out some defenseless Negro" (330). Advocating blind Party loyalty, Hilton fears the manipulation of the white-dominated police force and the anti-Communist American government. "[Man's] most dominant characteristic," according to Houston, "is an enormous propensity toward fear" (478) for which Cross, as he defines him at the end of the novel, serves as an anti-thesis:

> Today many sociologists say that the American Negro, having been stripped of his African tribal culture, has not had time to become completely adjusted to our mores, that the life of the family of the Western World has not had time to sink in etc. But with you, you are adjusted and more . . . You've grown up and gone beyond our rituals (562).

These racial inflections prop up Wright's pulp Gothicism. Although *The Outsider* is soaked with improbable occurrences, garish violence, horrid murders, and fast-paced actions (the pulp part), it effectively renders what Agniezska Soltysik has identified as a particular American-Gothic epistemology, that which "provides a complex intellectual and ethical reading experience" (2).[8]

But for Wright, the Gothic takes a form that not so much encompasses quests for racial identity as it signals Cross's political and ideological affiliations (and their racial consequences) that set him apart from the dominant culture. *The Outsider* challenges accounts of modern consciousness that fail to provide an examination of racial concepts embedded in popular culture forms. Gothically inflected, Cross's modern consciousness, "so infatuated by its own condition that it could not dominate itself" (149), "condition[s] his present and give[s] him those hours and days out of which he could build a new past" (114). Cross rejects the Western political and social ideology that forces him into a "subcultural allegiance" (Rabinowitz 83). In effect, *The Outsider* shows African Americans living in a Gothic world in which guilt, fear, and betrayal are the most important themes of their existence.

This world is inseparable from popular cultural forms.[9] Wright conjoins, for example, the Gothic urban worlds of Chicago and New York with the *femme fatale* motif to illustrate the limitations of conventional racial knowledge, at least when applied to gender.[10] Traditionally, the femme fatale's cultural shorthand trades on racial stereotypes, which in *The Outsider* Wright aims to counter. Paula Rabinowitz remarks in her study of the novel,

> In Richard Wright's inversion of film noir, white women offer black men the transgressive power of the femme fatale. Like the femme fatale, she is desirable because she is trapped. Jenny the Chicago prostitute, and Eva, the abstract expressionist in New York, are caught by systems controlling their desire; pimps and brothels, on the one hand, and the CPUSA, on the other . . . This is a community of betrayed women—[Cross Damon's] mother, his wife, his lover a prostitute—and of well meaning coworkers who sort mail during the night shift at the post office. (96, 94)

But scheming and deadly women, in the form of *femmes fatales*, pursue and betray Damon as well—or so he thinks—women he can't control or appease or escape. They await in the urban-Gothic dark: "What greater shame was there than to walk the streets cringing with fear of grasping women whose destructive strokes were draped in the guise of whimpers and accusations?" (48). Cross's women and his fear of them occur in a subterranean Gothic atmosphere, clouded by a constant uncertainty and trepidation. It is an African American recoding of a Gothic white city in which "tiny crystals tremb[le] lightly" on "dark faces" (4), a "frigid world" where Cross is "conscious of himself as a frail object which [has] to protect itself against a pending threat of annihilation" (21–2).

On the other hand, Cross *is* a betrayer (in pulp double-cross fashion) of black women who, like Gladys, Dot, and Cross's mother, are presented in turn as betrayers of Cross and as victims to their religion or race. His wife easily accepts him being out of her life because she can collect from his insurance policy; Dot, his mistress, wishes to take Cross to court for statuary rape to pressure him into marrying her or paying her off. White women such as Jenny, the Chicago prostitute, and Eva, the painter, languish in brutal urban-pulp worlds. Cross, himself a betrayer of these women (in his deceit towards them and abandonment of them), decodes the information presented to him via his impulses and interprets that information in light of his prejudices. Thus he impulsively abandons the women in his Chicago existence by taking on new identities in his New York life. He fools Jenny into thinking that he will take her to Hollywood, and lies to Eva about his marriage and murderous past. The fatal subway scene—a perfect example of pulp Gothicism—bridges Cross Damon and post-Cross Damon existences, in the symbolic form of a dead woman:

> [Cross] reached the window and saw that a young woman's body had been crushed almost flat just beneath it. The girl was dead, but, if he was to get through that window, he either had the choice of standing upon her crushed body or remaining where he was. He stepped upon the body, feeling his shoes sinking into the lifeless flesh and seeing blood bubbling from the woman's mouth as his weight bore down on her bosom. He reached for the window avoiding the jagged edges of glass. (97)

Foreshadowing his betrayal of Eva, the young woman's body serves as a Gothic-pulp reminder that Cross will let nothing stop his relentless quest to obliterate his present predicament.

At times the pulp elements of *The Outsider* supersede those of the Gothic. For example, the film noir talk that peppers the Chicago scenes.[11] Here is Cross, on the lamb, with the prostitute, Jenny:

> "Gotta match?" she asked, lifting a cigarette to her mouth and keeping her eyes boldly on his face.
> He caught on; she was selling herself. But was she safe? Was she stooling for the police?
> "Sure," he said, taking out his lighter and holding the flame for her.
> "You're new here," she said.
> "Yeah," he said. "I got in last night."
> "So I heard," she smiled.
> "Seems like news travels pretty fast around here."
> "Pretty fast for those who want to find out things," she said. (117)

Likewise, gangster descriptions of violent plottings and dead-end deals are part of the film noir–pulp mix that permeates the appropriately titled Book One, "Dread." Here, in ultimate despair and increasing isolation, is Cross contemplating suicide:

> He sprang to the dresser and yanked open a drawer and pulled forth his gun. Trembling, feeling the cold blue steel touching his sweaty palm, he lifted the glinting barrel to his right temple, then paused. His feelings were like tumbling dice . . . He wilted, cursed, his breath expiring through parted lips. (16)

Such talk and descriptions not only describe, but also elicit, the dangerous forces of modern propensities (i.e., when Cross severs all communal connections he becomes receptive to "anarchic violence," [Relyea 197]) and the symptoms of a troubled and unjust social system. All of the blacks are economically struggling in the novel; few of the whites are shown to be. The various crime stories of *The Outsider* easily elide into a social problem novel, departing very little, in this sense, from *Native Son* and *Black Boy*.

Congruent to the pulp-dominated sections of *The Outsider* are straightforward Gothic parallels. For instance, Cross's conflictual relation with his mother sets up a persistent Gothic motif—that of the living dead—or, more accurately, the living while dying.

> Without answering, she widened the door and he walked past her into a tiny, shabby room that smelt of a sweetish odor of decaying flesh that seemed to cling to the aged who are slowly dying while still living. (23)

Gradually Cross feels that this state applies to himself as well—he is already a dead man—even before the fateful tram accident: "He felt as though he were already dead and was listening to [Gladys] speak about him" (88). When Cross tumbles into an opportunity to "start all over again" (105), to become the Gothic revenant through falsifying his death in a tram accident, he comes to these conclusions:

> *He was dead* . . . All right . . . Okay . . . [. . .] Why should he refute it? Why should he deny it? He, of all people on earth, had a million reasons for being dead and staying dead! An intuitive sense of freedom flashed through his mind. Was there a slight chance here of his being able to start all over again? (105)

Cross's premature burial results in a opportunity that tilts towards evil: "to shape for himself the kind of life he felt he wanted, but he knew that that innocence was deeply forbidden" (109). In Gothic fashion, his imagination transports him beyond his bounded vision and existence into a past ("He would be a Negro who had just come up fresh from the Deep South looking for work") and a future (his new life in "New York") (111), and into a condition that his imagination has devised, situated in areas of constant liminality and transition.

But Wright, in a basic structural device of *The Outsider*, most frequently combines his visions of the criminal metropolis with Gothic echoes and motifs. Just following the aborted-suicide scene, this episode describes Cross's agony over his body having a life of its own and illustrates his emerging modern consciousness where self-alienation dominates:

> He was despairingly aware of his body as an alien and despised object over which he had no power, a burden that was always cheating him of the fruits of his thought, mocking him with its stubborn and supine solidity. (16)

Pulp and Gothic inflections intermingle to create in some instances a hybrid "hard-boiled stance" (Ellison 112) not *un*appropriate for an African American writer for such inflections have readily served to represent African American experience.[12] In *The*

Outsider, this experience is articulated by Ely Houston, Cross's alter-ego ("Cross could feel that Houston sensed the quality of the demonical in him, and he could feel the same in Houston," 170) and pursuer, and extended by Cross himself. In effect, *The Outsider* circles around a specific nexus in playing this drama out: Cross is looking for acceptance while at the same time remaining contemptible and individualized, a central problem in Gothic fiction (the individual recognizes only his/her existence to the exclusion of anything or anyone else: e.g., the narrator in Poe's "Black Cat").[13] In Gothic code as well, Cross cannot depict his wrongdoing as wrong because he lacks "a shared conceptual or moral framework" (Soltysik 9) that would assure his place in a community.

Wright's propensity, however, is never to go too far in any Gothic-inflected direction without returning to some kind of 1940s or 1950s popular-culture form.[14] For example, when Cross is at his lowest points, the form that relieves him the most (again reminiscent of Ellison) is African American music.[15] The blue-jazz that Cross listens to in "Part Two: Dream" is at once "a knell for those who are outsiders and who despair" (McCluskey 336) and a confirmation of Cross's only "emotional home" (337):

> Blue-jazz was the scornful gesture of men turned ecstatic in the state of rejection; it was the musical language of the satisfiedly amoral, the beginning of the contentedly lawless, the recreation of the innocently criminal. (178)

"One for whom all ethical laws [will be] suspended" (379), he listens to "raucous blue-jazz welling up from downstairs" at his rooming house (178) filling his ears with "the orgiastic culpability of jazz" (178). At the same time, Cross's identification with this musical form (i.e., above all, its power of "recreation") plunges him further into a "nonidentity," Gothically coded and appended by Wright as a form of haunting the world because unable to enter it: "To live amidst others without an identity was intolerable. In a strict sense [Cross] was not really in the world; he was haunting it for his place, pleading for entrance" (167). Cross is intensely aware of his longings and the fears it describes. His inner life, plagued by guilt and transgressions, pushes him toward extremes and excesses, but by immersing himself in popular cultural forms (e.g., "the blue-jazz")—Cross believes he can perhaps "still [a] fear of himself" (172) and take pleasure in self-abandonment by no longer having a self:

> The strains of blue and sensual notes were akin to him not only by virtue of their having been created by black men, but because they had come out of the hearts of men who had been rejected and yet who still lived and shared the lives of their rejectors. These notes possessed the frightened ecstasy of the unrepentant and sent his feelings tumbling and coagulating in a mood of joyful abandonment. (111)

II

Hybrid forms of a pulp-Gothic discourse underlie the epistemological premises of *The Outsider*. Wright's concern with the situation of black intellectuals in the West, and his increasing engagement (and disengagement) with existentialism,[16] is represented in Cross Damon's rejection of essentialist forms of identity. In the context of his own modern consciousness—and outside the confines of conventional racial ideologies—Wright, like Cross, wished to understand race not as biological necessity but as a social category. Thus Cross, early in the novel, tells us in a flat existential declaration, "[a] man creates himself" (65), though the novel both affirms and denies this assertion: social forces, beyond Cross's control, eventually destroy him. At the same time, Wright, despite his clinging to an independent (and racially conflicted) "outsider" status (as the narrators do in *Black Boy, Black Power*, and *The Color Curtain*), "never disavows his own experience of Black oppression and resistance" (West ix) and the oppressiveness of racism.[17] At this point in the novel, however, Cross tries to deny or ignore his relations to such forces and racial communities. He continues to be obsessed by "the insistent claims of his own inner life" (195). He withdraws from the world he has known in Chicago, suppressing past traumas and guilt. His journey to New York, his adventure of self-fashioning and desire, begins internally:

> The outside world had fallen away from him now and he was alone at the center of the world of the laws of his own feelings . . . he knew where his sense of dread came from; it was from within himself, within the vast and mysterious world that was his own and yet unknown. And it was into this strange but familiar world that he was now plunging. (148)

For Robert Chodat, despite or perhaps because of this internal journey, "*The Outsider* implies a world in which characters' lives are overwhelmingly shaped by circumstances beyond their control. Damon doesn't create his own narrative, and whatever Wright's stated beliefs, the limitations of existentialism grow increasingly evident in the text itself" (662). Like Bigger Thomas in *Native Son*, Cross is a "failed convert," killing and going against those who try to proselytize him (Wald 680)—for whatever political or philosophical reason. Indeed, eventually backing away from a self-serving existentialist existence, Cross finally recognizes the need for complicity with others ("The search can't be done alone," Outsider, 585) and, by implication, the impossibility of living in a de-ethnized or aracial world. In this regard, *The Outsider* opens the epistemological means of its own operation: Cross's "fatal flaw is ultimately his individualism" (Graham xxxi); he needs to understand how to "make a bridge from man to man . . .," for "Starting from scratch every time . . . is no good" (*Outsider*, 585).

But not before Cross becomes so self-absorbed and drawn into his interior world that he is submerged in a form of Gothic dread which partakes of a fear of himself (152):

> Imprisoned he was in a state of consciousness that was so infatuated by its own condition that it could not dominate itself; so swamped was he by himself with himself that he could not break forth from behind the bars of that self to claim himself. (149)

As Cross creates himself he creates a certain Gothic persona as well, someone whose state not only defines the fragmentation of a modern consciousness but who increasingly sees himself as "a little god" (308), a conventional Gothic trait:

> Cross had to discover what was good or evil through his own actions which were more exacting than the edicts of any god because it was he alone who had to bear the brunt of their consequences with a sense of absoluteness made intolerable by knowing that this life of his was all he had and would ever have. (157)

The Outsider, as Paul Gilroy notes, "elaborated a view of blackness and the relational ideologies of race and racism which support it . . . as metaphysical conditions of the modern world's existence that arise with, and perhaps out of, the overcoming of religious morality" (160). For Wright, though, Gothic horrors (including Gothic explanations and incomprehension) invariably accompany such a vision. Pursuing explanatory origins for the problem of evil and suffering in both the social and racial psyche, Cross is the Gothic figure of the undead returned to settle scores with the historical real of racial and ideological existence.[18]

As in the Chicago section, hybrid forms of pulp Gothicism illuminate the New York chapters to chronicle Cross's trajectory of aloneness, his increasing mistrust and suspicion of himself and those he meets, and "the questions of identity that haunt Gothic discourse" (Edwards xxiv). Once in New York, assuming a new identity as Lionel Lane and fleeing his wife, mistress, and the murder of his fellow postal worker, Joe Thomas, he takes consolation in "movie houses" (177) and he participates in more film noir–pulp episodes, as in this encounter with his landlord, Mrs. Turner: "At noon she knocked on his door. He made sure that his gun was ready . . ." (179). Similarly, in this bar scene, shortly before Cross finds a room at Mrs. Crawford's, he is convinced that "cops . . . were looking him over . . . He slipped his hand slowly into his overcoat pocket and grasped the gun . . . Both cops disappeared wordlessly into the rear and Cross felt his hot muscles relaxing. The bartender took a bottle of whiskey back to the cops. When he returned, Cross said in a whisper: 'I thought they were raiding the joint'" (200). Later, in trying to learn more about the deceased Lionel Lane, "[Cross] looked about in the sea of frightened snowflakes, full again of that old sense of dread and criminality" (208). "Dread" in *The Outsider* is constantly associated with Cross's Gothic-like disposition, which constantly combines with his pulp-like "criminality" to become the index of a terrible modernity. The Chicago and New York sections are connected mainly through Gothic-pulp images, which, in addition to evoking the limitations of human judgment, serve as interpretive frames for understanding Cross in the menacing tide of an industrial economy.

What accompanies Cross's quest is a racial and philosophical gloss that puts it in another category from what one contemporary reviewer called *The Outsider*'s story, "a cheap drugstore whodunit."[19] While listening to blue-jazz, for example, "[Cross] sensed how Negroes had been made to live in but not of the land of their birth, how the injunctions of an alien Christianity and the strictures of white laws had evoked in them the very longings and desires that that religion and law had been designed to stifle"

(178). Wright's Gothic discourse complicates the novel's various forms of pulp and hard-boiled fictions, opening up discursive spaces in which revisions of identity are possible, racial understandings can be clarified, and revisionary social ideas can be expressed. Wright needs this pulp–Gothic hybridity to reveal such spaces.

III

Gangster worlds, film noir and pulp images intensify in the New York sections of the novel, culminating in several grisly murder scenes and coinciding, not incidentally, with Cross's involvement with and revenge against the Communist Party.[20] Wright's depictions of the Communist Party in *The Outsider* take on gangster and pulp connotations that underscore Wright's prevailing view of the CPUSA at the time.[21] One of Eva's diary entries, for example, freely associates the Party with a gangster film:

June 21st
I've begun to notice things that I've never noticed before. Is this because Gil and the Party have done to me? I feel like a victim and everywhere I look I think I can see other victims in the making ... I've just come from a movie [...] It was a horrible gangster film with a tense melodramatic atmosphere. (281–2)

Containing its own melodrama and mawkishness, Eva's diary entries reveal her true thoughts about the Party: "I've got a knife with which I cut canvases and I sleep with it under my pillow. Gil will never touch me again, drunk or sober" (282). "Gil and the Party have opened my eyes and I see" (283). Cross is likewise secretive and dissembling about the Party, and eventually comes to detest it. He explains his reasons for joining this counter-organization, a counterpart to his dark and secret world:

He had no desire whatsoever to join the Communist Party, but he knew that he would feel somewhat at home with Communists, for they, like he, were outsiders. Would not Communism be the best temporary camouflage behind which he could hide from the law? Would not his secret past make Communists think that he was anxious for their help? (223)

Through a series of murders Cross testifies to the fact that like the Communist Party, he too wishes to test his ability as a little God, in the likes of Gil Blount, Eva's husband and a leading Party figure: "[Gil] acts like a God who is about to create a man ... He has no conception of the privacy of other people's lives" (237). Another CPUSA member, Jack Hilton, warns the radical organizer, and soon-to-be-deported, Bob Hunter: "You can't be expelled [from the Party] ... And the Party will blacklist you throughout the labor movement. The Party will kill you. You can't *fight* the Party!" (247).[22] Here Hilton is portrayed—in a pulp-like fashion—as a cold and calculating henchman; Gil is depicted as a potentially violent killer (299–302), and most Party members are shown to be cruel manipulators and crooks. Paradoxically, the description of the CPUSA in

The Outsider comes close to one of J. Edgar Hoover's comments about Communism in the 1950s: "In the beginning it seemed little more than a freak. Yet in the intervening years that freak has grown into a powerful monster endangering us all" (53).

Wright's 1950s thoughts on the CPUSA, however, come out most clearly through *The Outsider's* Gothic overtones and discourses.[23] Wright gives us details of the lurid crime scene when he kills both Gil, the Communist manipulator, and Herndon, the fascist owner of Gil's apartment:

> [Cross] reached down and seized hold of the heavy oaken leg of the table and turned and lifted it high in the air, feeling the solid weight of the wood in his hand, and then he sent it flying squarely onto the bloody forehead of Herndon. . . . Cross let go with the table leg, smashing it into the left side of Gil's head. Gil trembled for a spilt second, then fell headlong toward the fireplace where flames danced and cast wild red shadows over the walls. (303)

Heightened gesture, violent language, melodrama, and "godlessness" (274), seen in profusion here and throughout Book Three, become the organizing principles of *The Outsider's* pulp Gothicism. Cross adopts the seedy, unscrupulous, and vengeful codes of the CPUSA: "Like Hilton and Gil had acted toward Bob, so had he acted toward Gil and Herndon; he had assumed the role of policeman, judge, supreme court, and executioner—all in one swift and terrible moment" (308). In stock Gothic echoes, although Cross expresses no remorse for the murders of Gil and Herndon, he realizes that "[h]e had become what he had tried to destroy, had taken on the guise of the monster he had slain" (309). Shortly after, the narrator adds, "If the actions of Gil and Herndon were monstrously inhuman, then was not what he was doing also devoid of humanity?" (318). Congruently, Cross's revenge has racial and class implications—Bob is foreign, black and working class—and from this moment forward, Cross, in seeing through the Communist Party's ploys to use racial consciousness for its own empowerment (331), plays God to others.

Cross goes further into his monster/little God-like condition with the murder of Hilton, a friend to Gil and another CPUSA party member.[24] The description of the murder is hard-boiled and pulp:

> [Cross] dropped the corner of the mattress and lowered the volume of the radio. Hilton's hands still moved; a labored breathing went in and out of his thin lips; there was a groan and the form on the bed was quiet. Cross strained, listening. There were no sounds in the corridor. He had to get out of here . . . The .32 . . . Yes . . . He wiped it clean of fingerprints on the sheet of the bed and tossed it beside Hilton's hand. He paused, then forced the gun into Hilton's fingers. (405)

Wright uses the paranoia and isolation of the pulp genre in combination with Gothic overtones ("[Cross] was more concerned with getting away from the sight of that grotesquely grey face with its gaping mouth than with saving himself" (405–6)) to suggest that the 1930s language of collectivism had been tainted by Communism. The ideology Communism represents is devoid of civic purpose ("The essence of the Party was an open lawlessness" (470)) and humanism. Pulp fiction was a perfect form for Wright because it offered a populist moral critique of social corruption. But he used it for more than this. Wright recast the cultural and critical significance of the genre to focus on a Communist Party characterized by corrosive self-interest and a society dominated by racist oppression.

The Outsider is Gothic precisely because it attempts to speak the unspeakable and claims a retaliatory, monstrous, self shape-shifting into something new. It is Wright's unique development of the thesis novel or the novel as essay as inflected by his Gothic sensibilities. "Acting individually just like modern man lives in the mass each day" (563), Cross feels free to act upon the world in order to try to invest it with meaning but in so doing he accepts a kind of God-like responsibility and displays monstrous, demonic power (as the name Damon suggests). Although his demonism, as he is quick to tell himself, is "buttressed by [self-involved] ideals, a goal" (389),[25] it can be argued that *The Outsider*, like pulp, film noir, *and* the Gothic itself, "explores chaos and wrongdoing in a movement toward ultimate restitution of order and convention" (Lloyd-Smith 5). Cross ultimately *does* recognize his essential wrongdoing:

> He knew that he had cynically scorned, wantonly violated every commitment that civilized men owe, in terms of common honesty and sacred honor, to those with whom they live. That in essence was his crime. The rest of his brutal and bloody thrashings about were the mere offshoots of that one central, cardinal fact. (501)

In melodramatic-pulp echoes, he confesses to Eva his murders and asks her to be his judge:

> "I've killed and killed . . . Have mercy on me . . . Pity me, but not for what has been done to me, but for what I've done to others and myself . . . You can be the judge; you tell me if I'm to live now . . . Can you tell me . . .?" (523)

Further, he admits that "he was caught" (563) after Ely Houston, his alter-ego, reminds him of his *inhumanity*:

> You've grown up and gone beyond our rituals. I knew that you were beyond organized religion, but I didn't suspect that you were already beyond the family . . .
> And I said to myself: "This man *could* have killed Blount, Herndon, and Hilton . . . Only *he* could have done it. He has the emotional capacity—or *lack* of it!—to do it." (562)[26]

And finally, he is shot, most probably by the Party, confessing to Houston in his dying words, the necessity of needing "others": "The search can't be done alone . . . Never alone . . . Alone a man is nothing . . . Man is all we've got" (585). Cross appears to regret his psychological detachment, his absence of commitment, and his estrangement from family, community, and friends. Blinded by himself and his outsider status he is ultimately self-trapped but despite Houston's implorations (584–6), he cannot account for himself.

What Peter K. Garret terms the Gothic's propensity for "solitary subjectivity under stress" (3) is an especially apt description of Cross in this closing scene. For while the Gothic subverts judgment it can also, in complicating the reader's relation to the narrative, defy reader understanding. So too can it, because it lacks "shared paradigms" with society at large (especially in its American forms), "leave characters struggling to judge and make sense of things on their own" (Soltysik 26)—Cross's dilemma throughout the novel. Alan Lloyd-Smith argues that a standard feature of the Gothic form is that it "allows the thrill of readerly experience of transgression within a safe and moralizing pattern of closure. Because of the ongoing confrontation between these opposing forces, the Gothic situates itself in areas of liminality, of transition, at first staged literally in liminal spaces and between opposing individuals, but subsequently appearing more and more as divisions between opposing aspects within the self" (5–6). *The Outsider* adds a racial and popular-cultural dimension to this mix. It represents some of Wright's Left-wing mass pulp truths about American politics in the 1950s; it poses a challenge to postwar American middle-class complacencies and racial conformities; and it shows how Wright uses the Gothic to push this self beyond any acceptable ethical, or moral limits, to make Cross Damon irredeemable, unaccountable, and to expose the "devilish aberrations" still haunting post-World War II America.

Notes

1 Racial discourses have always been embedded in the American Gothic. For the terms "American Gothic" and "Gothic discourse," see Justin E. Edwards's *Gothic Passages: Racial Ambiguity and the American Gothic*, xviii–xxviii; for how the Gothic has been modified by the term "American," see Teresa Goddu's *Gothic America: Narrative, History, and Nation*. Given its racial and socio-cultural importance, the Gothic in Richard Wright's fiction and non-fiction has been undervalued and undertheorized. For notable exceptions, see Michel Fabre's *The World of Richard Wright* (Jackson: University of Mississippi Press, 1985), 27–33, and *The Unfinished Quest of Richard Wright* (New York: Morrow, 1973); Joseph Bodziock's "Richard Wright and Afro-American Gothic" in *Richard Wright: Myths and Realities*, ed. C. James Trotman (New York: Garland, 1988), 27–42; James Smethurst's "Invented by Horror: The Gothic and African American Literary Ideology in *Native Son*" (*African American Review* 35, Spring 2001), 29–41; Cedric Gail Bryant's "The Soul Has Bandaged Moments: Reading the African American Gothic in Wright's 'Big Boy Leaves Home,' Morrison's 'Beloved,' and Gomez's 'Gilda'" (*African American Review* 39, Winter 2005), 541–53; and Diane Long Hoeveler's "The Gothic (Literary Style)" in *The Richard Wright Encyclopedia* (eds Jerry Ward and Robert J. Butler, London: Greenwood Press, 2008), 153–6. The Gothic in *The Outsider* has gone largely untreated in Wright criticism.
2 See, for example, Stephen Soitos, *The Blues Detective: A Study of African American Detective Fiction* (Amherst: University of Massachusetts Press, 1996); Charles L. P. Silet, *The Critical Response to Chester Himes* (Westport: Greenwood Press, 1999); Sheree R.

Thomas (ed.), *Dark Matters: A Century of Speculative Fiction from the African Diaspora* (New York: Warner, 2000); and Reginald Martin, *Dark Eros: Black Erotic Writing* (New York: St. Martin's Press, 1997).

3   Inversing the more rural Gothic of a Faulkner or O'Connor, Wright's Gothic is a palimpsest for divergent responses to political and social oppression in which the dark places of cities (Chicago and New York) conceal irrational passions, and the threat of racial corruption. At the same time, he uses the mode to assert the possibilities—and dangers—of a "re-sacralization" (Brooks 17) of the individual in a phenomenal world. As we shall see, the Gothic thus becomes the base for Wright's racial recreation of an uncivil world.

4   For examples of Wright's use of these forms, see Joseph B. Entin's *Sensational Modernism: Experimental Fiction and Photography in Thirties America* (Chapel Hill: The Univeristy of North Carolina Press, 2007), 215–56 and Paula Rabinowitz's *Black and White and Noir: America's Pulp Modernism* (New York: Columbia UP, 2002), 82–102. This essay is indebted to both of these studies.

5   See, for example, Mae Henderson's "Drama and Denial in *The Outsider*" (*Richard Wright: Critical Perspectives Past and Present*, eds Henry Louis Gates and K. A. Appiah. New York: Amistad, 1993), 388.

6   As Wright states in his essay, "Tradition and Industrialization" (1956), "This contradiction of being both Western and a man of color creates a psychological distance, so to speak, between me and my environment . . . Hence, though Western, I'm inevitably critical of the West. Indeed, a vital element of my Westerness resides in this chronologically skeptical, this irredeemably critical outlook" (705).

7   A reviewer of Wright's *Native Son* made this comment about the novel that could easily pertain to *The Outsider*:

> the "extraordinary" aspect of the book is that it approaches difficult questions of race "through a criminal who commits such atrocities as are dealt with in the most sensational tabloids."
>
> (*Richard Wright: The Critical Reception*, ed. John M. Reilly.
> New York: B. Franklin, 1978), 52

8   See Agniezska Soltysik, *The Poetics and Politics of the American Gothic: Gender and Slavery in Nineteenth-Century American Literature* (Farham: Ashgate, 2010) and Peter K. Garrett, *Gothic Reflections: Narrative Force in Nineteenth-Century Fiction* (Ithaca NY: Cornell UP, 2003).

9   Michel Fabre argues, "One consistently finds traces in him of the poor black child who owes his spiritual survival in racist Mississippi and, in part, his vocation as a writer to detective stories, popular fiction, and dime novels" (Fabre, *World of Richard Wright*), 93. For specific examples of Wright's use of such forms, see Rabinowitz, *Black and White and Noir*, 85–6, 98, 102; and Margaret Walker, *How I Wrote Jubilee and Other Essays on Life and Literature* (New York: The Feminist Press, 1990), 33–49.

10 See Suzanne Schlangen, "Film Noir: Not Just Black and White." *The Image of the Hero II*. Eds Will Wright and Steven Caplan (Pueblo, CO; Society for the Interdisciplinary Study of Social Imagery, 2010) and Paula Rabinowitz, *Black and White and Noir*, 61–3; 73–4; 95–7.

11 As Andrew Spicer notes, "film noir is not only a list of textual conventions which reflected a wider social malaise," but rather "it is also the product of a multi-faceted

interaction between developments with particular genres" (*Film Noir*, Essex, England: Pearson Education, 2002), vii. Gothic melodrama is certainly one of the interacting players. *The Outsider* can usefully be treated as a literary version of such noir films as *Double Indemnity* (1944), *Kiss Me Deadly* (1954), *The Naked City* (1948), and *The Third Man* (1949) but with important differences from the conventional film noir. *The Outsider* is characterized by a certain anxiety over the existence and definition of race— in relation to, among much else, a 1950s "masculinity" and "normality."

12 See James Smethurst, "Invented by Horror: The Gothic and African American Literary Ideology in *Native Son*" (*African American Review* 35, Spring 2001), 29–41. For the purpose of my argument, I am taking my definition of "hard-boiled" from Walter Mosley who suggests that "hard-boiled" can be seen as eliding into a Gothic terrain, "The hard-boiled condition is when a man or a woman, or an entire nation of women and men, is pressed to physical, emotional, economic, and/or intellectual limits—past, present, and for the foreseeable future . . . In this world there are only choices between evils, and the secret, unobtainable rulebook was written by Satan himself" ("Poisonville," *A New Literary History of America*. Eds Greil Marcus and Werner Sollers. Cambridge: Harvard University Press, 2009), 598.

13 See Steven Bruhm, "The Contemporary Gothic: Why We Need It" (*Cambridge Companion to Gothic Fiction* Ed. Jerrold E. Hogle, Cambridge: Cambridge University Press, 2002).

14 Tellingly, one of the novel's most important events, the fortuitous subway accident and Cross's supposed death, is announced by a popular cultural form, the radio: "*Ladies and Gentlemen, the police have just informed me of the identity of the last victim taken from the subway crash at Roosevelt Road. His name is Cross Damon, a 26-year-old postal clerk who lived at 244 East 57th Street on the South Side*" (103). Throughout the novel Cross, on the lamb, reads about his own story in the Chicago and New York newspapers. For noir fiction in twentieth-century America, see Sean McCann, *Gumshoe America: Hard-boiled Crime Fiction and the Rise and Fall of New Deal Liberalism* (Durham, NC: Duke UP, 2000).

15 For useful histories of American blues and jazz, see the DVDs by Alan Lomax, *The Land Where Blues Began*, 2009; and Ken Burns, *Jazz: A Film by Ken Burns*, 2004.

16 For the ambivalence of Wright's relation to existentialism, see Jeffrey Attebury, "Entering the Politics of the Outside: Richard Wright's Critique of Existentialism" (*MFS Modern Fiction Studies*, 51.4, Winter 2005), 873–95.

17 For Wright, exile, and existentialism, see, for example, Michel Fabre, "Richard Wright and the French Existentialists" (*The Critical Response to Richard Wright*, ed. Robert Butler. New York: Greenwood, 1995), 111–21; Yoshinobou Hakutani, *Cross-Cultural Visions in African American Modernism* (Columbia: Ohio State UP, 2006) 101–19; and Amritjit Singh, "Richard Wright's *The Outsider*: Existentialist Exemplar or Critique?" (*The Critical Response to Richard Wright*, ed. Robert Butler. New York: Greenwood, 1995), 123–9.

18 As Marc Mvé Bekale points out, *The Outsider* expresses "Wright's disillusionment with the foundational values of Western societies, the evolution of which has resulted in [quoting from *The Outsider*] 'a kind of war against mankind'" (3). Cross Damon's "war" reflecting his "struggl[e] to make sense of the material values of Western society" (3) is reinforced and furthered by the pulp Gothic form of the novel.

19 Wright papers, Box 53, Folder 639. *Jet*, March 26, 1953.

20 See Finley C. Campbell's "Prophet of the Storm: Richard Wright and the Radical Tradition" (*Phylon*, Vol. 38, No. 1, 1977), 9–23, for a chronology of Wright's involvement with the CPUSA. By the time Wright quit the party (1944), he felt that it had become oppressive and dictatorial. He also held that it gave inadequate "attention to the fight against racism and the development of the individual" (Fabre, *The Unfinished Quest*, 231).

21 For a discussion of the Party dominating Cross's consciousness, see R. Baxter Miller, "From New Chicago Renaissance" (*Richard Wright: New Readings in the 21st Century.* Eds Alice Mikal Craven and William E. Dow, New York: Palgrave Macmillan, 2011), 21–2.

22 As Paula Rabinowitz notes in reference to *The Outsider* (*Black and White and Noir: America's Pulp Modernism,* New York: Columbia UP, 2002),

> The picture of the Communist Party that Wright paints … is one of venal deception and raw exploitation. When it needed a black face, the CPUSA was willing to take on a stranger and provide a new identity. But should that stranger question the discipline required of him, he would be left dangling—offered up to rivals, including the police, to protect the organization. (100)

23 Significant qualifications to this assessment: as Maryemma Graham has noted, "although Wright became disenchanted with the Communist party in the United States, he remained a Marxist with a revolutionary vision of societal change, continuing his activist commitments throughout his life" ("Introduction," *The Outsider*. 1953. New York: Harper Perennial, 2003), xviii. See also Alan Wald, "The City Was Unity: Communist and African Americans, 1917–1936" (*African American Review*. 34.4, Winter 2000), 716.

24 Significantly, the murder of Hilton is framed between "the dancing waves of jazz music that swirled around [Hilton's] room" and Cross Damon (Lionel Lane), immediately after leaving the hotel where the murder has taken place, purchasing *The Daily News* (405–6).

25 Reactions to the novel have generated various kinds of uncertainties and confusions. See Robert Coles, "Richard Wright's *The Outsider*: A Novel in Transition (*Modern Language Studies*. Vol. 13, No. 3, Summer 1983), 53–61. For *The Outsider* as an "abysmal flop," and the demise of Wright's career in Paris, "dragged down by the wreckage of *The Outsider*," see James Campbell, *Paris Interzone: Richard Wright, Lolita, Boris Vian, and Others on the Left Bank 1946–1960* (London: Secker and Warburg, 1994), 105, 106. I would attribute the claim that *The Outsider* is a failed novel partially to the fact that it has not been sufficiently understood as a pulp-Gothic text, one overflowing with multiple meanings and descriptive excess. As Judith Halberstam notes, the type of fear the Gothic produces in a literary text "emanates from a vertiginous excess of meaning … Within Gothic novels … multiple interpretations are embedded in the text and part of the experience of horror comes from the realization that meaning itself runs riot" (Halberstam 2). At certain moments, Cross's horror and fear result in a kind of epistemological overkill in which he has no sense of a past or a future, only the horrific realization that his monstrosity seems to emanate from within.

26 Cross's encounters with himself, Eva, and Houston emblematize perhaps his most terrible Gothic sin: his inability to feel, his hardness towards his mother's death, and the abandonment of his sons. In standard Gothic fashion, the family, a stable marker of social identity, is obliterated.

Works cited

Babb, Valerie. "Wright, Hurston, and the African American Novel." *The Cambridge History of the American Novel*. Ed. Leonard Cassuto et al. Cambridge: Cambridge UP, 2011. 798–812. Print.

Bekale, Marc Mvé. "Cultural Hybridity and Existential Crisis in Richard Wright's *The Outsider* and Cheikh Hamidou Kane's *L'aventure ambiguë*." *Transatlantica* 1/2009: 1–7. Web. Sept. 23, 2011.

Brooks, Peter. *The Melodramatic Imagination*. New Haven: Yale UP, 1976. Print.

Bruhm, Steven. "The Contemporary Gothic: Why We Need It." *Cambridge Companion to Gothic Fiction*. Ed. Jerrold E. Hogle. Cambridge: Cambridge UP, 2002. Print.

Chodat, Robert. "Philosophy and the American Novel." *The Cambridge History of the American Novel*. Ed. Leonard Cassuto et al. Cambridge: Cambridge UP, 2011. 653–70. Print.

Dietzel, Susanne B. "The African American Novel and Popular Culture." *The Cambridge Companion to the African American Novel*. Ed. Maryemma Graham. Cambridge: Cambridge UP, 2006. 156–70. Print.

Edwards, Justin D. *Gothic Passages: Racial Ambiguity and the American Gothic*. Iowa City: U of Iowa P, 2003. Print.

Ellison, Ralph. "The Seer and the Seen." *Shadow and the Act*. New York: Signet, 1966. Print.

Fabre, Michel. *The Unfinished Quest of Richard Wright*. 1973. Trans. Isabel Barzun. Urbana: U of Illinois P, 1993. Print.

—— *The World of Richard Wright*. Jackson: UP of Mississippi, 1985. Print.

Garrett, Peter K. *Gothic Reflections: Narrative Force in Nineteenth-Century Fiction*. Ithaca: Cornell UP, 2003. Print.

Gilroy, Paul. *The Black Atlantic: Modernity and Double Consciousness*. Cambridge: Harvard UP, 1993. Print.

Goddu, Teresa. *Gothic America: Narrative, History, and Nation*. New York: Columbia UP, 1997. Print.

Graham, Maryemma. Introduction. *The Outsider*. By Richard Wright. 1953. New York: Harper Perennial, 2003. xiii–xxxi. Print.

Hoover, J. Edgar. *Masters of Deceit: The Story of Communism in America and How to Fight It*. New York: Holt, 1958. Print.

Lloyd-Smith, Alan. *American Gothic Fiction*. New York: Continuum, 2004. Print.

McCluskey, John, Jr. "Two Steppin': Richard Wright's Encounter with Blue-Jazz." *American Literature* 55.3 (1983): 332–44. Print.

Rabinowitz, Paula. *Black and White and Noir: America's Pulp Modernism*. New York: Columbia UP, 2002. Print.

Relyea, Sarah. "The Vanguard of Modernity: Richard Wright's *The Outsider*." *Texas Studies in Literature and Language* 48.3 (2006): 187–219. Print.

Soltysik, Agniezska. *The Poetics and Politics of the American Gothic: Gender and Slavery in Nineteenth-Century American Literature*. Farham: Ashgate, 2010. Print.

Wald, Alan. "Steinbeck and the Proletarian Novel." *The Cambridge History of the American Novel*. Ed. Leonard Cassuto et al. Cambridge: Cambridge UP, 2011: 671–85. Print.

Walker, Margaret. *How I Wrote Jubilee and Other Essays on Life and Literature*. New York: Feminist Press, 1990. Print.

Ward, Jerry. "Everybody's Protest Novel: The Era of Richard Wright." *The Cambridge Companion to the African American Novel*. London: Cambridge UP, 2006. Print.

West, Cornell. Introduction. *Three Books From Exile:* Black Power, The Color Curtain, *and* White Man Listen! By Richard Wright. New York: Harper Perennial, 2008. vii–xiii. Print.

Wright, Richard. "How 'Bigger' Was Born." *Native Son*. New York: Harper Collins, 1993. Print.

—— *The Outsider*. 1953. New York: HarperPerennial, 2003. Print.

—— "Tradition and Industrialization." *Three Books From Exile:* Black Power, The Color Curtain, *and* White Man Listen! Intro. Cornel West. New York: HarperPerennial, 2008. 701–28. Print.

—— *Twelve Million Black Voices*. 1941. New York: Basic Books, 2008. Print.

10

Working the Underground Seam: Richard Wright's "The Man Who Lived Underground" in the Light of Percival Everett's *Zulus*

Michel Feith
University of Nantes, CRINI

Judging from his 2001 novel *Erasure*, Percival Everett is no great fan of Richard Wright's. In this text, *Native Son* is a major butt of the satire of stereotyped, "neo-minstrel" ghetto writing, whereas Wright's great adversary, Ralph Ellison, serves as a model to overcome such ethnic provincialism (Feith 74–5). Yet Everett himself confessed later that he may have been unfair both in praise and blame ("Interview" 225). We have all the more reason to dig further into Everett's intertextual relation with Wright since another of his novels, *Zulus*, written in 1990, seems to echo both "The Man Who Lived Underground" and *Invisible Man*, thus reconciling the "parent" and "ancestor" who are at loggerheads in *Erasure*.[1]

The underground as both topography and symbol pervades *Zulus*, as a summary of the plot will make clear. In a future dystopian society, whose advent is consecutive to some World War, and where women have been sterilized, presumably to prevent harmful genetic mutations and the birth of monsters, the only fertile woman left, obese Alice Achitophel, gets pregnant after being raped and decides to run away from the city to the abode of the "rebels" in the wilderness. She is smuggled out through a form of the Underground Railroad but is soon disappointed by the rebels' bigotry and instrumentalization of her fertility. The Messiah turned Devil goes back to the city, but under a different form. Fat Alice has turned into a cave of flesh that explodes, letting out a thin version of herself, still in ESP contact with her decaying former husk. When thin Alice gets pregnant by her black lover, Kevin Peters, her child is stolen. In her quest for her lover and child, she burrows deep into the underbelly of the city and is finally poised to destroy all human life by liberating a poisonous gas from a container worshipped by an enormous crowd in a roofed stadium.

The plot seems to belong firmly to the genre of popular science fiction, yet the theme of the underground also connects the novel with major milestones in the African American tradition, like Jean Toomer's *Cane*, Wright's "The Man Who Lived Underground," and Ellison's *Invisible Man*. As a matter of fact, Ellison is mentioned at least twice: once by name—"*E is for Ellison and his Optic White*" (*Zulus* 63)—and once indirectly—"*poetry out of being invisible*" (*Zulus* 119). One character in *Zulus* is called Sue Kabnis after the "underground" play revolving around the mute figure of an African ex-slave enthroned in a cellar, which constitutes the third part of *Cane*. Wright is not named: does this mean that his contribution to the theme is silenced or denied? It seems on the contrary that we can find many allusions to his work in *Zulus*, perhaps in the form of a "quiet tribute" similar to that paid to Chester Himes's *If He Hollers Let Him Go* in *Erasure*, not on the explicit level but "scattered throughout the book in a lot more subtle way" (Everett, "Interview" 225). Even though veiled in "invisibility," we may assume that Wright still underwrites the project of the novel, both filtered through the Ellisionian prism and for his own sake, as an underground "ancestor."

But it is impossible to deal fully with the underground theme without referring back to Fyodor Dostoyevsky's *Notes from Underground*, which had a deep impact on Toomer, Wright, and Ellison, as well as on Lewis Carroll's *Alice's Adventures in Wonderland*, presumably the intertextual motivation for the protagonist's first name; her adventures are those of Alice in the Waste Land. Starting from Dostoyevsky's novella, it might be interesting to work the seams—or the semes—down through time and see how they are rewritten by each black writer. Yet it seems to us that a chronological study of cumulative influences is not the only, or the best, way of dealing with intertextuality. My approach will be less linear and is inspired by Henry Louis Gates, Jr.'s vision of African American intertextuality as "Signifyin(g)," or creative parody and revision, according to which each new writer working the seam comments both on his or her predecessor and on the whole chain, reconfiguring the tradition by entering into a dialogue with it, sometimes setting off an "ancestor" against another, in a critical evaluation of the way each of them treated the theme (Gates 122). This implies a shift from the image of a chronological chain to that of a coextensive network, supporting a multidirectional analysis that allows the reader to reinterpret the works in the light of each other, actualizing or even creating potential meaning.

We will therefore study "The Man Who Lived Underground" as a hub in a polycentric intertextual network, a hub radiating in many directions but also modified by its relation with other texts. Our main focus will be on the convergence between Wright's novella and Everett's *Zulus*, yet Dostoyevsky and Ellison will constitute two other poles of this study, forming, so to speak, a virtual square of influences. Incidentally, we might remark that intertextual relations are not only established between literary texts but also include the works of critics like, in the present paper, Michel Fabre, Houston A. Baker, Jr., or Mikhail Bakhtin. The three lines of force that will allow us to set a course in the multiple ramifications of the intertextual field will be those of dialogism in narrative form; grotesque and carnivalesque elements; and the messianic language games at work and play in our texts. We might then be able to pinpoint transformational constants in Everett's refashioning of "The Man": strategies of radicalization and displacement, revolving around the body as a site of alienation and potential empowerment.

The stereophonic rabbit-hole: Dialogue and narration

Bakhtin's concept of dialogism has both an intratextual and an extratextual dimension: it implies first the presence of a dialogue of ideas within the work, in the form of exchanges between characters, for example, and, second, a dialogue between the work and other discourses, social or literary (Bakhtin, *Problems* 182–3). As far as narrative strategies are concerned, the four novels or novellas under study can be grouped into pairs. Dostoyevsky's and Ellison's are characterized by complex first-person narration and divided into two main parts, one "philosophical," the other narrative; each part calls out to the other, and the reader is explicitly addressed, thereby exploiting to the full the dialogical possibilities of the novel genre. On the other hand, Wright's and Everett's plots are presented in linear, chronological fashion, in the third person, in an apparently unsophisticated mode. If formal complexity were to be taken as an outstanding criterion of quality and literary merit, then *Notes from Underground* and *Invisible Man* would obviously be superior to "The Man Who Lived Underground" and *Zulus*. This is implied by Robert Bone: "Ellison succeeds in developing on a full scale themes which Wright treats only sketchily" (201–2). Why would such a self-conscious writer as Everett choose a sort of formal regression rather than further complicating the theme? We might have to reconsider our standards, especially as they affect the interpretation of Wright's work.

One of the possible readings of Wright's story is a naturalistic one, according to which Fred Daniels represents the black man as victim, the underground being a transparent allegory of the lower depths of society, illustrated by the opposition between light and darkness. The protagonist's murder at the hands of white policemen completes this "protest novel" dimension or, in a more affirmative way, converts him into a figure of black identity and resistance (Watkins 149; Young 15). It is precisely to avoid these deterministic definitions of identity from outside the individual, corresponding to third-person designation, that the anti-hero of Dostoyevsky's *Underground* writes a first-person confession, permeated with second-person addresses to his fantasized potential readers. This reactive streak helps explain his constant contradictions and shifts in positions: his monologue is a polemic dialogue, and his main objective is a refusal to be pinpointed to any stable location or essence, so as to keep his freedom (Bakhtin, *Problems* 53).

The prologue of *Invisible Man* is also a jumpy, agonistic monologue, exhibiting the conditions of production of the writing and replete with addresses to the reader. "The Invisible Man stands in relation to white American culture and *its* ideas and values as Dostoevky's Underground Man stands in relation to Western European culture. For the Invisible Man discovers that all of its definitions of himself, all the structures within which it wishes to place him as a Negro, violate some aspect of his own integrity" (Frank 47). Ellison's reverting to Dostoyevsky's technique of the dialogical monologue could be more than a bypassing, an implicit criticism of Wright's perceived naturalism. Yet the naturalistic interpretation of "The Man" is not the only, or the most rewarding, reading. Another possible plot is an existentialist fable, in which the protagonist, exiled from the strictures of the world aboveground, has a liberating insight into the human condition. More than a racial allegory, the represented situation is that of the individual in modern society, characterized by a feeling of universal guilt, not in the narrow legal sense but in the existentialist sense of "thrownness" into an absurd world (Fabre 100). His final discovery, a lay version of Christic redemption and messianism, is that a common guilt makes brothers of all human beings and that hierarchies and oppression have no ground for being anymore. "If he could show them what he had seen, then they would feel what he had felt and they in turn would show it to others and those others would feel as they had felt, and soon everybody would be governed by the same impulse of pity" (Wright, "The Man Who Lived Underground" [hereafter "MU"] 81).

Invisible Man is governed by a similar pattern of hibernation, resurrection, and shedding of illusions. Other elements in the prologue and epilogue of Ellison's novel recall Wright's text: the inversion of the values of light and darkness in the underground, the latter as a place for meditation on the human condition, and as a locus of artistic creation at one remove from everyday experience, symbolized in "The Man" by the theft of the typewriter. In a way, the Dostoyevskian bipartition of *Invisible Man* might not only be a tribute to the great "ancestor" but also a differential Signifyin(g) on Wright. Many episodes in the main narrative appear as critical reminiscences of *Black Boy* and the short memoir "I Tried to Be a Communist"; even though Ellison's evaluation of *Black Boy* was more positive than that of *Native Son*, he still deplored the author's "ideological" insistence on the depleted condition of black existence and culture (*Shadow and Act* 120, 140). By framing his own takes on Wright's realistic or naturalistic writing by allusions to the more self-reflexive "Man," Ellison might have encoded in his own work an implicit comparison between two facets of Wright's talent, subterraneously tipping the scales toward the underground side.

The above example reminds us that dialogism in a literary work does not need to be foregrounded in terms of form; it can also be present, as a "double-voiced" discourse, in ironic tension, in indirect speech, or in intertextual reference. Neither "The Man Who Lived Underground" nor *Zulus* necessarily lose in complexity for their linear story line and seemingly matter-of-fact third-person narration. In Wright's novella, a hidden polemic with the world aboveground is conducted more through things than through words. Fred steals objects, not for their exchange or monetary value, but for their aesthetic or "semiotic" value. This expresses fascination, of course, but also establishes a dialogue.

> He did not feel that he was stealing, for the cleaver, the radio, the money, and the typewriter were all on the same level of value, all meant the same thing to him. They were the serious toys of the men who lived in the dead world of sunshine and rain he had left, the world that had condemned him, found him guilty.
>
> ("MU" 47)

In Dostoyevsky's *Notes from the Underground*, words are acts; in the Freudian interpretation of dreams, words and things can become interchangeable; here, in this other dream-like world, things are words. They carry the weight of social discourses and practices: by using them against the grain, Fred frees their polysemy. Even though he is inarticulate and misunderstood when he emerges from the sewer, what he performs in his cave is a silent reappropriation of (symbolic) language through the medium of objects, what Baker calls "a countertext to the cultural discourse of the upper world" (169). This countertext hieroglyphically denounces the folly of mankind: the hidden polemic is a form of satire.

Zulus introduces another alternative to linear narrative: each chapter is introduced not by a number but by a letter of the alphabet—from A to Zulus—and a short paragraph, a rhapsodic succession of sentences whose key words start with the initial at hand and are often linked by associational logic.

> *A is for Achitophel. It was he who put Absalom up to the big naughty. Dryden called Achitophel a great wit. Not to blow Dryden off, but the wit was Solomon's. Sawing a babe in two? "And thin partitions do their bounds divide." So, A is for Solomon for there are better for S and because Solomon was small and a little queer. A is for Aristotle who learned from Plato. A is for Anaximander who said that the element of things is Boundless. (7)*

In the other three texts, the protagonist is at one moment or another shown in the act of writing, but not in *Zulus*. Perhaps as compensation, and echoing Fred's stolen typewriter, these chapter headings self-reflexively foreground the infrastructure of all novels, the alphabetic code. The text becomes a gigantic spelling bee, exhibiting the combinatory powers of language even below the semantic level. There is something playful in giving the character a name from this first, extradiegetic paragraph: it sets in relief the arbitrariness of fiction and characterization. Yet this language game is not purely gratuitous. Achitophel, the villain in John Dryden's 1681 satire *Absalom and Achitophel*, was a biblical flatterer who tempted King David's son Absalom into betraying his father; he is often seen as an antetype of Judas. He announces the many betrayals Alice will experience, but his forked tongue also hints at the intimate connection between language and deception, in a pointed take on the concept of "double-voicedness." The theme of duality, duplicity, and division is further pursued in the reference to Solomon's judgment: it foreshadows Alice's parturition by splitting. Her "double A" initials also spell division, all the more so since the meanings of her first and last names are at loggerheads: Alice comes from the Greek *Aletheia* "truth," whereas Achitophel is "Brother of Madness." Put together into one sentence, the components are even more ambiguous: is truth to be opposed to madness and duplicity, or is truth the "brother of madness," as the pessimistic ending seems to imply?

The novel functions simultaneously on at least two levels: the diegetic level of the linear science-fiction story and the symbolic level, characterized by an associational, radiating logic that feeds on intertextual references. This opposition, or dialectic, between a narrative superstructure and a "rhizomatic" infrastructure echoes the dichotomy between the aboveground and underground worlds; it also has a more fundamental, theoretical dimension. Fabre had already remarked that the topology of "The Man Who Lived Underground" was an exploration of "the nature of literary works"—a characteristic it shares with Dostoyevsky's *Notes from the Underground* and

Invisible Man—and that Fred's "transformations and wanderings underground reflect the winding becoming of a work in the unconscious" (106). Perhaps this analysis can be projected even deeper, into the very nature of language, if we follow Jean-Jacques Lecercle.

> As a consequence, I shall no longer treat language as a scientific object, susceptible of a comprehensive description in terms of system and coherence, i.e. in terms of Saussure's concept of *langue*. There is another side to language, one that escapes the linguist's attention, not because of his temporary failure or failings, but for necessary reasons. This dark side emerges in nonsensical and poetic texts, in the illuminations of mystics and the delirium of logophiliacs or mental patients I have called it 'the remainder'. (5–6)

This rhizomatic remainder, which is "in excess" of the rules of grammar, semantics, and narrative, is actually not a minor, residual part but the substratum of language, the underground chaos that rules are formed to discipline. It is, so to speak, the grotesque state of language. At this juncture, it seems possible to say that, out of the different threads of the underground tradition, Everett "sides" with Wright in his choice of narrative form, while radicalizing his criticique of the economy of the sign.

The grotesque and the GroText

Providing a different, distorted perspective on the world above, the underground has essential affinities with the grotesque: the word itself comes from "grotto," referring to the type of fantastic ornamentation brought to light during the excavation of Titus's baths in Rome, characterized by "the extremely fanciful, free, and playful treatment of plant, animal, and human forms. These forms seemed to be intervowen as if giving birth to each other" (Bakhtin, *Rabelais* 31–2). Moreover, Toomer, Wright, and Ellison are renowned for their use of grotesque imagery throughout their *œuvre* (Gysin). Compared to "The Man," *Zulus* is once more characterized by a radicalization and partial displacement of the grotesque theme. There is an actantial shift from a black male protagonist to a (presumably) white female; rather than simply being in a cave, she becomes the cave, explodes, and gives birth to . . . herself. But in both texts, the basis for all subsequent symbolic developments seems to be the body as a site of alienation, the body as a prison of flesh under the reifying gaze of the Other. The grotesque is in the eye of the beholder: blackness for Fred and obesity for Alice set them apart from the mainstream. This Platonician *soma/sema* (body/grave) may then become, with various degrees of success, a paradoxical site of liberation and empowerment.

Zulus is a freak show, full of grotesques: a Rabelaisian giant, and several midgets, like Alice's treacherous allies, her boss and helper Theodore and his girlfriend Lucinda Knowles. Physical caricature often points at another form of grotesque, the mental or spiritual kind, which Fritz Gysin defines as "a discordance between body and soul" (143). The city resembles T. S. Eliot's Waste Land, a land of death-in-life based on absurd repetition sponsored and controlled by the government. The rebel camp is defined by the same emptiness as the city (*Zulus* 101), becoming its grotesque mirror.

If the grotesque in our works often conveys caricature and satire, does it retain the positive, life-affirming dimension that is often associated with it since Bakhtin? As a matter of fact, the Russian critic connects the grotesque to the spirit of the carnival, a popular merry-making that suspends the laws and hierarchies of society in favor of an egalitarian spirit illustrated by the parodic inversion of the social order. This vision of the topsy-turvy world focuses particularly on the lower functions of the body (Bakhtin, *Rabelais* 20). Alice's explosive birthing has both somatic and social implications: it is a total upheaval and the ultimate act of rebellion against the rebels' narrow-mindedness; it also literally sets her free from the house where she had been confined.

Other Rabelaisian representations of Alice's body are to be found when she is examined by the rebel doctors and knows the humiliation of her stinking body (*Zulus* 89) or at the public bath, when she is caressed by the midgets who clean her, bringing her to an orgasm (*Zulus* 93). This ambivalent image of the body, which is both dirty and clean, decaying and life-giving—the smell could be caused by pregnancy, say the doctors—ties in very well with Bakhtin's analysis of the popular view of the grotesque:

> The grotesque image reflects a phenomenon in transformation, an as yet unfinished metamorphosis, of death and birth, growth and becoming. The relation to time is one determining trait of the grotesque image. The other indispensable trait is ambivalence. For in this image we find both poles of transformation, the old and the new, the dying and the procreating, the beginning and the end of the metamorphosis.
>
> (*Rabelais* 24)

There is a special affinity between the grotesque body and the earth, especially the underground, including graves and Hell, seen as sites of death and rebirth. "The essential principle of grotesque realism is degradation, that is, the lowering of all that is high, spiritual, ideal, abstract; it is a transfer to the material level, to the sphere of earth and body in their indissoluble unity" (Bakhtin, *Rabelais* 19–20). This paradoxical fusion of opposites and ambivalent topology is present in "The Man Who Lived Underground" even more than in *Invisible Man*. The sewers of "The Man" become organic, a mythical womb-and-tomb complex, as is made obvious by Fred's disappearance and reappearance through a "manhole," the presence of a dead baby in the waters, and a funeral parlor. Pipes and drains take on a bodily dimension: they are compared to veins and a throat ("MU" 22, 26). "The bottom of the sewer was a slopping V-trough" ("MU" 21), reminding of a uterus; in red light, water looks like blood ("MU" 31). High and low, light and darkness become inverted in what Baker calls a carnivalesque "transvaluation of values" (164): "The sun of the underground was fleeing and the terrible darkness of the day stood before him" ("MU" 75). The most striking example of this is the wonderful episode of the diamonds in the cave ("MU" 56–7). After stealing diamonds from a jeweller's safe, Fred divests them of their monetary value to use them in poetic and artistic ways. Comparing them to a lump of coal, he takes them back in time to their basic chemical elements; then, strewing them on the floor, he sees a sky of restless stars below him, then the "twinkling lights of a sprawling city," then images of the war the radio brings news of, and whose cause may very well be the cupidity of men for diamonds such as those (Capetti 7). The character's imagination seems to reach beyond mere metaphor, to initiate a process of metamorphosis that is applied to both himself and the cave. The reversibility of high and low, concerning the landscape, also involves Fred in a process of crowning and uncrowning, which, according to Bakhtin, is also typical of the carnivalesque spirit (*Problems* 124). From his state as a man, he becomes a god when watching cities and battles from above, and then a man again, in front of a meaningless pack of precious stones. The role-playing and laughter he indulges in in the cave just before this episode ("MU" 54–5) also evoke the masquerade and merry-making of the carnival, yet laughter turns to horror and anger as he feels trapped underground. When he re-emerges into the city, he is caked with mud like a newborn with blood and amniotic fluid ("MU" 66): his metamorphosis has affected both body and soul and has brought about the carnivalesque unity between organic and inorganic, man and matter.

This cosmic correspondence between the grotesque body and the earth is fully declined in *Zulus*, in a kind of Chinese-box, or *matryoshka*, effect. It starts with metonymic juxtaposition, goes on with metaphor, and ends up in a complete metamorphosis. The underground "scar" in the earth, which Alice walks along in her flight from the city, is also called a "vein" and almost absorbs her (*Zulus* 56–60). Then she feels reborn at the rebel camp, a place encircled with mountains, "and she felt safe nestled there as if in the arms of giants" (78): this isolated, womb-like landscape is that of all utopias. But the utopia soon becomes too good to be true: the rebel government, called the Body, is interested only in her (reproductive) body. This is a playful echo of the classical correspondence between microcosm and macrocosm, between the human body and the Body Politic. Interestingly enough, the same grotesque barrenness is to be found in the three concentric "bodies": human, social, and planetary. Alice, the only fertile woman, is a promise of renewal and salvation for all three. During the last stage of her pregnancy, she is, aptly, imprisoned in a dwelling situated behind the "Body House," another variation on a classical *topos*.

When she gives birth, metaphor becomes metamorphosis:

> The room became hot and wet with all the flesh, and the woman slipped into a hallucinatory state, seeing into her gut, observing the terrain of her interior and the growing creature within … She was a cavern, deep and wide and well-lighted and with pictures carved into the fat-walls of her cavity, pictures of houses arranged neatly in rows, of stick figures herding cattle and sheep, of men and women copulating, of crosses and arrows and swastikas and stars … And then the woman was breaking up, splitting as her body pressed into the walls of her confinement, breaking her into the light of day, while the earth quaked violently, and fingers pointed at the breaking woman, the opening body yielding the complete woman, full of the brain and emotions of her fat mother, earth mother, Alice Achitophel.
>
> (*Zulus* 108–9)

This episode is doubly grotesque: first, in the aesthetic sense, since "exaggeration, hyperbolism, excessiveness are generally considered fundamental attributes of the grotesque style" (Bakhtin, *Rabelais* 303); second, because the grotesque woman becomes a grotto where grotesques are inscribed, in a vertiginous *mise-en-abîme*. These graffiti read like a writing on the wall (of the body), down to the alphabet itself: the woman made of words bears on her paper flesh the very letters that make up her being and which introduce each chapter (*Zulus* 185). This *matryoshka* twist is textbook Bakhtin, further enhanced to encompass the body of the text and the body as text, an original variation on the "double body" of the grotesque:

> The grotesque body, as we have often stressed, is a body in the act of becoming. It is never finished, never completed; it is continually built, created, and builds and creates another body. Moreover, the body swallows the world and is itself swallowed by the world ... Eating, drinking, defecation, and other elimination ... as well as copulation, pregnancy, dismemberment, swallowing up by another body—all these acts are performed on the confines of the body and the outer world, or on the confines of the old and new body.
>
> (Bakhtin, *Rabelais* 317)

It also Signifies on Wright's underground topology, especially on the aforementioned passage in the cave: signs, cities, wars, a recapitulation of the whole history of mankind, from cave-dwelling and stick figures to modern cities and writing. According to Fabre, "The Man" has a certain closeness to Daniel Defoe's *Robinson Crusoe*: "the underground exploration represents the process involved in developing a culture" (104). *Zulus* deals with the reconstruction of a human, and possibly humane, culture after some cataclysm. Furthermore, the hallucinatory exaltation of the man in the sewer into a God and creator is rewritten in the feminine mode: Alice becomes an earth-goddess. This corresponds to the Paleolithic and early Neolithic cults of the Great Mother, illustrated by such iconography as the cave-dwellers' obese "Venuses" reminiscent of our own Alice and perpetuated in the myth of Demeter. The Greek goddess of the tilled earth retaliates to the kidnapping of her daughter Persephone by Hades, king of Hell, by making the earth barren. Persephone is restored to her mother for three-quarters of the year, the three months of winter being spent in the infernal regions with her husband. Alice's adventures underground, her fertility in a sterile world, and the final tier of her progress, in search of her ravished daughter and absentee lover, make her story a variation on that of Demeter.

This reversion to a "primitive" stage in the evolution of cultures ties in with a relatively coherent trajectory in the text. Alice moves first from a "developed," polluted, urban way of life to a small village smacking of the Puritan origins of the United States and then to a more elemental, "prehistoric" mentality. This equation of the carnivalesque to a form of elemental primitiveness to be rediscovered beneath the varnish of "civilization" is very Bakhtinian. Can we interpret it as an unveiling of the hidden Romantic premises on which our contemporary understanding of the carnival is based, as expressed both by Wright and Bakhtin? Another possible clue is more satiric and therefore in accordance with the semi-avowed genre of the novel: Alice has hallucinations and visions, and keeps a telepathic link with her older, discarded body. These phenomena of extrasensory perception remind us of the characteristics of shamanism and direct us toward Amerindian and African religious forms, whose spiritual contributions to American society appear to be more positive than those of Christianity and industrialization.

Furthermore, Alice's telepathic abilities actually endow her with a form of "double-consciousness," a split mind that is at the same time painful alienation and the visionary gift of "second sight." This take on W. E. B. Du Bois's definition of African American identity in *The Souls of Black Folk* (5) seems to inscribe *Zulus* firmly within the matrix of black literature. Should we then include it within the scope of Baker's triumphant definition of "The Man" as a black (w)hole in which the grotesque and carnivalesque are empowering subversive strategies that affirm black cultural and literary identity?

> Transliterated in letters of Afro-America, the *black hole* assumes the subsurface force of the black underground. It graphs, that is to say, the subterranean *hole* where the trickster has his ludic, deconstructive being. Further, in the script of Afro-America, the hole is the domain of *Wholeness*, an achieved relationality of black community in which desire recollects experience and sends it forth as blues. To be *Black* and *(W)hole* is to escape incarcerating restraints of a white world (i.e., a *black hole*) and to engage the concentrated, underground singularity of experience that results in a blues desire's expressive fullness.
>
> (Baker 151–2)

Messianic language games

According to Baker, this "fullness of black expression" is linked to two main figures: the folkloric trickster and Jesus Christ. Fred is identified with the former for his overall subversion of aboveground hierarchies in favor of "implicit antinomian and egalitarian underground norms" (Baker 171). He is then seen as a true Christic character, in opposition to the basement church worshippers' desire for atonement within the system: the form of redemption he illustrates is a "revised logos—a new 'Word' transforming chaos and death into a humane order of existence[,] a life of responsible human freedom" (Baker 169). Baker's conjunction of the trickster and Christ, which is quite close to Bakhtin's implicit infusion of carnivalesque egalitarianism with quasi-messianic fervor, leads him to discard Fred's death as a mere "ritual act": "As a primal, expressive Logos, a Word, he is no more dead at the conclusion of the novella than his Judeo-Christian archetype" (Baker 172).

There is only one problem with this upbeat finale: the Biblical Christ is not killed again after re-emerging from his three-day stint in his grave cave. Fred's lions' den is not the underground but the police station, which he does not leave unscathed. Textual irony establishes similarities between Fred's fate and that of another Christ, the one who comes back to earth in Dostoyevsky's "parable of the Great Inquisitor" from *The*

Brothers Karamazov. This character is expelled from the city by the inquisitor, because his message is too disruptive for the social order established by the Church, just as an inarticulate Fred is shooed away by the black congregation before being killed by white policemen. Fred is not really a figure of black empowerment, and Wright was hardly a novelist of black "expressive fullness": African American culture and vernacular forms were problematic to him, as illustrated by a famous passage from *Black Boy*:

> Whenever I thought of the essential bleakness of black life in America, I knew that Negroes had never been allowed to catch the full spirit of Western civilization, that they lived somehow in it but not of it. And when I brooded upon the cultural barrenness of black life, I wondered if clean, positive tenderness, love, honor, loyalty, and the capacity to remember were native with man. I asked myself if these human qualities were not fostered, won, struggled and suffered for, preserved in ritual from one generation to another. (37)

Moreover, at the time of "The Man Who Lived Underground," he was attempting to reach beyond questions of "race" and black cultural nationalism: he defined the novella as "the first time [he had] tried to go beyond stories in black and white" (Fabre 94).

The parodic dimension of his mud-caked, inarticulate, maniacally laughing Christ figure makes it less an ethnic trickster than a Dostoyevskian fool, a more or less grotesque figure uniting Christic suffering and compassion with a Quixotic desire to impart important knowledge to mankind. Bakhtin states that the Underground Man plays the part of the *iourodievyi*, the "holy fool," a simple-minded character of religious Russia, traditionally endowed with a prophetic gift and unlimited freedom of speech, and even granted some respect (*Problems* 231). Another version of this type of mystic, pathetic fool is Prince Mishkin in *The Idiot*.

Fred's laughter ranges from the carnivalesque, affirmative subversion of aboveground values to downright madness. He dies more like a fool than a Christ, yet he is also a wise fool, whose vision, even though lost and washed away with him into the sewer, is precious. In the finale of the story, the character does unremittingly die; if his survival is somehow ensured on the literary level, it is not as a Savior but as a work of art. The man vanishes; "The Man" remains; the word survives the Word. In fact, the carnival is but a short-lived period, after which the iron law of society takes precedence again, as symbolized by the uncrowning of the ephemeral King of Fools. Fred's most striking thought seems to confirm this metafictional twist. When at a loss to express his great revelation coherently, he finds a way to circumvent his inarticulateness: "What statement? He did not know. He was the statement, and since it was all so clear to him, surely he would be able to make it clear to others" ("MU" 68–9). There is irony in this passage, since Fred's message will remain misunderstood and unheeded. The irony becomes parody if we connect it with the Gospel notion of the Word made flesh. What does remain is a definition of Wright's "incarnational art," not in the line of Flannery O'Connor's Catholic vision but in a more modest, existentialist sense: truth is perhaps better reached not through abstract thought but by delving in physicality and existence, which, as we know, precedes essence. In literary terms, it might be translated as "trust the tale." This does not exclude the possibility, as in tragedy, of the character's fate and the text having a transformational effect on the reader and, more remotely, the world.

Everett displaces this religious theme by focusing on the Virgin rather than on the black Christ, and radicalizes Wright's critique of religion through parodic debunking. Alice's rape is set up as a parody of the Incarnation. The fat woman is a virgin, and the child will be considered a Messiah, at least at first. The conception takes place in winter, like Jesus's birth, and the rapist uses the pretext of watching the (virginal) snow from Alice's porch. His small penis represents an "insignificant entry" (*Zulus* 11), which is yet not an immaculate intercourse; his dirty hair and green skullcap make him a shabby Gabriel. The topic of the Annunciation pervades the description of the moments before the rape, rife as it is with polysemic words, words "pregnant" with meaning that shape the reader's expectations. There is a "knock" that "she'd been expecting"; the man was wearing a skullcap and "rubber kind of boots"; he had knocked on her door, stomped his feet on the porch "shaking the whole house like he thought she would be letting him inside. Well, if he thought that, he had another think [*sic*] coming" (*Zulus* 7). The Annunciation of her "knocking up" is made through the words of the text, thereby creating a "predestination effect," and the result is another form of "incarnational art," according to which words take on flesh—and fat. Alice Achitophel, as a character, is a paper being, a woman made of words, and this woman is impregnated by words: the only real Incarnation is that of the text becoming a body of work.

Religion is made a target of satire in several other episodes: the Heifer cult that Alice initiates in the city—"We heifers are dairyists and believe that God works in the cheese warehouses" (24)—the rebels who only wait for Alice's child to have a messianic religion (*Zulus* 99), and their condemnation of what they do not understand as devilish (*Zulus* 140). Religion seems to stem from despair and illusion, especially since, in the end, the novel's ersatz Virgin Mary destroys the world rather than redeeming it. Yet do not, as we tentatively concluded earlier, some forms of myth and spirituality fare better than Christianity? The text seemed to privilege "archaic" forms of spirituality like shamanism, nature religion, the worship of Great Goddesses, which are at one with nature, the body, and the Unconscious, over the—male? Manichean?—creeds of the light, such as Christianity or Platonism. In fact, both "The Man" and *Zulus* can be read as inverted Myths of the Cave, in which revelation comes from the depths (Baker 169). Yet the last of the large, illuminated caves Alice crosses in the end is the huge stadium with the poison-gas worshippers: this finale, which recalls the nuclear bomb cult in the film *Beneath the Planet of the Apes* (directed by Ted Post), identifies religion with the death drive.

> *V is for vacuity and eyes in hollow heads. V is for the vanities of religion, for verspertine strolls through valleys of death and full of bones.* "Et vera incessa patuit dea." ...
>
> (*Zulus* 235)

How should we interpret this juxtaposition of images of death and religion in the chapter heading? Is there an opposition between the life-denying impulses of Biblical faith and the cult of the Great Goddess, referred to through Virgil's line about Venus, "in her walk the true goddess is revealed"? Or is the antinomy blurred, announcing the fact that Alice, a fertility symbol, will presumably terminate the human race?

Once again, Everett clarifies and radicalizes a trend that is already found in Wright's text: a connection of the underground theme to the death drive. What seems in "The Man" an inadvertently courted demise becomes in *Zulus* conscious mass suicide. Carried away by his enthusiasm, Fred forgets all prudence and goes straight into the heart of danger, as if he were unconsciously pursuing his death. He ends up like the dead baby he had seen before, surrounded by ripples of water: eyes and fists closed, mouth gaping in a silent cry ("MU" 26, 83–4). The protagonist has come full circle, and death and birth once again exchange their qualities: Fred has come back into timelessness, into the mythical womb of Mother Earth, to absolute rest. Interestingly enough, Sigmund Freud, in *Beyond the Pleasure Principle*, identifies the death drive to "an urge inherent in all organic life to restore an earlier state of things," that is go back to the indistinct mineral state (36). This exhaustion and desire for rest might be due to the racism and oppression aboveground, but it seems to have a more fundamental root in the nature of human beings. After all, this state of indistinction is only the reverse side of the utopian egalitarianism Daniels had dreamed just before.

A similar ambivalence is to be found in *Zulus*; if Alice does switch the lever and release the deadly gas, it may be to wipe out the human madness—contained in the name of Achitophel—which leads men to kill and exploit each other and destroy the planet. Her hold on life becomes very tenuous in her final crawling through narrow fissures in the earth: "If she died there, right there, it would have been all right with her, and she hoped that someone would find her and bury her in the ground so that she could decompose and give something to the poor, sick, anemic planet" (*Zulus* 238). Even in the throes of the death drive, there remains a Christ-like sacrificial impulse and a trace of the life-giving impetus of the carnival, as the eradication of mankind might ensure a new lease of life for the earth. Even though both principles are present at the same time in a paradoxical way, it seems that Thanatos has the last word.

If the carnivalesque retains a crucial place in Wright's and Everett's underground texts, it seems far less optimistic and life-affirming than in Baker's analysis. Ellison, on the contrary, is more positive, since an emergence out of hibernation is clearly envisaged, and the Invisible Man, a writer, has a putative offspring in the novel we hold in our hands. Wright and Everett offer a much more negative, dystopian outlook in which decay, trash, and absurdity have the upper hand. They seem much closer to what Bakhtin called the Romantic grotesque, a subjectivized and alienated form that is divorced from the collective ethos of the people expressed in the carnival and in which laughter becomes satirical and sarcastic.

> The world of Romantic grotesque is to a certain extent a terrifying world, alien to man. All that is ordinary, commonplace, belonging to everyday life, and recognized by all suddenly becomes meaningless, dubious and hostile. Our own world becomes an alien world ... Images of bodily life, such as eating, drinking,

copulation, defecation, almost entirely lost their regenerating power and were turned into "vulgarities." ...

... [Medieval madness was festive.] In Romantic grotesque, on the other hand, madness acquires a somber, tragic aspect of individual isolation.

(Bakhtin, *Rabelais* 38–9)

Should this somber ethos, which *Zulus* seems to take over from "The Man," be construed as a comment on the continuation of racial, or human, alienation, in spite of apparent social and ideological change, from the modern to the postmodern condition? In any case, Everett's strategies of displacement and radicalization are key components of Signifyin(g) as self-conscious revision, paying tribute to Wright's critical awareness.

Coda: Literary parthenogenesis, or a figure of tradition

To alleviate *Zulus*'s dark ending, the most pessimistic one of the whole "underground seam," we must remember that it is a satire, concluding on a grotesque apocalypse. It may not have to be taken too seriously, less as a prophecy of doom than a warning against human and environmental depletion. The penultimate chapter (XY) fades out as Alice's hand is poised on the poison-gas lever. We literally never see her pulling the switch. So even if the drift of the story seems to lead to a tragic, nihilistic conclusion, the end remains open, and mankind might still stand a chance. But language continues in any case. The last "chapter," a heading without a text, amounts to a simple sentence: "*Z is for Zulus*" (*Zulus* 247). More than an Afrocentric statement, it recalls the second chapter: "*B is for blood. The river of life. Blood River, where the Boers were slightly wounded on 16 December 1838. Three hours of battle, leaving three hundred Zulus dead. Z will be for Zulus*" (*Zulus* 21). This history of colonization, exploitation, and massacres, besides being an indictment of Western civilization, can also show what mankind is capable of and confirm Alice's decision "to hang the whole human race and finish the farce" (Twain 283). The end of the text is also the end of the alphabet, which will go on carrying the memories of men and women beyond the term of their natural lives.

We have already seen the complex *mise-en-abîme* of writing in the novel, according to which the inside of Alice's exploded cave-like body is inscribed with drawings and letters.

> The drawings still covered the walls of her being, strange, primitive drawings and isolated words, some in languages she did not know, but there speaking to her ...
> Along one wide stretch she read the alphabet, A-through-Z, speaking to her and playing, toying with her, and she felt the tears rolling down her face to nowhere.
>
> (*Zulus* 185)

This baroque loop, or Mœbius strip, in which the alphabet is both code and referent, identifies Alice's body with the body of the text; she/it is a self-engendering language game, incarnated and memorialized in a book. The book is itself a paradoxical locus similar to a reversible cave, proceeding from—in the act of writing—and taking us back to—in reading—the author's skull and his conscious and unconscious thought processes.

Does this strong focus on language and form in *Zulus* imply a rejection of the relevance of "race" to Everett's writing, as the parody of Wright's *Native Son* in *Erasure* could indicate? *Zulus* is centered on a latter-day Alice, whose color is never mentioned but who could be presumed to be white, as the novel's jacket illustration has it. Obesity seems to have replaced "race" as the visible difference that manufactures invisibility, along Ellisonian lines. Yet the chapter headings tell a different story, as made clear by the reference to the Blood River massacre and to other aspects of the enslavement and exploitation of black people, which the misleading title of the novel symbolically foregrounds. The intertextual tributes to Toomer, Wright, and Ellison recognize an African American artistic filiation and an original tradition but also, like these predecessors, express a refusal of its ghettoization. Everett seems to yoke, like his fellow underground men, a preoccupation with form and a moral imperative rooted in, but not limited to, an ethnic situation. Dialogism in this case spells like hybridity and reminds us of the mixed, "double-toned" ancestry of black literature in the Americas. Alice Achitophel is a late variation on Gates's figure of tradition, the Signifyin(g) Monkey.

The novel's strange *matryoshka* births may then constitute a metaphor of intertextuality. Old Alice, a written cave, gives birth to a younger girl, who retains the memories of, and stays in mental contact with, the former; similarly, textual parthenogenesis creates a text of two minds. The biological and dialogical unite in a form of "genetic" code, fostering the "grotext" character and her world. Alice, in her many incarnations, can therefore be construed as a figure of transmission and a tribute to a tradition, both European and African American, of which, even though not explicitly mentioned, Wright is a key underground ancestor.

Note

1   "[W]hile one can do nothing about choosing one's relatives, one can, as artist, choose one's 'ancestors.' Wright was, in this sense, a 'relative'; Hemingway an 'ancestor' . . . I will remind you, however, that any writer takes what he needs to get his own work done from wherever he finds it" (Ellison, *Shadow and Act* 140–1).

Works cited

Baker, Houston A., Jr. *Blues, Ideology, and Afro-American Literature: A Vernacular Theory.* Chicago: Chicago UP, 1984. Print.

Bakhtin, Mikhail. *Problems of Dostoevsky's Poetics.* 1929. Ed. and trans. Caryl Emerson. Manchester: Manchester UP, 1984. Print.

—— *Rabelais and His World.* 1965. Trans. Hélène Iswolski. Bloomington: Indiana UP, 1984. Print.

Cappetti, Carla. "Black Orpheus: Richard Wright's 'The Man Who Lived Underground.'"
	MELUS 26.4 (2001): 41–68. Print.
Carroll, Lewis. *The Annotated Alice: Alice's Adventures in Wonderland and Through the
	Looking-Glass*. New York: Norton, 2000. Print.
Dostoyevsky, Fyodor. *Notes from the Underground*. 1864. Project Gutenberg, 1996.
	Web. Feb. 20, 2010. http://www.gutenberg.org/etext/600
—— *The Brothers Karamazov*. 1880. Trans. Richard Pevear and Larissa Volokhonsky. New
	York: Farrar, 1990. Print.
Dryden, John. *Dryden's Satire*. Ed. D. R. Elloway. London: Macmillan, 1996. Print.
Du Bois, W. E. B. *The Souls of Black Folk*. 1903. New York: Penguin, 1989. Print.
Eliot, T. S. *Collected Poems*. London: Faber, 1963. Print.
Ellison, Ralph. *Invisible Man*. 1952. Harmondsworth: Penguin, 1965. Print.
—— *Shadow and Act*. 1964. New York: Vintage, 1995. Print.
Everett, Percival. *Zulus*. Sag Harbor: Permanent Press, 1990. Print.
—— *Erasure*. New York: Hyperion, 2001. Print.
—— "An Interview: May 3rd, 2005." *Reading Percival Everett: European Perspectives*. Ed.
	Claude Julien and Anne-Laure Tissut. Tours: CRAFT, 2007. Print.
Fabre, Michel. "From Tabloid to Myth: 'The Man Who Lived Underground.'" *The World of
	Richard Wright*. Jackson: U Mississippi P, 1985. 93–107. Print.
Feith, Michel. "Ellison avec Barthes: Occultation et désoccultation du 'canon ethnique'
	dans *Erasure* de Percival Everett." *Revue française d'études américaines* 110 (2006):
	61–77. Print.
Frank, Joseph. "Ralph Ellison and a Literary 'Ancestor': Dostoevski." *Ralph Ellison's Invisible
	Man*. Ed. Harold Bloom. Philadelphia: Chelsea House, 1999. 45–59. Print. Bloom's
	Modern Critical Interpretations.
Freud, Sigmund. *Beyond the Pleasure Principle, Group Psychology and Other Works*. Trans.
	James Strachey. London: Hogarth Press, 1964. Print. Vol. 18 of *The Standard Edition of
	the Complete Psychological Works of Sigmund Freud*. 24 vols.
Gates, Henry Louis, Jr. *The Signifying Monkey: A Theory of African-American Literary
	Criticism*. New York: Oxford UP, 1988. Print.
Gysin, Fritz. *The Grotesque in American Negro Fiction: Jean Toomer, Richard Wright, and
	Ralph Ellison*. Bern: Francke Verlag, 1975. Print.
Lecercle, Jean-Jacques. *The Violence of Language*. London: Routledge, 1990. Print.
Toomer, Jean. *Cane*. 1923. New York: Norton, 1988. Print.
Twain, Mark. *A Connecticut Yankee at King Arthur's Court*. 1889. London: Penguin, 1986.
	Print.
Watkins, Patricia. "The Paradoxical Structure of 'The Man Who Lived Underground.'"
	Richard Wright: A Collection of Critical Essays. Ed. Arnold Rampersad. Englewood
	Cliffs: Prentice, 1994. 148–61. Print.
Wright, Richard. "The Man Who Lived Underground." 1942. *Eight Men*. 1961. New York:
	Harper Perennial, 1996. Print.
—— *Black Boy*. 1945. *Later Works*. New York: Library of America, 1991. Print.
Young, Joseph A. "Phenomenology and Textual Power in Richard Wright's 'The Man Who
	Lived Underground.'" *MELUS* 26.4 (2001): 69–93. Print.

Part Four

Richard Wright's Sweet Airs: Experiments with Performance Genres

11

Forgotten Chapter: Richard Wright, Playwrights, and the Modern Theater[1]

Bruce Allen Dick
Appalachian State University

Introduction

One of Richard Wright's first assignments after his long awaited transfer to the New York Federal Writers' Project in 1937 was a lengthy essay documenting African American life in Harlem. Titled "Portrait of Harlem," Wright's essay was part of a collaborative project on the social and political implications of the New Deal and would later be included as a chapter in a book entitled *New York Panorama*. In addition to offering an informative historical sketch beginning in 1626, when the first African slaves were brought to what was then known as New Amsterdam, the essay includes insightful commentary on the cultural achievements of New York City blacks, particularly in the field of drama. Wright traces the general development of African American theater in New York, from the establishment in 1821 of the first black theater on Mercer and Bleecker Streets to the radical social drama of the 1930s. He focuses specifically on the nineteenth century, arguing that "a growing antagonism toward the Negro" prevented most blacks from gaining access to the professional stage (134). Wright highlights the achievements of actors like James Hewlett, who performed in *Richard III* and other Shakespearean plays during the 1820s, but he also maintains that "fields of amusement and personal service offered the Negro his most promising opportunities for advancement" (137). In addition, Wright discusses African American drama in the early twentieth century, citing Willis Richardson's one-acts, Garland Anderson's *Appearances*, Wallace Thurman's collaborations on *Harlem* and other plays, and Langston Hughes's *Mulatto* as recent plays that had received critical acclaim. He also identifies Paul Robeson as "the outstanding Negro actor" of the day (145).

This apparently well-researched essay shows how Wright had cultivated a professional interest in drama long before the Panorama project as well as how he was probably revising material he had worked on or thought about for years. By the time he started composing "Portrait of Harlem," he had already immersed himself in theater literature. As early as 1932, he had read Shakespeare and Ibsen and discovered works by Eugene O'Neill and Paul Green. Wright had also befriended contemporary playwrights, among them Hughes and Theodore Ward, and by the spring of 1936 he had worked as an advisor for the Negro Federal Theatre of Chicago, which was producing controversial agitprop skits and one-act plays. In addition, during the mid-1930s he had written theater criticism, judged a theater contest, and attended Broadway shows. Not surprisingly, Wright had tried his own hand at playwriting, drafting a 17-page manuscript called *The Burkes*, which he would later rewrite into the opening scenes of *Native Son*.

Chronicling Wright's lifelong interest in theater, this essay examines both his successes and shortcomings as a dramaturge. Besides the more impressive accomplishments of his dramatic imagination in other genres, Wright's attempts at writing plays and related theater criticism also place him squarely in the American theater tradition and elsewhere. In fact, Wright's dramatic sensibility complemented and directly influenced his other creative work, especially his most important novel, *Native Son*. Both Wright's fiction and nonfiction can be read as anticipating many elements of performance studies, associated in particular with theoretical texts such as Judith Butler's *Bodies That Matter* and critical texts such as Catherine Rottenberg's *Performing Americannness: Race, Class, and Gender in Modern African-American and Jewish-American Literature*.

Performative autobiography and theatrical fiction

Although his formal involvement in drama began a few years before the Depression, Wright had been conditioned since his childhood to view the world theatrically. Oppressive social conditions helped shape this vision, leaving indelible marks that would affect his personality and influence the way he interacted with both blacks and whites. In the autobiographical *Black Boy*, Wright makes use of theatrical language to describe the general predicament of African Americans but also the personal hardships of his own troubled past. His more than 30 allusions to the word *acting*, for example, often characterize the behavior he and other blacks used in order to survive in the Jim Crow South. In one scene, Wright recalls the trouble he has with white co-workers and his friend's subsequent advice:

> "Dick, I'm treating you like a brother," [Griggs] said. "You act around white people
>   as if you didn't know that they were white. And they see it."
> "Oh, Christ, I can't be a slave," I said hopelessly.
> "But you've got to eat," he said.
> "Yes, I got to eat."
> "Then start acting like it," he hammered at me, pounding his fist in his palm. "When
>   you're in front of white people, *think* before you act, *think* before you speak.
>   Your way of doing things is all right among *our* people, but not for *whites*. They
>   won't stand for it." (184)

Clearly, Wright's use of the term "acting" evokes a range of association that goes beyond behaving in a particular way. Such acting relates to social forces that are evidenced throughout *Black Boy* and are indicative of the pressures upon young Richard and others to perform their identity against what Wright called "the ethics of living Jim Crow." Rottenberg argues that dominant "norms help shape who we are," underscoring how a writer like Wright is "compelled to identify with these norms" if he wishes "to maintain a [relatively] non-marginal existence" (7). By the time he left the South, Wright had already understood that addressing Southern whites meant figuring "out how to perform each act and how to say each word" (*Black Boy* 196). It entailed mastering basic components of performance, including pitching one's "voice to a low plane, trying to rob it of any suggestion or overtone of aggressiveness" (*Black Boy* 186) so as not to be threatened by racist whites.

Like other autobiographies, *Black Boy* conveys not only *what* Wright wants us to see but *how* he wants us to see it. Thus these references to acting and similar allusions to performance, speech, audience, silence, movement, and other ideas associated with theatricality supply highly charged language that evokes racial events in Wright's tormented youth as well as the domestic abuse he experienced growing up. For example, in *Black Boy* Wright recalls the day his mother withdrew him from a Memphis orphanage and insisted he bid his playmates farewell. Wright points to the dual role he was forced to play even among peers: "In shaking hands I was doing something I was to do countless times in the years to come: acting in conformity with what others expected of me even though by the very nature and form of my life, I did not and could not share their spirit" (37). Performativity also played out closer to home, as Wright recalls an altercation he had with a relative: "And now a strange uncle who felt that I was impolite was going to teach me to act as I had seen the backward boys act on the plantations, was going to teach me to grin, hang my head, and mumble apologetically when I was spoken to" (158). One can find dozens of such passages in *Black Boy* that use similar theatrical language to highlight the burden of living Jim Crow that Wright felt compelled to resist throughout his youthful years in the South.

A brief overview of Wright's imaginative writing demonstrates that he employed this same discourse in his major fiction in order to emphasize his main characters' dire predicament. To illuminate Bigger Thomas's plight in *Native Son*, he repeatedly invokes performance and the varied connotations associated with it. One of the most important scenes in the narrative comes at the beginning when Bigger and Gus "play 'white,' ... referring to a game in which [Bigger] and his friends imitated the ways and manners of white folks" (17). The scene foreshadows the novel's blatant racial divide as well as the disastrous night with Mary Dalton that seals Bigger's fate. In *The Outsider*, Cross Damon assumes multiple personas to avoid detection. When he is finally apprehended for murder, District Attorney Houston declares, "Boy, what an actor. You should have been on the stage" (559). More than once in *The Long Dream*, Tyree Tucker pays "humble deference to the white man," stupefying his son with flawless acting. By the end of the novel, Fishbelly finally understands his father, who convinces him that "the only way to git along with white folks is to grin in their goddamn faces ... then do what the hell you want to behind their goddamn backs!" (142).

These examples and others speak to what Rottenberg calls the "*regulatory ideals* that circulate and operate in the service of particular power relations" (7). Tyree Tucker knows that the "only" choice he has is to play the submissive role of Uncle Tom and bow down to racist whites, the same way Wright reveals that to avoid his mother's wrath, he must "act in conformity" to her and society's expectations. Performative identity is never absolute, however. Rottenberg points out how regulatory ideals rarely function "as monolithic entities" (9). The "attempt to embody a norm is always incomplete—norms are *ideals* that can never be embodied or accomplished once and for all" (11). Not only does Wright underscore the failure of dominant norms to determine an individual's behavior, but Wright's protagonists are often depicted as resisting the dominant hegemony. Throughout their respective narratives, Bigger, Cross, and Tyree perform subversively and, in some sense, challenge the system by grinning in the "goddamn faces" of white folks then doing "what the hell" they please "behind their goddamn backs."

Wright leaves the South not only to escape racism but also to avoid his family's authoritarianism. This, too, can be seen as a refusal to allow the racist Southern norms of white supremacy to determine his individual fate. If Wright uses theatrical language to help structure important scenes in his writing, he also utilizes such language to illustrate some of the powerful themes that made both his fiction and his nonfiction famous, among them the glaring inequities associated with social stratification. Moreover, Wright's strategic incorporation of tropes of theatricality and performance lays bare how challenging normative behavior has the potential both to liberate and destroy the individual.

Theatrical influences

Wright's interest in formal theater was initiated in 1925 when he discovered the world of literature, particularly H. L. Mencken's *A Book of Prefaces* and his six-volume series of *Prejudices*. He chronicles his introduction to Mencken in *Black Boy*, claiming that he was "jarred and shocked" by Mencken's style and wonders what motivated the Baltimore journalist to use "words as . . . weapons" (248). Wright mentions 40 writers he discovered during his early apprenticeship in Memphis, most of them after reading Mencken's work. The list is varied and includes Russian novelists, French poets, American essayists, and German philosophers. It also includes two European playwrights, Henrik Ibsen and George Bernard Shaw. His mention of these dramatists in such a distinguished group, among them Dostoevsky, Baudelaire, and Nietzsche, indicates that early on Wright recognized the collective nature of literature and that he saw all types of writers, including playwrights, as possible literary influences. He purchased a copy of Ibsen's *Works* shortly after his move to Chicago, and as late as 1945 he bought Shaw's *Pygmalion: A Romance in Five Acts.*[2] Given his devotion to Mencken as well as his reputation as a voracious reader, Wright presumably read representative samples of each writer's work. Also, judging by a handful of journalistic articles Wright wrote in the 1930s for *New Masses* and *Daily Worker*, where he uses "time," "character," "place," "scene," and other conventional dramatic devices to frame his writing, it is probable that Wright knew of Shaw's taste for lengthy prefaces and elaborate stage directions to explicate his drama.[3]

Wright's list of influences in *Black Boy* also includes Frank Harris, a Shakespeare biographer and promoter of erotically provocative writing. In *Prejudices*, Mencken maintains that innovative critics like Harris throw "all the old hocus-pocus ... overboard" and thus write "some of the soundest, shrewdest and most convincing criticism of Shakespeare that has ever been written" (406). Wright owned a copy of Harris's *The Man Shakespeare and His Tragic Life Story* and eventually purchased copies of the biographer's massive five-volume autobiography, *My Life and Loves*, which includes references to Shakespeare, Goethe, Oscar Wilde, Ellen Terry, Sarah Bernhardt, and other important figures associated with the stage. These books represent a small portion of Wright's varied Shakespeare collection, among them *Complete Concordance, or Verbal Index to Words, Phrases and Passages in the Dramatic Works of Shakespeare*; *Shakespearean Tragedy: Lectures on Hamlet, Othello, King Lear, Macbeth*; *Tales from Shakespeare*; *A Life of William Shakespeare*; and *The Lion and the Fox: The Role of the Hero in the Plays of Shakespeare*. During the Depression, he purchased a copy of *The Complete Works of William Shakespeare*, in 1944 *Shakespeare's Complete Works*, the following year *The Tragedies of Shakespeare*. He includes "Shakespeare" in a short list of books he wanted to take with him during his move to France in 1947. Wright continued to purchase critical texts on Shakespeare as well as various editions of his plays after he settled in Paris.[4] It is worth noting that he bought most of his books at the celebrated Paris bookstore Shakespeare and Company and spent hundreds of hours browsing among its shelves.

If Ibsen's and Shaw's influence on Wright is speculative, Shakespeare held Wright's unequivocal interest until the novelist's unexpected death in 1960. Wright alludes to Shakespeare in journal entries, interviews, epigraphs to novels, and informal conversation. In the late 1930s and 1940s, he also saw New York productions of *Hamlet, Macbeth*, and *The Tempest*. With his wife, Ellen, he traveled to New Jersey to see Paul Robeson in *Othello*. In a relatively unknown anecdote, writer Saunders Redding remembers the night he attended the production with Wright:

> I remember Dick from the fall of 1943. We met at the McCarter Theatre in Princeton, where Paul Robeson was doing *Othello*. During the course of the performance it was noticeable that Robeson was drooling, spitting really, in the faces of the other actors. At the intermission we were standing in a group, Dick, his wife, my wife and several friends, and one of the men criticized Robeson for losing his saliva. Dick got very mad about this and said, "Don't you know that Othello was an epileptic, and this is a conscious, a purposeful thing; this is part of the role."
>
> (qtd. in Hill 200)[5]

Keneth Kinnamon argues that Wright "demonstrated a close knowledge" of *Othello* in the late 1930s and "deliberately established close parallels to the play" in *Native Son*. He points specifically to the "sexual theme" in both works and claims that "Bigger Thomas is Othello to Mary Dalton's Desdemona" ("Richard Wright's Use of *Othello* in *Native Son*" 358). Also, Wright might have had the play in mind when composing "Long Black Song" several months earlier. When Silas returns home from selling cotton, he finds a soiled handkerchief on the bed he shares with Sarah, his wife. The evidence confirms Sarah's infidelity. As in *Othello*, the handkerchief leads to the couple's tragic end. A bloody handkerchief also incriminates Cross Damon in *The Outsider* and foreshadows his destruction.

Wright's reactions to other Shakespeare plays were also characterized by enthusiasm. After seeing *The Tempest* with theater friends Herbert Kline and Mark Marvin in the winter of 1945, Wright mentions Shakespeare's inspiration: "By God, how this Shakespeare haunts one! ... One is awed. And feels afresh the power of the spoken word and the power of the living image on the stage, and again I longed to try to do plays" (qtd. in Fabre, *Unfinished Quest* 269). Wright felt inadequate after seeing Shakespeare performed, but he also believed he too could write successfully for the theater. "I recalled when I saw *Hamlet* and told my friend that some day I'd make thunder like that on the stage, and by God, not a year had passed before *Native Son* was on that very same stage" (qtd. in Fabre, *Unfinished Quest* 269).

Before making "his thunder," Wright would involve himself in other aspects of the theater. In fact, the decade in Chicago and New York leading up to his Broadway success represents Wright's most productive in terms of working in playhouses, establishing contacts, and writing dramatic literature. Wright's earliest exposure to theater in the South most likely included variety acts like Silas Greene from New Orleans, which toured the South at the turn of the century. He reveals his familiarity with black minstrel shows in the early pages of *The Long Dream*, when he describes a barker, bawdy comedians, dancers, and other tent performers at a fairground on "Colored Folks' Day" (40–8). In an unpublished essay called "Memories of My Grandmother," Wright also documents his penchant for nightlife in Memphis, where he frequented Beale Street's Palace Theater, a popular entertainment hall for blacks that showcased big-time jazz bands, girly shows, comedians, shake dances, and the blues (18–19). In *Black Boy*, he also expresses his familiarity with city life on Beale Street. But it was in Chicago in the early 1930s where he sharpened his understanding of the stage, particularly left-wing political theater. Here he met an assortment of playwrights, actors, and producers who would influence his writing for years to come. With Nelson Algren, Studs Terkel, Katherine Dunham, and other Illinois-based writers and intellectuals, he joined the Chicago Repertory in 1933. Their primary goal was to make theater accessible to the city's poor, regardless of race. One of his first significant theater moments occurred after he joined the John Reed Club, the newly formed cultural division of the Communist Party. Across the country, local branches of the John Reed Club financed unemployed artists, organized art exhibits, and raised funds for Leftist publications. They also sponsored politically explosive plays and encouraged skits, chorus chants, and dramatic dialogues during fundraisers and meetings (Kinnamon, *Emergence* 51). Because Wright was a regular member of the Chicago branch and zealously attended weekly meetings, this broad range of productions represents his first consistent contact with live theater. That members eventually elected him "club leader" suggests his close association with these productions and that he understood their potential for solidifying party unity.

Rooted in the New Playwrights' Theater, the Workers' Theater, and similar agitprop drama from the 1920s, the John Reed performances also prepared Wright for the more professional Broadway productions he applauded during his first venture to New York, when he attended the First Writers' Congress in 1935. One night he saw a Jack Kirkland adaptation of Erskine Caldwell's controversial novel, *Tobacco Road*. Another evening he witnessed a psychological tale about a West Virginia coal mining strike by Albert Maltz called *Black Pit*. By the time he left New York, Wright had seen three more plays, including the extremely popular *Waiting for Lefty* by Clifford Odets and a shorter piece called *Till the Day I Die*, starring Elia Kazan and Lee J. Cobb. He also saw a three-act marathon called *Awake and Sing*, which focused on a Jewish family and their unwed, pregnant daughter trying to maintain social dignity. These Broadway productions introduced Wright to his first high-profile professional drama and familiarized him with the social and political themes that flourished in fringe theaters throughout the 1930s, including experimental playhouses in Chicago, where he lived for ten years. Attending the 1935 Congress also enabled Wright to interact with a host of playwrights and intellectuals associated with the theater, among them Mike Gold, John Howard Larson, Herbert Klein, Frederich Wolf, Peter Martin, Maltz, and Odets. In the last line of *Lawd Today!*, whose revised manuscript he finished a year after his Broadway sojourn, Wright pays homage to Maltz: "Outside an icy wind swept around the corner of the building, whining and moaning like an idiot in a deep black pit" (189). He also adapted this "black pit" metaphor in some of his best fiction, particularly the novella "The Man Who Lived Underground." Despite their political differences, Wright and Maltz remained friends for years. While he never developed a close relationship with Odets, he did seek Odets's advice in the early stages of dramatizing *Native Son*.

Wright's literary apprenticeship was also inspired by his friendship with other African American playwrights, most notably Langston Hughes. By 1934, Wright knew Hughes's writing well enough to present a formal lecture tracing his career through *The Ways of White Folks*. Two years later, Wright had acquired his own reputation as a writer and was asked to judge a theater contest sponsored by the local YMCA, which Hughes had entered. Titled *Soul Gone Home*, Hughes's play finished a distant third behind Paul Green's *Hymn to the Rising Sun* and Ward's *Sick and Tiah'd*.[6] During the 1930s, Wright saw other Hughes productions, including an agitprop history of black America called *Don't You Want to Be Free?* The Harlem Suitcase Theater performed the play in 1938, the same year Hughes attempted to dramatize Wright's prize-winning short story "Fire and Cloud." As an associate member, Wright joined Hughes, Theodore Ward, Powel Lindsay, Abram Hill, and several other playwrights to help form the Negro Playwrights Company. Based out of Harlem's Lincoln Theatre, the organization debuted Ward's *Big White Fog* in fall 1940. Hughes also tried to adapt Wright's "Bright and Morning Star" to the stage, but the project never materialized. The two remained friends long after Wright's departure for France, however. As Hughes remembers in "Richard Wright's Last Guest at Home," they discussed the theater until three days before Wright's unexpected death in Paris.

In Chicago, Wright also met Theodore Ward, a southerner who had recently relocated to the Windy City after a successful stint as a drama student at the University of Wisconsin. Born in Louisiana, Ward had also been a victim of racial discrimination. By the time he returned to Chicago a hardened man, he was prepared—in the spirit of Mencken—to lash out through his art. Wright shared his writing with Ward and encouraged the latter in his own creations, including a play about the impact of Marcus Garvey's teachings on the black middle-class. Ward called it *Big White Fog*, whose title appears on the first page of Wright's "Fire and Cloud": "We black folks is jus los in one big white fog" (*Uncle Tom's Children* 157). In April 1936, Wright and Ward helped form the South Side Writers' Group. This collective sounding board for young African American writers was one of several collaborations between the two authors. As a chorus member in the Broadway hit *Swing Mikado*, Ward followed Wright to New York in 1937. Three years later, Ward encouraged his friend to dramatize *Native Son* before Wright had even completed the novel.

Wright's friendship with Hughes, Ward, and other playwrights obviously broadened his understanding of drama and exposed him to the daily functions of the contemporary stage. Coupled with his reading, his innovative journalism, and his Broadway experience, they also prepared him for his appointment as literary advisor to the Federal Theater in spring 1936. Because Wright documents his days with the FTA in the closing pages of *Black Boy*, there is no need to elaborate on his employment here. However, it is important to point out that he took great pride in his new position—one of his first significant literary appointments—and that he earnestly tried to fulfill the Federal Theater's aim of performing select theater for Americans from diverse social and economic backgrounds. Wright defended rent-strike plays like Meyer Levin's *Model Tenements* and pushed harder for a production by Paul Green about life on a Southern chain gang called *Hymn to the Rising Sun*. In addition to *Black Boy*, Wright documents his involvement with Green's play in two places: an unpublished essay written in the winter of 1936 called "Hymn to the Sinking Sun" and a 1944 *Atlantic Monthly* article called "I Tried to Be a Communist," which later appeared in Richard Grossman's *The God That Failed*. Both pieces offer a rare glimpse into the numerous problems Wright encountered as a radical social reformer and help capture the contentious mood of the Chicago Federal Theater at the height of the Depression. According to *Black Boy*, the violent barrage of protests he received from the city's black actors denouncing *Hymn* frightened Wright so much that he requested a transfer.

Experimenting with dramatic form

Wright's earliest attempts at playwriting most likely coincided with his Federal Theater employment.[7] One of his most ambitious projects was a 17-page manuscript called *The Burkes*. The unfinished play focuses on a family's struggle with poverty in a Chicago tenement slum. The setting is Christmas Day during the Depression, and Ma Burke is worried that she will not have a turkey to cook for Christmas dinner. The early action centers on how her oldest daughter, Vera, tries to appease her wearied mother. The play opens with Ma Burke singing hymns and caring for Baby, her handicapped son. Baby is confined to a wheelchair and his insistent, guttural murmurings symbolize the family's ongoing anguish. Religious-minded Ma Burke attributes the family's suffering to God's will and laments her burden, but declares she will carry the Lord's cross until she dies. The other Burke children enter the stage at different intervals, mocking Baby and snickering at Ma Burke's incessant demands. Ma Burke berates her children for their selfishness and refusal to accept God. She levels her strongest rebuke at Hank, her sympathetic but ineffectual husband, who blames his unemployment on racist whites. Instead of turning to religion for direction as his wife insists, he puts his energy into the local Communist Party. His rants infuriate Ma Burke, who ends up grabbing Hank by the collar and then ramming him against the apartment wall.

Only Vera is able to communicate with her bereaved mother. The last child to enter the stage, she placates Ma Burke by reminding her of a precinct captain's promise to deliver a Christmas turkey. The mother's spirits are quickly diminished when the politician sends beef roast instead. Ma Burke orders everyone out of the apartment except Vera, and once again she bewails her sorrow. Vera tells Ma Burke that Willie Boy, her boyfriend, is dropping by for dinner and that his surprise Christmas present is a huge turkey. Ma Burke knows of Willie Boy's reputation as a street-gang thug and reacts angrily, but she is unable to convince her daughter of Willie Boy's wayward habits. At the same time, Vera informs Ma Burke that she is pregnant and that she and Willie Boy are getting married. Willie Boy walks on stage and the rest of the action centers on a heated exchange between Willie Boy and Ma Burke. Willie Boy belittles Ma Burke's religious proselytizing and boasts that he is the new provider of the Burke family. Ma Burke threatens Willie Boy with retribution if he lays a hand on her daughter. Willie Boy erupts in rage, heaving the turkey through an apartment window. The scene ends with Vera uttering a piercing cry.

This incomplete portrait of the Burkes noticeably resembles the opening pages of *Native Son* and foreshadows the family drama we experience in Wright's first published novel.[8] Bigger Thomas's mother also argues with her children as the story unfolds. Like Ma Burke, she bemoans her agony and pleads for mercy: "Lord, I get so tired of this I don't know what to do . . . All I ever do is try to make a home for [my] children and [they] don't care" (9–10). She too sings inspirational songs and insists that Bigger can find salvation if he turns his attention to God. Bigger Thomas could very well be Willie Boy reincarnated. Like Willie Boy, he aimlessly roams the city streets with friends. He is spiteful and prone to violence, and instead of helping his wearied mother overcome her misery, he vandalizes property and plots robberies of neighborhood stores. Bigger's mother chastises her son and tells him that "the gallows is at the end of the road [he's] traveling" (9). Her words echo Ma Burke's verbal assault on Willie Boy's violent ways. The other Thomas children also resemble their Burke counterparts. Vera, the only Thomas daughter and the sibling closest to her mother, actually shares the same name as the Burkes' oldest child. Additional similarities between the two works indicate that central characters and selected motifs in Wright's provocative narrative originated in dramatic form. Such an antecedent seems even more plausible considering Wright's declaration in "How 'Bigger' Was Born," where he discusses the origins of his violent antagonist: "I wanted the reader to feel that Bigger's story was happening *now*, like a play upon the stage" (*Native Son* 459). This declaration further demonstrates how theater and theatricality informed Wright's non-dramatic writing.

Around the same time he wrote *The Burkes*, Wright attempted another dramatic piece called "3314: A Play in 3 Acts." The numbers in the title are unclear but possibly refer to a street address in the play's setting. Like the Burke drama, "3314" is incomplete. Wright finished Scene One and part of Scene Two, Act One, but he left no traces of additional scenes or a second and third act. If the Burke drama alludes to certain events in *Native Son*, the "3314" manuscript parallels the violent tension in *Lawd Today!* In fact, except for a few stage directions and minor syntactic adjustments, most of the action and dialogue in the first scene of "3314" are incorporated into the opening chapter of Wright's first novel, published posthumously in 1963. While he left behind few specific dates, Wright composed at least nine additional outlines, sketches, and developmental drafts before leaving for permanent exile to France. The subjects of these dramatic transcripts vary and include a domestic worker's suicide, a murderer's confession, and a war hero's return home. These multiple attempts at playwriting fall far short of Wright's successful Broadway production of *Native Son*. At the same time, they embody an array of convincing characters and plausible dialogue. While the manuscripts lack development, they do reflect themes that interested Wright during his early career as a writer—urban poverty, political corruption, and the role of the Communist Party in the African American community. More importantly, they authenticate Wright's use of dramatic form and verify his continuing interest in the stage at a time when he was trying to find his own literary direction.

Native Son on stage

Native Son is Wright's magnum opus in the theater. Though the play is well documented and needs little introduction, it helps to remember that Wright's most significant dramatic venture was beset with problems and that the volatile atmosphere he encountered on Broadway was even more unsettling than the one he witnessed in the Negro Federal Theater of Chicago. Wright had turned down several offers to dramatize his best-selling novel before deciding on Paul Green, a North Carolina-born playwright whose *In Abraham's Bosom* won a Pulitzer Prize for Drama in 1927. He appreciated Green's *Hymn to the Rising Sun*, which he saw in Chicago, and argued later that Green's treatment of African Americans was authentic, honest, and sympathetic. Curtailing a summer honeymoon in Mexico with his first wife, Dhimah Rose Meadman, Wright agreed to stop in North Carolina on his way home to New York to meet Green and to begin discussions on how to condense the 450-page Book-of-the-Month Club novel into a play. He approached the collaboration with mild trepidation, however. Part of his concern centered on a return south. In a *True* magazine article he published in 1946 called "How Jim Crow Feels," Wright records his train ride from Raleigh to Chapel Hill, where Green was teaching. He remembers how he needed information on travel connections and turned to a black porter for help. The porter spoke to Wright in a normal voice, but when he asked a white conductor for assistance, the porter's voice "leaped at least two octaves higher" (51). Wright's second visit to Chapel Hill was marred by similar racial tension. More than one malicious letter to the editor denounced Green, a white southerner, for inviting a black man (and a Communist) to lodge at his home.[9] Even the administration at the University of North Carolina kept close tabs on faculty, students, and local citizens who attended social gatherings in Wright's honor.[10]

While the names associated with the stage version of *Native Son* read like a venerable "Who's Who in American Theater" (Orson Welles, John Houseman, Canada Lee, Paul Green), the overall production was fraught with dissent. Ironically, the trouble started with Wright and Green, who disagreed on how to portray Bigger Thomas on stage. Wright re-enacts the tension between the two writers in a four-act mini-drama called "The Problem of the Hero," written for a radio interview eight months after the Chapel Hill collaboration. The "White Man" in the play represents Green, the "Black Man" Wright. The White Man wants to turn Bigger into a tragic hero with Christ-like appeal; the Black Man agrees as long as the transformation is credible. The White Man also thinks Bigger should commit suicide in the end as a way of affirming his "new sense of humanity" (5). The Black man believes Bigger "must die the same agonizing death" as he does in the novel, arguing that humans have little control over their destiny as long as they are enslaved. The drama ends with the black man proclaiming, "There shall be heroes, when men are *free*!" (7). While he never published "The Problem of the Hero," it is noteworthy that Wright conveyed the collaborative tension, via airwave, in dramatic form. The article also points out the difficulty of dramatizing a disturbing psychological narrative like *Native Son*, even with a seasoned veteran of the stage.

As producer of *Native Son*, John Houseman sided with Wright. His written impressions of the collaboration appear unreliable, however. Curtis R. Scott has chronicled the flagrant misinformation in both Houseman's autobiographical *Run-Through* and an earlier piece Houseman wrote on the play for *New Letters* called "*Native Son* on Stage." Apparently, Houseman exaggerated his role in rewriting the drama and his claim that he helped transfuse "the blood of the novel back into the body of the play" by "cutting and fine-tuning Green's script" (Scott 6). Houseman also exaggerates Welles's haphazard participation, since the flamboyant director of *Citizen Kane* seems to have been informed of the dramatization from the start. Though it is unclear to what degree Welles helped write the final script, the version seen on Broadway differed considerably from the final revision Green worked on with Wright. Green hinted that he felt duped by left-wing propagandists and that he disagreed with the numerous edits of the script heard on stage. During final rehearsals, the writers, director, and producer met one last time to iron out differences. Apparently, Green left in disgust, and the feud was never resolved.

Ultimately the play prevailed. It was the first Broadway production of the season to garner a four-star rating. Reviewers praised relative newcomer Canada Lee's performance, citing his honest portrait of Bigger Thomas as nothing short of remarkable. In an unpublished tribute, Wright boasted that Lee's achievement surpassed that of other black actors trying to convey realistic portraits of urban life.[11] The supporting cast also received a critical nod, particularly Ray Collins as Defense

Attorney Paul Max. Most reviewers welcomed the return of Welles to the stage, extolling his unconventional style and ability to prolong suspense. In a March 2, 1941 article for *New York World-Telegram*, Wright also exalts the director's talent, calling him a "creative engine" and "warning all governments now engaged in war: One Orson Welles on earth is enough" ("What Do I Think of the Theatre?" 20). While reviewers encouraged audiences to read Wright's book in order to grasp the full effect of Bigger's tragedy, they also applauded the successful stage adaptation. Brooks Atkinson commented in the *New York Times* that Green and Wright had written "a forceful drama with thoughtful deliberation" (1). Other favorable views on Green, Wright, and Welles followed suit.[12] After successful runs in Harlem, Brooklyn, and the Bronx, the play toured several northern and mid-western cities, finally breaking even financially on October 7, 1941, 17 months after its Chapel Hill conception. With a little help from his friends, Wright had indeed wreaked thunder on the stage. In addition to being the country's foremost African American novelist, he could now count himself among new talents in American theater.

Performativity abroad

Wright traveled to France for the first time in May 1946. He moved there permanently the following year. Because he was by this time considered more of a novelist and global political commentator, it was probably more difficult for others to appreciate his strong interests in drama. He did involve himself in the theater, however, and continued to write professionally for the stage. Upon arrival in Paris, he was an instant celebrity and enjoyed his new role as cultural ambassador in France. He attended fundraisers, receptions, exhibitions, and other galas, many of them theatrical. As in New York and Chicago he surrounded himself with writers, artists, and intellectuals, including a colorful coterie associated with the French stage. During exile, he appeared with Antonin Artaud, Marcel Duhamel, René de Obaldia, Ionesco, and other theatrical celebrities. With Jean Cocteau, he initiated an international organization associated with theater and film. The event was sponsored by French radio and television in the summer of 1951. He remained friends with Jean Genet throughout the 1950s, and the French writer modeled his play *Les Nègres* after Wright's novel *Native Son*.[13] Wright also spent time with Jean-Paul Sartre, whom he had met briefly in New York in 1946. He admired Sartre's *La Putain Respectueuse* (*The Respectful Prostitute*), a drama based on the trouble surrounding the Scottsboro Boys. He saw the play shortly after his move to Paris and lauded Sartre's farcical commentary on American race relations in *Art and Action* the following year ("*La Putain Respectueuse*"). He also wrote a detailed reaction to a script of *La Putain* that Sartre wanted to adapt to film, offering constructive ways to authenticate the Scottsboro injustice.[14] Actor Marcel Duhamel expressed an interest in dramatizing *Native Son*, and while the play never materialized in Paris, it did have successful performances in other European cities. Years later, a stage adaptation of *The Long Dream* enjoyed a brief run in Philadelphia, New York, and New England.

As he had done in his early fiction and autobiography, Wright continued to couch both his imaginative writing and his nonfiction in theatrical tropes. In *White Man, Listen!*, he returns to the stage directions he had used in "Two Million Black Voices" and other 1930s works of political commentary to add clarity and direction to his writing. After framing the "time," "place," and "characters" at the beginning of "The Miracle of Nationalism in the African Gold Coast," the fourth essay in the collection, Wright states:

> I've commenced as though I were about to present a drama. But it's not quite that. Yet, in a sense, what I'm about to relate is a phase of the prime, central, and historical drama of the twentieth century, the most common and exciting drama that we know. All of us are caught up in its stupendous and complicated unfolding; all of us play some kind of role, passive or active, in it; and yet most of us are totally unaware that we do so. (112)

Wright thrusts Ghanian nationalism onto a metaphorical international stage, casting the world as unsuspecting participants. Finally, he composed "Man of All Work" and "Man, God Ain't Like That" in the 1950s as radio plays. Both works appeared in the posthumously published collection of stories called *Eight Men*.

While abroad, Wright's most ambitious venture in the theater was a five-act satire called *Daddy Goodness*. The project began in the summer of 1956 in a Paris café, where Wright remembers an unidentified woman asking him to read a manuscript by Louis Sapin, a journalist-turned-playwright who had worked with filmmaker Luis Buñuel in Mexico. In 1948, Sapin had also assisted Albert Vidalie in a successful radio adaptation of "Fire and Cloud." The woman explained that Sapin's play possessed "universal elements" and embraced "the lives of simple people everywhere" (VI). Wright was skeptical about its far-reaching appeal but agreed to read the play after the woman raved about its biting humor. Within a week he was praising Sapin, calling him a "French genius" and exclaiming that had Voltaire read the play, he would have "split his sides with guffaws" ("A Play Voltaire" 4).

The play, titled *Papa Bon Dieu*, centers on a rustic drunk with the same name who drinks rum every day in order to escape the misery of human suffering. One morning, his sister Ana opens her front door to find her brother dead from excessive drinking. On the way to his funeral a few days later, Papa Bon Dieu's body accidentally slides off a wagon and miraculously comes back to life. As it turns out, Papa Bon Dieu has only been dead drunk, and the sudden jolt has awakened him to his senses. Ana and the other villagers think otherwise, and bow down to their new Risen Messiah. By the end of the play, Papa Bon Dieu dies a second death—this time, a real one—but not before he has stripped the local ministry of its power, seduced the town prostitutes, and reaped a fortune from the village poor.

Wright saw striking similarities between Sapin's incorrigible hero and religious figures from his own past. "I was at once enthralled by this play ... arousing memories of the communities that vegetate in the black belts, the Negro sections of large cities," he wrote in 1958. "I only had to think ... of various black contemporary Messiahs to feel that this story ... was a true story, indeed" ("A Play Voltaire" 3). Without much hesitation, Wright set about adapting Sapin's story to his own. He placed his narrative in an unnamed southern town in the United States but modeled his main character after Harlem's Father Divine, who after experiencing an epiphany in 1914, proclaimed himself God. While living in New York, Wright had witnessed Father Divine's political and social commitments, including his views on integration that differed only slightly from those of the progressive reformers of the time. At the same time, Father Divine's self-deification made him a target of ridicule. Wright satirizes his sanctimonious ascension to power near the beginning of *Lawd Today!*, when Al tries to reason with Jake and other friends:

> ... so Gawd might have done made up his mind to show 'em that everybody's equal in his sight. So he might come down in a black skin, see; he come as a Jew the last time, and how come he can't come as a nigger now? You see, he'd fool all the white folks then. (69–70)

In his first novel, Wright satirizes the man behind the self-righteous proclamation. In *Daddy Goodness* 20 years later, he satirizes the entire Father Divine movement. Through a slate of social outcasts that make up Daddy Goodness's inner circle, including drunkards, crooked businessmen, and whores, he exposes the numerous hypocrisies and crimes behind Father Divine's organization that not only sent key members to jail but eventually forced the entire operation to disband.

Wright never saw his play produced in the United States. After several failed attempts to have it staged on Broadway, he gave up and turned his attention back to France. Despite the backing of the American Theatre Association in Paris, he had little success in his adopted homeland. After a few minor productions, the play floundered without critical review. Three days before Wright died, he handed a copy of the manuscript to Hughes, who was visiting Paris. Wright still believed the play had merit and asked his old friend to find a producer in the United States. Hughes's efforts failed.[15]

Conclusion

If Wright had been asked to revise "Portrait of Harlem" 23 years later in order to make it more inclusive, he would most probably have still left his name off the list of prominent African American playwrights. Despite his relative success with *Native Son*, he would have balked at ranking *Daddy Goodness* and his unfinished manuscripts beside the more impressive achievements of Hughes, Ward, and other contemporaries. Making thunder on stage only once would not have been enough. Wright's efforts at writing drama both in the United States and France never measured up to his fiction, which fostered his reputation. Moreover, when he completed a worthy manuscript, he relied on professionals like Green or a more convenient adaptation such as *Papa Bon Dieu*. As his unfinished manuscripts indicate, Wright had provocative ideas but had not found ways to see them through. Nonetheless, he maintained a fascination with drama throughout his life. In his article published in the *New York World-Telegram* in 1941, Wright wrote: "[Nothing] on earth, save perhaps religion itself, is more intriguing, more replete with the spirit of fun and adventure, of make-believe and illusion, of men and women giving bodily form and reality to their impulses and dreams than the theater" ("What Do I Think of the Theatre?" 2). Over the course of his career, Wright showed an uncanny interest in exploring new ground, and his desire to write plays as well as immerse himself in the world of theater show him to be the prototypical postmodern experimenter willing to commit himself unconditionally to his art. By rediscovering Wright's dramatic view of the world as well as his multiple associations with theater, we can acquire a more complete picture of both the writer and the man.

Notes

1 I'm grateful to Alice Craven, Catherine Rottenberg, Mark Vogel, and Leon Lewis for their careful reading of this essay and for the suggestions they made. Amritjit Singh, a comrade and colleague since 1992 when we first met in Paris, has been most generous with his time in helping prepare this essay.

2 See Fabre, *Richard Wright* 78, 145.

3 See "Two Million Black Voices" 15; "Mrs. Holmes and Daughter Drink from the Fountain of Communism"; and "How He Did It, and Oh!—Where Were Hitler's Pagan Gods?" 1.

   In his e-mail of March 11, 2011, Amritjit Singh speculates that sections such as Max's speech in *Native Son* and the debate between Ely Houston and Cross Damon during their train journey to New York are intended to have an effect similar to Shaw's extended prefaces and afterwords to spell out for the reader ideas that are being dramatized in Wright's novels.

4 See Fabre *Richard Wright* 143–5.

5 Othello passes out in act 4, scene 1 of the play. Iago tells Cassio that it is "epilepsy" and Othello had also had such a fit the previous day. The Folio version has the stage direction "Falls in a trance" (Shakespeare).

6 See Fabre, *Unfinished Quest* 132. Also, I tried to track down this information in the YMCA's national archives in Minnesota. Officials could find no record of the contest. Fabre told me in 1992 that he obtained his information from an interview he conducted with Theodore Ward. I never heard the interview.

7 See Fabre, *Unfinished Quest* 132.

8 At one point, Wright had intended the play to be a much longer work. A "Characters" list attached to the first page of the manuscript includes five additional players who do not appear in the script: "Clarence Day—Communist leader," "Sister Sanders—church going neighbor," "Rev. Patterson—preacher," "Hot Stuff—Pal of Willie Boy," and "Louise Taylor—Pal of Vera and Sally." Judging by the descriptions following their names, these individuals were designed to complement the characters already introduced. Moreover, Wright places an "Act I" at the beginning of his manuscript. Such a division suggests that he meant to extend the play by introducing other characters or new themes in a later act. Finally, Wright inserts no stage directions after Vera's cry to indicate the play's conclusion.

9   See August 9, 1940 anonymous letter to the editor in UNC Archives, University of North Carolina Library, Chapel Hill.
10 See the Paul Green Papers, #3693, in the Southern Historical Collection, University of North Carolina Library, Chapel Hill.
11 See Tribute to Canada Lee, JWJ Wright Misc. 784.
12 See, among other reviews, Brown; "Native Son"; and Fishback.
13 See McCall, who argues that Wright's *Native Son* greatly influenced Genet's *The Blacks*, which premiered in October 1959 in Paris (182–6).
14 See Fabre, *Richard Wright* 238–44.
15 See Hughes 94.

Works cited

Atkinson, Brooks. "*Native Son*: Orson Welles Has Staged the Drama by Paul Green and Richard Wright." *New York Times* April 6, 1941, IX, 1:1.

Brown, John Mason. "Orson Welles Presents Mr. Wright's 'Native Son.'" *New York Post* March 25, 1941. Print.

Butler, Judith. *Bodies That Matter*. London: Routledge, 1993. Print.

Fabre, Michel. *Richard Wright: Books and Writers*. Jackson: UP of Mississippi, 1990. Print.

—— *The Unfinished Quest of Richard Wright*. 2nd edn. Urbana: U of Illinois P, 1992. Print.

Fishback, J. M. "'Native Son' Programs" *New York Times* May 25, 1941. Print.

Green, Paul. Journals. Paul Green Collection. University of North Carolina at Chapel Hill, Chapel Hill.

Hill, Herbert, ed. *Anger, and Beyond: The Negro Writer in the United States*. New York: Perennial Library; Harper & Row, 1968. Print.

Houseman, John. "*Native Son* on Stage." *New Letters* 38.2 (1971): 71–82. Print.

—— *Run-Through: A Memoir*. New York: Simon & Schuster, 1972. Print.

Hughes, Lansgton. "Richard Wright's Last Guest at Home." *Ebony* Feb. 1961: 94. Print.

Kinnamon, Keneth. *The Emergence of Richard Wright: A Study in Literature and Society*. Urbana: U of Illinois P, 1972. Print.

—— "Richard Wright's Use of *Othello* in *Native Son*." *CLA Journal* 12.4 (1969): 358–9. Print.

McCall, Dan. *The Example of Richard Wright*. New York: Harcourt, 1969. Print.

Mencken, H. L. *A Book of Prefaces*. 1917. Garden City: Garden City Publishing, 1927. Print.

—— *Prejudices*. First-Sixth Series. 1919–27. New York: Library of America, 2010. Print.

"Native Son: Best-Selling Novel Is Turned into Tense Drama Strikingly Staged by Orson Welles." *Life* Apr. 7 1941: 94–6. Print.

Rottenberg, Catherine. *Performing Americanness: Race, Class, and Gender in Modern African-American and Jewish-American Literature*.

Scott, Curtis R. "The Dramatization of *Native Son*: How Bigger Was Reborn." *Journal of American Drama and Theatre* 4.3 (1992): 5–41. Print.

Shakespeare, William. *Othello*. Ed. Edward Pechter. New York: Norton, 2004. Print.

Wright, Richard. *Black Boy*. 1945. New York: Library of America; HarperPerennial, 1993. Print.

—— *The Burkes*. 1936. Unpublished. JWJ Wright Misc. 339.

—— *Daddy Goodness*. Unpublished. JWJ Wright 103.

—— *Eight Men*. Cleveland: World, 1961. Print.

—— "How He Did It, and Oh!—Where Were Hitler's Pagan Gods?" *New Masses* June 24, 1938: 1. Print.

—— "How Jim Crow Feels." *True* Nov. 1946: 25–7, 154–6. Print. First published in *Paris-Matin* June 27–July 2, 1946.

—— "Hymn to the Sinking Sun." Unpublished. JWJ Wright Misc. 411.

—— "I Tried to Be a Communist." *Atlantic Monthly* Aug. 1944: 61–70; Sept. 1944: 48–56. Print.

—— *Lawd Today!* 1963. Boston: Northeastern UP, 1986. Print.

—— *The Long Dream*. 1958. Boston: Northeastern UP, 1986. Print.

—— "Memories of My Grandmother." Unpublished. JWJ Wright Misc. 474.

—— "Mrs. Holmes and Daughter Drink from the Fountain of Communism." *Daily Worker* Sept. 7, 1937: 5. Print.

—— *Native Son*. 1940. New York: Library of America; Harper Perenniel, 1993. Print.

—— *The Outsider*. 1953. New York: Library of America; HarperPerennial, 1993. Print.

—— "A Play Voltaire Would Have Been Delighted With." Trans. Michel Fabre. *L'Avant Scene* 15 (1958): 3–4. Print.

—— "Portrait of Harlem." *New York Panorama*. Ed. New York WPA. New York: Random House, 1937. 132–51. Print.

—— "The Problem of the Hero." Unpublished. 1941. Text for a radio interview, Apr. 22, 1941. JWJ Wright Misc. 631–2.

—— "*La Putain Respectueuse*." *Art and Action*. New York: Twice A Year Press, 1948. 14–16. Print.

—— "Two Million Black Voices." *New Masses* Feb. 25, 1936: 15. Print.

—— *Uncle Tom's Children*. 1936. New York: Library of America; HarperPerennial, 1993. Print.

—— "What Do I Think of the Theatre?" *New York World-Telegram* Mar. 2, 1941: 20. Print.

—— *White Man, Listen!* Garden City: Doubleday, 1957. Print.

12

A Wright to Sing the Blues: King Joe's Punch

Steven C. Tracy

University of Massachusetts, Amherst

(And if you think Wright knew anything about the blues, listen to a "blues" he composed with Paul Robeson singing, a most *unfortunate collaboration!; and read his introduction to Paul Oliver's* Blues Fell This Morning.*)*

Ralph Ellison, "The World and the Jug"

Many blues scholars consider Mississippi to be the heart of blues country, perhaps the state where the blues first emerged. Though there is no definitive proof of that, surely there is evidence that it was among the earliest locations where the blues were heard and collected. W. C. Handy, for instance, heard them in Tutwiler in 1903 (though in fact Gates Thomas heard them in Texas and Handy in Alabama in 1890, and Handy again in St. Louis in 1892). Some of today's most revered blues performers among the first and second generations of blues singers to record commercially—Charley Patton, Son House, Mississippi John Hurt, and Robert Johnson, for example—hail from the state, though that reverence is in part because contemporary white critics and fans frequently came to the blues through either folk music, with its connections to the Popular Front-era guitar-strumming folk scene, or guitar-driven rock music that traces its parentage there. Urban blues singers like Mamie Smith, Bessie Smith, and Edith Wilson far outsold rural folk blues performers up until about 1926 or so, when the women had the primary attention of record industry executives intent upon replicating Mamie's commercial success by presenting, in many but not all cases, a composed, urban-oriented, sophisticated, and jazzy version of the blues accompanied by formally trained musicians. While stage-oriented blues was certainly a part of the blues scene of the era, it was hardly the folk material of the itinerant, frequently illiterate, and informally taught poor black musicians whose music found popularity among folk and rock-and-roll aficionados in the late 1930s–1950s and crystallized, perhaps, in the important release of Harry Smith's *Anthology of American Folk Music* in 1952. Blacks migrating from Mississippi to Chicago at the time of World War I and post-World War II also powerfully influenced the type of music associated with the Windy City in the 1910s and after. This included the folk interests of such white Chicago Renaissance figures as Carl Sandburg and those Chicago performers who also contributed to the birth and popularity of rock and roll through their influences on Chuck Berry, Bo

Diddley, and other performers from that era, the 1960s era of the British invasion, and beyond.

Richard Wright was born in Natchez in 1908, with the dire poverty, educational deprivation, sharecropping, and lynching environment firmly in place. Eighty-nine African Americans were reported lynched in the United States in the year he was born, with dozens being reported lynched per year up through 1927, the time Wright left the South for Chicago. Indeed, Wright knew the violence first-hand, his uncle Silas Hoskins having been killed by jealous and greedy whites who murdered with impunity, and hunger haunting Wright regularly throughout his childhood as well. Despite a population in Mississippi that varied between 75 percent and 90 percent black from 1910 to 1920, affected in major ways by the migration of some 148,000 blacks from Mississippi during those years, the stranglehold that planter-class whites held on African Americans resulting from the re-established hegemony resulting from the "Shotgun Plan of 1875" and reinforced by the Elaine Massacre of sharecroppers and tenants in 1919 remained strong. This region was H. L. Mencken's "Sahara of the Bozart," the South Howard W. Odum saw as having a "cultural index or plane of living . . . the lowest in the nation" (Young 262). But it was an environment where the materials of the oral tradition for a segment of the population barred from achieving literacy served as a powerful means of cultural expression and transmission that would ultimately produce some of the most important cultural materials of the twentieth century through the blues tradition's important music, lyrics, and approach to living. The spirit of the folk blues and the blues of tent shows was all around Wright in Mississippi, and the blues-inflected tradition of gospel music was beginning to emerge in Chicago at the time as well, crystallizing in the work of Chicago-based performer Thomas A. Dorsey.

Residence shortly thereafter in Memphis and West Helena, Arkansas, reinforced the saturation with Delta blues to which Wright would have been exposed before going back to Jackson, Mississippi, and then Memphis in 1925. These connections are all reinforced by the various highways (49, 51, and 61) and railways like the Illinois Central that passed through Mississippi into Memphis (and on to Chicago, being the train Muddy Waters caught to that destination in 1943). These avenues are seemingly ubiquitous, especially in pre-World War II blues lyrics. Between 1932 and 1943, there were 12 blues songs recorded with the words "Highway 49," "Highway 51, and "Highway 61" preceding "blues" in the title—and this does not count the many songs where references occurred internally. Jackson, in fact, is located roughly halfway between the home bases of blues legends Skip James in Bentonia and Tommy Johnson in Crystal Springs, some eighty miles from Muddy Waters' birthplace of Issaquena County, near Rolling Fork, Mississippi, in 1913. As such, one might expect Wright to have strong first-hand knowledge of not only the blues but also the similar-sounding Christian religious music of the sanctified tradition, and that it would inform his work in some way unless some major philosophical shift turned him aside from appreciating and employing the materials of the oral tradition, stories, toasts, and other genres as well as music, in his work.

In fact, over the years, various critics have suggested that Wright was influenced by and did employ the blues in his work. Hazel Rowley describes the "visceral excitement" with which he responded to blues and jazz once he left his grandmother's "puritanical prison" (43–4). Margaret Walker spoke of his love for "all kinds of black music—jazz, blues, gospels, and spirituals—especially on records," and noted his acquaintanceship with Alan Lomax, Lead Belly, and Count Basie" (313). Indeed, Wright wrote about Lead Belly for the *Daily Worker* in August 1937 (Goldsmith 96), the year that his important essay extolling the virtues of folk culture "Blueprint for Negro Writing" was published and the year before the appearance of *Uncle Tom's Children*. It was clear Wright "understood that the celebration of Lead Belly's traditional repertoire was in itself a political act" (Goldsmith 98), and this repertoire and style, much more rough-hewn than the stylings of Gertrude Saunders that Wright had enjoyed earlier, indicated a folk-oriented shift in Wright's aesthetic to the grittier music of his childhood environment. Wright's early attempt at a novel, *Lawd Today!*, while influenced clearly by James Joyce, John Dos Passos, and James T. Farrell, also includes references to such songs as W. C. Handy's "St. Louis Blues," "Handy Man," and "Two Old Maids in a Folding Bed" in a blues performing environment.

Critics have identified strong stylistic influences on Wright's prose as well. Gayl Jones referred to *Native Son* as "blues storytelling" (qtd. in Harper 369), and Edward Watson saw the speeches of Bessie in *Native Son* as being "in the tradition of Ma Rainey and Bessie Smith in the particulars of his depiction of fear, pain, and brutality in her life (55–6). Arna Bontemps describes the prose style of *12 Million Black Voices* as "belonging to the authentic tradition of the blues and spirituals" (*Reader* 145). Ralph Ellison himself asserted that *Black Boy* was "like the blues" in its refusal to offer solutions (144). Even Wright's sociological ideas have been compared to the tradition of blues criticism. Michel Fabre called attention to Wright's own parallel between Paul Oliver's *Blues Fell This Morning* and Wright's "Literature of the Negro in the United States" (620). And the blues has been identified as a source of strength, education, and maturity for the politically fueled literary artist. Arnold Rampersad has written that "[i]n embodying the blues, Wright had been able to endure and resist oppression, escape the trap of ideology and Communism although lured by it, and finally mature as an artist and a man" (188).

It seems clear that Wright encountered the blues in a number of different environments in his early life—Mississippi, Memphis, and Chicago's South Side were all hot spots for blues performance—and continued to be in touch with the blues as he traveled globally, writing poems, fiction, and nonfiction, including record liner notes and book introductions, that demonstrated a continuing connection to the blues. Still, Ellison, who called Wright "a personal hero, in the same way that jazz and blues musicians Hot Lips Page and Jimmy Rushing were friends and heroes" in "The World and the Jug" (164), later called into question the breadth and depth of Wright's knowledge about the blues—indeed, he also challenged Wright's knowledge of jazz and claimed Wright did not even know how to dance, indicating "he didn't possess the full range of Afro-American culture" (667). Ellison, in his quest to discredit Wright, may unfortunately be straying toward the stereotypical suggestion that all African Americans ought to have rhythm enough to dance. Of course, there is a time span of seven years between the essays that can help account for the change from associating

Wright with blues and jazz performers in an essay the title of which echoes a well-known traditional blues lyric to denigrating Wright's knowledge of the blues. The question that needs addressing is, just what did Wright know about the blues, how can we tell, and how did it manifest itself in his work?

When critics speak of the visceral importance of the blues to Wright's experiences and work, they must understand that the sources of the blues—slavery, Jim Crow, and their racism and discrimination—along with the will and determination to face down those forces and create a powerful, life-affirming spirit, were omnipresent. That omnipresence was also reflected in the variety of fashions in which these blues feelings and creations manifested themselves, in folk and commercial domains, as well as politically charged atmospheres—all of which affected the content of the blues form and necessitate an examination of the environment in which Wright was creating his "literary" blues, and the distance his aesthetic and work placed between him and his creations. Like the blues tradition itself, Wright's works manifest elements of the folk, commercial, and literary traditions, even as they express the concerns of the group in multifaceted individual voices that share experiences.

In his writing, Wright does not really relate much about the music in his life during his time in the South—Mississippi and Memphis, Tennessee, until 1927—though he recalled in the undated manuscript essay "Memories of My Grandmother" that shortly before he left for the South Side of Chicago in 1927, he would go to the famed Beale Street's Palace Theatre in Memphis to hear Gertrude Saunders sing the blues. This he contextualized by recalling his grandmother's unbending religious orthodoxy at the time. In the parlance of the time among black Christians, the blues was often the Devil's music, to be shunned and avoided by good Christians, though the sanctified music of the time had much in common with the blues. Saunders was not a low-down blues singer such as Bessie Tucker or Memphis Minnie, nor even one of the better commercial vaudeville blues singers such as Ida Cox or Rosa Henderson. Though certainly not a vocal challenge to Bessie Smith, she did help break up Smith's marriage to Jack Gee after he financed one of Saunders's shows with Bessie's money. In a career stretching from as early as 1914 into the 1930s, she recorded only six songs, the earliest in 1921 with James "Tim" Brymn (Brymn headed an African American Army Band during World War I, served as director of the Clef Club Symphony Orchestra, and led the Black Devils Orchestra, in addition to his songwriting). These earliest sides feature Saunders singing in a rather mannered soprano. Her later sides with a white studio orchestra (including composer, arranger, orchestrator, and Gershwin and Ravel collaborator Ferde Grofé in 1923) and accompanied solely by pianist Porter Grainger in 1927 presented better vocal performances, lower pitched and warmer in the manner of Alberta Hunter, but still not classics by any means. However, she was considered a talented actress and comedienne (common terminology on phonograph records for early blues singers who were stage performers), versatile and popular enough to sing solo, in quartet, and with choruses. She starred in a variety of shows, such as *Shuffle Along* in 1921, which she left not long thereafter, providing her replacement, Florence Mills, with a springboard to stardom, and provided voices in movie cartoons after her stage career was over. Wright's evocation of the music of Saunders seems indicative of what he considered to be a notable blues performance of the time, if Saunders performed live as she did in the studio. This was not the raw, low-down, gutbucket blues of the juke joint and dusty dirt back roads of Mississippi, nor the prison blues or work songs of Lead Belly with which Wright would become familiar in the 1930s. It was a sweeter blues, dressed up and placed on the stage among a variety of other musical and comedic acts that is some distance away from the experiences of itinerant laborers that made up the folk blues of the lower classes. But it is still the Devil's music that was anathema to Christian fundamentalists, and black music rather than white popular music—a link to his own past and present, in addition to that of many lower-class African Americans.

Chicago had been a percolating jazz and blues town with a fair amount of recording activity for several years by the time Wright arrived in 1927. Among the early New Orleans jazz bands to play Chicago in 1915 and 1916 were the Original Creole Band with Freddy Keppard and the Original Dixieland Jazz Band. The groups of Wilbur Sweatman, Dave Peyton, Frankie "Half Pint" Jaxon, and King Oliver worked such venues as the Grand, the Monogram, the Sunset, and the Plantation into the 1920s (Sengstock 15–18). Additionally, Tampa Red, Georgia Tom Dorsey, and Big Bill Broonzy were among the popular blues performers (and Dorsey became known as the "father" of gospel music) who came to perform in Chicago in the 1920s. Meanwhile, African American entrepreneur J. Mayo Williams worked beginning in the 1920s as a Chicago distributor and collection agent for the black owned and run Black Swan record label and a resourceful and influential record executive for Paramount, Vocalion, and Decca (Jasen and Jones 307–33), all labels that had setups in Chicago. White businessman Lester Melrose "opened a music store on Cottage Grove in 1922" (Rowe 17), helping to set the stage for the rise of RCA Bluebird Records in Chicago in the 1930s. A lively club and tavern scene, especially on Chicago's South Side, welcomed those many migrants who, on the encouragement of the *Chicago Defender* early in the twentieth century or the recommendation of relatives who had already made the northern trek, came up to Chicago, primarily from Mississippi, to seek their fortunes in the land of milk and honey (or milking the workers with honeyed lies).

In Chicago beginning in 1927, Wright's literary and political activities were very much intertwined. His membership in the John Reed Club and later the Communist Party coincided with work on two novels, short stories, and a number of poems, the latter of which began to appear in leftist journals such as *Left Front, The Anvil,* and *New Masses.* Work as an editor for *Left Front* in 1934 preceded his involvement with the Federal Writers' Project, and both also increased Wright's literary and political connections and gave him more time to write. In 1936, he was making the rounds with a draft of his novel *Lawd Today!,* which went unpublished until 1963. Stylistically experimental in the modes of Joyce, James T. Farrell, and John Dos Passos, the novel interpolates snippets from folklore, a variety of media, and daily events in a manner intended to mirror the ambience of the city as well as the racial, social, and political pressures at work on the minds of Wright's protagonists, Jake Jackson, Slim, Al, and Bob. Among the dozens, toasts, and pop songs Wright employs in the text are several blues tunes, including W. C. Handy's "St. Louis Blues," "Handy Man" (variations of the song recorded by Ethel Waters, Victoria Spivey, and Edith Wilson in 1928 and 1930), and "Two Old Maids in a Folding Bed" (recorded by Billy Mitchell, Monette Moore, and Jimmy La Rue in 1936). These songs, though, tend more toward composed or pop-blues than down home folk material, another reflection of the way that a capitalist and consumer-driven media presented folk materials to the general public about which Wright was commenting in the novel.

In an African American bar setting in the text, Wright refers to "crooned snatches from a popular blues song," as well as ejaculations from the crowd that recall material from contemporary blues lyrics: "The hottest stuff in town" is also the title of a recording by Whistling Bob Howe and Frankie Griggs from 1935, and "Look at that salty dog" recalls the folk tune recorded by Papa Charlie Jackson in Chicago in 1924 and Clara Smith in New York City in 1926 (among others). Exploring as the novel does the lives of four black postal workers on the South Side of Chicago, with their mixtures of comedy and tragedy in their lives (itself a hallmark of the tone of and responses to the blues), it is natural for Wright to utilize the contemporary commercially recorded songs. A number of them deal blatantly with sexuality: a handy man is someone who demonstrates sexual dexterity and competency; the two old maids in a folding bed are lesbians; the hottest stuff refers to genitalia; a salty dog is someone who wishes to have sex without a relationship. As such, Wright employs the snatches from blues songs to reflect the men's preoccupations with sexuality, among other things, as they waste away their lives in dissipation. However, their references to these commercially recorded blues songs, which have attitudinal subject matter, and stylistic roots in African American vernacular music, demonstrate the ways in which the music unites them but reflect also the changing nature of the music in a capitalist marketplace. Thus the use of the blues here is for "local color," in a sense, in that it portrays the strong presence of certain elements in the community that find expression in popular art that in turn reflects the soul of the residents and the arc of their attitudinal changes.

When Wright arrived in New York in 1937, shortly before the start of the American Writer's Congress, he was ready to make an aesthetic statement regarding the relationship between folk materials, African American literature, and radical politics. He found his outlet in the revival of Dorothy West's *Challenge* journal as *New Challenge*, a literary organ approved by the Communist Party with West and Marian Minus at the helm and Wright, Claude McKay, Langston Hughes, and Henry Lee Moon among its group of writers and decision makers, and in the *Daily Worker*. Lawrence Gellert had published his *Negro Songs of Protest* with the Popular Front-affiliated American Music League in 1936, reinforcing notions of the strong rebellious black worker sometimes portrayed by Lawrence's brother Hugo in his art. Leadbelly, who had logged time in prison in Texas and then later at the Louisiana State Penitentiary, secured his release from the latter facility with the help of John and Alan Lomax in 1934. After a stint with the Lomaxes as chauffeur and performer, Leadbelly recorded a variety of sessions in New York City in 1934 and 1935, but after they parted ways, he signed with service station manager Joe Townsend and Townsend's mother, and rolled back into New York City in March 1936 for his re-emergence in the public spotlight. By this time the Leadbelly legend had been disseminated in the press, and he was becoming an important symbol for the burgeoning Leftist folk song movement at the height of the Comintern's Popular Front (1934–9). Within three years, John Hammond's *From Spirituals to Swing* concerts, staged with support from the *New Masses*, would provide a launching pad for folk performers like Big Bill Broonzy and Sonny Terry in a new arena and help change the reception of African American music and performers in the American mainstream forever. This Leftist folk song movement, directed by white Leftist intellectuals, differed from the market for "Race" recordings provided by major labels at the time. The popular market was driven more by generalized blues about the relations between men and women in an increasingly urban environment, frequently without direct mention of the larger social and political forces controlling the means of production. Blues songs recorded for "Race" labels in this template outsold most recordings made for the Leftist folk song market. They were more commercial and more commercially available.

Around this time, Wright's publication of *Uncle Tom's Children* signaled his interest in carrying out some of the aesthetic prescriptions laid out in his manifesto "Blueprint for Negro Writing." In that important manifesto, Wright signaled an interest in employing cultural materials drawn from the church and African American folklore in order to both reflect and reach the black masses. Wright felt that the folklore reflected the details and spirit of black life in America for the race in general, and he felt that given the perspective of the majority of colored peoples populating the world and the requisite social consciousness and nationalism, African American writers could take on their proper roles as agents of cultural reclamation. This would make writing by African Americans more crucially related to the lives of all blacks. For Wright, "[e]very first-rate novel, poem, or play lifts the level of consciousness higher" (402). And in folklore, one finds best expressed "a Negro way of life in America" (397). The social organization presented in the strong, hierarchical, and decisive actions of the church members in "Big Boy Leaves Home," coupled with the copious folk references to the important symbol of the train, including folk-song hero Casey Jones, demonstrate some of Wright's application of his blueprint to the work in that volume.

But Wright was now poised to utilize the popular recording idiom to spread his ideas concerning African American culture through the enlightened viewpoint of the politically informed literary artist with connections to the Popular Front recording market. Although the number of blues and gospel releases by commercial labels per year had fallen from the 1930 high of around 500 that year to less than 300 near the start of 1941, the industry had not yet reached the low that wartime shellac rationing and the 1942 Petrillo ban would soon bring (Dixon and Godrich 104–5). Indeed, the triple threat combination of Robeson, Basie, and Wright (fresh off of the success of *Native Son*) might well have been calculated to consolidate five audiences into one— concert, jazz, literary, boxing, and political.

As the quotation from Ellison in the epigraph points out, Ellison considered Wright's collaboration with Count Basie and Paul Robeson on the recording of "King Joe" to be a failure. So did Paul Oliver, who found that "[t]he lyrics themselves struck a false note" and that the recording "was a failure," due especially to the "wooden" delivery of Robeson (*Blues Tradition* 161). Contemporary reviewers were somewhat kinder. The critic from *The New York Times* called the record "mighty good jazz," with the *New Masses* critic calling it "swell music to dance to." The record sold in excess of 40,000 copies, to the delight of Wright, who was "proud of their collaboration" (Rowley 257).

Boasting that he had written 13 stanzas in three hours (Fabre 237), there was only time for eight of them on the two-sided OKeh recording, cut on October 1, 1941, just a week after the Basie recording of the classic "Take Me Back, Baby" with vocalist Jimmy Rushing.

The title, "King Joe," is interesting in itself. Of course, we encounter many references to royalty in blues and jazz *noms du disques*—the Empress of the Blues (Bessie Smith), Queen of the Moaners (Clara Smith), Queen Victoria Spivey, Queen Elleezee (Lizzie Miles), Queen of the Blues (Susie Edwards, Sara Martin), Queen Bea of Blues Singers (Wee Bea Booze), the Uncrowned Queen of the Blues (Ida Cox), Princess of the Blues (Olive Brown), King of the Jukeboxes (Louis Jordan), King of the 12-String Guitar Players of the World (Leadbelly), King of the South/King of Zydeco (Clifton Chenier), King of the Blues (B. B. King), Harmonica King (George Smith), King Solomon Hill, King Kolax, Count Basie, and Duke Ellington, to name a few, though some were likely invented by record companies for promotion. Many songs, especially in gospel music, refer to Christ as "King Jesus" as well. The use of royal nicknames, particularly among the lower classes in a reputed democracy that has subjected certain groups to an inferior status, is one way of claiming for oneself a status unrecognized or granted only grudgingly by the dominant socioeconomic classes of society. Although democracies are not supposed to have such royalty, there are in fact elements of American society that are more "equal" than others; this naming practice recognizes inheritance and pedigree in a way that was denied by white American society to African Americans presumed to have only a degraded cultural background and history, and is associated with a kind of wealth and power—not usually monetary—that yet establishes the figure as a superior person in a world that insists upon his or her inferiority.

There were, of course, other recordings by African Americans that lionized Louis. After all, as the fifth child of tenant farmers who grew up to be world heavyweight boxing champion, Louis provided a much-needed symbol of black strength and determination. Songs like "Champ Joe Louis," "Joe Louis is the Man," "Joe Louis is a Fighting Man" (the latter two emphasizing his status as a man, not an animal), "Joe Louis Strut" (which he decidedly did not do in the ring), and "He's in the Ring (Doing that Same Old Thing)" were all recorded at the height of Louis' success as a boxer and testify to his status as a genuine folk hero among blacks. As such, Wright's choice of Louis, especially after he came back to defeat German boxer Max Schmeling in the shadow of World War II, was particularly appropriate in terms of integrating into contemporary commercial blues trends.

The recording was one of Robeson's rare and earliest recorded blues vocals. He had recorded "St. Louis Blues" in 1934 and Gershwin's bluesy "Summertime" in 1938, as well as the "John Henry" blues ballad later in 1945 (five years after his successful performance in the disastrous five-day run on Broadway of Roark Bradford's *John Henry*). Wright himself had referenced the ballad earlier in the manifesto "Blueprint for Negro Writing" (397). The delivery of "King Joe," by a stiff and stentorian Robeson, recalls and justifies

Carl Sandburg's 1927 assertion that he would "rather hear a Negro in the cornfield or on the levee or in a tobacco factory, than to hear Galli-Curci grand-operize" (Songbag 224). Zora Neale Hurston echoed and particularized Sandburg's sentiments to contemporary concert artists who included spirituals on their programs, commenting that she would rather hear the singing of some "cathead man in Florida" than that of Roland Hayes or Paul Robeson because of the trained singers' inabilities to produce the proper "effect" (Hemenway 54).

There is little lyric or melodic variation in his delivery, and scant rhythmic verve or energy. The Basie band is its usual impeccable self: the admirable gentle swing of the walking bass and call and response passages between trumpeter Buck Clayton and the trombones, high brass, and saxes in the 12-bar interlude on Part One turn up the juice markedly in contrast to the energy of Robeson's vocals—the contrast between the rooted, cooperative, syncopated exchanges of the band and the plodding formalism of Robeson is startling. Robeson's leaden tones drag heavily against the swinging syncopation of the Basie band, too much like the molasses he describes in one stanza, and not peppy enough to capture the trickster spirit of the rabbit. The warmly wise voice of Rushing, with its beautiful blend of wistful sadness and sinful celebration and in-the-pocket groove matching that of the Basie band, might indeed have carried off the lyric more successfully—and Rushing was there in Liederkranz Hall at the session, as was Wright (Fabre 237). What were they thinking?

Wright likely chose Robeson for several reasons. Robeson was by this time a public figure whose achievements (1) educationally (Rutgers, Columbia Law School), (2) vocationally (lawyer, concert artist, actor), and (3) physically (professional athlete) were well known. By this time, he had appeared in Eugene O'Neill plays (*All God's Chillun Got Wings* and the sensational *The Emperor Jones*), DuBose and Dorothy Heyward's *Porgy*, Jerome Kern and Oscar Hammerstein II's *Show Boat*, and a London production of *Othello*, in addition to making a number of films. And he was a concert artist known for his "all Negro" musical programs. Robeson reflected, in a way, two burgeoning impulses of the time: the desire of the black middle class to improve the image and heighten the profile of African Americans and their cultural productions and the desire of whites to explore the stereotypes of primitivity and sentimental images imposed by them upon African Americans. It was an unfortunate and uneasy situation in that it pressed folk materials in a concert mould that robbed the music of much of its folk-based strength and vigor in favor of the studied polish of the classical tradition.

One does not normally associate the singers of the African American vernacular blues tradition with Phi Beta Kappa valedictorians with 15 varsity letters from Rutgers who practice law and appear on the concert and theater stage and in film internationally, though, of course, those people are not automatically disqualified from singing the blues. He was, after all, still a black man in America, and as the folk story in Hurston's *Mules and Men* reminds us, the refrain "remember, you're a nigger" follows blacks indiscriminately and interminably. Still, if the blues does express autobiographical experiences—though indeed sometimes they are dramatic monologues—the spirit of Robeson's blues would be of New Jersey, the Spanish Civil War, and the theater proscenium in London and the radicals and intellectuals who drew them together into a political *cause célèbre* and fashioned their own concepts of the "folk" to express them—hardly staples of blues lyrics. This is not to say that the blues or the singers that sang them were apolitical—certainly there are explicit and implicit references to political situations in blues songs. But Robeson was a more public figure with organizational connections. Robeson had become a political figure by this time, too, traveling to Berlin, Moscow, and Spain, and portraying Toussaint L'Ouverture in a play by C. L. R. James. Wright's political activities, as well as his desire to reach the masses and employ folk materials in his work (as expressed in "Blueprint for Negro Writing"), likely drove his impulse to record with Basie using Robeson. Of course, the fact that both Wright and Robeson had Party associations must have been a major factor as well, since their memberships indicated institutional and political connections. The producer of the recording session, John Hammond, who had helped arrange the *From Spirituals to Swing Concerts* at the end of the 1930s (at which the Basie band appeared), was known for his involvement with Leftist causes as well, including soliciting the *New Masses* to help sponsor the 1938 concert. However, the lyrics seem woefully out of context with the Basie band's performance and Robeson's rendition of the lyrics.

It would be interesting to know exactly who chose the stanzas to be included on the recording. Unlike most blues compositions, the song is not in the first person, removing something of the personal and autobiographical elements that the first person lends to blues recordings, though they are not always literally autobiographical. As such, the song is more of a ballad utilizing the AAB blues stanza pattern—a blues ballad such as "Dupree Blues" (recorded separately in 1930 by Kingfish Bill Tomlin and Willie Walker, as well as by a Chicago performer also known to Langston Hughes, Georgia White, in 1935, who also recorded a "New Dupree Blues" in 1936)—than a traditional blues lyric. Moreover, it is a nodal ballad, celebrating certain important characteristics rather than following some strict chronological order (though the songs do open with mention of his birth and end with a reference to his quitting the ring). This makes it easier, perhaps, to make personal identifications between Louis, the author, and the audience by not having to concentrate on narrative historical markers in the text.

The lyrics are, indeed, not very strong but self-consciously rustic, more like folk tales than the blues, especially when contrasted with accompaniment by an urban uptown and mellow wall of horn sound by the Basie band. The first and last stanzas of part one use rural imagery, as does the last stanza of part two, all of which frame the song in a properly proletarian political setting. References to black-eyed peas talking to cornbread, rabbits talking to bees, and bull frogs talking to boll weevils lend a rural agrarian touch that Wright likely seeks, and certainly one can find references to most of these elements in contemporary blues songs, though the enumerative depictions here seem more like folk-tale than folk-song references. These elements are more likely, though, to be referenced in blues songs in the third person as objects rather than being speaking characters in the blues themselves (though they are not unprecedented in the blues). They are appropriate, perhaps, politically given Wright's connection to the Popular Front politics and the desire to broaden the reference and appeal to the masses through the use of folk music. Significantly, two of the eight stanzas begin with the words "they say," introducing statements that are either critical of Louis or offer false opinions, whereas what the animals and insects say is more positive, upbeat, supportive of Louis and his strength. The "they" here clearly refers to outsiders not as familiar with Louis, and people who, perhaps, do not identify with his strength and achievements as much as the folk do.

There are some strengths in the lyrics, real connections to the blues tradition in addition to Wright's use of the common AAB stanza pattern. For example, Wright uses the common blues lyric "you sure can't read his mind" in stanza three—a slight variant contained, for example, in Clara Smith's 1923 recording of "Every Woman's Blues"—and a characteristic reference to the bee's stinger as a phallic symbol—very common in blues such as Memphis Minnie's "New Bumble Bee":

> I got a bumble bee don't sting nobody but me
> I got a bumble bee don't sting nobody but me
> And he makes better honey any bumble bee I ever seen.

Interestingly, the arrangement of lyrics in the Basie recordings separates the bee stinger reference, which ostensibly refers to Louis's stinging punches, from one that alludes to Louis's nocturnal activities clearly partaking of sexual innuendo, by placing the former as the last stanza on part one, and the latter as the first stanza on part two. This sexual punch is perhaps telegraphed by the boxing reference in stanza two, which calls attention to Louis's "rolling" in the ring—also a common blues sexual metaphor. Wright also couples this rolling with rocking his opponents to sleep, using the rock and roll phrase, also sexual, in combination with "sleep" in the final line of the stanza to emphasize the sexual connection. Given the audacious *double entendre* bawdiness of a great many recorded blues and hokum tunes, it seems hard to believe that the record company would have been responsible for this separation, but did Wright, Hammond, or someone else see the necessity, or was the separation merely a function of time constraints imposed by the length of a 78 RPM record? Might they have expected that the combination of the very public figure of Joe Louis with Wright, Robeson, and the Basie band might produce an expanded audience with which they wanted to be careful, especially with regard to the stereotypes of the sexuality of African Americans? It seems impossible to know at this point whether this was a conscious decision, and who the "they" were if it was.

Other images from the blues tradition turn up as well. Texas Alexander's version of a common lyric in blues songs, "They cook cornbread for their husbands, and biscuits for their men," turns up in stanza one, though Wright's personification seems labored as opposed to the sexuality of the blues lyric. Alan Lomax reports the blues lyric from "Big Fat Mama," "But a jet-black woman make a jack rabbit hug a hound," extolling the sexual powers of the dark-skinned woman; Blind Lemon Jefferson reports how

> Blues jumped a rabbit, run him one solid mile.
> Blues jumped a rabbit, run him one solid mile.
> This rabbit sat down and cried like a natural child.

In each case, the rabbit is a kind of underdog, to a woman and to the blues, though it strives mightily to resist, and thus one identifies with the rabbit, perhaps as a potential trickster figure—or identifies with the singer, who exposes the rabbit's helplessness and is thus a trickster himself. Wright again personifies, making his rabbit talk to his bee, and missing in some ways the folk symbolism and commentary on interpersonal relationships in the folk or commercial blues. The bull frog, too, is a common enough folk image, employed in a surreal question posed by William Harris in his 1928 recording "Bull Frog Blues": "Have you ever woke up with them bull frogs on your mind?" In her "Bull Frog Blues," Jenny Pope uses indirection, blaming bull frogs for drinking up her wine and generally being in the way around her house. Further, there are some 22 songs recorded by African Americans before 1944 with some variant of "Boll Weevil" as the title, since the destructive pest was prominent in the minds of agrarian sharecroppers and farmers worried about the reduction of crops. However, Wright's boll weevil is mostly a prop character who talks to a bull frog, not a powerful folk symbol that might have been used in a more essential way. Still, in a land where cotton was king and the boll weevil the chief threatening contender for the throne, to have the boll weevil call Joe Louis the king does have some particular significance in its reclamation of power for poor sharecroppers, especially black ones, who need to see someone black as an officially crowned king.

Wright shows a desire to turn Louis into a folk hero and to foster pride in Harlem as Louis's home and a place of unprecedented celebration and excitement when Joe wins. This is another obvious reference to the importance of solidarity and pride, which one can find in Cleveland, St. Louis, and Chicago—without reference to race or neighborhood—but encounter best in Harlem, obviously setting aside a prominent place for black pride within the context of Popular Front politics. The emphasis on action over literal talk in stanza three—"They say Joe don't talk much, but he talks all the time"—is clearly a call to action along the lines of Clifford Odets's "Strike, Strike, Strike!" in *Waiting for Lefty* and Langston Hughes's "fight, fight, fight!" in *Don't You Want to Be Free?*, though far more implicit than explicit in the song.

Perhaps most important of all the recorded stanzas is stanza two, where the singer indicates that he knows the secret of Joe's skill and dominance. That secret is itself never revealed in the song, but coming on the heels of a stanza that suggests that Louis's strength stems from his place of origin—where he was born—the assumption is that his strength comes from his African American folk origins and heritage, represented by the gustatorial images of black-eyed peas and cornbread. Fed on good old downhome cooking, Joe can not help but be the king. This is no middle-class "bougie" afraid to be seen eating chitlins; this is the person who embraces the stuff of the African American diet, nourished—as Wright had called for in "Blueprint"—by the folk heritage. The notion that the secret must be kept—the singer says "swore I'd never tell"—testifies to its importance strategically and politically—as if, like Frederick Douglass's refusal to discuss the most dramatic climax of his story in *Narrative of the Life of Frederick Douglass*, his escape, something crucially important, is being protected from the enemy—the route for others to follow.

Fabre reports two stanzas that are interestingly not included on the recordings, likely because they are too pointed and confrontational since no other stanza veers explicitly this close to controversy:

Old Joe wrestled Ford engines, Lord, it was a shame;
Say Old Joe wrestled Ford engines, Lord, it was a shame;
And he turned engine himself and went to the fighting game . . .

Wonder what Joe Louis thinks when he's fighting a white man
Bet he thinks what I'm thinking cause he wears a deadpan. (237)

Going head to head with the dehumanizing assembly line symbols of the machine age, mentioning Henry Ford by name (though this is not unprecedented in folk music), and literally transforming oneself into one of them in order to transcend his status, effectively projects Wright's notion that one must wrestle with one's barriers and gain strength from them in order to overcome them. The relation of human being to machine was a preoccupation for both high modernists and surrealists, two elements of literature in which Wright was also interested and which influenced his aesthetic at the time—indeed, Wright even explicitly connected surrealism to the blues, as Eugene E. Miller points out, especially in the juxtaposition of materials without rational connections and their associational structure (79–81). Franklin Rosemont connects the machine in blues and surrealism to physical desire and revolution:

It is not accidental that this fundamentally revolutionary erotic orientation is combined, in blues and surrealism, with a conception of *machines* that is as far from traditional romantic fear and mistrust as it is from the futurists' idiotic worship. For blues-singers and surrealists, machinery (like everything else) exists to be used *poetically* for the realization of *desire*. This conception in turn is inseparable from the theory of the revolutionary proletariat: The present intolerable state of affairs, in which millions of men and women are the slaves of machines owned by a handful of exploiters, must be ruthlessly overturned, because only the abolition of wage slavery will enable the machine to be placed at the service of genuine human creativity. (24)

The machine (Ford engine), desire (Louis's nocturnal activities and the stinger), and the revolutionary proletariat buoyed by Louis's example and victories are all elements touched upon in Wright's blues lyric, demonstrating that Wright at the time was making connections between surrealism, blues, and Leftist politics even in works that are minor in his *oeuvre*.

Interestingly, it has been remarked before that Joe was advised not to delight in or celebrate in the ring his defeat of white opponents—something about which Wright had obviously heard—but presumably this lyric was deemed too inflammatory for general public consumption, particularly when Wright makes an explicit connection between Louis's superiority as a symbol of the black man's strength and accomplishment behind an emotionless mask. Certainly, the strategy is emblematic of the situation of African Americans in this country that necessitated a kind of masking referenced by Douglass in his *Narrative* and Paul Laurence Dunbar in his poem "We Wear the Mask," but summed up most succinctly in the blues lyric to "You Don't Know My Mind Blues" recorded by Josie Miles on January 19, 1924. Significantly, part of the lyric already discussed in stanza three of part one dealing with not being able to read Louis's mind is echoed in the lyrics of this common blues stanza as well:

You don't know, you don't know, you don't know my mind, this mornin'
You don't know, you just don't know my mind
Now you see me laughin, I'm laughin to keep from cryin.

This identification of the blues singer with the boxing hero and the strategy of masking and its relation to laughing to keep from crying points out an important role of the blues singer and the blues to express the contradictions, difficulties, strategies, celebrations, and successes of African American lives, to unify and overcome, to assert and indemnify, to wear a "dead pan," in the contemporary slang a lifeless or expressionless face, while demonstrating vigor and communicating identity in an individual and distinctive yet communally identified way. Here Wright unites the folk, the boxer, and the art form in a politically meaningful gesture of understanding and solidarity. Though all of these elements are not handled as well as someone more knowledgeable of the folk might handle them—Sterling Brown comes immediately to mind—if one can put aside some of the incongruities, Wright brings the lyrics to a salient point. Unfortunately, these are the lyrics not performed on the recording. One can only surmise that this is a concession to the commercial market, ironic given the parties involved and their connections to radical politics.

This phase of Wright's career reflected his interests in folk and popular culture as they could manifest themselves in politically meaningful—though not politically uncomplicated—statements. Certainly Wright's ambivalence toward the Communist Party is reflected in the lyric he put forward, even if it was not included on the recording, concerning a black man fighting a white man, which clearly veers from purely class issues to the race issues that were bothersome to the Party's line. Wright's "Notes on Jim Crow Blues" for an album of recordings by Josh White would be more uncompromising, with White's and author Waring Cuney's "social militancy," as Wright put it (Liner Notes), indicative of an indigenous strain in the blues. Wright's experiment with popular blues recording cannot be judged an unqualified success, sometimes because of his own inadequacies, though the choice of Robeson instead of Rushing as vocalist is the primary drawback. Rushing would have served the record-buying public's interests better, and made a more aesthetically pleasing statement. And it would have been more pleasing for the aficionado of the blues and sweet science, though not the hoped-for brawl, that would have pleased the Leftist leadership of the masses.

Works cited

Bloom, Harold, ed. *Major Literary Characters: Bigger Thomas*. New York: Chelsea House, 1990. Print.

Brooks, Tim. *Lost Sounds: Blacks and the Birth of the Recording Industry, 1890–1919*. Urbana: U of Illinois P, 2004. Print.

Dixon, Robert and John Godrich. *Recording the Blues*. New York: Stein, 1970. Print.

Ellison, Ralph. *The Collected Essays of Ralph Ellison*. Ed. John F. Callahan. New York: Modern Library, 1995. Print.

Fabre, Michel. *The Unfinished Quest of Richard Wright*. 2nd edn. Urbana: U of Illinois P, 1993. Print.

Goldsmith, Peter D. *Making People's Music: Moe Asch and Folkways Records*. Washington, DC: Smithsonian, 1998. Print.

Harper, Michael. "Gayl Jones: An Interview." *Chant of Saints: A Gathering of Afro-American Literature, Art, and Scholarship*. Urbana: U of Illinois P, 1979. 352–75. Print.

Hemenway, Robert E. *Zora Neale Hurston: A Literary Biography*. Urbana: U of Illinois P, 1977. Print.

Jasen, David A. and Gene Jones. *Spreadin' Rhythm Around: Black Popular Songwriters, 1880–1930*. New York: Schirmer, 1998. Print.

Jones, Gayl. *Liberating Voices: Oral Tradition in African American Literature*. Cambridge: Harvard UP, 1991. Print.

Miller, Eugene E. *Voice of a Native Son: The Poetics of Richard Wright*. Jackson: UP of Mississippi, 1990. Print.

Oliver, Paul. *Blues Fell This Morning: Meaning in the Blues*. 1960. 2nd edn. Cambridge: Cambridge UP, 1990. Print.

—— *The Blues Tradition*. 1968. New York: Oak, 1970. Print.

Rampersad, Arnold. *Ralph Ellison: A Biography*. New York: Knopf, 2007. Print.

Rosemont, Franklin. "The Machinery of Mad Love." *Living Blues* Jan.–Feb. 1976: 24. Print.

Rowe, Mike. *Chicago Breakdown*. London: Eddison, 1973. Print.

Rowley, Hazel. *Richard Wright: The Life and Times*. New York: Holt, 2001. Print.

Sengstock, Charles A., Jr. *Jazz Music in Chicago's Early South-Side Theaters*. Northbrook: Canterbury, 2000. Print.

Walker, Margaret. *Richard Wright: Daemonic Genius*. New York: Amistad, 1988. Print.

Woods, Clyde. *Development Arrested: The Blues and Plantation Power in the Mississippi Delta*. London: Verso, 1998. Print.

Wright, Richard. *Black Boy*. 1945. New York: HarperCollins. Print.

—— "Blueprint for Negro Writing." *New Challenge* Fall 1937. Rpt. in *Voices from the Harlem Renaissance*. Ed. Nathan Irvin Huggins. New York: Oxford UP, 1976. 394–401. Print.

—— "King Joe, Parts One and Two." OKeh 6475, 1941. On Count Basie, *My Old Flame*. Centurion Jazz IECJ315, 2004.

—— *Native Son*. 1940. New York: HarperCollins. Print.

—— "Notes on Jim Crow Blues." *Southern Exposure*. Keynote Album 107, 1941.

—— *Richard Wright Reader*. Ed. Ellen Wright and Michel Fabre. New York: Harper and Row, 1978. Print.

—— *Uncle Tom's Children*. 1938. New York: Harper. Print.

Young, Thomas Daniel. "Introduction to Part Three." *The History of Southern Literature*. Ed. Louis D. Rubin, Jr., et al. Baton Rouge: Louisiana State UP, 1985. 261–3. Print.

Part Five

Transnational Shifts: Silence and Sentiment

13

Richard Wright's "Island" of Silence in *The Long Dream*

Alice Mikal Craven
The American University of Paris

Living the tensions of the Franco-Algerian war vicariously as well as enduring the witch hunts spawned by a Cold War environment fueled a collective paranoia for the African American exile community in which Richard Wright found himself in the late 1950s. Collective paranoia has an allure that has greatly enhanced the personal legacies of authors such as Wright, William Gardner Smith, and Chester Himes. Sadly, it has also often marred critical assessment of their literary output during the time period in question (Maxwell 256; Harrington 3–20; Stovall 189–92). Critics of Wright's *The Long Dream*, his last published novel, broadly asserted that the work was fundamentally weak and flawed as a result of his exiled experience (Hakatuni 276). This particular period in Wright's literary production, however, should be examined in light of the balance he constantly sought between aesthetic and political concerns. Through an analysis of *The Long Dream*, as well as his unpublished manuscript "Island of Hallucination," I argue that literary appreciation of Wright's nuanced transnational voice is paradoxically to be found in noting Wright's insistence on protagonist Fishbelly's *need* for silence.

In order to develop a literary critique of Wright's decisions to go public with *The Long Dream* and turn from an unfinished "Island of Hallucination" to other projects, Fishbelly's silence, or lack thereof, remains key. While it has been argued that posthumous publication of the manuscript "Island of Hallucination" would be the best way to have full access to Wright's attitudes towards his exile and his political *milieu* at the end of his life, the more pressing revelation for his literary legacy is what I am calling Wright's literature of silence, his presentation of a protagonist in evolving states of a need to *remain silent*. The human need to withdraw into silence or exercise one's right to silence is created with a greater sense of aesthetic balance in *The Long Dream* than it is in "Island of Hallucination" where the ultimate authorial intentions for Fishbelly's characterization are not fully developed. Whereas *The Long Dream* balances Wright's mastery of naturalistic tendencies with a burgeoning modernist perspective, "Island" forays into caricatured depictions of the Negro in Paris, which Wright ultimately rejected as being beyond his aesthetic scope at the time. Had there been time for him to complete and polish this manuscript, it might have proven to be Wright's most progressive novel.

Fishbelly's daily struggles *in Paris* never did make it to press as a result of a conscious choice by Wright to turn to other projects rather than complete the manuscript. Even so, depicting the life of Fishbelly in Paris was an important thought experiment for Wright with respect to his own future creative directions. *The Long Dream* project, conceived as a trilogy and "considered as a stepping stone into the future and not a retreat into his childhood which is all the American critics found in it," encompasses *The Long Dream* as well as Wright's manuscript, "Island of Hallucination" (Fabre, *Unfinished Quest* 527). The third part of the trilogy would have been set in Africa but was also never completed (Hamalian 120). To allow a reading of the "Island" manuscript to overshadow the critical assessment either of *The Long Dream* or Wright's mindset at the time completely is to discount the public and controlling place of *The Long Dream* in the trilogy as well as to privilege the allure of the collective paranoia of Wright's last days when determining the quality of his work.

Wright's explicit concentration on the literary dimensions of *The Long Dream* was indeed fashioned in tumultuous times, against the backdrop of the 1956 First Congress of Black Writers and Artists, notably, against Fanon's warning not to place "too much faith in purely literary and artistic endeavors"—in "the culture of culture" (Jules-Rosette 59). "Island of Hallucination" was put aside by Wright in its initial phases as being insufficiently thought through with respect to the proper balance between "culture of culture" and political positioning. As James Baldwin's essay "Alas Poor Richard" indicates, debates about balance between aesthetic and political concerns was a central one for the exiled African American community at the time (161). Much of the *essay* writing around this debate, reliant as it has always been upon supposed direct quotation by members of the exiled community, mimics the shadow of collective paranoia and perhaps muddies rather than clarifies what the stakes of the game really were. The veracity of the supposed conversations that took place and which are reported in such essay writing can never be fully determined. The essays only bear witness to the pressing need to be proven right within the terms of the debates. A critical analysis of the crucial literary elements of Wright's last novel, *The Long Dream*, can ultimately serve as an alternative mode for discovering Wright's position in the debates in question.

In a similar vein, the disputes surrounding the potential publication of "Island of Hallucination" as a *roman a clef* have ironically made of it a very public document. Despite its unpublished nature, the temptation to look for answers about Wright's last days is great indeed, just as essays that resort to argument on the basis of direct quotation of oral statements carry an emotive force of truth but do not necessarily clarify Wright's authorial intention. In Richard Gibson's own recently published account of the contexts informing "Island of Hallucination," he concludes by remarking that "while I do not think that 'Island of Hallucination' is a great book, it is a very important document about Richard Wright's state of mind at the end of his life and reveals as in a cracked mirror the tensions and sad delusions that moved some leading figures in the African American community in Paris in the 1950's" (917). Gibson's call for publication of the document is understandable, but it is crucial that the manuscript is regarded as a *document*, not as a finished novel written and acknowledged by Wright. It cannot provide the answers to Wright's *literary* achievements at the end of his life in the same way that *The Long Dream* does.

Most biographical readings of the political contexts covered in the manuscript grant that Wright's literary activity was checked by his fear of reprisal from governments, from colleagues, and from friends, and that therefore the paranoiac reactions of Fishbelly throughout "Island" are rooted in factual experiences (Gibson 913). The works of biographers Rowley, Fabre, and Campbell indeed affirm that Wright felt plagued by criticisms from all sides. As Tyler Stovall asserts, "This silence [of Richard Wright on the subject of the French-Algerian conflict] provoked increasing criticism toward the end of the great writer's life; those who argued that Parisian exile had cut him off, both creatively and politically, from his American roots could now also contend that his new internationalist vision had some serious blind spots" (191).

Most notably, Wright's ability to function as a publicly honest writer of protest literature or politically vibrant fiction was stifled by his lack of a suitable public platform from which to comment upon the racial tensions of his adopted home, Paris. In the *Times Literary Supplement* of June 2008, reference to the unpublished "Island" manuscript is used quite perspicaciously by James Campbell in his overall assessment of Wright's legacy. Like others, Campbell suggests that Wright's legacy rightly or wrongly suffered from his inability to engage in topical issues at the end of his literary career and that therefore his particular strengths as a writer were muted (1).

Literary criticism separates political from aesthetic concerns only with great delicacy, but Wright's characterizations of a protagonist who needed to keep silent in *The Long Dream* blends literary technique skillfully with the representation of an individual caught in a state of compromise very similar to Wright's own in those last years. Wright's literature of silence, as structured in *The Long Dream*, shares strong affinities with other prescient transnational works as well, notably Bernard Dadié's *Un nègre à Paris* and Smith's *The Stone Face*. The motif of individuals making decisions about what they should or should not say about their situations is crucial to all three novels and comparison of the works would indicate that Wright's *aesthetic* development was not as arrested at this point in his career as has been assumed, but was rather part of a generic trend towards constructing a transnational literary voice through deeper explorations and through literary perspectives on immigrant voices and silences— narratives of "cultural displacement and longing" (Jules-Rosette 8).

Fishbelly's longing and belonging

Fishbelly's voice evolves in *The Long Dream* into a transnational voice and shifts the focus of Wright's intentions away from the naturalistic tendencies for which his earlier fiction is so appreciated. Even those who championed the "compelling" naturalism of Wright, such as Henry Louis Gates, Jr., have remarked upon his contribution to shaping literary modernism. Wright's late experiments in characterization even drift radically towards an absurdist vein in much of "Island" with figures such as Mechanical, or in anecdotal episodes such as one in which an old woman refuses to leave a Parisian restaurant for mysterious reasons. To Fishbelly, her stubbornness is initially read as a typically French behavioral pattern until he eventually discovers that she has dropped her false teeth and is ashamed to ask anyone to reach under the table to fetch them for her. This constitutes one of many episodes where Fishbelly bears witness to the Parisian world he confronts.

While reflecting upon certain truths about the Parisian culture he was witnessing, Wright was also shaping a compelling commentary on the absurdity or grotesqueness of the new world confronted by Fishbelly. Tensions between when one can speak or when one must remain silent are already hinted at in the structure of such anecdotal episodes, but Wright's control of them is not established. In the second half of the novel, Fishbelly realizes that there are many who would like to "buy his silence" (214). Trotskyist leader Cato even suggests at one point that Fishbelly could help their political cause simply because he was a "silent one" (426). Had time allowed, the literature of silence, which is so deeply structured in *The Long Dream*, would no doubt have been continued and perfected in "Island of Hallucination" as these and other instances in the manuscript indicate.

As it stands, Wright's exploration of an increasingly modernist aesthetic through his motif of the right and need to remain silent, while tenable in *The Long Dream*, remains uncontrolled in the unfinished manuscript. In the preface to his collection of Wright essays written in 1993, Gates ventures that "Wright may also have been responsible for the shaping of literary modernism" (xiii). This perspective is easily girded by examples of characterization and events in "Island" had it been completed and is certainly supported by critical examination of *The Long Dream*, Gates does not choose to expand in this direction, given the overwhelming importance of Wright's legacy as an author of "compelling" protest fiction in the naturalist vein, but one can glean that finding continuity between *The Long Dream* and "Island" requires that one see Wright's overall creative purpose as a foray into a modernist aesthetic. By contrast, to insist on the manuscript as a semi-autobiographical index of the day-to-day activities of the African American exile community is to dismiss Wright's own creative purposes for beginning the manuscript (i.e., as a second part of an overall trilogy of novels rooted in an exploration of a literature of silence).

Cynthia Tolentino argues that "even as Wright appropriates sociological modes of analysis to develop his literary technique, he also struggles to distinguish his literary production from communism and sociology" (7). Tolentino's focus is on social and political contexts of Wright's American fiction, but her arguments are useful in analysing the exile fiction as well. Fishbelly's need to remain silent as a controlling trope of *The Long Dream* appears as part of a shift into an explicit modernist aesthetic in Wright's literary production. The trope becomes a controlling one at a crucial moment in Wright's coming to terms with his Parisian setting. For him to be wary of his public image in that domain and to exercise discretion was a constant and pressing need. Paris indeed serves ironically as the solution to Fishbelly's problems in *The Long Dream* but precisely as Wright's urban nightmare at this point in his career.

By the time Wright rejected "Island" as a viable project, Paris had ceased to be an urban setting where he could successfully continue to create "new ways of understanding the effects of urbanization on the human condition" (Joyce 139). As a writer, his constant search for ways to translate the fictional characterizations that emerged from his own life experience into an aesthetic articulation of an authentic human voice had not yet allowed him to think the "voice" of the Parisian Negro. Wright ultimately withdraws from certain types of characterization or from physical spaces such as the Parisian urban landscape when he ends his work on "Island" and turns back to a treatment of the Chicago urban landscape in *A Father's Law*. As editor Julia Wright quotes in the opening pages of her introduction to *A Father's Law*, Wright expressed an exhilarating freedom to his friend Margrit de Sablonière when he shifted his attention from "Island" to the new geography of the novel he ultimately would not have time to complete, *A Father's Law* (v).

As a character, Fishbelly remains consistently aware of his longing to belong in his new environment, at the same time that he recognizes the impossibility of ever doing so:

> In Paris he went in and out of bars, offices, cafés, hotels and restaurants free of that dogging racial constraint that had been his all his life.
>
> Yet he was not free . . . deep down, he had to admit that he was not truly *in* or *of* France; he knew he could never be French even if he lived in France a million years. He loved France and the French, yet France was always *psychologically distant* in his mind. Had he come too late?
>
> ("Island" qtd. in Rowley 482–3; emphasis added)

In this passage from "Island of Hallucination," Fishbelly admits that though he inhabited the urban space of the French, he would always remain on the outside of their dark secrets. In *The Long Dream*, Fishbelly was able to join the world defined by his father Tyree once they shared the dark secret of Tyree's world. Fishbelly rejects that world out of hand as essentially inhumane before moving on to Paris and to a new national culture. Just as Fishbelly abandons the United States in order to find his voice, Wright abandons Fishbelly and his struggles in Paris once the character can no longer help him to find his own voice.

The Long Dream reads as a coming-of-age novel, which shifts midstream into a modernistic treatment of a father-son pair who "share a dark secret" (27). Once the secrets are shared, the father and son can live a narrative sequence of "justified lying" (18). Tolentino notes in her study of the fictions of sociology that "coming-of-age narratives" lent themselves easily to a treatment of characters emerging from the Black Belt by authors who were themselves part of that social phenomenon. Wright used this genre successfully in his early years, but he transforms the genre beyond recognition in *The Long Dream*. The reality that a protagonist must learn about and accept in a coming-of-age narrative never materializes in *The Long Dream*. Similarly, in "Island of Hallucination," Fishbelly continuously summarizes for himself the lessons he has learned but then admits in a much quieter voice that he has not learned his lesson at all.

This is a particularly prominent pattern in the first half of the manuscript. When he realizes that a young white woman, Nicole, has betrayed him and duped him into believing in a color-blind France, his reaction is to stare in silence at nothing, "shame protecting him from the meaning of what had happened. It was as though he had struck his thumb with a hammer and was waiting for the numbness to thaw out and the searing pain to come" (44). Rather than becoming internalized, this lesson is increasingly caricatured later in the manuscript; Fishbelly claims that each time he hears people speaking good sense about business, he just "shuts his mouth and listens" (286). The more he rejects the others' attempts to draw him into their political troubles, the more he characterizes himself as being the "business" man his father taught him to be back in good old racist Mississippi. Business talk is the only way he finds to silence "race talk," a subject to which I will return.

The reality that Fishbelly confronts in *The Long Dream* is one that must be rejected as politically unjust and in need of replacement. The reality Fishbelly leaves behind when he takes the plane to Paris seems harshly inhumane and the justifications for abandoning his home terrain are rooted in political debates on American racism that were already familiar to his readership. But like Wright, *The Long Dream*'s Fishbelly is driven by a need to remain silent in order to feel free in relation to this inhumanity, and *explicitly* to be free to have his voice resonate at a later point in time within the context of the racial debate. The "Island" Fishbelly constantly assesses the extent to which his own personal vanity has been injured as a result *not* of racial inequalities but rather as a result of others who are willing to exploit Fishbelly's *belief* in racial inequalities for their own personal gain. His enemy is not racial prejudice—it is human greed, his own included.

Being willing to break silences and to engage in "race talk" thus plays a different role in *The Long Dream* and "Island of Hallucination." In the former, one of the types of talking that Fishbelly is most adamantly against is "race talk." Fishbelly repeatedly asks his friend Sam and others around him to stop all their "race talk" as he feels it drowns out other kinds of talking that need to be done (357). When Sam says at an early point in the novel "You-all just 'shamed of being *black*," Fishbelly responds "nervously" by saying "Aw Sam, stop that kind of talk" (33). Fishbelly continually delivers admonitions against race talk in *The Long Dream*, a novel created at the same time that Wright was positioning himself in relation to confused "race talk" of the 1956 Congress of Black Writers and Artists. *The Long Dream* responds to the debate concerning the pros and cons of a "culture of culture" by framing references to race talk in a constantly evolving protagonist. Ironically, Fishbelly is characterized in "Island" as only seeming normal when he's talking about race:

> "Crap," Fishbelly sneered. "[The French] are prejudiced! Now tell me: are they prejudiced against us because we're black or because we're Americans or both?"
> "There he goes!" Zeke yelled, laughing. "When he's talking race, he's normal!" (65)

As the above quotation suggests, Mississippi Fishbelly and Paris Fishbelly are discontinuous entities but certain structural continuities in the two novels indicate some of the directions Wright might have taken in joining them up eventually. *The Long Dream* is ostensibly built on a structure of dreaming: daydreams and night dreams that eventually transform into a waking dream in the final section of the novel. As Hamalian has stressed in her article "Richard Wright's Use of Epigraphs in *The Long Dream*," the novel is forcefully literary, with its exquisite use of the epigraph (120). In the "Island" manuscript, many of the chapters are introduced by an underlined passage that reads as if it were the recounting of a dream. The underlined passages seem to serve the same purpose as the epigraphs in *The Long Dream* (i.e., to introduce and structure the chapter divisions). Though the manuscript still retains traces of epigraphs from authors Mark Twain and Herman Melville as well as the Bible, the dream sequences are more deliberate in their development. Even so, the structuring of the two works argues that there is an attempt to let literature speak for itself and to insist on an aesthetic distance even in the case of what might ultimately be regarded as a form of protest. Critical comments on the "Island" manuscript, particularly those by Gibson, belie the fact that Wright's ultimate objective was not yet clarified in the second part of the trilogy.

The dominant narrative feature in question involves lessons in learning to be silent, which runs parallel to the structure of dreaming. Tyree's early advice to Fishbelly to "dream only what can happen" (79) is consistent with the fact that the plot is constructed as a series of very loosely connected memories of events in Fishbelly's life until the moment when he must act or speak in ways that can have concrete consequences on the directions his life will take. Events in the novel become more tightly woven together and the plot becomes more driven by Fishbelly himself as he internalizes his father's lesson. Fishbelly's most sustained action in the novel leads him from dreams that cannot happen to one that can and does happen, namely, his dream to move to Paris. This dream is only realizable as a result of Fishbelly's strategic gesture of remaining silent during the entirety of his incarceration and beginning to speak only when the time is right.

This transformative moment is made possible through his ability to remain silent about the existence and whereabouts of the checks that would have implicated police chief Cantley in the crimes for which his father was killed. The fact that Fishbelly has no physical space in which he can exercise his "right" to remain silent about the checks reinforces the idea that even being able to remain silent is a right for which one must be prepared to fight. The only space for freedom of speech that finally offers itself is Paris, as Wright himself remarked upon his own arrival there (Stovall 198). Wright's insistence on remaining silent about "race talk" was a right only grudgingly granted to him in those last years, but one that he zealously provides for Fishbelly.

The Long Dream mirrors Wright's increasing awareness at this point in his life that he had perhaps become a prominent writer but he would always be an American Negro in the eyes of the world. As he points out in his letter to James Holness dated July 7, 1959, when he declines an invitation to attend a cultural festival in London, "I shall state my case honestly. I'm an American Negro. We American Negroes who live abroad live under tremendous political pressure ... Hence I must keep clear of entanglements that would stifle me in expressing myself in terms that I feel are my own." Narrative structuring of this pressing need to remain silent builds progressively in *The Long Dream* and echoes Wright's struggle to express himself in ways that are his own. In the first half of the novel, the main thread linking episodes is an inability to express one's thoughts. Fishbelly is told to "shut up" (126); he "yearns to talk" (122) when he knows he shouldn't; he "holds his tongue" (97); he has "no more words" (146) or realizes that "he could never put what he was feeling into words" (63). When remaining silent finally becomes a matter of life and death for him, he is able to refrain from speaking.

Wright continually brings Fishbelly back to the idea of a dark secret whose meaning must be revealed before one can belong together with others who share that secret. He reconfigures the need for silence as a learning process, where each moment of mastery becomes the base for yet another lesson to begin. Fishbelly frees himself at the end of *The Long Dream*, only to realize that his newfound freedom serves as the trap that opens the second part of the trilogy. France was too psychologically distant and was a constant reminder that, for an American Negro, to dream to become French was to dream something that could never happen. In the absence of a possibility to become French, the groundwork for establishing a transnational voice is laid, and psychologically strong characterization is its foundation. As Wright himself puts it in a comment quoted by Fabre in *Richard Wright: Books and Writers*, he saw himself as a "psychologist" no matter how crudely he might practice such psychoanalysing (9). That he stresses the psychological distance felt by the character reinforces Wright's own need for a deep understanding of his characters in order to create authentic voices for them. In this sense, his work on *The Long Dream* trilogy is uncannily aligned with the other narratives of longing and belonging that characterize creative production in Paris at the time.

Airplane cabins for transnationals

Both *Un nègre à Paris* and *The Long Dream* are narratives of longing and belonging whose authors have witnessed the new cultural world they confront by "assuming an ethnographic and journalistic gaze on their social environments" (Jules-Rosette 186). Dadié defines the struggle he faced in writing his novel *Un nègre à Paris* as one where he had to recognize the "essential dichotomy between the aesthetics of joyous expression and the social responsibility of the artist" (Jules-Rosette 186), the very dichotomy that has repeatedly divided critics in their judgment of Wright's legacy and that dominated the central debates of the 1956 Congress on Fanon's culture of culture. Benetta Jules-Rosette highlights the ultimate questions posed by black artists such as Dadié and Wright in 1956 and that resonate with the ones asked about Wright's legacy today: "Should the writer be an activist, a witness, or an engaged artist?"(189).

Seeking equilibrium with respect to these questions, both authors stress metaphors of spatial relations that mimic the pain caused by racial otherness and that reinforce the controlling trope of a call for silence in such spaces. The physical space of the airplane cabin replaces the segregated worlds of the two protagonists and opens up new realms of possibility for them. For Fishbelly, being in the airplane cabin "was the first time in his life that he had sat surrounded by white men, women and children with no degrading, visible line marking him off. His knees were held stiffly together, as though he expected his presence to be challenged" (378). Though he tries to avert his gaze, he eventually succumbs to the temptation to look at the beautiful and luxurious head of hair of the woman in front of him. His joy at this vision is coupled with anxiety as he witnesses "the charming trap that could trigger his deepest fears of death" (378). His subsequent experience of the plane ride and his discussion with the Italian American next to him who wants Fishbelly to articulate his true feelings about being a Negro from America lead the protagonist to withdraw into a silence, which does not contest the Italian American's own image of the American Dream but belies the fact that Fishbelly is "not yet emotionally strong enough to admit what he had lived" (380).

Fishbelly knows enough to be able to refute what the Italian American believes to be true but needs to remain silent about his knowledge in order to gain entry into the French world to which he is fleeing. The closing pages of the novel emphasize exhilaration at potential entry into a new cultural experience coupled with the anxieties of longing to know in advance he will belong to the world he is entering. As a result, metaphors of silence prevail. As he muses, "that man's father had come to America and found a dream; he [Fishbelly] had been born in America and had found a nightmare" (380). Unlike the other passengers on the plane, Fishbelly "sat looking at the dream images of his life with wide-open eyes." He rejected the "curtain of dreams shielding [their] hearts from the claims of waking hours" (382). He had learned, finally, to dream only what could happen and to do so involved a certain amount of necessary silence.

Dadié's protagonist expresses joyful enthusiasm about possessing a plane ticket to go to Paris but is quickly subdued when he giddily takes his seat and realizes that no one will sit by him precisely because he is black. When someone finally does have the courage to sit beside him, the protagonist equally realizes that they will spend the entire journey in silence. In *The Long Dream*, Fishbelly enters the airplane cabin with a new-found sense of freedom but by the time he leaves the airplane in "Island of Hallucination," he too recognizes that the freedom he thought he had gained was only a pipe dream and that the talking in which he engaged on the plane was never authentic. The preface to his realizations is given in the opening words of the "Island" manuscript, which stress silence:

> Inside the craft, the lights are dimmed, and, save for an occasional half-asleep, nervous cough, and the steady muted drone of the four powerful motors, there was silence. (1)

The desire and need for silence pervades narratives of longing and belonging. The reader is introduced to a silent but dreaming Fishbelly in seat number 17 (7) and to a young ten-year-old boy who is thinking about how terrifying it will be if he runs into any French people in Paris who "talk politics" (3). Discrepancies in characterization in *The Long Dream* and "Island" notwithstanding, questions posed by his critics and by

Fishbelly himself concerning the relative value of remaining silent in the face of specific racial dilemmas keep coming to the surface. What was the correct response of the socially responsible African American at this point in time? This was the incessant issue nagging Fishbelly, Wright, and the entire African American community exiled in Paris. Was Wright convinced of an ethical need to keep silent or was he simply in a process of opting for creature comfort over social responsibility?

Smith, in a *supposedly* direct quote, remarks that Wright was adept at unsettling the nerves of European whites in those tense times of the late 1950s with such quips as "Don't worry about a thing. When the Africans and Asians invade Europe, I'll put in a good word for you and you won't be shot or raped. After all, I'll have some influence we're all colored brothers together" (*Return* 69). Rather than reconfirming Wright's own sense of creature comfort amongst European whites, these observations perhaps illustrate Wright's realization that there was not necessarily any real power in being all colored brothers together, as sentiments of his presentation at the 1956 Congress, "Tradition and Industrialization: The Plight of the Tragic Elite in Africa," attest (356). In this address, Wright directly called into question whether or not the cultural unity of blacks in Africa, America, and elsewhere could overcome other pressures in the modern world such as the compelling force of technology (Jules-Rosette 58).

Like Wright, authors such as Himes and Smith wanted to create socially responsible novels but were constrained by the interdiction against speaking about racial tensions and, in particular, about Franco-Algerian racial problems. Whereas Wright's solution was to explore the emotional impact of a need to keep silent in *The Long Dream*, Smith ultimately ignored these constraints and Himes eventually catered to a readership hungry for caricature in the satiric detective novels written while he lived in France (Craven 39). Each of these authors seemed bent on finding a plot, a thematic, or a setting that could allow them to confront the dichotomous relation between the types of characters they wanted to create and the ones they were expected or allowed to create. What is regrettable is that those wanting to dismiss Wright's late fiction as socially negligent cite Smith's 1963 novel, *The Stone Face*, as a direct confrontation with the Franco-Algerian "race talk," which they claim Wright was too cowardly to address (Stovall 191).

Smith departs from the directions taken by Wright and Dadié in his willingness to create Algerian characters that are "re-imagined" as African Americans, thereby asserting a similarity between the plights of the Algerian immigrants and the American Negro. Despite Smith's care with making necessary distinctions between Algerians and American Negroes in his dialogue, the thematic thread upon which his novel depends is a reduced logic of oppressor and oppressed, which echoes the sentiments expressed at the 1956 Congress concerning the history of colonialism. For the face of the oppressors, he claims, "They were all the same face. Wherever this face was found, it was his enemy; and whoever feared or suffered from, or fought against this face was his brother" (*Stone Face* 1964, 176). The uncompromised likening of Algerian immigrant to American Negro was rejected by Wright, given the complexity of identity politics in Paris during the Franco-Algerian war (Smith 57; Stovall 194; Ross 225).

Smith succeeds in making a social statement about the Franco-Algerian racial issues he confronts, but he does little to advance the aesthetic evolution of a transnational voice in his novel. It would certainly be counterproductive to criticize such a step, but it is clear that *The Long Dream* is finally better positioned to be analysed in terms of its literary representation of a transnational voice than is *The Stone Face* for this very reason. In its current state, the "Island" manuscript seems to have abandoned the question of balancing aesthetic and political concerns in order to explore the absurdist veins of characterization that dominate in its pages. One telling example of grotesque political positioning is when Fishbelly asks Yvette to "be France" for him. Her aim is to engage Fishbelly in a political positioning and his response is to ask that France and all of its politics be substituted for by the love of a woman (112). We realize in this instance that France, as represented in the figure of Yvette, is more likely an escape from politics than anything else for Fishbelly.

Wright's legacy is ultimately dependent on his place with respect to the literary tradition and to the debates on the racial and human conflicts of his time. In his last years, Wright certainly witnessed extraordinary tensions for the African and Algerian populations in his Parisian home and in his carefully orchestrated travels to Africa, but he was spared the violence of the Algerian massacre of October 1961, which invaded the physical spaces he had chosen to depict in one of his final fictional works. Conversely, the massacre is the pivot upon which Smith's characterization rests in *The Stone Face* precisely because it no doubt played a large role in motivating the novel's creation. In writing *The Long Dream*, Wright chose to look back at his past in order to figure out how to move forward, but was unable to retrace the reminiscent journey any further than his flight to Paris, at least not in published form. Looking at the balance between his formal education and the education he received under the cloaks of silence throughout his lifetime therefore remains etched in the mental development of Mississippi Fishbelly, a character that is part of Wright's literary legacy.

In his speech at the American Church of Paris a few weeks before his death, Richard Wright describes this dichotomous education as follows:

> Suppose Negro literature in the United States were no longer under the control, direct or indirect, of institutions influenced by religion or *Negro leadership*, enjoying its prestige by being subsidized by guilt ridden whites? *What would literature say?* But you'd like to ask, why had I or how had I escaped such influence?
>
> ("The Negro Intellectual" 3; emphasis added)

Wright stresses that it is not his own voice *per se* but the voice of "literature" that somehow miraculously escaped the control of institutions, a fact that was paramount throughout his existence, and a truth to which he clung at the end of his life when he was pressed to defend his own life choices. His tone throughout this last address suggests that he still insisted on the freedom of the literary voice. Though it might be political in its nature, "literature" did not have to answer to political constraints or to the constraints that might ultimately be imposed on a Negro writer. As he suggests, "You have the right to say that what I've written is good or bad but you cannot say that it was controlled by the influences extant in the black belt" ("The Negro Intellectual" 3–4).

Wright insists that it is his own life of reading that allowed him to construct an identity free from control and conditioning through the rigid ideologies of the place from which he originates, the deeply racist Southern United States. Wright's voice was a voice of protest, even in the sentiments of this last speech, but one that relied upon his ability to be a literary craftsman who could establish an aesthetic distance and engage freely in experimentation with stylistic considerations and generic forms. His literature was one that spoke, not controlled by "influences extant in the black belt" but as a result of his having remained silent in the face of those controlling influences long enough for him to find his own way to control them. Unlike the indifferent Mississippi school system, historical accounts show that national governments, colleagues, and Black Congresses alike were not at all indifferent to what Wright might or might not say by the time he became a writer in exile. They bore resemblance to the ubiquitous and unyielding police chief one encounters in *The Long Dream*, who dogs Fishbelly even to his jail cell, as did the CIA and FBI in their employment of any and all African American expatriates willing to exchange information for money or favors (Maxwell 258).

Wright's speech on "The American Negro Intellectual and Artist in the United States Today" established that he had not stopped thinking about the literal place of the American Negro in the world and his or her role in the construction of a transnational discourse. Yet he knew that were it to consume his creative practice or derail his intellectual journey, this would short-circuit any influence he might have on future generations of American Negroes who would be introduced to his work. The value of Wright's work rests on his ability to remain silent until he learned how to speak and on his insistence that he spoke best through literature. This insistence places his exile novel *The Long Dream* in line with the literary experiments of African writer Dadié as well as with his fellow American, political novelist Smith. Comparative analysis of these three authors puts Wright's journey towards speaking in a transnational vein in perspective. It also speaks against a contemporary desire to find Wright's own authentic voice in a manuscript he did not publish.

Works cited

Baldwin, James. "Princes and Powers." *Nobody Knows My Name: More Notes of a Native Son.* London: Penguin, 1961. 24–55. Print.

Campbell, James. "Black First." *Times Literary Supplement* June 11, 2008. Web. Mar. 23, 2010. http://entertainment.timesonline.co.uk/tol/arts_and_enteertainment/the_tls/article4112123.ece

Craven, Alice Mikal. "A Victim in Need Is a Victim in Deed: The Ritual Consumer and Self-Fashioning in Himes' *Run Man Run.*" *Questions of Identity in Detective Fiction.* Ed. Linda Martz and Anita Higgie. Newcastle: Cambridge Scholars Press, 2007. 37–58. Print.

Dadié, Bernard. *Un Nègre à Paris.* Paris: Présence Africaine, 1959. Print.

Fabre, Michel. *Richard Wright: Books and Writers.* Jackson: UP of Mississippi, 1990. Print.

—— *The Unfinished Quest of Richard Wright.* Champaign: U of Illinois P, 1973. Print.

Gibson, Richard. "Richard Wright's 'Island of Hallucination' and the 'Gibson Affair.'" *Modern Fiction Studies* 51.4 (2005): 896–920. Print.

Hakutani, Yoshinobu. "Richard Wright's *The Long Dream* as Racial and Sexual Discourse." *African American Review* 30.2 (1996): 267–80. Print.

Hamalian, J. B. "Richard Wright's Use of Epigraphs in *The Long Dream*." *Black American Literature Forum* 10.4 (1976): 120–3. Print.

Harrington, Oliver W. *Why I Left America and Other Essays.* Ed. Thomas W. Inge. Jackson: UP of Mississippi, 1993. Print.

Joyce, Joyce Ann. "Richard Wright's *A Father's Law* and Black Metropolis: Intellectual Growth and Literary Vision." *Richard Wright: New Readings in the 21st Century.* Ed. Alice Mikal Craven and William E. Dow. New York: Palgrave Macmillan, 2011: 129–46. Print.

Jules-Rosette, Benetta. *Black Paris: The African Writer's Landscape.* Urbana: U of Illinois P, 1998. Print.

Maxwell, William. "African American Modernism and State Surveillance." *A Companion to African American Literature.* Ed. Gene Jarrett. Oxford: Blackwell, 2010. 254–68. Print.

Ross, Kristen. *May '68 and Its Afterlives.* Chicago: U of Chicago P, 2002. Print.

Rowley, Hazel. *Richard Wright: The Life and Times.* Chicago: U of Chicago P, 2008. Print.

Sainville, Léonard. "Le roman et ses responsabilités." *Présence Africaine* 27–8 (1959): 37–50. Print.

Smith, William Gardner. *Return to Black America.* Englewood Cliffs: Prentice Hall, 1970. Print.

—— *The Stone Face.* New York: Farrar, 1963. Print.

—— *The Stone Face.* New York: Pocket Cardinal, 1964. Print.

Stovall, Tyler. "The Fire This Time: Black American Expatriates and the Algerian War." *Yale French Studies* 98 (2000): 182–200. Print.

Tolentino, Cynthia. *America's Experts: Race and the Fictions of Sociology.* Minneapolis: U of Minnesota P, 2009. Print.

Wright, Julia, ed. Introduction. *A Father's Law.* By Richard Wright. New York: Harper Perennial, 2008. Print.

Wright, Richard. *A Father's Law.* Ed. Julia Wright. New York: Harper Perennial, 2008. Print.

—— "Island of Hallucination". TS. Box 34, folder 472. James Weldon Johnson Collection, Yale Collection of American Literature. Beinecke Rare Books and Manuscripts Library, Yale University, New Haven.

—— Letter to James Holness. 7 July 1959. Michel Fabre Papers. Manuscript, Archives, and Rare Book Library, Emory University, Atlanta.

—— *The Long Dream.* Chatham: Chatham Booksellers, 1969. Print.

—— "The Negro Intellectual and Artist in the United States Today." Typescript of speech given at the American Church (prepared by Clayton Machmar and Helen M. White). Special Collection. American Library in Paris, Paris.

—— "Tradition and Industrialization: The Plight of the Tragic Elite in Africa." *Présence Africaine* 2nd ser. 8–10 (1956): 347–60. Print.

14

Expanding Metaphors of Marginalization: Richard Wright, Sharankumar Limbale, and a Post-Caste Imaginary[1]

Sudhi Rajiv
Jai Narain Vyas University

I

In his influential essay "Imaginary Homelands," Salman Rushdie makes a powerful case for the critical relevance of diasporic writing, helping us to make sense of Richard Wright's work in his years of exile. At one point, Rushdie states, "It may be argued that the past is a country from which we have all emigrated, that its loss is part of our common humanity . . . I suggest that a writer who is out-of-country and even out-of-language may experience this loss in an intensified form . . . This may enable him to speak properly and concretely on a subject of universal significance and appeal" (12). As a diasporic South Asian writer in the United Kingdom, Rushdie claims that he and others like him "will not be capable of reclaiming precisely the thing that was lost; that we will, in short, create fictions, not actual cities or villages, but invisible ones, imaginary homelands, Indias of the mind" (10).

Amritjit Singh notes a similar thematic vein in Wright's works. As Singh states,

> In non-fictional works such as *Black Power* and *Color Curtain*, as well as in fictional works such as *The Outsider, The Long Dream* and *Eight Men*, Wright was doing precisely that—creating his own imagined communities, his imaginary homelands, envisioning a world in which freedom and economic justice would touch every individual life in the world, where former slaves and other colonized peoples could "catch the full spirit of Western civilization."[2]

In his introduction to *Black Power*, Singh further observes that "For Wright, measuring the humanity of Africans by the yardstick of Western values such as freedom, individualism and democracy was an effective way of countering the continuing distortions of Africans and other people of color in the West" (xix). Both Singh and Rushdie stress the importance of exile writing as a source of inspiration, but Rushdie goes further in "Imaginary Homelands" and mentions both Wright and Ralph Ellison as possible models for his work. Viewing his own and other diaspora writings in adversarial terms, Rushdie posits his novel *Midnight's Children* as "one way of defying the official, politicians' version of truth" (14) in keeping with lessons learned from Wright and Ellison. He acknowledges in particular the influence Wright's proposed frameworks had on his writing. Wright's early recognition that black and white Americans were engaged in a war over the nature of reality helped Rushdie to understand that "their descriptions were incompatible. So it is clear that re-describing a world is the necessary first step towards changing it" (13–14).

Clearly, Rushdie speaks in his essay primarily for himself and possibly for other diasporic South Asian writers in the UK and North America, writers such as Meena Alexander, Chitra Divakaruni, and Jhumpa Lahiri in the United States and Rohinton Mistry and M. G. Vassanji in Canada. But since the 1970s, black American writing has also reached academics and writers who live and work in India. This is largely because of Singh's influence and mentorship as well as the support of various institutions. For example, thanks to the American Studies Research Centre (ASRC) in Hyderabad, now called the Osmania University Center for International Programmes (OUCIP), scores of doctoral dissertations have been completed for over half a century at Indian universities in the fields of African American literature, history, and politics. While there is no reliable systematic survey of Indian scholarship in African American studies, readers will likely find a broad indication of the kind of work Indian scholars are doing in the following two essays: Singh's "Beyond the Mountain: Langston Hughes on Race/Class and Art" and Manju Jaidka's "The Road to Hyderabad: MELUS in India." Even more directly relevant to the subject is an essay by Darius Krishnaraj: "Difficulties and Dead Endings in Teaching African American Literature in Indian Universities."

In "Beyond the Mountain," Singh narrates his surprising success at being able to introduce young graduate students at a small rural university in North India to the poetry of Langston Hughes. On the other hand, in "Difficulties and Dead Endings," Krishnaraj is discouraged by factors such as lack of financial resources as well as lack of cultural awareness in the development of African American studies in India. He complains about the Indian scholars' lack of openness to multiple critical methodologies but welcomes their growing "intellectual independence," adding, "In the field of criticism of African American literature, excepting a few scholars like Amritjit Singh, one does not encounter many worthy personages" (58).

Today, while research in American studies is not as vibrant in India as it was 20 years ago, Indian universities are no longer as financially strapped, and there is a steady interest in reading and teaching African American writers such as James Baldwin, Alice Walker, Toni Morrison, Ralph Ellison, Amiri Baraka, Gwendolyn Brooks, and W. E. B. Du Bois, the grandfather of African American studies. Some of the same figures have long fascinated writers from oppressed backgrounds in India, a country that is still marked by caste hierarchies and class divisions, as well as by religious and linguistic diversity.[3] In short, African American writing has clearly influenced Indian scholars in their abilities to redescribe their reality—that necessary first step to changing their reality and to challenging oppressive versions of reality imposed upon them by their own culture.

II

Saunders Redding writes in his 1931 introduction to Du Bois's *The Souls of Black Folk* that the book "may be seen as fixing that moment in history when the American Negro began to reject the idea of the world's belonging to white people only, and to think of himself, in concert, as a potential force in the organization of society" (ix). Redding's reading of *Souls* recognizes how Du Bois questions the white supremacist structure, even as he provides an analysis of the impact of the antebellum and Reconstruction eras on African American personality and community. In particular, Du Bois theorizes the notion of "double consciousness" as part of the black American struggle for complete personhood. It was in the context of this long struggle that Du Bois had pronounced that the twentieth century would be the century of the color line. The history of the twentieth century in different parts of the world corroborates his prophetic pronouncements. Later in his career, Du Bois widened the scope of his analysis to include a critique of imperialism and capitalism on the global stage.

Du Bois's career and writings have influenced generations of people throughout the world who are still struggling to come to terms with "double consciousness" or the double bind. In his nonfictional books from the 1950s, Wright extended Du Bois's perspectives to connect with and make sense of the lives of colonized populations in Africa and Asia, and by implication elsewhere around the world. This essay extends the implications of Du Bois's "color line" to include the Dalits in India and ventures to examine Wright, in a comparativist perspective, with Sharankumar Limbale, an Indian Dalit writer, with special reference to their autobiographies and their concerns for the role race and caste have played in the lives of oppressed peoples and in the stages involved in "the process of liberation" (Kapoor 5344).[4] These autobiographical writings display a pattern of "emergence, crystallization and growth of . . . consciousness" (Rajiv 151). While there may not be a point-by-point correspondence between Wright's and Limbale's thinking on marginalization, the two writers share a broad framework for these struggles. They both focus on the marginalized populations as they move from the rejection of the imposed, socially constructed self to the creation of a new assertive self that can transcend the binaries of caste/race. Of course, the sense of confinement experienced by both blacks in the United States and Dalits in India is not just a product of race or caste alone. Indeed, it involves deeply entrenched and systemic social, economic, and political structures.

The idea of "double consciousness" as defined by Du Bois in *Souls* has great critical relevance to the issues of identity as explored by Wright in his autobiography, *Black Boy (American Hunger)*. In his autobiography, Wright documents in searing detail the dual existence he was forced to live in the midst of the harsh racial realities of the deep South: "I was quickly learning the reality—a Negro's reality—of the white world. One woman had assumed that I would tell her if I stole, and now this woman was amazed that I could not milk a cow, I, a nigger who dared live in Jackson ... They were all turning out to be alike, differing only in detail. I faced a wall in the woman's mind, a wall she did not know was there" (142). At each point of discovery and realization, the young Richard begins to see himself and his place in the world differently. His autobiography suggests that blacks in Mississippi were safe as long as they accepted the conditions of existence prescribed for them. Any attempt to alter the social conditions would be met with resistance, even violent death.

The way whites in the South limit Richard's experiences and aspirations becomes clear when he goes to work for a white family. The lady of the house asks him about his future plans, and young Richard replies,

> "Well, I want to be a writer, . . ."
> "A what?" she demanded.
> "A writer," I mumbled.
> "For what?"
> "To write stories," I mumbled defensively.
> "You'll never be a writer," she said, "Who on earth put such ideas into your nigger head?"
> "Nobody," I said.
> "I didn't think anybody ever would," she declared indignantly. (141)

Through such prescriptions, white Southerners attempt to limit the opportunities of African Americans. In confronting a racist society, a black girl or boy's consciousness is damaged for life. Although the US Constitution guaranteed equal opportunity for one and all, African Americans "knew unerringly" through their daily experiences "what to aspire to and what not to aspire to" (188). But Richard decided he must learn to fight back, knowing well his sense of powerlessness against individuals and forces surrounding him: "I resolved that ... if I were ever faced with a white mob, I would conceal a weapon, pretend that I had been crushed by the wrong done to one of my loved ones; then, just when they thought I had accepted their cruelty as the law of my life, I would let go with my gun and kill as many of them as possible before they killed me" (71).

Wright turns his emotional response to these oppressions into an elaborate intellectual structure as his writing evolves. He realizes that the only freedom he can find from the concrete realities of color and race is through reading and writing. The books that he manages to read give him the idea that life could be different and could be lived in a fuller and richer manner. He discovered that authority could be challenged. Words could be used as weapons. Wright ends the original 1945 edition of *Black Boy* with a powerful resolve to "hurl words into the darkness and wait for an echo, and if an echo sounded no matter how faintly, I would send other words to tell, to march, to fight, to create a sense of the hunger for life that gnaws in us all, to keep alive in our hearts a sense of the inexpressibly human" (135).

In discussing the problem of perspective in his manifesto, "Blueprint for Negro Writing" (1937), Wright raises a number of questions for black American writers:

"Should they be called upon to preach? . . . Must they write propaganda?" His answer is "No, it is a question of awareness, of consciousness, it is above all a question of perspective" (87). For Wright, perspective is that "fixed point in intellectual space where a writer stands to view the struggles, hopes and sufferings of his people" (88). In Wright's view, Marxist thought would provide such a perspective for black writers broadly. Achieving distance and objectivity as a writer would involve the will to change the existing system and thereby to create a meaningful picture of the world, an "imaginary homeland" in Rushdie's terms. In his magnum opus, *Native Son*, and his autobiographical works, *Black Boy* and *American Hunger*, Wright explores his experiences of oppression as an African American against the US historical context, and in *Black Power* and *The Color Curtain*, he internationalizes those black American problems by including colonized populations from Africa and Asia in his expanding metaphor of marginalization. In the process, long before V. S. Naipaul and Rushdie, Wright had carved out for himself the role of a global intellectual and created a means whereby he could provide hints and directions to other marginalized individuals and groups.

In a way, Wright set the agenda for the twenty-first century, making antiracism and anti-imperialism the central issues of his career in the 1950s. He knew that soon after World War II, with the looming independence of former colonies in Asia and Africa, the world was fast becoming globalized and interactive, and he felt that the shared knowledge of caste/race and class oppression throughout the world could be transformed into a movement to counter Western domination. He also warned against falling into the trap of absolutist definitions of race, nation, ethnicity, and gender to demonstrate the power of hybrid identities. As Paul Gilroy argues in *The Black Atlantic*, Wright prepared a meeting ground for "a global, coalitional politics in which anti-imperialism and anti-racism might be seen to interact if not to fuse" (4). Wright also enlarged the expressive possibilities for black life, or for the life of the oppressed, by employing strategies thrown up by modernist culture, without compromising the basic issues of freedom and social justice.

The discursive strategies that Houston A. Baker, Jr. finds in Booker T. Washington's "mastery of form" (31) and Du Bois's "deformation of mastery" (56) show how modernist techniques and perspectives have been incorporated into African American writing by Wright and others. In his chapter on Wright in *The Black Atlantic*, Gilroy shows how Wright uses modernist discursive strategies to his advantage and how his "extended exercise in intercultural hermeneutics" has an important effect upon his theories "about 'race,' modernity, identity and their interrelation" (150). As Singh suggests in his introduction to the 1995 reprint edition of *Black Power*, Wright invites his readers to join his heuristic projects in books such as *Black Power* and *The Color Curtain*, opening up the possibility of learning from diverse global sources and locations and at the same time using the lives of black Americans as "emblematic of the struggles of exploited and oppressed human beings in general" (Gilory 154).

According to Singh, "to recognize the changing nature of this paradigmatic representation from his early books [to the] later works" is to begin to understand Wright's insertion of a diasporic link through "a common heritage of suffering and a hunger for freedom" (Introduction, *Black Power* xiv). Wright's "travel writings" assimilate

Africa and Asia into the discourse of alterity and at the same time give due credit to the drive for national liberations. In works such as *Black Power, The Color Curtain* and *White Man, Listen!*, Wright, along with Frantz Fanon, becomes a pivotal writer and intellectual for the newly emerging independent countries in Africa and Asia—long before Edward W. Said's *Orientalism* was recognized as a foundational text for postcolonial studies.

Wright's experiences and perspectives as a descendent of slaves in the Americas gave him a special understanding of the status of the African Americans, whom he regarded as "'intrinsically a colonial subject"' (qtd. in Singh, Introduction xviii). His use of a Marxist lens, even after he relinquished his membership in the Communist Party, gave him an insight into the working of societies and the predicament of the "wretched of the earth." In his afterword to *The Color Curtain*, Singh underscores the global nature of all of Wright's career and observes how Wright

> saw the struggle for Civil Rights in the U.S. as inextricably linked to the full freedom for peoples of color throughout the world. So, while others participated in the boycotts and marches at home, [Wright] was convinced that he was fighting the same battle in global contexts by participating in debates on Negritude and Pan-Africanism and supporting movements for freedom in Africa and Asia. (225)

Quite early in his career, Wright had begun to identify the suffering African Americans with the colonized peoples in Africa and Asia, through their shared record of suffering and hunger for freedom. At the same time, Wright did not ignore the dissimilarities between black Americans on one hand and Africans and Asians on the other. He recognized what a stupendous challenge Africans and Asians had in their struggle to reclaim what they had lost under colonial rule and to establish a fair economic and political order.

Wright's reach as a thinker undoubtedly became wider as his "outsider" perspective from his sojourn in France forced him to confront much more than African American history and experience. His visits to Africa (Gold Coast/Ghana) and Asia (Bandung, Indonesia) enabled him to observe the cultural displacement in the two major continents caused by imperialism and the uncertain idea of development faced by leaders such as Jawaharlal Nehru and Kwame Nkrumah. At the heart of his nonfictional books from the 1950s are questions of culture, freedom, and equality, as well as of individuals and peoples as they confront the consequences of political and economic oppression over centuries. As Michel Fabre notes in the afterword to the original 1977 edition of *American Hunger*, "Wright not only addresses the materialism of the South, of the United States, of Western culture; he speaks to the whole of mankind in calling for radical awareness and change" (146).

III

Wright observed how the oppressed throughout the world have common experiences, face similar problems, and hence share a language. Each oppressed group is strengthened by the realization that their struggle for claiming the human space finds resonance with other similar struggles around the globe. While M. K. Gandhi refined nonviolent civil disobedience first in South Africa and then in India, African American leaders like Frederick Douglass and Du Bois devised their own strategies to fight against discrimination and oppression. All of them became in their own distinctive ways a shaping influence upon oppressed groups around the world, pushing them to think afresh about social relationships and human dignity.

Dalit writers have always been drawn toward black American writers precisely because the long suffering of African Americans strikes a chord in them, as does their tenacity to fight against physical and psychological oppression. Daniel Immerwahr in his essay "On B. R. Ambedkar and Black–Dalit Connections" mentions an undated letter from Ambedkar to Du Bois in which Ambedkar writes that "there is so much similarity between the position of the Untouchables in India and of the position of the Negroes in America that the study of the latter is not only natural but necessary" (2). Dalits have also been inspired by the questions African American artists and intellectuals have raised at each stage of their struggle, especially since the Harlem Renaissance.[5] There are specific references in the essays and commentaries by Dalit writers to Hughes, Wright, Toomer, Margaret Walker, Claude McKay, Ellison, and Baldwin. Limbale wrote his PhD dissertation on the aesthetics of African American literature, finding equivalence in Dalit aesthetics and discovering an echo in Dalit writings of black American approaches to life and literature.

Limbale's book *Towards an Aesthetic of Dalit Literature: History, Controversies and Considerations* (2004) carries a full chapter comparing Dalit literature with African American literature. In Limbale's view, "the similarities and contrasts between the two literatures will have to be investigated, for such an endeavor can create a hospitable environment for the development of literature" (82). In the foreword to the Hindi translation of his autobiography, *Akkarmashi* (*The Outcaste* 1991), Limbale compares his situation as a writer from an oppressed community with that of African American writers. He writes that blacks in America "are like my mother-father, brother-sister. The common bond between us is the imposition of inhuman slavery. Therefore, all those who are slaves, who are opposing slavery are like my own. The question that the blacks faced was 'Who am I?' The same question of identity haunts me" ("From the Writer" 8; my translation).

Questions of identity influenced not only individuals but movements as well. The Black Power movement (including the Black Panther Party), the violent phase of black liberation, inspired the Dalit Panther Movement founded by Namdeo Dhasal in 1972 in Bombay. Like the Black Panthers, the Dalit Panthers called for self-defense and self-determination. In India, however, primarily writers spearheaded the Dalit Panther Movement. The writings of Dhasal, Baburao Bagul, and other activists provided the much-needed impetus to Dalit writing. Limbale writes that this "vast movement looked like the sun. We were becoming aware of a great struggle ahead and felt the need to organize to meet the challenge" (*The Outcaste* 1991). Like Wright, some members of the Dalit Panther Party were attracted to Communism and like Wright again, a few of them dissociated themselves from it in later life.

The tension between the psychologically forced subservience and the defiance leading to assertiveness is as real in Dalit writings as it is in black American literary and journalistic works. Both black American and Dalit writers show the determination to challenge the definition of reality imposed upon them by the dominant race or caste. Like Du Bois, who prescribed a framework for the liberation of his people in Chapter 3 of *The Souls of Black Folk*, Ambedkar offered a freedom manifesto in his famous essay, "Annihilation of Caste." Ambedkar avers, "Caste is a notion, a state of the mind. The destruction of caste does not, therefore, mean the destruction of a physical barrier. It means a notional change" (1: 68). In Rushdie's terms, it should lead to the creation of an imaginary homeland.

Limbale draws on a long tradition of Dalit consciousness, beginning with medieval saint-poets (such as Kabir, Guru Nanak, Chokhamela, and Ravidas) as well as Mahatma Jyotirao Phule, the nineteenth-century social activist who frontally attacked the *savaran* (upper-caste) manipulation of Dalit lives (Shudras and Ati Shudras) and worked to uplift them. Other influences on his thought include Periyar, Narayan Guru, and most of all Ambedkar, who not only analysed the Indian past responsible for their degradation but also provided an ideological basis for raising a movement against caste discrimination. Because of these powerful Du Bois-like influences on their thinking and actions, the Dalits can now challenge and reject the forces that are out to subdue them continually. Ambedkar's thought in particular provides a "perspective" to Limbale, although he does not disregard the Marxist position completely. In fact, he talks both of caste and class. For Limbale, the "aesthetics of Dalit literature rests on the following: first, the artist's commitment; second, his life-affirming values present in the artistic creation; and third, the ability to raise the reader's consciousness of fundamental values like equality, freedom, justice, and fraternity" (*Towards an Aesthetic* 120).

Dalit writings question and examine the experience of their "untouchable" peoples and formulate alternative modes of discourse, change, and identity formation. In order to create a new tradition, Dalit writers must establish a connection between their culture and their lived experience. Limbale does not view his story as purely personal and individualistic. Like Wright, he talks not just about his own community but also about the entire society. His agony, he says, is "the pain of millions in India" (*Outcaste* x).

Apparently, Wright is much more specific than Limbale in his writings on the economic organization of society. In building on Du Bois's concerns, Wright questions the larger goals of American society and its pretensions to humanistic concerns. In his interview with Alok Mukherjee, Limbale similarly argues that the Dalits and high-caste Hindus (the *savarans*) can coexist when caste is no longer a social reality. A post-caste Indian society will be based on what Ambedkar called Equality, Liberty and Fraternity, ideas Ambedkar thoroughly internalized as a law student at Columbia University from 1913 to 1915.

Du Bois placed the predicament of his people in the context of history and made them see their common suffering and attempted to prepare African Americans to deal with the formidable social and political forces surrounding them. One can see a similar move in Ambedkar, who painstakingly analysed the intricate and destructive caste system in his book on untouchables and Shudras (*avarans*, without a "varna," hence low caste).[6] He expected that armed with this knowledge, his people would find a way "'to educate, organize and agitate"' (*Outcaste* xvii). In many ways, both Wright and Limbale seem to have benefited from the thought and direction of torchbearers like Du Bois and Ambedkar. Like Wright, who had been assigned the role of a "non-man" (*Later Works* 233) in the South, Limbale starts with a negative image of himself. He strives to destroy this nonexistent image and to establish his identity in a society that does not accept him.

The Outcaste is a bitter critique of the realities of the bondage of caste, creed, and class and also reveals endeavor for manumission from these fetters. Limbale vividly describes his experiences of being discriminated against and his sense of internalized inferiority. He recalls how his classmates ostracized him and made him sit outside his classroom lest his touch should contaminate them. He is not even allowed to touch his teacher's shoes as it "may taint their sanctity" (*Outcaste* 5). He becomes aware of the differential treatment meted out to the Dalits when he goes for a picnic in the woods with both high-caste and low-caste students. From a distance, he watches the high-caste boys and girls playing games among themselves. Being marked as a low-caste Mahar boy, he cannot join them. The rigid caste segregation creates a strong sense of alienation in him.

Though a Hindu, Limbale could not go to a temple, could not bathe in a river, could not draw water from a well meant for the higher castes, could not take tea from the same cup in a public eating place. He was an *akkarmashi* (half caste)—an illegitimate child of a father from the privileged high caste and an untouchable Hindu mother. His interminable quest for identity makes him question his roots: "How can I be high caste when my mother is untouchable? If I am untouchable, what about my father who is high caste? I am like Jarasandh [a mythical character in the epic Mahabharata, whose body even if torn asunder, would reunite]. Half of me belongs to the village, whereas the other half is excommunicated. Who *am* I? To whom is my umbilical cord connected?" (*Outcaste* 38–9). He is infuriated that the higher-caste drunkards would accept "liquor from the house of a Mahar [a low caste] but not water. They had affairs with Mahar women but wouldn't accept the food they cooked" (*Outcaste* 35). He feels ostracized both in and outside the village.

This realization of the situation leads the untouchable "Other" to question the hierarchical, purity-conscious social codes that mandate absolute and divine superiority of the "twice-born," upper-caste patricians, as also the lines drawn between one group of untouchables and another. The neo-literate boys use their power to protest and challenge the social set-up. When served tea in cups and saucers kept outside a hotel for untouchables, he and his friend decide to take action against the owner. They take the tea to the police station, where the inspector stares at them for their audacity. Limbale's threat of complaining to the Chief Minister and writing to the Prime Minister forces the inspector to take action. Parallel to the African American resistance to Jim Crow laws, Limbale and his cohorts succeed in breaking through their own cultural codes of oppression.

The awareness of his predicament, brought about by the education that he received due to the government's policy of caste-based "affirmative action," makes him recognize the nexus between the ruling/capitalistic and *savaran* (upper-caste) classes that perpetuates inequality. He finds it strange that even God discriminates between man and man and "makes one man rich and the other poor. One is high caste, the other untouchable. What kind of God is this that makes human beings hate each other. We are all supposed to be the children of God, then why are we considered untouchable. We don't approve of this God, or this religion, or this country because they ostracize us" (*Outcaste* 62). Limbale's rejection of Hinduism and his adoption of Buddhism represent acts of empowerment, forcing a reconsideration of his old religious beliefs and revealing new possibilities of freedom from social injustice. This desperate attempt to understand a society where birth determines worth motivates Limbale to fight for basic civil rights and to actively participate in Dalit political movements like the Dalit Panther Movement.

Limbale deals with the larger societal issues and closely examines the all-powerful and immutable caste values that coerce the Dalits into ritualized servility. One such incident in which he feels dehumanized is when he cannot find a room to live in because of his caste, which follows him "like an enemy" (*Outcaste* 106). Every town and person is caste conscious. "I ... had become a Brahmin by attitude, but high caste people didn't even allow me to stand at their doorsteps" (*Outcaste* 107). That Limbale and other Dalits have to conceal their caste and live under an assumed name to survive speaks volumes for caste oppression in India.[7]

The Outcaste raises questions of religion, tradition, and culture through the problem of identity. It shows that although the outcastes follow the high-caste culture, they are relegated to the margins of society. They are said to be both part of and apart from the mainstream culture. They cannot relate to a tradition because they are denied access to it. The internalization of the oppressive beliefs has affected them to such an extent that though they are aware of and can analyse their predicament, they have to struggle to anticipate bigger challenges. However, their daily experiences serve as a wake-up call to the Dalits to do something "to change the Touchable Hindu" (Ambedkar 5: 3), as also a call to the *savaran*, the upper-caste Hindus, to mend their ways. Thus, what we see is an assertive but nuanced empowerment in a complex, multilayered Indian democracy.

The Outcaste gives a heartrending commentary on the events and incidents highlighting the suffering common to three oppressed groups: Dalits, women, and Muslims. He wonders how man has lost himself in the intricate web of caste, religion, breeding, and family. "What kind of religious burden do we carry like a porter his load?" (*Outcaste* 105). He raises the question regarding an egalitarian society in which Hindus and Muslims have an equal place. He believes that both Hindus and Muslims have human rights. At the end of the autobiography, Limbale thinks of his "dada," his grandfather, who was a Muslim, on Eid, the Muslim festival (his grandmother was a Hindu[8]). He agonizes about who in a fragmented society would perform the last rites for his grandpa when he dies. "Will Muslims attend his cremation? How can they perform rituals after his death? Where would they bury his body?" (*Outcaste* 113). He rails against social structures that support so much baseless discrimination. Through this interrogation, he visualizes an ideal society where discrimination against the oppressed may cease to exist.

African American writers use the consciousness of their predicament in order to analyse and diagnose America's racism and to explore ways out of the existing race relations. They posit an alternative to the materialistic civilization that is satisfied with the acquisition of trinkets and trash. The question that Wright had posed—"Could the Negro ever possess himself, learn to know what happened to him in relation to the aspirations of Western society? ... [Could he] save a confused, materialistic nation from its own drift toward self-destruction?" (*Later Works* 284)—was taken up by later black writers, thinkers, and scholars who not only provide a critique of white society but also offer an alternative vision of a new society based on equality and justice. Dalit writers in India posit a similar critique of their society and project a society free of caste and exploitation.

The role writers can play is not limited to the racial or caste question. It takes them beyond anger and protest to a hope for change, a vision of freedom, and a life of dignity for the oppressed. Both Wright, the participant-observer, and Limbale, the writer-activist, work for a reconceptualization of the pre-existing notions of identity and difference to include people situated outside the cultural and socially constructed frontiers of race, caste, gender, and nation.

In his later works, Wright expanded this consciousness to include the consciousness of people similarly placed in the Third World and beyond the Atlantic. His own voyage beyond the shores of America allows him to posit new identities and alternative worlds in which race and caste have no meaning. Wright's works lead to global literary traditions, which might work towards self-affirmation at both political and aesthetic levels. The same trajectory is reflected in Limbale's literary works and social activism. Limbale realizes that his duty toward his own community calls for stronger and newer strategies. In an interview with me at Pune in August 2003 published in *Literary Voices* (2007), Limbale stated, "This movement cannot be strong if run only by Dalits. A movement, a struggle, succeeds when it finds strength from a large number of people" (131). Limbale recognizes that it is not only the consciousness of the subalterns that has to be changed but also the dominant ideology. Like Wright, he looks at oppression from a global perspective. In his interview, he stated, "So far we had been writing against a limited society/village for not letting us go to school, fetch water or enter the temples. Now it is the entire world where, on the one hand, is the master order [capitalism] and, on the other, is the slave order. How to see it at the international level and how to strengthen it? ... The casteist fight alone would not stand on the international level" (131).

Wright critiqued both the state and capitalism, and Limbale questions the discrimination (state) and the master order (neocapitalism). In his interview with Mukherjee, Limbale underscores the struggle "between the capitalists and the dispossessed," suggesting that the Dalits must "fight for the end of both the caste system and the feudal system" (*Towards an Aesthetic* 138), and that they must "include the entire Bahujan [people from many castes] society ... and speak to all the dispossessed, wherever they may be, whichever country, whichever community" (*Towards an Aesthetic* 137). In fact, from my ongoing phone conversations with him, it is clear that Limbale the humanist has moved beyond the boundaries of religion. Parallel to

Wright's struggle against oppression in the 1950s, Limbale is concerned today with fighting oppression on the larger South Asian, international scene so as to expand his vision to include the Scheduled Castes, Scheduled Tribes, Other Backward Classes, Bodh Dalits, Muslim Dalits, Sikh Dalits, and women even if they belonged to the upper class not only in India but also in Nepal, Pakistan, Bangladesh, the UK, and the United States—in fact the whole world in an expanding metaphor of marginalization.

IV

Both Wright and Limbale create a literature wherein not only do they rehabilitate themselves but they also envision a world free of race and caste barriers, a world in which they see the urgent need for freedom and economic justice for all individuals. In their capacious engagement with issues of marginalization, they move beyond racial/ caste territories to include other marginalized groups in their imagined communities. Their broad framework for fictional and life narratives is indicative of the inspiration and influence of Du Bois on African Americans and of Ambedkar on Dalits in India.

Both Du Bois and Ambedkar spoke fearlessly against racist and casteist structures as well as against capitalism as they envisioned a society free of hunger and oppression. Inspired by these leaders, Wright's and Limbale's evolution as writers allows them to pass from the well-defined stages of liberation to a painful awareness of their situation, through a rejection of the imposed image, and finally to the affirmation of their full humanity. Since they doggedly refuse to accept limits to their experience and existence, they subject the workings of dominant race and caste to brutal examination. Both fight inhuman structures, political as well as economic, in order that ordinary mortals may have access to the full spirit of civilization and can overcome its hypocrisy.

Notes

1   I would like to thank the three editors of the volume and anonymous readers for their many suggestions in helping me to revise this paper for publication. I am especially grateful to my former teacher, still my guru, Professor S. D. Kapoor, in directing me to expand several points of my analysis. Professor Amritjit Singh has been, as always, a valuable guide in developing my argument. He continues to inspire me and many other Indian scholars with his insights as well as his uncompromising high standards.

2   From an e-mail dated February 23, 2013, from Amritjit Singh to Sudhi Rajiv. It must be noted that Singh is the most important scholar responsible for generating a sustained and serious interest in African American studies in India. Singh's contributions to American literary studies in India are indeed multifold: as Deputy Director of the American Studies Research Center (ASRC) from 1974 to 1977, he helped to build the research collection in African American and ethnic studies as well as in women's studies; he was an attentive and supportive mentor to many research scholars during his nine years of professional life in India (1974–83); since 1983, when he returned with his family to the United States, Singh has continued to assist scholarly work in

India through his annual homeland visits and has also helped and inspired new research even from his US locations in Rhode Island and Ohio.

3   Also worth noting are visits to India since the 1980s by well-known African American writers such as Sherley Anne Williams, Michael S. Harper, and Gloria Naylor, as well as the willingness of many black American scholars and other African Americanists to participate in conferences and seminars in South Asia. Jean Toomer, the author of *Cane*, was deeply disillusioned with India at the end of his six-month spiritual journey there in 1939–40. Saunders Redding traveled to India in 1953 at the invitation of the State Department and recorded his experiences in *An American in India* (1954). Novelist Charles Johnson, a practicing Buddhist, has had a deep interest in Indian philosophy and religion, but has never visited India.

4   "Dalit" stands for the oppressed and exploited people. The word "Dalit" is derived from the Sanskrit word "dal" which means to crack open, split, crush, grind. Today, "Dalit" invokes people subjected to discrimination, oppression, and exploitation. The phenomenon of caste as a "status marker," comparable with "race" (in contrast to "class"), is a distinctive feature of Indian society. In *Un/Common Cultures*, Kamala Visweswaran notes that "Since caste is constructed through the social experience of casteism, it could thus seem that we have a socially constructed notion of caste that mirrors Du Bois's understanding of the caste-like nature of racism in the US. Caste, like race, is not an essence or identity but a product of social forms of discrimination" (150).

5   Ambedkar had read most of Du Bois's works and wanted to bracket the experience of Dalits with those of the blacks in America. He wrote a letter to Du Bois requesting copies of the petition from black Americans to the United Nations so that the Dalits could follow suit (Immerwahr).

6   In his essay "The House the Hindus Have Built," Ambedkar defined caste "as a social group having (a) belief in Hindu Religion and bound by certain regulations as to (b) marriage, (c) food and (d) occupation" (5: 158). He further explains, "A Hindu is born in a caste and dies as a member of that caste. There is no Hindu without caste, cannot escape caste and being bounded by caste from birth to death, he becomes subject to social regulations and traditions of the caste over which he has no control" (5: 159). The stigma of caste has suppressed the talent of the oppressed and impeded the growth of Indian society.

7   In his essay "Slaves and Untouchables," Ambedkar suggests that the source of difference between the black and Dalit experiences resides in the difference between slavery and untouchability. Slavery, he says,

> makes the slave conscious of his enslavement and to become conscious of slavery is the first and most important step in the battle for freedom. But if a man is deprived of his liberty indirectly he has no consciousness of his enslavement. Untouchability is an indirect form of slavery … It is enduring because it is unconscious. Of the two orders, untouchability beyond doubt is worse. (5: 15)

8   In India it is customary for people to marry within the same religion and caste. Marriage between a Hindu and a Muslim is especially frowned upon.

Works cited

Ambedkar, Bhimrao Ramji. *Dr. Babasaheb Ambedkar: Writings and Speeches.* 17 Vols.
     Bombay: Education Department, Government of Maharashtra, 1989–2003. Print.

Baker, Houston A., Jr. *Modernism and the Harlem Renaissance.* Chicago: U of Chicago P,
     1987. Print.

Fabre, Michel. Afterword. *American Hunger.* By Richard Wright. New York: Harper, 1977.
     136–46. Print.

Gilroy, Paul. *The Black Atlantic: Modernity and Double Consciousness.* 1993. Cambridge:
     Harvard UP, 1999. Print.

Immerwahr, Daniel. "On B. R. Ambedkar and Black–Dalit Connections." April 2008. Web.
     June 2, 2013. http://faculty.wcas.northwestern.edu/daniel-immerwahr/Ambedkar.pdf

Jaidka, Manju. "The Road to Hyderabad: MELUS in India." *MELUS* 29.3/4 (2004): 481–98.
     Print.

Kapoor, S. D. "B. R. Ambedkar, W. E. B. Du Bois and the Process of Liberation." *Economic
     and Political Weekly* Dec. 27, 2003: 5344–9. Print.

Krishnaraj, Darius. "Difficulties and Dead Endings in Teaching African American
     Literature in Indian Universities." *MELUS* 18.4 (1993): 53–61. Print.

Limbale, Sharankumar. "From the Writer." Foreword. *Akkarmashi.* By Limbale. Hindi trans.
     Suryanarayan Ransumbhe. New Delhi: Granth Akademi, 1991. 7–10. Print.

—— *The Outcaste: Akkarmashi.* Trans. Santosh Bhoomkar. New Delhi: Oxford UP, 2003.
     Print.

—— *Towards an Aesthetic of Dalit Literature: History, Controversies and Considerations.*
     Trans. and ed. Alok Mukherjee. New Delhi: Orient Longman, 2004. Print.

Rajiv, Sudhi. "Sudhi Rajiv in Conversation with Dr. Sharankumar Limbale." *Literary Voices,*
     2007: 124–33. Print.

—— *Forms of Black Consciousness.* New York: Advent, 1992. Print.

Redding, Saunders. Introduction. *The Souls of Black Folk: Essays and Sketches.* By W. E. B.
     Du Bois. 1903. Chicago: McClurg, 1931. viii–xi. Print.

—— *An American in India: A Personal Report on the Indian Dilemma and the Nature of
     Her Conflicts.* New York: Bobbs Merrill, 1954. Print.

Rushdie, Salman. "Imaginary Homelands." *Imaginary Homelands: Essays and Criticism
     1981–1991.* 1991. London: Granta, 1992. 9–21. Print.

—— *Midnight's Children.* 1980. New York: Penguin, 1991. Print.

Said, Edward. *Orientalism: Western Conceptions of the Orient.* 1978. New Delhi: Penguin,
     2001. Print.

Singh, Amritjit. Afterword. *The Color Curtain.* By Richard Wright. 1956. Jackson: UP of
     Mississippi, 1995. 223–45. Print.

—— "Beyond the Mountain: Langston Hughes on Race/Class and Art." *Langston Hughes
     Review* 6.1 (1987): 37–43. Print.

—— Introduction. *Black Power: A Record of Reactions in a Land of Pathos.* By Richard
     Wright. 1954. New York: Harper Perennial, 1995. xi–xxxiv. Print.

Visweswaran, Kamala. *Un/Common Cultures: Racism and the Rearticulation of Cultural
     Difference.* New Delhi: Navayana, 2011. Print.

Wright, Richard. *American Hunger.* New York: Harper, 1977. Print.

—— *Black Boy.* New York: Harper, 1945. Print.

—— "Blueprint for Negro Writing." *African American Literary Criticism 1773–2000.* Ed. Hazel Arnett Ervin. New York: Twayne, 1999. 82–90. Print.

—— *The Color Curtain: A Report on the Bandung Conference.* 1956. Jackson: UP of Mississippi, 1995. Print.

—— *Later Works: Black Boy (American Hunger), The Outsider.* New York: Library of America, 1991. Print.

—— *Native Son.* 1940. New York: Signet, 1965. Print.

—— *White Man, Listen!* 1957. New York: Harper, 1995. Print.

—— *Eight Men: Stories.* 1961. New York: Harper, 2008. Print.

—— *The Outsider.* 1953. New York: Harper, 2008. Print.

—— *The Long Dream.* 1958. Boston: Northeastern UP, 2000. Print.

15

Culmination in Miniature: Late Style and the Essence of Richard Wright's Haiku

Sandy Alexandre
Massachusetts Institute of Technology

Everybody got style. Style ain't nothing but keeping the same idea from beginning to end.

> Toledo (from August Wilson's *Ma Rainey's Black Bottom*)

[T]he work of some great artists and writers acquires a new idiom towards the end of their lives—what I've come to think of as a late style.

> Edward Said, "Thoughts on Late Style: A Lecture"

In what one might call the post hoc method essay that explained how Bigger Thomas, the main protagonist of Richard Wright's *Native Son*, was originally conceived and eventually developed—appropriately titled "How 'Bigger' Was Born"—Wright revealed that Bigger is thus named because he represents a composite of several rebellious and reckless young black men whom Wright had encountered at various points in his lifetime.

> The birth of Bigger Thomas goes back to my childhood and there was not just one Bigger, but many of them, more than I could count and more than you suspect [...] Bigger, as I saw and felt him, was a snarl of many realities; he had in him many levels of life. (999)

Through this shocking and horrifying creation, Wright hoped to make an unprecedented and profound impact on his intended audience—the world, that is. After all, Wright had declared that in creating Bigger he hoped that *Native Son* would be considered "so hard and deep that [white readers in particular] would have to face it without the consolation of tears" ("How 'Bigger' Was Born" 454). Wright took such a tough stance because, as he explained, he no longer wanted to be associated with his former writing self—that is, the man who had written what eventually proved to be a cathartic book, *Uncle Tom's Children*, which had, apparently, made people weep. Wright had effectively redeemed himself by giving birth to a bigger and badder creation in penning *Native*

Son. Bigger is Wright's creature creation—the monstrosity of the gigantic, both in name and in composition.

I begin by revisiting Wright's (essay) formulation of what Edward Said would have likely designated a "beginning intention," because what I ultimately want to discuss is Wright's later (haiku) formulation of what Said would also have designated a "late style." If "How 'Bigger' Was Born" constitutes a premeditated formulation not only of Bigger Thomas's beginnings but also of Wright's revisionist narrative about his own early style, then what do Wright's haiku (in light of their minimalist aesthetic and miniature form—debiggered, if you will—their speculative and forward-looking qualities, and especially their terminal position in the timeline of Wright's complete *oeuvre*) suggest in the way of a companion method essay that one might call something like "How Smaller Was Born"? This is the question I will attempt to answer in this article. In belaboring this point about size, which Wright's most famous protagonist so obviously invites, I certainly do not wish to trivialize my argument. My aim, rather, is to avoid discussions about the psychological roots of Wright's turn to haiku by focusing more particularly on the form of haiku themselves.[1] Borrowing from Said's and Theodor Adorno's respective theories regarding the late works of artists, I argue that a combination of the formal conventions of haiku, their anomalousness and terminal place in the overall scheme of Wright's literary corpus helps him to propose a wishful thought—to realize a last-ditch fantasy—of transforming himself as an artist and disaffiliating from both his historical context and, concomitantly, the plight of an oppressed African American community. Wright's haiku constitute the medium through which he is empowered to divest himself of the weight of his socio-historical and racial circumstance; consequently, through this deliberate act of self-alienation and generic unencumbrance, he is able to propound futurity—that is, a quixotic vision of another world.

My main reason in considering what the relationship might be between Wright's knowledge of his imminent death and the anomalousness of haiku in the context of his *oeuvre* is that the juxtaposition of Kenneth Warren's recent book *What Was African American Literature?* with recent studies regarding so-called post-racial trends in American literature and culture has me thinking retrospectively about where exactly in time an African American dying artist is ideologically situated in relation to his cultural context and to his culture's literary history. Is that artist, who is under such particularly dire circumstances, consequently rendered "post" any and all identity markers before his time? Could that exceptional temporal locus, occasioned by knowledge of one's imminent death, have a transforming influence on that artist's work?

Warren's courageously searching and provocative book reads the category "African American literature" as a necessary and collective counter-response to the degradations of Jim Crow. As such, the combination of African American literature's coherence and its initial *raison d'être* necessarily has a shelf life. The situation of Wright's imminent death serves as a fitting and instructive parable for Warren's argument regarding the demise of the African American literature enterprise. Thus the advantage of analysing the work of a writer whose late work is more than likely shaped by the approach of his own death is that it reveals the ways in which such a writer might challenge and explode the notion of compulsory allegiance to the African American literature cause. The late style of a dying black American writer might also reveal exactly how an artist attempts to transcend the particularities of his socio-historical context. Is it through a deliberate act of anomalous art in which he puts an unexpected finishing touch to his otherwise consistent corpus? Or is it through a thematic focus on otherworldliness?

In this essay, I intend to situate Wright in a future that he had himself created through his collection of haiku—one that enlarges the vision of what African American literature could be and do as well as where it could go if Jim Crow was not a pressing and influencing concern for a black American artist. Wright's haiku—that seemingly oxymoronic juxtaposition—represent a visionary literature particularly because of the way in which they exhibit an aspiration to global literature and introduce possibilities for universal humanism and ecological holism. This visionary literature allows readers to witness an artist in his most subjunctive mood as he makes a bid to think beyond the various and sundry constraints of his oppressive social context, his obligations to "his people," and his failing health in order to demonstrate to the world that he will soon leave behind new ways of making art, thinking, and living. Three years before he died, Wright was already thinking about what African American literature could look like if, without the constricting impositions of Jim Crow, African American writers were allowed to express themselves—not as a defense mechanism, but freely—without the sense that Jim Crow dictated the direction of art created by black Americans.

> If the expression of the American Negro should take a sharp turn toward strictly racial themes, then you will know by that token that we are suffering our old and ancient agonies at the hands of our white neighbors. If, however, our expression broadens, assumes the common themes and burdens of literary expression which are the heritage of all men, then by that token you will know that a humane attitude prevails in America toward us.
>
> (*White Man, Listen!* 105)

Here, Wright articulates the wish for African American literature's obsolescence that Warren rightly argues is the ultimate goal of any enterprise created for and committed to the sole purpose of pursuing social justice.[2] Wright's dream of obsolescence is subjunctive, which means it temporarily removes him from his immediate reality and situates him in another world that is created, if even in the abstract, by wishful thinking. This spatiotemporal straddling is how Said described "late style"—as being "*in*, but oddly *apart* from the present" (*On Late Style* 24). As far as I see it, in Wright's subjunctive mode—that is, in his haiku—he recontextualizes himself and his art, in time and space, through the authorial fiat of a writer who can dare to imagine boldly, futuristically, and originally, precisely because he knows he is dying and is therefore in probably the most opportune position to throw everything—from caution to national and local allegiance—to the wind and truly be visionary and pioneering. As Said notes, "[E]ssentially unrepeatable, uniquely articulated aesthetic works written ... at the end of a career can ... have an influence on what comes after them" (*On Late Style* 17–18). The crisis of approaching death not only creates productive urgency (Wright wrote more than 4,000 haiku by the time of his death, after all),[3] but it also propels the dying artist into a different world, thereby granting him a more farsighted perspective than, say, his hale contemporaries who, in contrast, may have been rendered imaginatively lax by what they assume is the guarantee they have of another tomorrow to live. One haiku, in particular, suggests this link between knowledge of approaching death and elevated consciousness:

Leaving the doctor,
The whole world looks different
This autumn morning.

(no. 243)

For Wright, at least, the impulse to futurity is certainly a consequence of his knowledge of death's approach, but also of his dissatisfaction with the current state of racial politics around the world, especially in the United States. Perhaps the most significant, even if disenchanting, contribution that the particularity of Wright's late style brings to Adorno's and Said's exploration of the topic is the sense that post-raciality can only ever be realized through textual fiat, by dint of speculation and wishful thinking, and by "passing"—in both senses of that term. On the one hand, Wright must pass into another world through death (or at least through unequivocal knowledge of his imminent death). If by mere virtue of when they were written, Wright's haiku retain and represent an aura of death.[4] On the other hand, he must pass as a writer of what would seem on the face of it to be non–African American literature. That there can be no real-life category of experience discernable as truly post-racial means that it is important to preserve the distinction that race will always be and can only be a lived and embodied human experience—until death and (in Wright's case) until late style.

*   *   *

Critics, reviewers, and biographers alike have all submitted their various and sundry theories about Wright's turn to haiku. Most recently, Jianqing Zheng has edited a collection of essays exclusively on this very subject in *The Other World of Richard Wright*. With the exception of the last essay in the collection, which reveals the various flaws in Wright's haiku, the essays can essentially be divided into two camps: the social activism camp and the Zen Buddhism camp. That is to say, one camp finds Wright's haiku literarily continuous with his earlier works, while the other considers the haiku anomalous. For example, Richard Iadonisi insists on seeing an old Wright even despite this completely new poetic form that he has chosen to adopt; Iadonisi reads Wright's haiku as "revolutionary poetry that offers and then savagely undercuts the possibility of Zen oneness" (179). With varying degrees of difference, Wright scholars Robert Tener, Sanehide Kodama, Michel Fabre, and Jean-François Gounard have all touted a post-racial, transcendent narrative regarding the haiku—one in which they suggest that the poems represented an opportunity for Wright to finally let go of his anger over the issues of racial inequality, social injustice, and oppression still plaguing American society. And finally, penning them as he did and as many as he did while he was dying, biographers Hazel Rowley and Jennifer Jensen Wallach have interpreted his obsession with haiku, along with its formalistic strictures and pastoral content, as a ritualistic form of therapy. I contend that if writing haiku was in fact a salutary practice for Wright, it was therapeutic precisely because he used this poetic form to imagine the implications of Jim Crow's abolishment for fearless African American artists such as himself. He used haiku to think outside the confines of a world and a body that he would soon be leaving behind anyway. Indeed, the explanation for Wright's turn to haiku inheres in the failure of his body, in the kind of artistic risk, freedom, and virtuosity that imminent death could endow an artist, and finally in trusting in the ability of art to linger long after that body has passed away. To think of Wright's haiku as a Hail Mary pass of sorts is to grant that deathbed literature does visionary work in the service of a "bigger (albeit miniaturized) picture."

Haiku as representations of future possibility

By exceeding the boundaries of the United States in his appropriation of a Japanese poetic form, by frustrating our expectations of him as a writer, and by suturing seeming antinomies in the haiku, Wright renders the notion of belonging (and by extension citizenship) more virtuosic and certainly more worldly than the nation-state's limited and localized definition of it. His haiku make world citizens out of his readers. In the Andersonian vein of "imagined communities," Wright imagines community through a literary form (Anderson 6). And the process that has enabled him to create these communities in haiku form is a combination of his own worldly life experiences and what I would like to call his geographical consciousness—or, in short, his heightened ecological awareness, as an African American, of the politics of occupying space. Fabre describes this African American sixth sense of place as Wright's "incessant battle against all that prevents an individual from fully belonging to the world" (54). Indeed, when asked by his wife how exactly he planned on reporting "twenty-nine [Asian and African] nations meeting together" at the 1955 Bandung Conference, Wright cited the worldly wisdom he had acquired, by virtue of his race and experiences as an American (both within the United States and from a self-exiled vantage point), as an obvious qualification: "I feel that my life has given me some keys to what [these nations] would say or do. I'm an American Negro; as such, I've had a burden of race consciousness. So have these people" (*The Color Curtain* 15). For Wright, as this response suggests, he would be reporting from a sense of kinship—from the standpoint of one who, like his fellow Africans and Asians, is ever aware of his DuBoisian twoness, at best, and his Fanonian wretchedness at worst.

In preparing for his trip to Bandung, Indonesia, for this unprecedented conference, Wright formulated a questionnaire of over 70 questions, which he fully planned on using to gather information from the conference's participants. But the Asians and Africans were so willing to divulge their political opinions about their current situation in the world and their hopes for a better future that Wright jettisoned the questionnaire after only his fifth informal interview. The participants were as excited as Wright was for the possibilities they imagined the conference could engender. The continuing influence of the Bandung conference on Wright's thinking and eventually his work is quite clear and certainly most evident, as I would argue, in his haiku. While at Bandung, Wright had already had a keen, if not optimistic, understanding of what this conference of African and Asian nations meant. For Wright, Bandung meant (or seemed to promise, rather) a major shift in thinking about how the human race should be organized. Imagining that the conference could mean the beginnings of what he called "a de-Occidentalization of mankind" (*The Color Curtain* 203) and therefore the end of the dichotomous notion of East and West as we know it, Wright was deeply interested in dismantling racial and national hierarchy in order to achieve "a universal humanism that [could] bind men together in a common unity" (*The Color Curtain* 24). Although as far as he knew, there was no culture "in the world today [that seemed] the most promising candidate to champion such a humanism," Wright did not want to sit idly and wait for a culture to realize an ambition he could just as easily actualize through his creative work (*The Color Curtain* 24). His approaching death would intensify rather than undermine that ambition.

Wright's enthusiasm about the conference, along with his overall sense of optimism regarding its significance, is a consequence of his belief that ideas could serve as templates or springboards for action in the real world. In *The Color Curtain*, he asserts the following: "Today as never before, it can be seen that the future of national cultures will reside in the willingness of nations to take up modern ideas [including the multi-nationalisms of national cultures] and live out their logic" (199). For Wright, it was the Bandung Conference's very actualization of the idea of blending nationalisms and cultures that he found most refreshing and modern. He would re-create this modern idea (of blending, of universal humanism, and of a new kind of nationalism) through his recognized bailiwick—literature. But he would modernize his old writerly habits through the novelty, portability, accessibility, and modernity of haiku. As Constance Webb notes, "Wright had to study [haiku] to find out why it struck his ear with such a modern note" (387). By enacting a universal nationalism by poetic fiat, Wright's haiku represent an homage to the Bandung Conference, which he viewed as "a racial and religious system of [Asian-African] identification manifesting itself in an emotional nationalism which was now leaping state boundaries and melting and merging one into the other" (Webb 222). Wright locates this traveling and ever-inclusive community at the venue of a poem. Indeed, Wright's collection seems to acknowledge as much in its subtitle: *This Other World*. Thus it is important to consider the kind of "great beyond" that Wright envisions his haiku as either creating or enabling.

The conceptual spaces that Wright's haiku create introduce possibilities for both universal humanism and ecological holism. In populating the haiku less with human characters than creatures of the natural world, Wright shifts the reader's attention away from human dramas in order to focus on what one might observe if one stopped to smell the proverbial roses. As a dying artist, Wright is certainly in a position to do exactly that; death's approach endows him with a new perspective on everything. In one haiku, he speaks of the literal and (as I am suggesting) the figurative importance of smelling roses, particularly to one who, although convalescing, might not ever be able to smell roses again:

> While convalescing,
> The red roses have no smell,
> Gently mocking me.
>
> (no. 224)

Who else but a sick person cannot smell the roses? Wright must strive in spite of his illness to perceive what otherwise remains neglected, unseen, and underappreciated. Incurable in this world and in his body, he creates this *other* world in order to be able to smell roses again, but to smell them differently—with instruction in mind. Wright deploys the haiku as a collective antidote to the problem of the human world being too much with us. He avoids his typical themes of dissension among races, classes, and ideological communities of people by creating what I will call "the common scene"— the observable sight, which becomes the center of attention:

> Heaps of black cherries
> Glittering with drops of rain
> In the evening sun.
>
> (no. 58)

> The moon has gone down,
> But its gleam is lingering
> On magnolias.
>
> (no. 545)

> Flitting through the trees,
> Some snowflakes cling to the twigs,
> Others flutter free.
>
> (no. 699)

> One crow on a limb;
> Another goes to join him,
> Then both fly away.
>
> (no. 805)

In these and other haiku in his published collection, Wright imagines an unidentified observer whose main concerns center on the exterior world outside of himself. That common denominator—that sight to see—subsumes all of its observers under the neutral and passive category of those who bear witness. Indeed, it renders them quiet, respectful observers who are cultivating an elevated—a humane and even objective— perspective.[5] This is not to suggest that there is nothing political or subjective to be found or reflected back in the various sights of the natural world, because as Camille

T. Dungy rightly reminds us in the introduction to the anthology *Black Nature: Four Centuries of African American Nature Poetry*, "Many black writers simply do not look at their environment from the same perspective as Anglo-American writers who discourse with the natural world" (xxi). While I completely agree with Dungy, my claim here is that Wright's quixotic fantasy of true artistic freedom and a brighter future—sparked precisely because he is in the throes of dying—is to shed seeing of all of its ideological bases, including race. Through their style of poetic reportage, enlightened observers situated in the worlds of these haiku present us with the answer to what Adorno argues is the question that forms the basis of true self-effacement and disinterestedness, which is "what and how one may sing of the absolute without deceit" ("Alienated Masterpiece" 577). And perhaps in writing so many haiku, Wright avoids selective observation in order to strive to be as inclusive and, therefore, as honest as possible.

In addition to this de-emphasis on human-centered dramas, the haiku's leitmotif of harmonious integration, especially between built and natural environments, demonstrates Wright's deep understanding of his place in the world as well as his acceptance of the variables that concatenated to create him and everything around him. Whether a consequence of his proximity to his own mortality or the result of the accretion of all of his life experiences, the vast collection of Wright's haiku reveals the interconnection and reciprocity of all things:

> I am paying rent
> For the lice in my cold room
> And the moonlight too.
>
> (no. 115)

> Merciful autumn
> Tones down the shabby curtains
> Of my rented room.
>
> (no. 174)

> Spring dawn is glinting
> On a dew-wet garbage can
> In a city street.
>
> (no. 177)

> The low of a cow
> Answers a train's long whistle
> In the summer's dusk.
>
> (no. 387)

Disparate objects coexist in surreal juxtaposition and make peace with one another. They all have a place in which they belong in the microcosm of the world that Wright has captured or created in each poem. The simultaneously revolutionary and sentimental quality of these reconciliations seems to be symptomatic of imminent death.

Adorno wrote that "the late works of significant artists ... show more traces of history than growth" ("Late Style in Beethoven" 564). This observation is certainly true of Wright's haiku, demonstrating as they do that an optimistic adaptation of George Santayana's famous quote, "Those who fail to learn history are doomed to repeat it," is long overdue: Those who know history (and are almost "history" themselves) are bound to learn from it and create new and improved temporalities in light of it. Wright's maturity as an artist manifests itself in the way in which he is able to use his historical knowledge to a pioneering end—to create other worlds. Interestingly, Said pits the way Adorno views late works as expressing their maturity in "a new spirit of reconciliation and serenity often expressed in terms of a miraculous transformation of common reality" against the way he views late works—as "intransigence, difficulty, and unresolved contradiction" (*On Late Style* 6, 7). Said, however, is mistaken in his assumption that these two modes are mutually exclusive. After all, a transformation of common reality can very well be an act of subversion. Change is, of course, difficult, especially for those left behind who now have to try to reconcile the late work with the rest of the artist's *oeuvre*. In other words, it seems to me that the inability to see resolution in the anomalous is Said's and our problem.

But the anomalousness of Wright's haiku does not begin and end at the genre of poetry under which they fall. I would argue that the very size of haiku itself could be folded into Wright's ability, if not intention, to jar and confound his loyal readers. Because if the concept of "bigger" constituted the form of his beginnings, then smaller could be said to constitute the form of the future he imagined before his death. But, for me, what the choice of the word "Bigger" does as a creative act of naming a fictional character is to indicate, if even retrospectively, Wright's deep-rooted concerns with matters of scale:

The dazzling spring sun
Dwindles the glittering sea
And shrinks the ships.

(no. 542)

"Let's make a scarecrow!"
But after we had made it,
Our field grew smaller.

(no. 543)

The sudden sunrise
Made the blossoming apple tree
Distant and smaller.

(no. 546)

A layer of snow
Is pulling the mountains nearer,
Making them smaller.

(no. 547)

So, the question with which I started the paper—"How does one go from Bigger to Haiku?"—is not only about an affective shift, but also a shift in scale—from the vastness of the novel to the conciseness of a three-line, 17-syllable literary form, which Wright had himself described as a delicate spider web. Here, I find Susan Stewart's argument about the miniature very helpful in trying to understand the ideological implications of Wright's generic downsizing. As Stewart writes, "the miniature, linked to nostalgic versions of childhood and history, presents a diminutive, and thereby manipulatable, version of experience, a version which is domesticated and protected from contamination" (69). This version of experience is one that he has himself created in order to counter the awful experiences that had been forced upon him and to claim the beautiful experiences that he had been denied. According to Wright's daughter Julia,

> Back in the forties, [my father] had written in his journal how much he disliked the countryside because it reminded him of the physical hunger he had experienced as a poor black child in one of the world's most fertile landscapes. And so these haiku not only helped him place the volcanic experience of mourning under the self-control of closely counted syllables, but also enabled him to come to terms with the difficult beauty of the earth in which his mother would be laid to rest. (xi)

In mediating his intranational experiences along the US North/South axis and his international experiences through haiku, Wright continued even on his deathbed to speak for a wider community. Wright's turn toward the practice of mastering this delicate craft demonstrates how a writer can actualize the integrity of community in small steps, through the miniature scale and the micro worlds of haiku.

But Wright's vision for the possibilities inherent in smallness does not end at the level of a haiku's size; it also includes the ways in which smallness operates (and indeed has the ability to reign) in an ecological context. Wright does not want us to underestimate the power of small, delicate things in the larger scheme of existence.

The dog's violent sneeze
Fails to rouse a single fly
On his mangy back.

(no. 20)

The path in the woods
Is barred by spider webs
Beaded with spring rain.

(no. 76)

A train crashes past:
A butterfly still as stone
On the humid earth.

(no. 158)

The darting fire-flies
Are dragging the river along
To where the sun went down.

(no. 242)

These examples emphasize the awe-inspiring quality of otherwise neglected and imperceptible small things—a perspective, which, at least in Western literary traditions, is often gained after a life-altering event. For example, after killing an albatross, Samuel Taylor Coleridge's ancient Mariner learns that "all things both great and small" need to be respected and loved by human beings (pt. 7). And after discovering a world of endangered Lilliputian people, who he finds a difficult time getting others to believe actually exist, the elephant in Dr. Seuss's *Horton Hears a Who!* begins to spread the message to all of his naysayers that "a person's a person, no matter how small." In other words, the knowledge that one possesses regarding the significance of small things is often construed as a consequence of a revelation. The greatness of small things is a post hoc consciousness, and, as such, it transports the individual who now bears that knowledge to an elevated, enlightened, and progressive realm or time. Colin Milburn, a professor who researches the cultural relations between literature, science, and technology, has captured the essence of this connection between smallness and revelation in the term "nanovision," which he coined to describe a way of seeing that is occasioned by nanotechnologies. As Milburn states:

> Nanotechnology entails a way of seeing, a perspectival orientation to the world, that operates through a productive dynamic of blindness and insight. [...] It is a way of seeing that lyses the membrane between the technological present and the nanotechnological future. (13)

Nanovision, in other words, is the amazing grace that allows the blind to see and, by extension, the ailing body to transcend its limitations. That grace and foresight comes in the form of our newly committed relationship to these nano things, these small things. Or as Stewart writes of the miniature:

> The miniature offers us a transcendent vision which is known only through the visual. [...] We are able to hold the miniature object within our hand, but our hand is no longer in proportion with its world; instead our hand becomes a form of undifferentiated landscape, the body a kind of background. Once the miniature world is self-enclosed [...], we can only stand outside, looking in, experiencing a type of tragic distance. (70)

Through his haiku, Wright suggests that, for him, nanovision is precipitated by the onset of his eventual death. The contrast or friction between the early style of bigness and the late style of smallness creates a porthole to the future, and, as far as Wright sees it, the future looks like reconciliation in miniature wherein small things can hold their ground against the bigger and ostensibly formidable things. Thus the nanovision of Wright's late style is at once retrospective and forward-looking. That is to say, it seems that Wright wants to balance out his "Bigger" beginnings with a smaller late style in order to share his ethical and forward-thinking revelation about nanovision to the world. Highlighting the power of small things projects him forward to the realm of revelations, anoints him enlightened as a consequence, and enables him to write prophetically—or at least without false consciousness.

Haiku as evidence of disaffiliation

Yet the smallness of the form of haiku and of the nonhuman characters that people them does not only betoken a new and innovative way of seeing things; it also denotes a separation, particularly from one's own ego. According to Fabre, "Wright attempts to [completely suppress subjectivity] as much as possible in many of his haiku" (qtd. in Hakutani 9). This kind of ego shedding *of* and *by* self-omission is half the story, because (in the words of Walt Whitman) "missing me one place [one must] search another" (sec. 52). Like Whitman, Wright—anticipating his inevitable death—bequeaths himself to (ecological) things that are more important than his mere mortal self, and he sets this tone immediately in his published collection of haiku.

> I am nobody:
> A red sinking autumn sun
> Took my name away.
>
> (no. 1)

In this opening haiku, Wright seems to summarize the purpose of the entire collection by suggesting what Benedict Anderson describes as "that remarkable confidence of community in anonymity which is the hallmark of the modern nation" (36). In order to achieve community and to confer on others the ability to think progressively or presciently, even after his death, Wright knows to make himself small—to become self-effacing. In a gesture either of self-dignity or selflessness, he takes himself out of the proverbial picture before he is taken out of the picture by his illness. In doing so, he intentionally advocates for and privileges the longevity of art over the brevity of mortal life. In describing how and why subjectivity is necessarily absent from the late work of (dying) artists, Adorno points out that

> [t]he power of subjectivity in the late works of art is the irascible gesture with which it takes leave of the works themselves. It breaks their bonds, not in order to express itself, but in order, expressionless, to cast off the appearance of art. Of the works themselves it leaves only fragments behind, and communicates itself, like a cipher, only through the blank spaces from which it has disengaged itself. Touched by death, the hand of the master sets free the masses of material that he used to form—its tears and fissures. Witnesses to the finite powerlessness of the I confronted with Being are its final work.
>
> ("Late Style in Beethoven" 566)

For Adorno, Being, the longevity of art, and both the beauty and possibility of "a red sinking autumn sun" are the realms of truth to which subjectivity dissipates. The same notion holds true for Wright as well. Wright tenders his enlightened or pre-emptive de-emphasis on himself (and "the self," in general) as a lesson for the living to adopt. His self-imposed separation from this world through textual fiat is at once an acknowledgment of his approaching death and an attempt to project himself into another world methodically—that is, in such a way as to first access the new perspective available only there and then to subsequently share it with others. Wright's haiku, as well as the lessons contained within them, are the accessible and compact intermediaries between the present and the future—between this world and "this other world."

In many respects, the theory at the root of this notion that his haiku constitute a different world and a different temporal register is indebted not only to Adorno's and Said's work on the subject of late style, but also to Helen Vendler's *Last Looks, Last Books* in which she examines how "older poets (who still imagined a world beyond this one) found a style adequate to the interface of death and life" (6). But unlike Vendler whose main interest is in what she calls the "binocular style" of deathbed poets—that is, their way of ocular straddling, with one eye focused on the optimism of life and the other on the despair of death—Wright's haiku reveal the kind of idealism and innovation that can inhere in the deathbed work of an artist. What Vendler views as the "creative predicament" of poets on their deathbed I see as the moment in a poet's life where they seize the opportunity to throw caution to the wind and reinvent both themselves and creativity itself for their contemporaries and for a next generation (Vendler 24). In other words, these deathbed artists' visions are more telescopic (and perhaps even more crystal-ballic) than merely binocular. But what Vendler's binocular metaphor does, at least, is confirm the way in which late style seems to operate under an ocular logic. In the case of Wright's haiku, which, so far in this article, have generated discussions about observers and their perspectives, compelled an adoption of Milburn's notion of "nanovision," and summoned up Adorno's conclusion that *witnesses* constitute the final work of artists at the late style period of their careers, sight is a gift that is revitalized and enhanced by Wright's imminent death. Seeing anew becomes a metaphor for having "crossed over," in both meanings of that phrase—that is, for transporting oneself to another world, on the one hand, and for changing one's artistic style in such a way as to appeal to a wider audience, on the other hand.

But Wright's telescopic sight is not only facilitated by a real or perceived change in location; it also has philosophical roots. Wright's ability to see and create in a different way from his African American contemporaries and from how he, himself, had been previously writing might also be a result of his experiences with existentialism during the last decade of his life. His expatriate years in Paris (1946–60) were marked by his close associations with key figures in the French existentialist movement, including Simone de Beauvoir, Albert Camus, and Jean-Paul Sartre himself. But it seems to me that Wright's stylistic transition from Bigger to haiku follows a Sartrean existential logic only insofar as it abides by Sartre's existential creed that "existence precedes essence." That living through the various and sundry complexities of life precedes one's reflection on it as well as one's natural compulsion to fashion a lapidary or simple meaning out of that re-examination does not strike me as a premise that is only specific to French existentialism. In other words, Wright did not need French existentialism to come to understand that existence is big whereas essence is small—the bare essentials. Thus Wright's transition from the "snarl of many realities" of which Bigger is composed to the whittled-down realities of his haiku attests to a universal human tendency to reason deductively by proceeding from a multiplicity of options in order to arrive eventually at a distilled nugget of truth—the needle-like essence in the haystack of existence. And as Nina Kressner Cobb has suggested, Wright's existential philosophy of living was one acquired not necessarily from his associations with existentialism's top names, but from his own outsider relationship to "his family, community, and race" (374). As Cobb justifiably argues, "Wright's awareness of the nexus between freedom and alienation was the source of his existential insights" (374). Wright simulated that nexus in the novel that many scholars have touted as demonstrating Sartre's influence on his work—*The Outsider*. In the novel, the main protagonist, Damon Cross, escapes his past and begins a new life, under a new identity, by faking his own death. Wright's own impending death, expressed as haiku, creates that nexus—that interface of this world here in the present and this other world in the future—where he can be honest with impunity, freely odd, and possibly far-seeing as a consequence. Wright's late style (as haiku) is the result of his wishful thinking and fantasizing about what it would mean if, like a Damon Cross, he could reinvent himself anew through death yet right before it—that is, through an imagined death precipitated by his very real approaching one. Said interprets Adorno's definition of late style as "a kind of self-imposed exile from what is generally acceptable, coming after it, and surviving beyond it" (*On Late Style* 16). This is the liminal place that Wright has the once-in-an-imminent-death opportunity to occupy.

Many things could be said about Wright's ostensibly bizarre turn to haiku—a poetic genre focused generally on the natural world. Of course, throughout his career, he struggled with the meaning of one's physical surroundings via his naturalistic fiction of environmental determinism, but the tone in these works remained pessimistic. Such pessimism has greatly dissipated in his haiku. I attribute that newfound optimism to historical changes and to Wright's perceptual remove as a deathbed artist. First, in a brief passage from *The Environmental Imagination*, Lawrence Buell concludes that phases of national belonging correspond to geographic phases of African American culture's lifespan:

> The displacement of Richard Wright's *Native Son* by Hurston's *Their Eyes* as the most often cited precontemporary African American novel suggests the greater readiness of African American intellectuals, having won a certain state of national acceptance, more assertively to reimagine the rural phase preceding urbanization as culturally formative. (18)

The shift from a decidedly urban text to a rural-oriented novel—to represent what might be characterized as the state of African American culture—charts an evolution in the way African Americans began to view themselves in relation to their history's rural beginnings. Once African American intellectuals and expressive artists believed that they had achieved more than a modicum of national acceptance, they began to view these otherwise embarrassing rural beginnings in a respectable light and to salvage them as an essential component in what could be considered a more comprehensive story about the formation of African American identity. Second, the assumption of such a mutual relationship between national belonging and geographical location suggests that Wright's turn to haiku is an act of aspiration and prescience in which he wills racial justice and complete national acceptance through writing about nonracial themes and the universal theme of the physical world of nature. Indeed, some of the haiku in his published collection might very well be described as distilled interpretations of actual chapters or what could have been chapters in *Their Eyes*. Wright, in other words, had come a long way from his anti-Hurston period (and whatever he thought she and her work stood for).

Enough of dawn light
To show pearly pear blossom
Burning from within.

(no. 219)

A black woman sings:
Filling the sunlight with steam,
Bubbling molasses.

(no. 452)

A radiant moon
Shining on flood refugees
Crowded on a hill.

(no. 467)

She has departed:
All the globes of golden pears
Are pointed in pain.

(no. 599)

If you will recall, Wright had originally thought that Hurston's *Their Eyes* pandered a little too much to the simple appetites that white readers seemed so suddenly to adopt when presented with literature written by and about black people. His excoriating 1937 review of *Their Eyes* revealed the extent to which such pandering offended his political sensibilities:

Miss Hurston *voluntarily* continues in her novel the tradition which was *forced* upon the Negro in the theatre, that is, the minstrel technique that makes the "white folks" laugh. Her characters eat and laugh and cry and work and kill; they swing

like a pendulum eternally in that safe and narrow orbit in which America likes to
see the Negro live: between laughter and tears.

   . . . She exploits that phase of Negro life which is "quaint," the phase which evokes
a piteous smile on the lips of the "superior" race.

("Between Laughter and Tears")

Displaying in this criticism his keen understanding of how whites perceived blacks as
always-already caricatural, Wright did not want, therefore, to be viewed as a black
writer who tailored his work in such a way as to ingratiate it with this particular brand
of white readership. For Wright, that "quaint phase" of black life was inseparable from
the rural sites in which Hurston located that black life. Thus, for him to adopt the
features and conventions of rural life in his deathbed work—his late style—is to write
the Negro subjunctively into national belonging by eradicating (albeit only thematically
and generically) the "old and ancient agonies [that blacks suffer] at the hands of [their]
white neighbors"; it is to create the possibility and the world in which "a humane
attitude prevails in America toward black people." While this other world may only
exist in Wright's (quixotic, deathbed) head, in writing it into existence he ultimately
wills it to us so that we can at least try to reify it.

Notes

1   According to Adorno, it is "the formal law of [an artist's late work] that must be
discovered, [. . .] if one disdains to cross the line that separates art from document"
("Late Style in Beethoven" 564).
2   Warren writes, "As an instrument for pursuing social justice, the literature was forced at
least to contemplate its own wished-for obsolescence" (18).
3   Wright prepared 817 haiku for publication, and they were posthumously published in
the collection *Haiku: This Other World*. He decided on the poems he wanted published
during the 18 months when he was on his sickbed trying, unsuccessfully, to recover
from amebic dysentery before his death in 1960. By that time, he had actually written
more than 4,000 haiku.
4   However, I should make it very clear that, through his haiku, Wright sees and uses
death optimistically—as a means to an end—rather than a depressing end of life or a
foreclosure of all future possibilities.
5   It would be interesting to think of Wright as envisioning each haiku as the individual
reportage of several thousand observers, because he would, in essence, be granting
each the opportunity to create a world by stopping to observe and report on some
small aspect of it.

Works cited

Adorno, Theodor. "Alienated Masterpiece: The *Missa Solemnis*." 1959. *Essays on Music*.
Berkeley: U of California P, 2002. 569–83. Print.

—— "Late Style in Beethoven." 1937. *Essays on Music*. Berkeley: U of California P, 2002. 564–8. Print.

Anderson, Benedict. *Imagined Communities: Reflections on the Origin and Spread of Nationalism*. New York: Verso, 2006. Print.

Buell, Lawrence. *The Environmental Imagination: Thoreau, Nature Writing, and the Formation of American Culture*. Cambridge: Harvard UP, 1995. Print.

Cobb, Nina Kressner. "Richard Wright: Exile and Existentialism." *Phylon* 40.4 (1979): 362–74. Print.

Coleridge, Samuel Taylor. *The Rime of the Ancient Mariner*. Ed. Paul H. Fry. Boston: Bedford, 2000. Print.

Dr. Seuss [Theodor Seuss Geisel]. *Horton Hears a Who!* 1954. New York: Random House, 1982. Print.

Dungy, Camille T. Introduction. *Black Nature: Four Centuries of African American Nature Poetry*. Ed. Dungy. Athens: U of Georgia P, 2009. Print.

Fabre, Michel. *The World of Richard Wright*. Jackson: UP of Mississippi, 1985. Print.

Hakutani, Yoshinobu. "Wright's Haiku, Zen, and the African 'Primal Outlook.' " *The Other World of Richard Wright: Perspectives on His Haiku*. Ed. Jianqing Zheng. Jackson: UP of Mississippi, 2011. Print.

Hurston, Zora Neale. *Their Eyes Were Watching God*. 1937. New York: Harper Collins, 2000. Print.

Iadonisi, Richard. " 'I Am Nobody': The Haiku of Richard Wright." *MELUS* 30.3 (2005): 179–200. Print.

Milburn, Colin. *Nanovision: Engineering the Future*. Durham: Duke UP, 2008. Print.

Said, Edward W. *On Late Style: Music and Literature Against the Grain*. New York: Pantheon, 2006. Print.

—— "Thoughts on Late Style: A Lecture." *London Review of Books* 26.15 (2004): 3–7. Print.

Stewart, Susan. *On Longing: Narratives of the Miniature, the Gigantic, the Souvenir, the Collection*. Durham: Duke UP, 1993. Print.

Vendler, Helen. *Last Looks, Last Books: Stevens, Plath, Lowell, Bishop, Merrill*. Princeton: Princeton UP, 2010. Print.

Warren, Kenneth W. *What Was African American Literature?* Cambridge: Harvard UP, 2011. Print.

Webb, Constance. *Richard Wright*. New York: Putnam, 1968. Print.

Whitman, Walt. "Song of Myself." *Leaves of Grass*. 1855. Mineola: Dover, 2007. Print.

Wilson, August. *Ma Rainey's Black Bottom*. New York: Plume, 1985. Print.

Wright, Julia. Introduction. *Haiku: This Other World*. By Richard Wright. Ed. Yoshinobu Hakutani and Robert L. Tener. New York: Arcade, 1998. Print.

Wright, Richard. "Between Laughter and Tears." Rev. of *These Low Grounds*, by Waters Edward Turpin, and *Their Eyes Were Watching God*, by Zora Neale Hurston. *New Masses* 5 Oct. 1937: 22+. Print.

—— *The Color Curtain: A Report on the Bandung Conference*. Jackson: UP of Mississippi, 1956. Print.

—— *Haiku: This Other World*. Ed. Yoshinobu Hakutani and Robert L. Tener. New York: Arcade, 1998. Print.

—— "How 'Bigger' Was Born." *Native Son*. 1940. New York: Perennial Classics, 1998. Print.

—— *Native Son*. 1940. New York: Perennial Classics, 1998. Print.

—— *The Outsider*. 1953. New York: Perennial, 2003. Print.

—— *Uncle Tom's Children.* 1936. New York: Harper Perennial, 2008. Print.

—— *White Man, Listen!* 1957. Garden City: Anchor, 1964. Print.

Zheng, Jianqing, ed. *The Other World of Richard Wright: Perspectives on His Haiku.* Jackson: UP of Mississippi, 2011. Print.

Contributors

Sandy Alexandre is Associate Professor of African American literature and culture at MIT. Her first book, *The Properties of Violence: Claims to Ownership in Representations of Lynching* (UP of Mississippi, 2012), explores the connections between various representational forms of lynching and the issue of black dispossession. She is conducting research for her second book, trying to determine if slavery's discourse of black thinghood—chattel, cargo, property, etc.—ultimately inspires ethical representations of black people's own relationships to material objects. She has published several scholarly articles in her field in journals such as *Virginia Quarterly Review, Transition, Modern Drama*, the *Journal of American Drama and Theatre, Mississippi Quarterly*, and *Signs: Journal of Women in Culture and Society*.

Marc Mvé Bekale was born in Gabon and lives in Paris. He is Assistant Professor at the University of Reims, France, and member of the research group Centre d'Etudes Africaines-Américaines et Diasporiques (CEAAD). He graduated from the University of Nancy with a doctoral dissertation on Richard Wright's literature. Apart from contributing scholarly papers to international reviews of comparative literature and African and African American studies, Marc Mvé Bekale has been active in the cultural and political debates about French–West African relations. The author of five books, among which is the highly acclaimed *Traite négrière et expérience du temps dans le roman afro-américain* (Harmattan, 2007), he is currently working on an essay (*Méditations senghoriennes. Essai sur l'esthétique africaine et afro-américaine*) that reassesses Léopold Sédar Senghor's interpretation of African aesthetic paradigms.

Laurence Cossu-Beaumont is Maître de Conférences at the Université Sorbonne Nouvelle – Paris 3. She is a former Ecole Normale Supérieure student and teaching assistant at the University of Harvard. She wrote her PhD thesis in 2004 on the works of African American writer Richard Wright. Through the study of his archives at Yale University, she reviewed the main sources of influence of his writing, such as 1930s radicalism or his 1950s exile, but also the black vernacular and literary tradition, and addressed the publishing conditions and reception of his works on both sides of the Atlantic. Her research now focuses on book history and the book industry in connection with African American studies. Her publications include "Book History and African American Studies," co-authored with Claire Parfait (*Transatlantica*) and "Orality in Richard Wright's Short Stories: Playing and Surviving" (*Journal of the Short Story in English*). She has recently published *Marie ou l'esclavage aux Etats-Unis* (Les editions Aux Forges de Vulcain, 2014).

Alice Mikal Craven is Associate Professor of Comparative Literature and Film Studies at The American University of Paris and Chair of Film Studies. She has published articles on the works of Chester Himes, on race and spatial dimensions in the film *In the Heat of the Night* for the *Tamkang Review*, and on issues of race and otherness in *Titus Andronicus* for the journal *Shakespeare*. Alice Craven's article on James Baldwin's readings of race signs in the cinema has been published in a special issue of the *African American Review* on James Baldwin (Winter 2013). Her article on Richard Wright's influence on Parisian *banlieues* aesthetics is forthcoming in 2014. She is co-editor, with William E. Dow, of *Richard Wright: New Readings in the 21st Century* (Palgrave Macmillan, 2011).

Anthony Dawahare is Professor of English at California State University, Northridge. He is the author of *Nationalism, Marxism, and African American Literature Between the Wars: A New Pandora's Box* (UP of Mississippi, 2003), as well as articles on twentieth-century American writers Nella Larsen, Langston Hughes, Tillie Olsen, Richard Wright, and Alain Locke, among others. He has recently completed a book manuscript on dialectical philosophy, proletarian literature, and Tillie Olsen.

Bruce Allen Dick is Professor of English at Appalachian State University, where he teaches African American literature, Latino literature, and film. He has co-edited books on Rudolfo Anaya and Ismael Reed, including *A Critical Response to Ishmael Reed* (Greenwood, 1999). He also published *A Poet's Truth: Conversations with Contemporary Latino and Latina Poets* (U of Arizona P) in 2003. In 2008, he co-wrote and directed a documentary called *Offside(s): Soccer in Small-Town America.*

William E. Dow is Professor of American Literature at the Université Paris-Est (Marne-la-Vallée) and teaches at The American University of Paris. He is the Managing Editor of *Literary Journalism Studies* (Northwestern UP) and has published articles in such journals as *Publications of the Modern Language Association, The Emily Dickinson Journal, Twentieth-Century Literature, ESQ: A Journal of the American Renaissance, Critique, The Hemingway Review, MELUS, Revue Française d'Etudes Américaines, Actes Sud, Prose Studies,* and *Etudes Anglaises.* He is the author of the book *Narrating Class in American Fiction* (Palgrave Macmillan, 2009) and co-editor of *Richard Wright: New Readings in the 21st Century* (Palgrave Macmillan, 2011). Recent contributions include the chapter on Richard Wright for *The Cambridge Companion to American Novelists* (2013). He is currently completing a book-length study on American modernism and radicalism entitled *Reinventing Persuasion: Literary Journalism and the American Radical Tradition, 1900–1941.*

Michel Feith is Associate Professor of American Literature at the University of Nantes, France, and a member of the Center for Research on National Identities and Intercultural Studies (CRINI). After a doctoral thesis entitled "Myth and History in

Chinese American and Chicano Literature" (1995), his publications include articles on Maxine Hong Kingston, Gerald Vizenor, John Edgar Wideman, Percival Everett, and the Harlem Renaissance. On the latter subject, he edited, with Geneviève Fabre, *Jean Toomer and the Harlem Renaissance* (Rutgers UP, 2001) and *"Temples for Tomorrow": Looking Back at the Harlem Renaissance* (Indiana UP, 2001). He has also edited three collections on nationalism and regionalism at the University of Nantes, the latest being *Nationalismes et régionalismes: Amériques, modes d'emploi* (CRINI Editions, 2008). A volume of conference proceedings entitled *Paroles de vainqueurs, paroles de vaincus: Réécritures et revisions* was released in 2012, also from the CRINI.

Barbara Foley is Professor II of English and American Studies at Rutgers University, Newark. She has published widely in the fields of Marxist criticism, literary radicalism, and African American literature. Her books include *Telling the Truth: The Theory and Practice of Documentary Fiction* (Cornell UP, 1986), *Radical Representations: Politics and Form in Proletarian Fiction, 1929–1941* (Duke UP, 1993), *Spectres of 1919: Class and Nation in the Making of the New Negro* (U of Illinois P, 2003), and *Wrestling with the Left: The Making of Ralph Ellison's* Invisible Man (Duke UP, 2010). Her most recent book, provisionally titled *Jean Toomer: Race, Repression, and Revolution*, will be published by the University of Illinois Press in 2014. She is a member of the MLA Radical Caucus and the Marxist Literary Group and serves on both the editorial board and the manuscript committee of *Science and Society*.

Shoshana Milgram Knapp is Associate Professor of English at Virginia Tech. She has published articles on a variety of nineteenth- and twentieth-century figures in French, Russian, and English/American literature and culture, including Napoleon Bonaparte, Anton Chekhov, Victoria Cross, Fyodor Dostoevsky, George Eliot, John Fowles, W. S. Gilbert, Victor Hugo, Henry James, Ursula K. LeGuin, Vladimir Nabokov, Ayn Rand, George Sand, Stephen Sondheim, Herbert Spencer, W. T. Stead, John Steinbeck, Leo Tolstoi, and E. L. Voynich. She is also the author of introductions to editions of *Toilers of the Sea* (Paper Tiger, 1993) and *The Man Who Laughs*, by Victor Hugo, as well as *The Seafarers* (Paper Tiger, 2002), by Nevil Shute, and *Graustark* (Norilana, 2006), by George Barr McCutcheon. Her current long-term project is a study of Ayn Rand's life from birth until 1957.

Sudhi Rajiv is Professor of English at Jai Narain Vyas University in Jodhpur, India, and Director of the Kamla Nehru College for Women. She is the author of *Forms of Black Consciousness* (Advent, 1992) and many essays on South Asian literature, African American literature, Global English, women's studies in India and the United States. During 1993–4, she was a senior Fulbright Fellow at Harvard University. In 1997, she was honored as a Dr. Ambedkar Fellow by the Bharatiya Dalit Sahitya Academy, New Delhi, for her commitment to social justice and equality. Rajiv was also a Visiting Fulbright-Nehru Professor in English at Ohio University in 2010.

Charles Scruggs is Professor of American literature at the University of Arizona. In addition to writing books and articles on African American literature and film, he is recently co-author (with Gary Holcomb) of *Hemingway and the Black Renaissance* (Ohio State UP, 2012).

Amritjit Singh, Langston Hughes Professor of English at Ohio University, has published well over a dozen books, including *The Novels of the Harlem Renaissance* (1976), *The Harlem Renaissance: Revaluations* (1989), *The Magic Circle of Henry James* (1989), *Conversations with Ralph Ellison* (1995), *Memory and Cultural Politics* (1996), *Postcolonial Theory and the United States* (2000) and *The Collected Writings of Wallace Thurman* (2003). Past President of MELUS (The Society for the Study of Multi-Ethnic Literature of the United States), SALA (South Asian Literary Association), and USACLALS (Association for Commonwealth Literature and Language Studies), he currently serves as an Associate Editor of *South Asian Review*. An internationally known literary critic and scholar, Singh has lectured and/or taught in many countries in Asia, Africa, and Europe. In 1995, he edited the reprint editions of *Black Power* and *The Color Curtain*.

James Smethurst teaches Afro-American Studies at the University of Massachusetts, Amherst. He authored *The New Red Negro: The Literary Left and African American Poetry, 1930–1946* (Oxford UP, 1999), *The Black Arts Movement: Literary Nationalism in the 1960s and 1970s* (U of North Carolina P, 2005), and *The African American Roots of Modernism: From Reconstruction to the Harlem Renaissance* (U of North Carolina P, 2011). He co-edited *Left of the Color Line: Race, Radicalism and Twentieth-Century Literature of the United States* (U of North Carolina P, 2003) and *Radicalism in the South Since Reconstruction* (Palgrave Macmillan, 2006).

Cynthia Tolentino is Director of Special Programs, Paris, for the University of Oregon. Her publications include a book, *America's Experts: Race and the Fictions of Sociology* (U of Minnesota P, 2009), and several articles on ethnic American literature and US empire. She is a visiting scholar at L'Institut d'histoire du temps présent (IHTP), a center for contemporary studies in Paris, and teaches cultural studies courses at Sciences Po University.

Steven C. Tracy is Professor of African-American Studies at the University of Massachusetts, Amherst; Visiting Professor of English at the School of Foreign Languages and Chu Tian Scholar at Central China Normal University; and a Fulbright Senior Specialist. He is the author, editor, co-editor of numerous books in American and Afro-American literature and culture. Translations of his texts *Langston Hughes and the Blues* (U of Illinois P, 1988) and *Going to Cincinnati: A History of the Blues in the Queen City* (U of Illinois P, 1993) into Chinese are forthcoming. *Going to Cincinnati* was winner of the ARSC Award for Excellence in Historical Recorded Sound Research, 1994 (Jazz, Blues, and Gospel category). He has also authored over 60 encyclopedia entries and book chapters and 50 CD liner notes. A singer and harmonica player, he has appeared with B. B. King, Muddy Waters, Sonny Terry and Brownie McGhee, and many others, and has recorded with his band, Pigmeat Jarrett, Big Joe Duskin, Albert Washington, and the Cincinnati Symphony Orchestra.

Index